The Promise of
Phenomenology

The Promise of Phenomenology

Posthumous Papers of John Wild

Edited by Richard I. Sugarman
and Roger B. Duncan

LEXINGTON BOOKS

A Division of
ROWMAN & LITTLEFIELD PUBLISHERS, INC.
Lanham • Boulder • New York • Toronto • Oxford

LEXINGTON BOOKS

A division of Rowman & Littlefield Publishers, Inc.
A wholly owned subsidary of The Rowman & Littlefield Publishing Group, Inc.
4501 Forbes Boulevard, Suite 200
Lanham, MD 20706

PO Box 317
Oxford
OX2 9RU, UK

British Library Cataloguing in Publication Information Available

Library of Congress Cataloging-in-Publication Data

Wild, John Daniel, 1902–1972.
    The promise of phenomenology : posthumous papers of John Wild / edited
by Richard I. Sugarman and Roger B. Duncan.
        p. cm.
    Includes bibliographical references and index.
    ISBN-13: 978-0-7391-0942-7 (cloth : alk. paper)
    ISBN-10: 0-7391-0942-1 (cloth : alk. paper)
    ISBN-13: 978-0-7391-1366-0 (pbk. : alk. paper)
    ISBN-10: 0-7391-1366-6 (pbk. : alk. paper)
    1. Phenomenology. I. Sugarman, Richard Ira. II. Duncan, Roger B. III. Title.
B829.5.W55 2005
191—dc22   2005026707

Printed in the United States of America

♾™ The paper used in this publication meets the minimum requirements of
American National Standard for Information Sciences—Permanence of Paper for
Printed Library Materials, ANSI/NISO Z39.48-1992.

In memory of John Wild
1902–1972

Contents

Preface

America has produced both innovative thinkers and those at home in the history of philosophy. In the life and thought of John Wild (1902–1972) there was a convergence of original philosophical vision and a mastery of the Western philosophical tradition that earned him an international eminence rare among American philosophers. The restlessness that propelled his search along so many adventures of philosophical exploration, and was to take him back to the very beginnings of philosophy, always aimed at an understanding of the world of contemporary human existence.

The essays included in this volume have been selected from his posthumous papers with the aim of furthering an appreciation and understanding of existential philosophy and phenomenology. John Wild was recognized as the foremost advocate of existential phenomenology in the United States prior to his death in October 1972. Wild believed that the essence of philosophy was dialogue. He addresses himself in these posthumous reflections to readers of varying degrees of philosophical sophistication. The same kind of clarity, originality and sense of urgency that made Wild's published work so accessible to beginning students of philosophy is found in these essays. At the same time, advanced students of phenomenology will find fresh and original approaches to issues that, to borrow from the apt title of one of Wild's own essays included here, are on the very "frontiers of phenomenology."

Wild's unpublished works are characterized by careful scholarship, clarity of expression and cogency of argument. What distinguishes the style of the posthumous papers is a greater freedom from the personal reserve that is always associated with Wild's meticulous published scholarship. Here we gain a much more direct sense of Wild's personal, philosophical beliefs on critical issues. Still, the reader will notice that some of these essays are more polished than others. At other times the reader will see reflections that appear somewhat fragmentary, unfinished and episodic. However, we believe that there is a directness and freshness, a sense of urgency that richly compensates the reader in the essays enclosed. We see Wild at work, thinking at times almost aloud in his reactions to important thinkers and ideas. Where he finds himself unable to resolve philosophical tangles and paradoxes, he sketches imaginative approaches to problems, the very formulation of which initiates the process of moving toward resolution. It should be noted that a number of the essays published here for the first time were originally given as public talks at universities or colloquia. There is, therefore, perhaps, a greater degree of orality to Wild's reflections that can be seen here. This is especially true of the part that we have entitled, "Conversations, Reflections and Beliefs." Above all, in some of these more personal reflections, we gain a clearer idea of how John Wild regarded himself as a philosopher.

Among the essays included in this volume are several that John Wild was clearly and specifically preparing for publication toward the end of his life. He specified in notes made in Gainesville, Florida, in 1970 that the following essays he regarded as finished or almost finished: "The Other Person: Some Phenomenological Reflections," "The Rights of the Other as Other," "The Perceptual Time-lag and Lived Time," and "An Empirical Approach to the A Priori." There are other essays that might have been selected by other editors which for various reasons we felt did not belong here, either because they were outside of the context of what Wild regarded as his most mature thinking, or because such essays were extremely difficult to follow. In the first category, among many others, is an eighty-page, single-spaced manuscript entitled "Science of Philosophy-Metaphysics." This manuscript (see bibliography, A. 7.01), a virtual tour de force of metaphysics, reflective of Wild's Realistic phase, does not reflect the significant changes in Wild's thinking in his existential, phenomenological period. However, this essay will be of interest to any students of philosophy interested in studying a realistic, systematic metaphysics. In the second category is an essay called "Secondary Qualities and the Life-world" (see bibliography, A. 2), which we regarded as less complete and more fragmentary than Wild himself had categorized it. Still, it is an important work for students of John Wild, in particular because it shows Wild attempting to preserve the strands of George Berkeley's thinking that he regarded as having an empirical dimension. What Wild attempts in this very difficult piece is to situate Berkeley's thought within the radical empiricism of phenomenology. In a way this shows a return to his magisterial work, *George Berkeley* (Harvard University, 1936).

We have chosen, however, to arrange the posthumous papers in such a way as to integrate them into the existential unfolding of the last phase of

Wild's career. Our aim is less ambitious than to disclose a fully integrated portrait of Wild's development as a philosopher. We readily acknowledge that we are indebted to other students of philosophy who have already published works on John Wild. This includes an excellent, book-length study by William E. Kaufman, *John Wild: From Realism to Phenomenology.* Kaufman's book argues for continuity as well as points out differences between the Realistic and Phenomenological phases of Wild's career. It also has an interview in which Wild describes his own intellectual development. Here Wild comments on the influence of George Herbert Mead on his own thinking, especially as it relates to the other, a subject that would preoccupy him in the last phase of his career. What was not available to Kaufman and others were the reflections by Wild enclosed here and published, with one exception, for the first time. We are republishing here, with the permission of Professor Anna-Teresa Tymieniecka, John Wild's commentary on Emmanuel Levinas's *Totality and Infinity,* "Speaking Philosophy," which appeared in *Philosophic Inquiry* (2000, Volume 24). This work forms a very important sequel and expansion, we believe, to Wild's introduction to the English addition of *Totality and Infinity,* published in 1969 (Duquesne University Press). This piece was very likely the last publication by Wild to appear in his lifetime.

We have divided this book into four parts, appended letters and an appended bibliography. We begin with a part titled "Explorations of the Human Life-world," which draws upon several of the essays that Wild was preparing specifically for publication, and includes a couple of others that we believe help to form a clearer idea of the task that Wild has set for phenomenology. Each of these essays is preceded by a short explanatory note that aims at situating the essay within contemporary continental thought and, at times, within the history of philosophy. Our purpose is to clarify the questions before him, the conditions under which Wild was writing and, most important, perhaps, the direction in which his thought was moving.

Part two, which we have called "Conversations, Reflections and Beliefs," brings to light for the first time a journal that Wild kept while on his second Guggenheim Fellowship (1957–1958). During this period, Wild meets, converses with and reflects upon his encounters with some of the most prominent figures in the world of Anglo-Saxon philosophy and continental thought. It is important, not only in terms of the personalities whom Wild engages and the issues which he undertakes to discuss but also for his ambition, at the time, to build a bridge between ordinary language philosophy and phenomenology. At the same time, we see him engaged in conversation with some of the luminaries of the continental philosophical world, who helped to fill out part of Wild's own vision for the tasks that he saw ahead of him for the remainder of his philosophical career. Appended at the end of this part is a philosophical credo written in close proximity to the conclusion of his European tour that makes Wild's beliefs and views more clear to himself and to others.

The two essays that comprise part three, "Toward a Phenomenology of Transcendence," deal with Wild's re-visioned understanding of the religious dimension of the human life-world. Wild was a "religious philosopher" in the sense that his philosophical judgments and concerns in all phases of his career granted an important place to the human relationship with the Divine Mystery, which is only to say that he was a true philosopher in the Western tradition. In his early period he was associated with the Aristotelianism of the Thomist revival—his *Introduction to Realistic Philosophy* was widely used in Catholic colleges and seminaries. In his later view, the meanings of "faith" and "reason" complexified, and in any case faith and reason were less separable than the Thomists allowed. For Wild this meant a liberation into new possibilities of dealing directly with religious issues as a philosopher, and that is what we see him doing here.

The fourth and last part of our book, "New Directions, A Philosopher at Work: Toward a Phenomenology of the Other," deals with Wild's preoccupation with the other. Wild's concern with the other predates his encounter with the philosophy of Emmanuel Levinas. However, his reflections on the subject are clearly deepened and, to a degree, altered by his engagement with the thought of Levinas. The two essays that Wild authored on the other are accompanied by a monograph-length commentary on Levinas's *Totality and Infinity*, which we have entitled "Speaking Philosophy." It continues and deepens Wild's published reflections, presented in the introduction of the English version of *Totality and Infinity*. Readers of Levinas, as well as students of John Wild, will find this a remarkably clear and compelling commentary, perhaps the most lucid written on *Totality and Infinity* by a major American philosopher.

In the essays assembled here, Wild charts new areas for philosophical inquiry in his approach to some of the dominant and emerging problems of our time: the phenomena of ethical relativism, human subjectivity and corporeality; the human experience of the passage of time; inter-subjectivity and the problem of establishing a just relation with the other; the crisis of contemporary religious life; the relationship of science to philosophy; the possibility of an autonomous domain for philosophical inquiry. Each of these problems is approached here with Wild's unique blend of passion, discipline and erudition. In most cases these essays are completely developed and finished products, which could have been published in leading philosophical journals. We have chosen to publish them together because they provide a dramatic climax to the career of one of America's most important and influential philosophers.

Appended to the book are several relevant letters and a complete bibliography of Wild's posthumous papers now at the Beinecke Library at Yale University, open to the public as of January 1, 2006. In our general introduction to *The Promise of Phenomenology* we describe Wild's development as a philosopher, with special emphasis given to the illumination deriving from his posthumous papers.

Acknowledgments

The editors' first debt of gratitude is to our teacher John Wild who introduced us to the study of phenomenology, and to each other, some forty years ago. The Talmudic dictum that it takes a student forty years to understand his teacher has taken on a new meaning for us through the research leading to the publication of this book. The essays and reflections included here represent approximately ten percent of the total collection of John Wild's posthumous papers. We would like to thank the Beinecke Rare Book and Manuscript Library at Yale University for preserving Wild's posthumous papers, and for their cooperation and assistance over many years.

We would also like to express our appreciation to the late Catherine Wild for helping us to contextualize Wild's writing in the midst of his life. We are indebted to John Wild's daughter, Mary Wild-Roy, who encouraged us with our project and supplied valuable insight into pivotal moments in Wild's life and career.

Among the many students of John Wild who encouraged us to persevere with our work, we would like to acknowledge Calvin O. Schrag and John K. Roth in particular.

For helping with the process from collecting to collating to transcribing to preparing this manuscript for publication, we would like to thank the late Dawn Lawrence, Linda Sugarman, Steven Shaw, Professor Robert J. Anderson, Asher Crispe, Matthew Geiger, Tim Shepard, Erin Menut, Annika Ljung-Baruth, Nika Graci, Benjamin Beck, Amy Coleman, Lisa Obrentz, Rose McGovern, Ian Nagel and Jessica French.

We would also like to thank Professor William Paden of the Department of Religion at the University of Vermont and the Dean's fund of the College of Arts and Sciences. Furthermore, we would like to thank the editors of Rowman & Littlefield and Lexington Books.

General Introduction:
John Wild's Philosophical Itinerary

John Wild's teaching career spanned more than forty years at Harvard, Northwestern, Yale and a last year at the University of Florida, Gainesville. He was the author of nine books and over one hundred articles. In addition to his pioneering efforts in existential philosophy and phenomenology, John Wild was a recognized authority on classical philosophy, the philosophy of religion, ethics and the history of philosophy. As a historian of philosophy he was regarded as a distinguished scholar whose research and interpretations focused on such diverse thinkers as Plato, Aristotle, Spinoza, Berkeley, James, Heidegger and Merleau-Ponty.

John Daniel Wild was born in Chicago, Illinois, on April 10, 1902. He studied at the University of Chicago where he received his bachelor of philosophy degree in 1923. After receiving his master's degree in philosophy from Harvard University in 1925, he returned to the University of Chicago where he earned his doctoral degree the following year. In 1927, he was appointed to the faculty at Harvard where he taught until 1961. From 1961 to 1963 he served as chair of the Department of Philosophy at Northwestern University, before moving to Yale University where he taught until 1969. He retired from teaching in 1970, having spent his last year on the faculty at the University of Florida in Gainesville.

His major publications include: *George Berkeley: A Study of His Life and Philosophy*, Harvard University Press, 1936; *Plato's Theory of Man*, Harvard University Press, 1945; *Introduction to Realistic Philosophy*, Harper and Row, 1948; *Plato's Modern Enemies and the Theory of Natural Law*, University of Chicago Press, 1953; *The Challenge of Existentialism*, Indiana University Press, 1955; *Human Freedom and Social Order: An Essay in Christian Philosophy*, Duke University Press, 1959; *Existence and the World of Freedom*, Prentice-Hall, 1963; and *The Radical Empiricism of William James*, Doubleday, 1969.

His professional honors include the presidencies of the American Philosophical Association, 1960–1961, the Metaphysical Society of America, 1953–1954, and the Association for Realistic Philosophy, which he helped found in 1947. In addition, he was the prime mover in helping create the Society for Phenomenology and Existential Philosophy (SPEP) in 1962. John Wild was twice the recipient of the prestigious Guggenheim Fellowship. In 1957–1958, with the support of the Guggenheim Fellowship, Wild traveled extensively in England and Europe engaging many of the most celebrated of his philosophic contemporaries in dialogue and discussion. The journal, which Wild kept during this period, is presented in this volume for the first time. It serves as a model of philosophical research cutting across the sectarian and provincial boundaries that have tended to handicap the pursuit of authentic philosophy in our times.

It was, however, Wild's first trip to Europe in 1930–1931, also as the beneficiary of the Guggenheim Fellowship, which was to permanently alter his concept of philosophy. Wild spent most of 1930–1931 at the University of Freiburg in Germany attending the lectures of Martin Heidegger, whose path-breaking work in phenomenology, *Being and Time*, had appeared just four years earlier. In his lectures Heidegger admonished students intoxicated with contemporary trends in phenomenology that the future of philosophy depended upon a capacity to reckon with its inner history. A genuine comprehension of Nietzsche's thought, according to Heidegger, required an understanding of Aristotle that could not be gained without fifteen years of study. The course that most impressed Wild was one in which Heidegger spent the entire semester commenting upon the implications of the first paragraph of Aristotle's *Metaphysics*. Wild, too, would develop an almost unrivaled enthusiasm for the accurate rendering of vital texts, a disciplined passion that was to find its way into his teaching as well as into his written work.

Wild was one of the few students to heed Heidegger's words, to begin with the strenuous project of reclaiming the past of philosophy in order to secure a surer foothold along the path of meaning set in motion in its ruling beginnings. Wild's sense of the limits of American Pragmatism, which he had studied at the University of Chicago, had already prefigured his own search for an ultimate description of reality in which the best part of pragmatism could be preserved but the subjectivism that he associated with it would be corrected. As William E. Kaufman points out in his excellent book, *John Wild: From Realism to Phenomenology* (Peter Lang, New York: 1996, 6), Wild had already indicated in his doctoral dissertation, "The Science and Metaphysics of Symbolism" (University of Chicago, 1926), a need for "a genuine epistemological beyondness." As Kaufman correctly indicates, this is an anticipation of his turn to classical Realism and an intimation of a concern with 'otherness' that Wild would focus on at the very close of his career. It is worth pointing out that an interest in classical philosophy was awakened in him by his studies with Etienne Gilson, with whom he studied at Harvard.

In resisting the call to take up the task of phenomenology in the early 1930s, Wild proceeded to follow a longer, more arduous path. The best sources that we have available to document Wild's initial reaction to his encounter with Heidegger are his elaborate and extensive notebooks from the period 1931–1936 (see bibliography). The notebooks contain lucid, extensive and penetrating commentaries on the central works of a number of philosophers, Aristotle in particular (see bibliography, A.1). We see Wild teaching himself Greek, mastering the rudiments of Aristotle's complex philosophical vision and finally emerging as an acknowledged authority, presenting creative and contemporary reinterpretations relevant to the predicament of man in modern, mass society. These years of intensive, scholarly study of ancient texts culminated in his becoming the acknowledged force behind the return to classical realism in the United States in the 1940s. In *Plato's Theory of Man*, Wild convincingly argued that a searching look at the Dialogues would show that Plato had sketched out virtually every major philosophical problem, and that the Dialogues taken together presented a coherent and defensible concept of being human that could be challenged only by coming to grips with the same fundamental issues that confronted Plato himself. As a public personality within the field of American philosophy during this time, he is remembered for helping rescue Plato from the near hysteria with which Karl Popper and others sought to discredit Plato's Dialogues as veiled political totalitarianism. Wild's famous polemic, *Plato's Modern Enemies and the Theory of Natural Law*, not only successfully took issue with the view represented by Popper but argued persuasively that philosophic positivism, by denying the validity of ethical discourse, was a sure invitation to ethical chaos and political totalitarianism.

As the fruit and culmination of Wild's inquiry into the Greek philosophic tradition, a desire to consolidate and update the results of this tradition emerged. Wild began to envision the prospect of a philosophic movement in the United States that would inventory the experience of the contemporary world through the translucent lens of philosophical realism. Tirelessly, Wild dedicated himself to the writing of essays, which examined in fastidious detail multifaceted problems that had not yet received satisfactory philosophical resolution. He sought to uncover the disorientation and dislocation that had arisen from the Cartesian transformation of modern thought, now dispossessed of the concept of final causality. At the same time, he wished to give full recognition to the reality of the modern scientific and technological revolutions. Along with a number of co-workers and students, Wild founded the Association for Realistic Philosophy in 1947. Out of this period in Wild's career emerged *The Introduction to Realistic Philosophy* (published by Harper and Row in 1948) and *The Return to Reason* (edited by Wild and published by the Henry Regnery Company in 1953).

THE TURN TO PHENOMENOLOGY

What has perplexed scholars, surprised students of John Wild and even dismayed some of his former colleagues in the Realistic Movement is the seemingly inexplicable and apparently abrupt change in his philosophic direction in the early 1950s from classical philosophy to existentialism and phenomenology. His former close associate in the Association for Realistic Philosophy, Henry Veatch, refused to take responsibility for a long interview with Wild that he helped to conduct for the book *Philosophical Interrogations: Dialogues with Martin Buber, John Wild, Paul Tillich, Paul Weiss and Others*. "One colleague, indeed, who conducted a most interesting and spirited interrogation, now amiably but resolutely wishes to be disassociated with his name. He is Professor Henry Veatch. Between the time when Veatch first solicited queries and the time when his author, Wild, prepared replies, Wild, who has always been a seeker in philosophy, had developed fundamental doubts concerning his former realistic beliefs and had shifted toward phenomenology and existentialism" (*Philosophical Interrogations*, p. 5). Wild's keen sense of irony and good humor helped to defuse some of the personal dimension of the philosophic controversy that accompanied his strong advocacy of new positions in philosophy.

What makes Wild's turn even more difficult to grasp is his basic acceptance of Heidegger's phenomenological approach to philosophy some twenty years after his apparent rejection of it. What tends, however, to be discounted by critics of his turn is that Wild's approach to the history of philosophy had always been radically existential and phenomenological. For Wild, every past thinker has living significance just insofar as he stands in relation to the one who looks to him from out of his own present hour for guidance; or, as he has said, the authentic project of the history of philosophy is carried out when an approach is undertaken, "which recognizes its own historical perspective and tries to carry on a living dialogue with some thought of the past from its own point of view" (*PI*, p. 121). The interrogation of John Wild by some leading philosophers of the day situates Wild's responses to both his changing views of the task of philosophy and what has remained constant in his thought. Wild's responses are carefully composed and quite revealing. The subjects that he comments on range from his views on the history of philosophy to ethics, epistemology, metaphysics and the role of philosophy in the contemporary world.

He acknowledges, in his written response to a question by Professor Herbert Spiegelberg, that his views on the theory of knowledge have been modified in the intervening years since Spiegelberg asked this question: "How does your 'direct realism' differ from other forms of realism?" Wild's response takes on added weight given the fact that Spiegelberg was widely regarded at the time as the authoritative historian of the phenomenological movement. Wild states: "The naïve realism of common sense is primarily concerned with things, and takes their presence in experience for granted as though it made no difference whatsoever. Hence, it is uncritical in confusing presence with what is present, and world with things in the world. Since you first submitted your inquiry phenomenology has taught me to be more critical of this naïve realism, which constantly forgets that things are revealed in a finite world horizon in relation to a corporeal, personal center. I am now much clearer on this point . . . I hold, precisely as a phenomenologist, that this relational context can be revealed as it is with no noetic distortion" (*PI*, p. 138). Wild shows that he is very much aware of the fact that his views on the theory of knowledge have evolved. However, the careful reader will note that Wild wishes to preserve a direct access to what Aristotle called "reality," but he does so by employing the methods of "radical empiricism." For Wild, this means that there is a primary experience of the world in which we find ourselves positioned, stretched out into temporal and spatial fields. Too much has been gained in his lifelong fight against philosophical idealism for Wild to abandon his realistic position altogether. In fact, just as he wanted to find an empiricism more truly empirical, i.e., faithful to direct experience, than the empiricists, so he might also be said to be looking for a more accurate realism than that professed by the Aristotelians. The classical categories distort the rich world of immediate experience by way of abstraction. And, Wild was to discover, it does not help to simply replace the abstractions of the classical tradition with a solipsistic a priori that excludes the shock of confrontation with the other more than the Aristotelians ever did, no matter how "existential" such a philosophy may be. On the basis of this dogged "realism" we can begin to understand why Wild was so receptive to the philosophy of Levinas later on, though not without critical sifting. In any case, he expands on these epistemological themes in various places in the interrogation before us, as well as in his published and unpublished works. There is one more point that is worth mentioning. In a last question that Spiegelberg directs to Wild, Spiegelberg asks, "What are the precise implications of the time-lag in sense perception for the epistemology of direct realism?" Wild indicates that he can only begin to answer this question in his response and states that "this question requires an extended answer." Included in this volume is an essay that almost certainly originated with Spiegelberg's question. The essay is titled, "The Perceptual Time-lag and Lived Time." It is published here for the first time.

We have said that for Wild the history of philosophy is an ongoing dialogue with the past: "It is not wholly mine or yet wholly yours, but a living tissue between, which belongs to both of us. The being of a thinker includes his thought, and his thought is communicated to other minds where it expands and grows . . . They are meanings which must be understood. And meanings cannot be understood without being set in a new horizon . . . A commentator may think that he is recapturing the real Descartes as he was, but what is actually written down is something of the commentator's own, a selection, an evaluation, the result of a dialogue. Why should he try to reduce himself to zero or to pretend that he is not himself in history?" (*PI*, p. 122). Wild's many in-depth explorations of seminal figures of philosophy appear to have been guided by his vision of the inner logic of the history of philosophy as a living dialogue in which the past lives in the aspirations of the present.

Responding to a provocative question from the famous rationalist Brand Blanshard on ethics, freedom and value, Wild indicates that there is a difference between human freedom and arbitrary preference. Building on this distinction, Wild argues that human freedom is "aware of the ambiguity of existence" (*PI*, p. 130). Moreover, Wild has already demonstrated a commitment to an ethics of pluralism and, at the same time, a rejection of the metaphysics of monism. Anticipating Levinas, Wild argues for the importance of genuine communication as itself, the dialogue that constitutes the history of philosophy. This is the only way, according to Wild, that we can escape from human isolation, establish our personal being and recognize the centrality of the spirit of freedom in Western philosophy: "Those who doubt its existence should consider the history of Western philosophy, where the spirit of freedom has expressed itself not only in worldviews which are radically divergent, but in disciplined modes of communication between them which constitute the very history itself" (*PI*, p. 130).

Only if we recognize the existential, social and political horizon within which Wild's thinking moved do the phases of his career and his concept of the task of philosophy in relation to its own history become evident. Just as there is a fidelity to "Direct Realism," or more precisely his lifelong antagonism to philosophical idealism, that persists in Wild's phenomenological period, so too does his preoccupation with existentialism and phenomenology predate what is commonly referred to as "Wild's Realistic Period." Already in the spring of 1937 we find Wild teaching a course at Harvard on phenomenology. We are indebted to Professor

Lester Embree for publishing correspondence between Wild and Dorion Cairns at a time when Cairns was helping to pioneer the study of Husserlian phenomenology at the New School for Social Research. The correspondence begins with Wild's response to Cairns on February 22, 1937, and indicates that Wild had already begun to teach Heidegger as well as Husserl at Harvard. He mentions that he will be teaching material dealing with Husserl's critique of psychologism found in the *Logical Investigations* and, pursuant to advice from Cairns, spending three meetings of his seminar on the Cartesian Meditations. He goes on to say that "in April I shall start on Heidegger—where I suppose we part company. But to my mind certain features of Heidegger are essential to purge phenomenology of the unfortunate solipsism or subjectivism arising from what seems to me to be a too exclusive emphasis on Husserl's part" (*Research in Phenomenology* 5, 1975, p. 155). Some twenty-five to thirty years later Wild will find similar problems with Heidegger to those he had situated in Husserl, and hence his final emphasis upon the correctives of Heidegger's thought by Levinas.

As early as 1940 Wild published articles and book chapters dealing with the importance of the phenomenological approach to philosophy. See, for example, "Husserl's Critique of Psychologism: Its Historic Roots and Contemporary Relevance" (*Philosophic Essays in Memory of Edmund Husserl*, edited by M. Farber, Cambridge: Harvard University Press, 1940, pp. 19–43). Also during this same year, Wild wrote an article on "The Concept of the Given in Contemporary Philosophy—Its Origin and Limitations." The following year, Wild authored a long piece, "On the Nature and Aims of Phenomenology," for Philosophy and Phenomenological Research. Both articles show Wild searching for an empiricism radical enough to penetrate beyond naturalism to the basic patterns of human experience.

In 1940, Wild had already published an article discussing the importance of Kierkegaard for philosophy and religion. In his article "Kierkegaard and Classic Philosophy," Wild recognizes the influence, seriousness and contribution of Kierkegaard as a thinker. Wild credits Kierkegaard for using a "descriptive technique" that helps us to uncover "phenomena such as death, choice, anxiety, and fear, usually relegated by modern philosophers without much further consideration to the limbo of psychology . . ." ("Kierkegaard and Classical Philosophy," *Philosophical Review* 39, 1940, p. 542). At this time in his career, however, Wild sees Kierkegaard's "lasting contribution" as a "recovery of classic insight," which is the kind of questioning Socrates himself engaged in (p. 551). Wild points out Kierkegaard's obsession with the claims of Hegel and sees this fascination causing Kierkegaard "to believe that his whole position was irrational and paradoxical" (p. 542). However, Wild tries to rescue this original vein of

Kierkegaard's thought by resituating it in relation to the history of philoso-phy, thereby weaving it into "the fabric of a truly philosophical psychol-ogy" (p. 551). Subsequently, Wild revalues his understanding of Kierkegaard as the beginning of the existential revolt against objectivism. As he puts it, "Kierkegaard's suggestions have been developed and rede-fined by his living disciples, the existential disciples of Western Europe" (*Challenge of Existentialism*, 1955, p. 29). Kierkegaard, furthermore, is not seen merely as philosophical psychologist but as the beginning of a new way of approaching philosophy that is governed by a method now charac-terized as radical empiricism. In other words, the descriptive technique is seen as a precursor to the methods of phenomenology.

What is distinctive about the latter phase of Wild's career is the manner in which he advocated for an existential phenomenology, preserving a version of the realism of his earlier views on epistemology, while at the same time arguing for a more radical method, phenomenology, in terms of approach. This radical empirical approach would help to lay bare a phenomenology of existence, thus paving the way for a systematic explo-ration of the life-world. In other words, Wild appears intent upon devel-oping a theory of human existence through using the methods of phe-nomenology as opposed to more orthodox Husserlian views advocated by Aron Gurwitsch, Cairns and others. Wild is in the process of develop-ing a new school in continental philosophy, one that would subsequently be known as "Existential Phenomenology." In retrospect, we can see that Wild's earlier interests in Husserl, Kierkegaard and Heidegger, previously two strains in his thinking, are coming together in ways that are progres-sively more definitive. The reader is encouraged to explore *John Wild: From Realism to Phenomenology* by William E. Kaufman, an important book, which, however, appears to have overlooked Wild's earlier separate interests in phenomenology and existential philosophy and their subse-quent coming together (Peter Lang, 1996). Some of the fruits of Wild's labors in exploring the life-world are found in part one in previously un-published essays that complement and augment published material on this same subject.

To summarize, Wild's advocacy of existential philosophy is prefigured by an earlier, expressed interest in each field separately, and is marked by a merger of the contents of existential philosophy with the approach of phenomenology. Wild's battles in this area have been hard fought, not only with others but especially with himself. As an acknowledged au-thority on so many historic figures within the Western philosophic tradi-tion, with the culmination of John Wild's philosophical turn, the move-ment of existential phenomenology was given an authority in America that it had previously lacked. When asked about the reason for his em-bracing existential philosophy, he liked to reiterate something that troubled him from his neo-Aristotelian period. For Aristotle, there can be no knowledge of the individual as such. He is always subsumed under a species and that species under a genus. In this way, Wild came to believe that it was necessary to take an existential position if one were to fulfill the ancient Socratic maxim which bore the very imprimatur of philosophy: "Know thyself."

JOHN WILD'S PHILOSOPHICAL LEGACY

Wild's early interest in the existential implications of philosophical theory informed his decision to write his dissertation on the pragmatic stakes of the new concern with symbolism in philosophy. Wild was searching for a concept of praxis and meaning responsive to the growing challenges presented to human experience by the advancing of scientific understanding of the world. The social cast of Wild's thinking in the middle and late 1920s, influenced by his teacher George Herbert Mead, was partially a response to the need for a generalized sense of 'otherness' that Wild continued to search for throughout his career, reaching a dramatic climax in his encounter with the thought of Emmanuel Levinas.

The rise of totalitarianism in Nazi Germany and the excesses of Stalinism undoubtedly were determining factors in Wild's search for the fundaments of a natural law that would hold a true and eternal course in the midst of the ravaging currents threatening to drown the island of civilization that reason had labored so long to build. His interest in Berkeley is not a tributary leading to a quiet stream for an isolated thinker to rest near, but rather an attempt to secure a worthy vessel for the scientific pursuit of eternal philosophical truth. Wild believed this could be achieved if he was able to prove that there was a nascent radical empiricism in Berkeley's thought that, despite its limitations, promised a method adequate to exploring the contingent facts of human experience.

In the Preface to *Plato's Theory of Man*, Wild makes Plato responsive to the shattering questions that have arisen out of a world whose foundations have crumbled beneath it. The existential dimension of his reflections on Plato and Aristotle show that Wild believed that a practical philosophy of human life could be elicited and systematized from the writings of the ancient Greek thinkers; we can focus on the human dimension of abstract problems without compromising the logical rigor of the subject matter. His vast writings on ethics, epistemology, metaphysics and the philosophy of culture testify to this fact.

In his introduction to *The Challenge of Existentialism*, first delivered as the Mahlon Powell Lectures at Indiana University in the early 1950s, Wild gives a revealing clue to the social and political reasons that determined his decision to reject his realistic past and to take up the cause of existentialism: "There are many present indications of a serious breakdown in the basic enterprise of philosophy throughout the Anglo-Saxon world. At a time when there is a desperate need for the wide dissemination of sound and appealing cultural aims, academic philosophy at least seems bankrupt" (*The Challenge of Existentialism*, p. 3). Wild is indicating here his fierce desire to advance a philosophy that is informed by rather than divorced from life.

At the same time Wild was motivated by the politically liberal desire to find a grounded philosophy and sophisticated alternative to Stalinist Communism: "We find ourselves engaged in what is primarily an ideological war against a formidable enemy, well equipped not only with physical weapons but with ideological armament as well. These ideas are not a mere jumble. They are ordered into a systematic philosophy, a coherent whole technically known as dialectical materialism, one of the great world philosophies which has drawn from the deepest springs of modern reflection" (*The Challenge of Existentialism*, p. 5). The lifelessness of academic philosophy came to be a more enduring object of Wild's enmity than did the deformation of dialectical materialism.

Just as John Wild refused to separate academic philosophy from the questions arising from everyday life, so too were his own life and thought very much bound up together. We are indebted to John Wild's daughter, Mary Wild-Roy, for generously sharing with us the answers to some of the often-asked questions about Wild's life that have remained largely unanswered.[1] Two dimensions of his life that have received insufficient comment concern both his religious and political views, neither of which could be separated from his existential, philosophical outlook.

One of Wild's best-known students was Charles Malik, who wrote his doctoral dissertation on "The Nature of Time in Heidegger and Whitehead" while studying under Wild at Harvard in 1936. Malik subsequently became a member of the Association for Realistic Philosophy founded by Wild in the late 1940s. Malik was responsible for drafting the U.N. Charter on Human Rights. Wild's own thinking on the subject of human rights is found most explicitly in one of his posthumous essays published here for the first time, "The Rights of the Other as Other." While showing agreement with the U.N. charter in fundamental respects he also is somewhat critical of the absence of phenomenological reflection needed to elucidate general principles. Furthermore, Wild begins his own reflection on the subject by challenging the attempt to reduce the other to the same, and emphasizes a more explicit pluralism and a need to express general principles in a more embodied way. Malik went on to become the president of the General Assembly of the U.N. According to Mary Wild-Roy, the two maintained contact over the course of many years, and it was Malik, then president of the American University of Beirut in Lebanon, who invited Wild to teach philosophy there in the spring semester of 1967, where Wild held the position of Centennial Professor of Philosophy.

John Wild was publicly active in supporting the candidacy of the Progressive former Vice-President Henry Wallace in the 1948 presidential campaign. According to Mary Wild-Roy, Wild's Cambridge home was often a gathering place for liberal and progressive intellectuals who met informally to discuss the important ethical, political and cultural issues of the time. This circle included among others, according to Mary Wild-Roy, the movie producer Dore Schary and a young Harvard instructor by the name of Timothy Leary. During the McCarthy era the group was infiltrated by a government agent. Mary Wild-Roy remembers she, along her late sister Cynthia Wild Cowgill and their mother, Catherine, lived in a climate of fear and were anxious that John Wild might lose his tenured position at Harvard. While Wild was, perhaps, less outspoken on political issues after this time, he did not refrain from pursuing the social and political underpinnings of human oppression in his teaching and writing.

Regarding his positions and views on religion, Wild had been an active member of the Episcopal church while at Harvard. Wild gave a number of sermons while in Boston, drafts of which can be found in the archive of his posthumous papers now at the Beinecke Library. For a period of time, he expressed a desire to unify what he perceived to be the strongest elements of both the Anglican and Catholic traditions. In fact, he left a credo on his views, "Things I Am Clear About in Religion and Theology," which parallels a similar paper on his philosophical beliefs, "Things I Am Clear About in Philosophy." We have not included the religious credo in this book because we have chosen to focus our attention on work that is exclusively philosophical in character. It is for this reason that we have not included any of his theological reflections. His enthusiasm for the Anglo-Catholic project appears to have waned, at least publicly, in the last decade of his life.

However, John Wild did not give up his interest in religion, but seemed to move in a more existential direction with a recognition of the importance of transcendence and the other, which found a prominent place in his later writings. In part three, "Toward a Phenomenology of Transcendence," we have included two previously unpublished sections by Wild dealing with his phenomenological and existential approach to religious life.

Wild's move from Harvard to Northwestern after thirty-four years of teaching has been the subject of some conjecture. There is little question that Wild felt progressively less comfortable in the emerging Harvard philosophy department whose direction was set by the analytic philosophy of W. V. O. Quine. For the last six or seven years of Wild's tenure at Harvard, he taught a number of classes at the Divinity school, or cross-listed his courses between the philosophy and Divinity schools. He undoubtedly felt a greater sense of freedom to teach philosophy as he understood it in the Divinity school than he did in the increasingly oppressive atmosphere of Harvard's Department of Philosophy. Several of Wild's most prominent colleagues, senior members of the department Raphael Demos, Donald Williams, Henry Aiken and Roderick Firth wrote him a letter, appended to the end of this book, in April of 1960, appealing to him not to leave but recognizing that this was likely inevitable. It seems clear that Wild's colleagues recognized that the philosophical scene at Harvard was moving away from the ultimate questions that had long been associated with philosophy toward a narrower view of philosophic inquiry. Wild's departure would mean that the most outspoken member of the department and critic of this change in direction would signal a change at Harvard with rippling effects for American philosophy.

In moving to Northwestern, Wild was influenced by the fact that he and his wife Catherine were originally from Chicago and had attended the University of Chicago as undergraduates. Also, his cousin, Payson Wild, an upper-level administrator at Northwestern hoping to enhance the prestige of his own university, offered Wild the chance to build up a department specializing in Continental philosophy with Wild serving as chair. In the span of three years, Wild had not only transformed the Northwestern Department of Philosophy into the leading institution in the United States for the study of phenomenology and existential philosophy but also worked tirelessly to make existential phenomenology an integral part of the American philosophical curriculum. It was to this end that he initiated and served as general editor of the Northwestern University Studies in Phenomenolgy and Existential Philosophy, a position that he held until his death. Consulting editors included Aron Gurwitsch, Emmanuel Levinas, Paul Ricoeur, Calvin O. Schrag, Herbert Spiegelberg and Charles Taylor among others. This became the most important English-speaking press devoted to Continental philosophy in the United States. At the same time, he served as co-founder of the Society for Phenomenology and Existential Philosophy (SPEP), which continues to occupy an important place on the international philosophical scene.

It was Paul Weiss (1901–2002), then Sterling Professor of Philosophy at Yale, according to Mary Wild-Roy, who initiated the successful attempt to lure Wild away from Northwestern. Weiss and Wild had known each other from their graduate school days at Harvard and, while having very different philosophical world outlooks, had maintained a friendship that spanned decades. They admired each other's philosophical work, and their families were quite close. Weiss believed that Wild was the best teacher of philosophy in America, a view that was shared by many of his students.

At the time he came to Yale in the fall of 1963, the Yale philosophy department was widely regarded as one of the best anywhere. It was known for its pluralism and for its formidable philosophical personalities. Wild's original colleagues at Yale included Brand Blanshard (who had just retired), a well-known advocate of philosophical rationalism; F. S. C. Northrup, an eminent philosopher of law; and Wilfred Sellers, the celebrated neo-Kantian philosopher and philosopher of science. Also included among Wild's initial colleagues at Yale were Robert Brumbaugh, one of America's better known Platonists; John E. Smith, philosopher of religion (who may have also played a role in encouraging Wild to come to Yale); and younger colleague Richard J. Bernstein. Promising scholars who would make their mark at other institutions included William McBride, who was to become an internationally known scholar of Marx and Sartre; young scholars of phenomenology, Edward Casey, David Carr, David Hoy, and Allen Paskow; and Holocaust scholar John K. Roth.

However, while Wild remained a popular teacher and his scholarship showed no sign of letting up, it was not clear that he was altogether at home at Yale. Mary Wild-Roy believes that Wild had some second thoughts about having left Northwestern. Wild's blunt spoken manner, his unqualified support for his students and his greater obligations to the existential, phenomenological movement that he headed all combined to make Wild feel like something of an outsider at Yale. Wild did not enjoy the same free hand in shaping the direction of the department of philosophy as he had as Northwestern. However, he did once again manage to create a circle of students and colleagues around him that met at his New Haven home on a regular basis to present papers on and discuss issues within phenomenology. This circle included the eminent Hegel scholar J. N. Findlay, Robert Ehman, David Carr, William McBride, Alan Paskow, Richard Sugarman and others. Wild's graduate seminar on Heidegger's *Being and Time*, taught in the fall of 1965, had forty-four students, the largest graduate seminar to be taught during those years.

Wild was a passionate advocate for his philosophical point of view and a major figure at Yale during this time who had established an international reputation outside of the world of Yale. In 1964, Wilfred Sellers and his close friend, the logician John Anderson, left Yale for the University of Pittsburgh in a successful effort by Pittsburg to establish itself as a prominent department of philosophy. The Yale Department of Philosophy was severely shaken by the departure of Richard J. Bernstein, at that time a highly popular teacher who became the first victim of the "publish or perish" syndrome. Wild was on sabbatical during this time and was not permitted to vote in the Bernstein case. Wild had significant regard for Bernstein and

Bernstein's work, and a keen admiration for one of Bernstein's primary mentors, Paul Weiss. In a rare public appearance noted by the *New York Times*, Weiss spoke to over a thousand people, most of them Yale students, in support of Bernstein. Fissures began to appear in the department between students and faculty and even between faculty members. In 1968, Weiss was forced to retire from the post that he occupied as Sterling Professor of Philosophy. Wild was much more interested in advancing the cause of phenomenology than he was in the university politics of the day. When the University of Florida approached him with an offer to forge a new graduate program in philosophy that he would head and could shape according to his interests, Wild accepted. At the University of Florida he was reunited with his old friend and colleague Charles Morris and found a receptive body of undergraduate students interested in Continental philosophy. Here, he taught his last courses, one devoted to Emmanuel Levinas's *Totality and Infinity*.

An important fact of Wild's career is that he not only championed his own ideas and seriously entertained those of his colleagues, including his critics, but was also extraordinarily devoted to his students. Oftentimes he could see scholarly promise in them, which would eventually be realized, that other teachers could not detect. Wild always made time for his students. He showed an unusual willingness to go out of his way to advocate on behalf of students, and not exclusively those who studied with or under him. He educated several generations of students. Wild's students were well represented in departments of philosophy in mid- to late-twentieth-century America. For example, Calvin O. Schrag, George Ade Distinguished Professor of Philosophy Emeritus at Purdue University and one of the leading figures in contemporary North American Continental philosophy, was a graduate student of John Wild's at Harvard in the late 1950s. Schrag credits Wild with playing a decisive role "leading to my opting for the 'Continental' track in philosophy" (*Journal of the Canadian Society for Hermeneutics and Post Modern Thought*, Spring 2004). Another graduate student of Wild's at Yale in the 1960s, John K. Roth, Edward J. Sexton Professor of Philosophy at Claremont McKenna College, praises Wild for his great interest in his students, and states that, ". . . he served as a kind of model for my own career aspirations." Roth also gives us a sense of the way that many students related to John Wild: "He had a kind of winsome combination of gruff directness, shyness, and passion. He was a bit awesome to me, but I also felt that I could always go to him for guidance and help" (Correspondence, 5/28/05). Wild not only taught but touched the lives of many of his students, going out of his way to help them with their own research and careers. He encouraged each student to find his or her own way, while at the same time advancing the common cause of philosophy. The enduring influence of John Wild continues not only in his own writings but in the lives and works of his students, whose numbers were exceeded by few philosophers in the United States in the twentieth century.

A typical day for him at Yale, while already an internationally recognized philosopher of stature, consisted of his arriving at his office at 9:30 a.m. and staying until 6:30 at night, his door always open. During the course of this time, students were free to come and go as they wished while Wild took notes in preparation for courses he was teaching or for manuscripts or books he was working on. One of the noteworthy aspects of Wild's meticulous preparation for class consisted of his rewriting material for classroom lectures and discussion, sometimes exceeding one hundred pages, even on thinkers and texts on whom he had already published books or extensive articles. In other words, his ideas were always fresh, and, while he remained a passionate advocate of phenomenology in particular, his own readings of the text were made contemporary with those of his students. After returning home, he would begin another part of his day: writing in his comfortable book-lined study until late at night. This was repeated day after day. In the summer of 1970, John Wild suffered the first of a number of strokes that left his gait and vision somewhat impaired. To his dismay, in August of 1970, he determined that he would be unable to return to his duties at the University of Florida. However, his mind remained sharp until the very end of his life.

Evidence of the stature that Wild had achieved as the preeminent American philosopher of Continental thought is visible in a book of essays in his honor, *Patterns of the Life-world*, edited by three colleagues and former students of Wild, Professor James M. Edie, Francis H. Parker and Calvin O. Schrag (Northwestern University Press, 1970). Contributors to this volume included, but were not limited to, Paul Ricouer, Mikel Dufrenne, Wilfrid Desan, Maurice Natanson, William McBride and the philosopher/psychiatrist Erwin Straus as well as the editors and his old student/collaborator, Henry Veatch. Two other contributors of note who were influenced by Wild, having been students of his at Harvard: the late Samuel Todes and Hubert Dreyfus. Dreyfus, who has become well known for his work on artificial intelligence, collaborated with John Wild in the late 1950s on a partial translation of Heidegger's *Being and Time* (see bibliography 7.04).

NEW DIRECTIONS, A PHILOSOPHER AT WORK: TOWARD A PHENOMENOLOGY OF THE OTHER

The existential positions of Kierkegaard, Heidegger, Merleau-Ponty and Sartre led Wild to seek a notion of responsibility that would compensate for the now absent concept of unchanging justice that had been at the center of his aspirations to found a realistic philosophy of culture. Wild recognized, as did Sartre, the necessity for adequately explaining the concept of oppression and the idea of history. Following the lead of Merleau-Ponty and Sartre, Wild envisioned the possibility of an existential concept of the human being, compatible with the aspirations of the early Marx, in explaining the multiple layers of human alienation and the ways to their overcoming.

However, Wild's search for an authentic concept of democracy and a version of freedom that was compatible with the idea of responsibility remained firmly set against all attempts to totalize man's experience of his own life-world. Too much had been given up in Wild's break from classical realism, and too much learned from his encounter with Plato and Aristotle, to believe that the dualism of Sartre's ontology or the monism of Heidegger's metaphysics could portray the full promise of the human condition without distortion. Philosophy, on the frontiers of phenomenology, has its own terrain to explore.

The essays included in the present volume show Wild's long search for an adequate method to describe the variegated regions of human existence. We see him undertaking important new explorations of the invariant concrete, patterned structures of the life-world. Again and again we see an anterior quest for a new horizon adequate to frame the life-world itself as a meaningful whole without subjugating the Other or inhibiting the restlessness that makes man long for religious self-transcendence.

The essays included here passionately argue for human existence as the central subject of authentic philosophical reflection. Wild believed that the task of the true philosopher required the courage to inquire after man's place and promise in the scheme of things despite the progressive amputation of the limbs of philosophy by the natural and social sciences. He believed and argued for a position that asserted the autonomy of philosophic inquiry, both in its approach and in its subject matter.

The idea that human existence can itself be held open for radical inspection is a relatively recent one in the history of philosophy. It was an idea whose time was long delayed in coming by an earlier position, established from the time of Aristotle, that the existence of an individual being is intelligible only insofar as the essential traits of that being as a member of a species could be determined. The philosophical understanding of man remained impenetrably general and universal; the specifically human freedom and privileged access to being (at least to human being) are ignored. The being of a man, for Aristotle, could be adequately understood from the consideration of its analogy with the being of a dog and that of a tree. Just as the dog is a full expression of the life of the puppy and just as a tree is the full expression of a sapling, so too is man's own being, given by nature. Every being and everything and every action, as Aristotle makes clear in the opening of his *Nichomachean Ethics*, aims at a given end. To deliberate, to choose, is always to consider only the action that will lead to those given ends. The magnificently integrated Aristotelian concept of man had no more formidable or passionate expositor than John Wild.

For almost twenty-five years Wild believed that the answers to the modern human predicament depended on our ability to reclaim and update the wisdom of the ancient classical philosophical tradition. This viewpoint reached its political climax for Wild sometime after its philosophical basis had been secured and its metaphysical underpinnings explored in fastidious detail by him in the late 1930s and through the 1940s. The convulsions of modernity that, with the advent of World War II, had shaken Western civilization to its very foundations no longer made it credible or at least compelling to believe that the world was designed in such a way that man naturally tended toward an end given by nature. Wild came to reject the notion expressed by Aristotle and defended by him that the most accidental aspect of any being was its irremediable singularity.

Human contingency became the essential fact of man's being. Recognizing the inevitability of his finitude, the apprehension and concern over the meaning of his existence affirmed for Wild the fact that ends were not given by nature alone but rather decided upon by each man. Existence, far from being an ultimate accident that befalls man, constitutes his very essence. The task of phenomenology is to lay bare the patterns that belong to everyone by virtue of a shared humanity but whose expression is in a decisive way lived out by each one. The human body must be retrieved from anatomy and physiology and described in its living orientation as the aperture through which we grasp hold of the world and gropingly make our way through it. The phenomenon of the lived body, as Wild makes clear, has patterned structures that define it and are in fact presupposed by every scientific interpretation. However the world may look to a dispassionate observer, man is not indifferent to the vicissitudes of daily life mapped out by the geography of his lived-body. The time of man's lived existence is irreducible and makes claim of its own, even when confronted by the perplexities and paradoxes of the advancing sciences.

The relativistic tendencies of modern philosophy, affected by the discoveries of anthropology and cross-cultural investigations, open rather than close an existential dilemma for phenomenological reflection. Wild tackles the difficult problems presented to philosophy by the historical, cultural and ethical variations of a world that no longer finds the drama of its own existence immediately compelling or credible. These questions must be resolved by living reason on the terrain of existential facts that circumscribe the global patterns of meaning of the human life-world.

Wild himself remains convinced of the authentic demand for and promise of a religious horizon to ground the life-world of human existence. The
dominant conception that man has of himself, his values and beliefs, his
sense of what is right and what is errant, have been, Wild believed,
shaped by his religious historicity and aspirations. The Biblical concept of
man is given weight in Wild's thinking that is set in dialogue with the
Greek concept of the human condition. Wild argues that there are existential signposts pointing toward human self-transcendence.

Despite his passionate concern with existential problems that we see
mirrored throughout the whole of his career, emphasized in his continuing
fascination with and sympathy for the life of Søren Kierkegaard, Wild is
not indifferent to the technical problems that both beset and preoccupy
modern philosophy. We see him arguing for the flexibility and adequacy
of human language to reveal and inform understanding of problems that
will not disappear even when the proper rules of philosophic syntax are
followed. Wild's early respect for the possibilities of logic endures in his
sensitivity to the limits that perception places upon our language about the
world—a recognition that guards against unbridled speculation.

The passionate advocacy of phenomenology, which dominated the last
phase of Wild's career, is not impervious to its deficiencies. Wild is sensitive to the anthropocentrism that often accompanies phenomenology in
its single-minded attempt to reposition man in the center of his own
world. He resists the idea advanced by Hegel and modified in its continuation by Heidegger that the inner history of philosophy is capable of an
univocal rendering under the rubric of a single dominating concept or
idea. Wild's substitution of the concept of "world" with many independent analogically related versions is a self-conscious attempt to accom-
modate the insights expressed by Heidegger in *Being and Time* without
succumbing to a tyrannical concept of Being that would divest each being
of its uniqueness and alterity. This does not mean that Wild understood
the history of philosophy as undiluted progress. He had fought strenu-
ously in his realistic period to secure the eternal truths from Plato and
Aristotle over against the "Cartesian deformation of modern thought."

The trajectory of John Wild's philosophical career lead him to a serious
encounter with the thought of Emmanuel Levinas in his last years. Wild's
willingness to modify his previous positions testifies not only to his restlessness as a thinker, always wishing to come closer to the truth, but also
to a personal and intellectual humility. The reader should keep in mind
that while Wild and Levinas were virtual contemporaries, Wild was significantly better known, at least in the United States, than Levinas at the
time that he wrote his introduction to the English edition to *Totality and Infinity*. Nevertheless, as the reader will see in Wild's posthumous commentary on *Totality and Infinity*, Wild was remarkably open to the new

ground broken by Levinas in phenomenology and philosophy. This does not mark as radical a turn as his movement away from Aristotle and toward existential philosophy. What it does show, however, is that right up to the very end of his active career, Wild remained, above all, a philosopher at work—that is, laboring tirelessly in search of wisdom. It is clear that Wild recognized that philosophy in the twenty-first century would find its first task in confronting the radically original thought of Emmanuel Levinas.

Wild is, however, unwilling to accept Levinas's assertion that history always belongs to the domain of totality because it objectifies existence under the regime of political power, modified only by the concept of enduring influence determined by survivors. Wild's enthusiasm for Levinas's project is circumscribed by his concern for finding a philosophy that is adequate to the demands made by mass society living under the domination of technology and guided by the spirit of scientific inquiry. Wild, then, rejects the enlightenment concept of unlimited progress, Hegel's notion of necessary evolution toward freedom, Heidegger's concept of regression from primal contact with being and Levinas's foreclosing of the idea of even an open philosophical system.

He agrees with Levinas that the other person always escapes our attempt to thematize his being. The doctrine of intentionality, so valuable in recovering an oriented awareness of perceptual existence and conceptual possibilities, is not adequate to describe the world that we inhabit with others when we recognize the genuine otherness of the other. In his commentary on Levinas and in his own phenomenological reflections on the other, we see Wild critically re-examine the history of philosophy and its contemporary landscape in search of a phenomenologically based description that will do justice to our meeting with the other. In this respect it is essential, he urges, that we recognize that the existence of the Other transcends our capacity to subject the Other to a conceptual system derived from our own needs and intentions.

The rich, manifold, variegated world of human experience necessitates that philosophy, for John Wild, while capable of stable results of lasting value, whose mandatory nature is dictated by the inescapability of its task, is always in need of correction and revision. The future of philosophy depends upon its capacity to reckon with the past and to appreciate the clear voices that continue to speak on behalf of human reason while doing justice to the full reach of human promise.

NOTE

1. Interview with Mary Wild-Roy, March 1, 2005.

Note to the Reader

The Promise of Phenomenology was a collaborative endeavor almost from its inception. The editors were both students of John Wild at Yale, and he introduced them to phenomenology and to each other. Richard I. Sugarman and Roger B. Duncan are responsible for collating, transcribing, editing and annotating the papers included in this volume. The original project, begun over thirty years ago, envisioned a longer work including unpublished papers from the earlier Realistic phase of Wild's career, as well as the focus of the present book, on phenomenology and existential philosophy. The preface, the general introduction and the explanatory notes reflect the editors' understanding of Wild's philosophical itinerary, positions, views and beliefs. However, the editors have published only those essays that they believe reflect Wild's most mature thinking.

Part I: Explorations of the Human Life-world was edited and annotated primarily by Richard I. Sugarman, who also provided the explanatory notes. Part II: Conversations, Reflections and Beliefs was a collaborative endeavor, with Sugarman focusing on Wild's discussions with figures in continental philosophy and providing the explanatory notes for those sections. Roger B. Duncan is responsible for the sections on Wild's religious thought and the relation between philosophy and theology, for which he provided a historical context as well as the explanatory notes. Sugarman and Duncan researched, discussed and annotated Wild's attempts to bridge phenomenology and analytical philosophy over the course of many years, culminating in August of 2004 in a tavern in Oxford, England. Part III: Toward a Phenomenology of Transcendence was edited and introduced by Roger B. Duncan. Richard I. Sugarman is responsible for editing, annotating and introducing Part

IV: New Directions, A Philosopher at Work: Toward a Phenomenology of the Other. The papers listed in the bibliography appended at the end of this volume can be found in the Beinecke Rare Book and Manuscript Library at Yale University, available for public study and research as of January 2006.

Part I

Explorations of the Human Life-world

1

Some Reflections on the Human Life-world

EXPLANATORY NOTE

"Some Reflections on the Human Life-world" is an important transitional piece showing John Wild reluctantly, but forcefully, substituting his phenomenological conception of the human life-world for his earlier Realism. This essay examines the question of the metaphysical status of the life-world. Wild argues, above all, that the life-world is not a system, at least a closed system in the logical or realistic sense, or even in some combination of the latter two. The life-world is, for Wild, both irreducible and unsurpassable. By insisting on its irreducibility, Wild is not arguing against logical or organismic systems, but rather argues that such systems have meaning only within the *Lebenswelt*.

This paper was clearly a preliminary reflection that appears to have been given as a talk in the academic year 1956–1957. Readers familiar with Wild's work will notice his substitution of the *Lebenswelt*, so important in later Husserl, for Being, as in Heidegger. Here, Wild is struggling with himself in the presence of others to demonstrate that the life-world makes it possible to understand both Aristotelian realism and Hegelian idealism. He argues that both of these views are inadequate to deal with human existence in its concreteness.

Subsequently, Wild modifies his position against all systems by arguing for the distinction between "closed" systems, which are unacceptable, and "open" systems, which are inescapable. This distinction of the world and its multiple versions is amplified in his popular book, *Existence and the World of Freedom* (1962). Later, one of Wild's primary disagreements with Levinas, whom he so much admires, has to do with the inescapability of what he calls "open systems." Such a view as he is here first articulating also permits us to see the very origin of his break from his Realistic period. He can no longer accept Aristotle's assertion that there is no knowledge or "science" of the individual as such. Such awareness that the individual has of himself is always in a world but, at the same time, is direct in the sense that William James speaks of "knowledge by acquaintance" as opposed to "knowledge about." Wild will continue to argue for direct apprehension of what he will later call "world facts" as opposed to "scientific facts" (see *Existence and the World of Freedom*). Despite its unfinished character, it is valuable in yet another respect—it shows Wild formulating his thinking as he moves toward conceptual refinements.

When we think of an individual human being, it is natural for us to think of him as a substance enclosed within the limits of his bodily organism, and capable of existing apart from other beings within these limits. He may depend on other beings, like the air that he breathes and the earth that supports him. But his own being lies within the boundaries of his body, and what lies beyond these boundaries is, strictly speaking, something other than him. He might therefore be conceived without them in his essence, being in himself alone.

This assumption has been questioned in the past by great philosophers like Spinoza and Hegel, who have asserted that man is essentially or internally related to other things beyond him, in a total system that governs all of its parts. This thesis has been defended by all the great monistic system builders of our Western past. Recent phenomenological thinkers also have questioned this assumption in the recent past, but in a different way, leading them to very different conclusions. Man is not a substance capable of existing in himself alone. He exists only in a "world," as it is called. And without this world, including other things and persons, man cannot be understood or even properly conceived. But this world is not a total system determining and regulating each of its component parts. It certainly possesses a certain unity and wholeness of its own, but in such a way that room is left for human freedom and autonomy, flexibility and free-play in its various parts. In this paper, I wish to examine the nature of this world in which we live and exist, and the many ways in which it differs from those other types of order we call systems. If what we mean by the world is not a system, what type of order is it? If we cannot think about it systematically without reduction and distortion, how then are we to think about it adequately? I think that these questions need to be raised, for much of the concrete phenomenological thinking is now directed to the human *Lebenswelt*, as Husserl called it, and to its manifold phenomena, regions and structures.

THE WORLD IS NOT A SYSTEM

I shall now divide systems into three types: the logical, the real, and those which claim to be both logical and real (like that of Hegel), and shall argue that the world belongs to none of these three classes. I believe that this is an exhaustive list. But if other types of organizations can be found to which the word 'system' properly applies, I am prepared to argue that what we call world also falls outside of this class. If there are readers who hold that I am arbitrarily restricting the range of the term 'system,' which legitimately applies to any form or order whatsoever, I shall not quarrel with this usage. If I can show that the term 'system' is being used in a significantly different sense when it is applied to the world in which we exist, my conclusion will still stand, and I shall not confuse the issue by using the same term 'system' for the different types of order.

By a logical system, I mean a set of concepts and propositions which are brought together into a unity by such logical relations as class inclusion and/or implications of some type. Thus, the traditional Aristotelian scheme of classification which adheres to class inclusion, from individuals falling under their proper species to higher general categories, and finally to the supreme, analogous concept of being, constitutes a unified logical system with a supposed ground in the real facts of nature. Also, a set of propositions, all of which may be deduced from a small number of primitive propositions, makes up a unified logical system of this kind. In so far as this logical system can be shown to be exemplified in certain facts, real relations become (merely) logical expressions of these facts. [In a side note, Wild asks "Does this mean that these facts reduce to mere logical relations?"]

By a real system, [I] mean a set of real entities which are brought into a unity by real relations such as that of causality, which make the action of one part dependent on that of another in such a way that the different, interdependent activities fit together to achieve a unified result. A machine and an organism are unified real systems of this kind. Each part of a machine performs a special partial function. When functioning together they achieve a unified result, like the cutting action of a lathe. The relations between the different cells of a living organism are probably not causal in the same sense, and are more complex. But they are mutually interdependent, and when functioning together normally, they achieve a complete and unified result, the sustaining of normal life. The same is true of human institutions maintained by the cooperative action of different individual members. When functioning adequately, these different activities work together to achieve a complete and unified result, like the collection and delivery of mail by a post-office. These are different types of unified real systems.

We have given examples of systems that have been supposed to be both real and logical, like the traditional hierarchy of species and genera in the Aristotelian tradition. Existing human individuals, for example, possess rational natures which are actually similar in *rerum natura*. The mind is then able to separate the abstract forms of rationality from the individual differences and to predicate this of different individuals in the same identical sense. This is also true of the higher genera such as animals, and living organisms, and of the highest analogous form of being. This hierarchy of logical predicates is, therefore, based on the real similarities of existing individuals.

Another system which is both logical and real is defended in the Hegelian philosophy. Here, concepts are related dialectically by the relations of negation and synthesis, as in the cases of being, nothing, and becoming, and logic, nature and spirit. This process by which a concept negates itself or objectifies itself, and then returns to itself in a richer form, can be thought through logically. But it can also be observed in the dynamic processes of history where the necessary relations of reason become concrete and real. This is no doubt the best known and the most influential case of a system for which the claim is made that it is both 'rational logical' and real. It is one because every distinct phase is immediately related by reason to other phases, and necessarily passes into them by the creative advances of history. It is complete because the absolute Idea which includes all partial phases is gradually developed and articulated by the historical process itself.

Now the human *Lebenswelt* has been clearly focused and carefully studied by many phenomenologists, including Husserl, Heidegger, Sartre and Merleau-Ponty. These thinkers markedly differ in many ways, but there are also significant points of agreement in their different studies. For instance, not one of them, I think, would deny that the oriented space of the *Lebenswelt* is different from any purely objective or geometric space. In the light of these studies, I shall now argue that this *Lebenswelt*, while it possesses certain patterns of its own, is not a system in any of the three senses we have just examined (the rational, the logical, and those that belong to both). I shall have to be brief in presenting the evidence to keep this paper within bounds, and [presuppose] some familiarity with the most recent phenomenological literature referred to.

In the first place, the *Lebenswelt* does not refer to a purely conceptual system which is first thought out in terms of concepts before a search is made for real examples. It is the other way around. I am directly familiar with the world in which I exist, as I am directly familiar with myself. In fact, the two belong together and I cannot be familiar with the one unless I am familiar with the other. This familiarity involves feeling and perception, and does not require concepts. It is found wherever man is found, and seems to belong to human existence. The young child is acquainted with the movements of his hand before he has words for them, and men were directly familiar with their life-world and its structures (like space and time) long before they had made any conceptual analysis of it. And this familiarity continues after such an analysis has been made. No intellectual statement, no matter how accurate it may be, can ever take the place of this direct acquaintance, or know-how, as we sometimes call it, by a phrase which emphasizes its achievements rather than its being. Our human being-in-the-world involves patterns of meaning. But if they are patterns of life or patterns of the world they cannot be logically abstracted. They must also exist. Hence, we may say that the world itself is an existential pattern, neither abstract meaning alone, nor bare existence without meaning, but a union of existence with meaning. Hence, such patterns can be sustained and broken down neither by brute force alone nor thinking alone, but only by meaningful or responsible action bearing meaning. Concepts of action may be abstract. But a real and new act, like the pressing of my finger on a typewriter key, or my moving to another chair and sitting down in it, are never separate and alone. Thus, I cannot press the key without singling out this one from the other keys, the keyboard from the rest of the machine, the machine from the table and the remainder of the room, the room and the house from the out-of-doors, and so on to the limits of the world. Any act bearing the real tang of reality occurs in this widening context, which always surrounds it as a real happening in this context which I call the 'world.' A happening or an act that lacks this hazy surrounding fringe is the thought of a happening or an event, not a real event. The world is not a set of abstract thoughts with no fringes.

Now, in the second place, the world which fringes real acts and events is not a real system in the sense in which machines, organisms and institutions are real systems actually found in the world where we exist. Each of these systems is a thing, something existing either in or out of its position in the world. This world, on the other hand, is not a thing of this kind. It is the indeterminate ground on which they appear, and with respect to which they are in or out of place. But the world has no place in a more ultimate ground. It is already the ultimate ground. Hence, it makes no sense to inquire for the place of the world, nor to ask, for example, whether it is in or out of its place. This sharply distinguishes the world from the three kinds of things we have mentioned (machines, organisms and institutions). The world itself is not a thing or a system in the world. But in addition to this basic difference there are other characteristics which distinguish the world from each of the three in turn. In the case of any machine, like the arrow or the chariot, we know that there were men who preceded it and existed without it. No artifact is essential to man, and thus coeval with him. But while we can readily conceive of men existing in very simple worlds quite different from our own, or any with which we are familiar, we cannot conceive of men not inhabiting any region, and not existing in any world. Whatever we may mean by the world, it is essential to man, and not made by him, but coeval with him. This marks the world off from any machine or artifact.

This difference does not apply to the notion of organism. Even though we may believe that science may soon succeed in synthesizing living compounds, we cannot believe that man is the original maker or creator of living forms. In fact, we know that highly developed living forms are procreated by other organisms. We cannot believe, therefore, that the earliest men came into being without other organisms producing them. Why, then, can we not think of the world as a great living organism which has produced the successive generations of living men as its component parts or cells? As a matter of fact, many thinkers have used this analogy in thinking of the world that we inhabit, and we need only turn to Hume's *Dialogues on Natural Religion* to find telling arguments against it. But it is now possible to formulate other arguments grounded on recent phenomenological studies. For example, each cell or organ of the entire organism requires the support of the others in performing its special function, which is necessary for the achievement of a single determinate result. This is not true, however, of man in relation to the rest of the world. He cannot live without the "functioning of the other parts." So far the analogy holds. But then it breaks down. Different "natural" functions have been assigned to man which he supposedly must perform to achieve the single overarching purpose of the universe. Different definitions of this overarching purpose have been given. But not one as yet has been demonstrated. These require different functions to be performed by man and by individual men. But men have acted in very different ways throughout recorded history, and yet not one of those has as yet been shown to be necessary for the normal life of the world as a whole, nor has anyone come even close to showing what this might be like as "a single determinate result." Here, the organic analogy completely breaks down. If certain cells of a living organism act in deviant ways the result is disease, and the life of the whole is threatened. But men have acted in very deviant ways, and the world goes on supporting them. The parts of a living plant and animal do not possess autonomy of this kind.

The world is not like a natural organism which requires certain determinate functions to be performed by virtue of its highest and guiding parts. At any rate, men who exist in the world like parts have a freedom and autonomy which does not fit with this conception. Perhaps it is not a natural system, like an organism, which has evolved independently of man, and now confronts him with certain fixed laws and structures which he must obey or suffer disastrous consequences. Perhaps these laws have originated in the mind of man and were imposed on nature by human toil and labor. In this case, we should look at the world not as an order imposed on man from the outside, but rather as developing creatively in history and imposed by man upon nature, and also upon himself. This would account for many known facts: for example, that different human groups and even certain individuals in what we call free societies inhabit very different worlds, and that worlds pass away in human history and are then replaced by other worlds with different patterns and forms of meaning. The world, then, is not a natural fact that simply has to be recognized and accepted, but rather a construction of man that arises and disappears in history, an expression of human freedom and autonomy. Why should we not think of the world in this way? There are several reasons.

There is, no doubt, some truth in this conception. The world is more like an institution, a system formed by man, than an organic system that is simply found in nature. But this characterization is also inadequate. The while of human existence from birth to death is included within the world. It is not included within any institution like a university or a post-office. The original forming of the institution, for example, is a project of human existence. But it is not included in the system which is not yet there to include it. The world is a far broader and richer horizon. This is a first basic difference. There is another which is closely connected; we shall call it rational comprehension, or englobement. In the case of any organization established by man, such as a post-office or a heating system, it is possible for a single mind to understand the meaning of very different functions that are being performed, no matter how manifold and complex they may be. Each of them fits with the rest in a system that achieves a single purpose—the transfer of written communications within a geographic area, or the providing of heat for a community. Each worker can understand the nature of what he is doing, and how it serves the common aim. Every action is pervaded by this common purpose, and can, therefore, be clearly understood. This is what we mean by rational englobement. Even though these human systems must be accounted for, the world cannot be comprehended in this way. All of them are in the world, have their places and their regions in the world, and each of them can be comprehended. Why, then, should we not think of the world itself as a comprehensive system pervaded by a single purpose in terms of which all these subordinated orders can be clearly understood? Many monistic thinkers have followed this line of thought. But as we have noted, this conclusion is out of line with the facts. The situation seems to be this: Human thought and labor have ordered certain natural elements and areas into meaningful regions. Thus, the factory is a region for the production of goods of a certain kind, the store is a place of exchange, and the town is a region for human dwelling and life. So far all is clear. Each place and region is pervaded by a meaning that has been imposed on it by human toil and can be clearly and unequivocally understood. This is the case as long as we assume that we know what man is for. But as soon as we raise this question, the issue becomes more problematic . . .

2

Frontiers of Phenomenology and Existential Philosophy

EXPLANATORY NOTE

The essay "The Frontiers of Phenomenology and Existential Philosophy" serves as a virtual prospectus of the phenomenological investigations that would occupy John Wild for the last phase of his career. This essay is perhaps John Wild's clearest, most cogent introduction to phenomenology and existential philosophy. Many of the themes that Wild would go on to explore in much greater detail are introduced here against the backdrop of traditional philosophy.

Wild believed that "living philosophy" involved a continuing dialogue with the great thinkers of the past. In order to understand the tasks that await the philosopher, he must be cognizant of the traditions that form the framework of the discussion into which he enters. It is, in good part, for this reason that Wild's views on engaging new approaches, methods and previously overlooked dimensions of philosophy were taken with such seriousness by philosophical traditionalists. Wild believed philosophy must remain rigorous in its approach, timely in its questioning and alert to explaining its positions in the face of its critics.

Wild shows why he rejects Cartesian rationalism and British empiricism. The former, he argues, is impervious to human experience as it is lived and reduces the human person to an indifferent spectator of his own world. British empiricism of the kind found in Hume, on the other hand, is insufficiently radical to describe what Wild calls "world-facts" that map out the human life-world. The human life-world, according to Wild, has a logic of its own that is not merely formal in character. Wild refers to this logic as the existential or empirical a priori. The invariant patterns of the *Lebenswelt* provide philosophy with an autonomous domain of enquiry. Lived body, lived time and lived space belong to the human life-world before we become consciously aware of it. The subjects that Wild analyzes in "The Frontiers of Phenomenology and Existential Philosophy" focus on, but are not limited to, giving an overview of the basic patterns of the human life-world. It is in this sense that we gain a clear idea of what Wild regards to be the task urgent and proper to philosophical exploration. In an essay found later in this book, "An Empirical Approach to the A Priori," Wild discusses this subject systematically and elaborates upon its importance. What is at stake here is no less than the claim that philosophy still has an autonomous domain of enquiry. The human life-world is the primary subject of investigation for phenomenology.

The "lived body" is necessary to explain how we can make our way through a world of oriented time and space through our lived-experience prior to conceptual reflection. In the essay before us, Wild gives a number of lucid and important illustrations of the way that the "lived body" is different from and presupposed by scientific discourse on the anatomical body. Wild connects the lived body to our awareness of the relation of appearance to reality. In so doing, he provides a novel resolution of what has been called the bent-stick problem in epistemology.

In addition, Wild becomes particularly animated in discussing the contributions phenomenology has already made to psychiatry and psychology, and is beginning to make to the other human sciences. He closes "The Frontiers of Phenomenology and Existential Philosophy" by introducing the notion of the world and its multiple versions. This discussion prefigures another essay of Wild's that we have included in this section, "A Phenomenological Approach to Relativism."

This essay was originally given as a lecture to the Department of Philosophy at Yale, most likely in the fall of 1962. This was exactly one year before Wild moved to Yale from Northwestern University. It is probable that Wild was giving this talk in anticipation of the possible decision to relocate.

Like so many of Wild's reflections, "The Frontiers of Phenomenology and Existential Philosophy" is of value to a continuum of students ranging from novices to university professors to scholars of philosophy.

One of the most important results of this exploration of the life-world is a growing skepticism concerning the traditional dualism of soul vs. body which was strongly emphasized by Plato, still defended, with certain qualifications, by Aristotle, and revived in an even more exaggerated form in modern times by Descartes. This radical dualism has now crept into our common speech, and into our common sense modes of thinking. It conflicts with evidence that has been brought into the light by recent scientific and philosophical studies of man. Hence, there is a widespread sense of the inadequacy of this traditional separation of the so-called soul from the so-called body, and of the need for overcoming it. But the meeting of this need is an arduous enterprise which will involve new approaches to the world of our lived existence, the forging of new concepts and meanings, and, ultimately, of radically new world perspectives quite different from those with which we are now familiar. It is one thing to reject this dualism in a purely abstract and theoretical manner, and quite another to show how it may be rejected actually by new meanings and new ways of thinking and speaking which neither presuppose it nor conflict with the facts. One such concept is that of "the lived body," which has emerged from recent phenomenological and psychiatric investigations. This concept is still being developed and clarified. But it has already led to exploratory investigations on the frontiers of phenomenology which have revolutionary implications for our understanding of man and the world in which he exists, and which I shall now attempt to summarize.

It has long been known that I do not know my own body merely as an object, lying there before the senses and the mind. Thus, when presented with pictures of five pairs of hands, I cannot normally pick out the pictures of my own. And yet, of course, I know my own hands—but not as objects from a visual or spectatorial point of view. I know them and feel them rather by operating with them, in the very act of handling and manipulating things; and the lived body, known in this way, is very different from the objective body as known by an external observer, even the trained physician. It is so different that in certain disturbed conditions, well known to the psychiatrist, the paralyzed person does not recognize his helpless extended limb as his. It belongs to the doctor! The living person does not exist in the objective perspective of a detached observer, but in an entirely different horizon that has to be understood, if it is to be understood at all, in a very different way. This world is centered in his lived body, and this body, as he operates it and lives it, is given a functional unity which is not visible to an objective observer. He does not face the world and operate by means of a set of isolated limbs and organs which are merely joined together. It is not merely by his hand and arm that he picks up the book. The posture of his whole lived body is involved.

The tradition has certainly been right in separating the active person from the objective body which can be observed as an inert, extended mass from a detached point of view. But it has been mistaken in inferring from this that the active "self" is to be identified with a disembodied spirit. This grievous error has led it to a neglect of what we are calling the lived body that has brought forth not only artificial problems which never should have been raised but misleading "solutions" of legitimate questions that have engendered further errors. The self who behaves and actively pursues his chosen projects in the world is an embodied self. This fact is now clearly recognized not only by critical phenomenologists like Merleau-Ponty, but by many of the more advanced British analytical philosophers, including Gilbert Ryle. Indeed, this can be shown by a reference to the ways in which we refer to human behavior in our ordinary language.

Thus, it is not a particular faculty, or an isolated limb, but the whole human person who normally acts and behaves. Hence we use personal pronouns in referring to acts of this kind, and we say: I am speaking; he is taking a walk by the river; or she is now in this room. But it is evident that these instances of behavior cannot be performed without the active body. It is only with this lived body that I can achieve my purposes and behave in these ways.

It is certainly improper to follow Marcel in speaking of the self as a being incarnated in a body, for there is no evidence pointing to a disincarnate self. Aristotle's early image, in which he compared the soul's relation to the body with that of the pilot to his ship, is unacceptable, since, as long as we exist in the world, we cannot leave this "ship." Our living language does not fit with the notion of the body as an instrument, even as a necessary instrument. For we do not say that I walk by means of my limbs, or by means of my body. We simply say: I walk. The Cartesian view, for example, that I fall down stairs only by accident is definitely odd.

Neither does it fit the facts to say, with some existential philosophers, that the body as a thing in the world is a link which enables me to deal with other things in the world. This is wrong for several reasons. First, as we shall see, the body is not only a thing in the world to be regarded objectively, it is also something more. By its movements, and by its way of being in the world, it helps to order or constitute this world-field in which it exists. I am also in the same world with my body, located with it where it is, projected in a direction of the spatial field constituted by its motions, and actually moving when, and where, and in the direction toward which it is moving.

Traditional images and phrases are too dualistic. If we are to follow the evidence, the only phrase which will do justice to the situation is something like: I am my body, not the extended object which can be observed by someone else, or even myself as a spectator, but the active body as I live it and exist from the inside. (Of course, this does not mean that I am the purely objective body of traditional materialism, whose motions are externally observed.)

Why then, it may be asked, has dualism, if it has no genuine empirical foundation, played such a central role throughout the whole course of our Western history from its beginnings in ancient Greece down to our own time? Why are we humans so prone to dualistic theories of this kind, if there is no empirical evidence from them? In working out their answer to this vital question, phenomenologists have, of course, looked for such evidence, and they have found it. When we are tired and weary, the body, as we say, resists our efforts. It is at such times that the phenomenon of willing to persist in our course arises. This can easily be interpreted as the act of an immaterial faculty. But there is no real need to accept an unverifiable hypothesis of this kind. The lived body is a complex affair, in which certain functions, less fatigued, may work against others, more fatigued. Also, in many kinds of illness, including frostbite and paralysis, parts of the body may sink to the level of an inert, unfeeling, extended mass, while verbal thinking still persists. This more extreme phenomenon of self-division can be accounted for in the same way, without the acceptance of any form of psycho-physical dualism.

Dualistic theories are based upon departures from an original mode of existence which is not divided against itself. The lived body is normally active, and moves itself as an integrated whole. In doing this, it is wholly in the world, and yet at the same time it is the constitutive center of this world. In the past, these constitutive, ordering functions have been attributed to an immaterial mind or spirit. In our time, however, the groundlessness of such theories has been clearly seen, and in medicine we find non-dualistic, psycho-somatic approaches to illness well under way. Philosophy still lags behind. We are desperately in need of a psycho-somatic philosophy, psycho-somatic categories, and modes of speech. This is a new frontier, and in phenomenology a bare beginning, at least, has been made. Shortly before his death, Merleau-Ponty made a statement in which he recognized this need, and outlined his plan for a book along these lines, which he was never able to finish. But the need is widely recognized, and several exploratory studies have been made both by psychiatrists like Erwin Straus, of the Veterans Hospital, Lexington, Kentucky, and by philosophers like Samuel Todes, a teacher at the Massachusetts Institute of Technology, now Santayana Fellow in Philosophy at Harvard.

In the whole literature of classical philosophy, and even of past phenomenology, no careful attention has been paid to the lived body, and to the essential role of bodily functions and habits in constituting the lifeworld. I am originally on my way and engaged in the world. Detached reflection is derivative and emerges later. The life-world is the field of my bodily needs, and it is divided into its different regions of production, eating, sleeping, education, recreation, etc. in accordance with these needs. The meaning of any thing, or activity, is its place in this world-field which is centered in the lived body. The education of the child consists in learning these meanings, and the habits that are required to satisfy his desires and needs. Our desires are restricted by the facts. We cannot desire the impossible. But a need is stronger than a desire. It is a desire that must be satisfied if the life-world is to endure.

As long as we live, we are engaged and seeking, that is, we are moving toward the satisfaction of some desire or need. It is through this bodily movement that the spatio-temporal structure of the life-field is actually constituted. This life-space is not a mere geometric spread in which there are no directions and all points are alike. As we have noted, it is oriented into forward and back, right and left, up and down, with respect to the different places and directions towards which my body is able to move. If I am to respond adequately to the independent things and persons around me in this life-space, I must develop habits of anticipation which will enable me to prepare for what they will do in the future. This future is what I face ahead of me—before me. As I move ahead toward this future I am constantly passing by things. What I have passed by lies behind me in the past.

Dr. Erwin Straus, in a recent and highly significant article, "The Upright Posture" (*The Psychiatric Quarterly*, October 1952) has shown how the upright posture of the body has enabled man to gain a distance from the primary objects of his care, has firmly established the "distance" senses of sight and hearing in the exercise of their guiding functions, and has greatly increased the range of our anticipatory responses to the things and events that we face in the future. So long as I maintain the delicate balance between the forces that threaten to upset me, I can make my own way, freely and with poise toward the things that are coming, and for which I am prepared. When I lose my poise, my movements become awkward or backward, and I lose control of the situation. In awkward, or backward, movement I cannot foresee the things that are to come. As a matter of fact, I get to know them only after I have passed them. I no longer face the future, and my knowledge, like that of a detached spectator, is restricted to what I have already passed. I lose the initiative in my active engagement with the forces around me. My actions become more and more fumbling and awkward, until I can no longer initiate any motion of my own, and am reduced to the status of an inert object in the fields of other, active agents.

It is only though bodily movement that I get a sense of the global, oriented space in which objects can be located, and of a global time, centered at the moment when I now am, stretching before me into the future toward which I am moving, and behind me into the things that I have passed. At this moment, I can come to a stand, and in this stance (instant) I can turn around, without moving ahead or passing, to survey the things and the forces that now lie around me, as I stand at the center of my circumstances. Our action always takes place in a field of circumstances, and we cannot pass out of one set without moving into another. This spatio-temporal field is centered in a living, moving body that maintains its identity. It is constituted as an integral whole, so that there is a necessary connection between its parts. Insofar as we continue to pursue our way with integrity, it is one field, and we live one life within it. But this field is generated by our capacity to move, and anything that restricts our motion also restricts the field.

Thus, the motion of the man in prison is restricted. Hence, unless he can develop special projects of his own, his field of action becomes so narrow and confined that it is in constant danger of collapsing. The whole world of motion, where things are going on, seems to lie outside his cell. He can inaugurate no motion of his own, he has difficulty in keeping track of objective clock time, its measure, and simply drags out his days in an endless immobility. He faces no future. He cannot be on a way of his own which will enable him to pass things by. Instead of this, everything that is going on in the "external" world seems to be passing him by. He is reduced to the role of a spectator who sees only what is passed and now lies in the past.

Todes makes some interesting comments on the phenomenology of pain, which also interferes with motion, and, in its more extreme forms, may suppress and swallow up the whole world-field. Thus, the pain in my wounded and immobilized foot is partly objectified. It is not in me; it is rather in my foot, an object lying there before me. Such pain is an intermediate stage in the gradual loss of bodily area. Later on, it may become numb and irresponsive, and finally a mere corpselike, bodily mass that I carry with me wherever I go, like the famous ghost in a dead machine. The excruciating pain which wracks my whole body is no longer in me. It is rather true that I myself, and my whole world-scheme are swallowed up in it. I lose all mobility, and can no longer generate a world-field by my action. Only my visual view remains, but this also is taken up into the pain in which my world simply disappears. In this experience, both I, myself and my world are lost in the torture of my body.

The traditional mind-body dualism has enabled objectively minded thinkers to discount such experiences, together with the whole field of our lived existence, as a train of subjective sensations, ideas, and volitions contained within an immaterial soul or mind. According to this theory, the real world is not centered in man. It is purely objective and uncontaminated by any subjective factors whatsoever. Phenomenology has now shown that this oversimplified conception is totally false to the facts of our lived existence. As Erwin Straus says in his article: "The idea of a mind-body unit demands first of all a revision of those traditional concepts of psychology which are shaped in accordance with the theory of a mind-body dichotomy. Experience can no longer be interpreted as a train, accumulation, or integration of sensations, percepts, thoughts, ideas, volitions occurring in the soul, the mind, the consciousness, or the unconscious, for that matter. In experiencing, man finds himself always within the world, directed towards it, acting and suffering" (p. 32).

This world, which is presupposed by all purely theoretical and objective thinking, has peculiar structures of its own which are neither purely physical nor purely mental in the traditional senses of these terms. It offers us a new approach to the problem of the a priori synthetic. The world in which we exist is not unified by objective structures which are merely observed from a detached point of view. This fails to account for the human factor that is present in all thinking and knowing, as well as for the a priori that is necessarily present in its roots. But neither is it a mere mental integration of elements in consciousness, over which the mind has complete control. This fails to account for the hard factuality of the existence into which we have been thrown, and the resistant circumstances out of which our bodily activity arises. Phenomenology is now suggesting another alternative, not subject to the many difficulties which have been found in these traditional views. This does not mean, of course, that all mystery has been eliminated. But the situation is changed. Dualism presents us with three mysteries, that of matter, that of pure mind, and how the two can work together. The last two may now be eliminated. What remains is the mystery of the lived body, the *corps vécu* and its openness to the world.

The life-world of the individual person is centered in his lived body which is surrounded by independent things, events, and forces which also exist with him in the world. It is by the intentional movements of this active body that he constitutes a spatio-temporal field, and organizes a meaningful world around his projects. Many alternatives are always open, but certain conditions, laid down by the structure of the human body, remain fixed. These conditions are not only physical. They are psycho-physical, in that they determine a priori both the patterns of physical action, as well as those of the awareness that dwells in this action.

Thus, in his revealing essay, Straus shows in detail "the correspondence between human physique and the basic traits of human experience and behavior" (p. 32). For example, the upright posture, which is peculiar to man, gives him a distance from things on the ground, and frees his arms and hands from their supporting and locomotive functions. But these are also correlated with changes in human awareness. "The horizon is widened, removed; the distant becomes momentous . . . In the same measure, contact with near things is lost . . ."(p. 10). Also "the hand becomes an organ of active, gnostic touching, the epicritic, discriminating instrument par excellence . . . and now ranks with the eye and the ear" (p. 16). As Straus remarks, "this intimate interpenetration of sensorium and motorium is well expressed in words like 'handling', 'fingering', 'thumbing', 'grouping', each of which combines the active and noetic meaning of toughing into one" (p. 18).

We see here a new conception of the a priori synthetic coming into the light. I do not know that my lived body is the center of my life-world by an induction, or observation from a detached point of view. Whether I ever succeed in conceptualizing it or not, I know this a priori by the awareness that dwells in my bodily intentions and acts. Hence, Hume, from his purely spectatorial point of view which reduced the lived body to an object, and disintegrated it into a mere set of contiguous organs and limbs, was unable to discover any necessary connections between these objective impressions. These necessary connections come from the active, living body which I am. Thus, I know that as long as I can move and act, I will be surrounded by an "active" (Straus) oriented space, that as I move forward I will face a future, and will leave behind me in the past all the circumstances I have passed. As long as my body persists, and is able to move, I know that there will be a thread of continuity running through my disparate experiences. Each new occurrence, no matter how unique it may be, will be experienced by the same body seeking to satisfy the same bodily needs. There must be a minimum uniformity in this world, or I could not survive at all.

Hence, in making my way through the world, I do not follow Hume in discounting the active knowledge that I find in my habits, and in the anticipatory acts that they lead me to perform (as in catching a ball, for example). This is a logical and mathematical perfectionism. It is only through these habits, and their indwelling knowledge, that the world becomes habitable. As long as I exist, therefore, I must maintain a general trust in them. When formulated in propositions, and subjected to an objective scrutiny, this trust is, of course, not logically necessary. But it is existentially necessary. As long as we exist, we must believe in those objects and structures which constitute the world, and which make it endurable. It is only under endurable conditions that we can endure. What it would be like for us to be enduring in an unendurable world is beyond our powers of imagination and comprehension.

It is in this sense that the basic structures of what Husserl called the life-world are necessary and a priori. Traditional philosophy has discounted it as "unstable," "irrational," "subjective," and "ineffable." But phenomenology has shown that these epithets are unjustified. This so-called "immediate experience" is not a mere chaos of subjective impressions contained within a mind. It is a vast and far-ranging world horizon with a place not only for our innermost feeling and thoughts, but for all the objects of the sciences, and with peculiar structures of its own. It is prior to, and presupposed by, all special, theoretical investigations. It is known pre-objectively and pre-conceptually by the awareness that dwells in our bodily intentions and acts. But modern phenomenology has found ways of penetrating to some of is structures, and of expressing them in a meaningful language. The disciplined exploration of the life-world has only just begun. But it has already suggested new approaches to basic traditional problems like that of the a priori element in knowledge which we have just considered. Other new conceptions have also been developed.

Let me now consider one epistemological concept emerging on the frontiers of phenomenology, which has aspects of genuine originality. This is the concept of an awareness dwelling in our bodily acts and intentions which we have noted in Straus and other contemporary phenomenologists. It has played an increasingly important role in phenomenology after Husserl, and breaks with traditional assumptions in several respects, the most important of which is the following. On the whole, the traditional philosophy of the West has maintained that knowledge is primarily concerned with its object, and only indirectly and obliquely with its own peculiar, immaterial acts. In Aristotelian terms, each noetic faculty is determined by its formal object. Thus, sight, strictly speaking, knows only its formal object, color; hearing knows sound; and the intellect knows objective forms and relations. We can obtain no clear and direct grasp of consciousness itself, but only of its objects.

There is no awareness dwelling in our bodily acts. The only way we can clearly know a conscious intention, or any self-originating act, is to make it the object of another intention, which in turn remains unknown until it can become the object of a further intention, and so on. This traditional view was taken over by Husserl, and is clearly expressed in his *Cartesian Meditations*. The conscious center of experience, therefore, can never be directly known. Rather, it must be inferred by peculiar inference as a transcendental condition of the objects we experience.

There have been several important exceptions to this centrifugal type of epistemology, as we may call it, in the history of Western philosophy. Thus, Augustine and his mediaeval followers defended an opposite centripetal type of theory, according to which the human agent has a direct, non-objective knowledge of himself and his own acts. But in the long controversy to which this opposition gave rise, Aristotoelian Thomists emerged victorious, and the centripetal view was submerged, until the coming of Descartes and his principle of the *cogito ergo sum*. Descartes makes it clear that he is not referring to any knowledge of myself as an object. He does not mean *cogito me cogitantem*. At the very time that I am doubting, in the very act, I directly and immediately know myself. This notion was further developed by some of his French successors as a new approach to human existence which came to be called reflexive analysis. But with the coming of Kant and German idealism this important movement was submerged by centrifugal transcendental trends of thought until recent times.

Thus Sartre, in his book *The Transcendence of the Ego*, made a penetrating criticism of transcendentalism, and defended the Cartesian conception of a self-revealing consciousness which he called "non-positional awareness." Since this time, it has played an increasingly important role in phenomenological research, and, as we have seen very recently on the frontiers of present day phenomenology, it has been separated from the traditional notion of an immaterial consciousness, and has been, at last, identified with the psycho-physical awareness that dwells in our bodily acts. For a good account of this development, one should read the third essay of Thévenaz in his book *What Is Phenomenology?*, recently published by the Northwestern University Press.

Our consciousness is not locked up in a mental container. It is joined to our bodily acts which reach out to their objects. Hence, it reveals not only our intentions, but also something about the real things and persons with which they are concerned. When we reach out our hand, we are guided by an anticipatory habit which leads us to expect something, though we may be only exploring, and this expectation is either confirmed or disconfirmed when we carry out the act. This discovery of a revealing awareness that inhabits our bodily acts and intentions has led to recent investigations that, I believe, have shed a new light on how we distinguish between appearances and real things, a traditional problem of modern epistemology.

In our perceiving of things and persons in the life-world, we are not passive receivers of random impressions that impinge upon us from the outside. We are actively engaged in the pursuit of some project, even though this may be one of exploration. This bodily activity joined with a revealing power makes certain things appear in the direction on which our attention is focused. As we turn our eyes or move our hands in a certain direction, we bring certain appearances into existence. As Husserl first clearly showed in his well-known account of *Abschattungen* (profiles), these appearances of real things are always partial and perspectival. The whole table may finally come to appear to me at a given moment, but only through its profile.

I cannot deny any appearance that appears to me while it appears. But the actual investigation of a real thing in the life-world requires activity on my part, and this takes time. By such activity I may also make certain illusory appearances disappear. This disappearing is not the same as sheer non-being. Only what appears can be made to disappear. I must look at the table from a different position. If problems arise, I will crawl under it, open its drawers, walk around it, and feel its different surfaces. If, as in this case, these are the appearances of a real thing, they will fit together and hold up in time, so that I get a sense of the style of the whole things as it passes from one profile to another. This real independent thing always resists me both physically and mentally. I never exhaust its manifold depths and aspects. No matter what I find, I know that there is something further there to be revealed, beyond what is momentarily appearing. But once I get a grasp of its style, I see the whole thing through its profile, and I know that it is what I have all along taken it to be. I can make the profiles of the past interlock with those I am now revealing, and with those I anticipate in the future, and I can give the thing a real place in the field of my experience.

An illusory appearance, at its moment, appears just like a profile. But it does not hold up in time. If my exploratory movements are properly directed, I can make them disappear. Take the bent appearances of the famous straight stick, held partly under water. At the given moment when they appear, they are like real profiles. But they do not hold up in time as I actively investigate them with my body. If I run my fingers along the stick, or lift it out of the water, I can make them disappear. I do not deny that they were once present. But they do not fit with the real profiles of the stick. They are somehow relevant to it, and were found in the neighborhood of the stick. But they do not belong to it as real. I can give them no enduring place in my spatial field. They are illusions.

We must note that this distinction depends upon my engagement in actively perceiving throughout a span of time. If I were to fall back into the attitude of a purely detached spectator, I could not make this distinction. One appearance would simply succeed another at different moments, and it would be easy to reduce veridical profiles to the status of separate impressions, or illusions. Without the exploratory movements of the living body, the distinction between reality and illusion cannot be made. Hence, it is not surprising that Hume, who in his official philosophy adopted the detached point of view of a spectator, could make no sense of it. Veridical profiles had to be reduced to logical atoms in the neighborhood of certain logical constructions which are not actually perceived but nevertheless called real, like Locke's famous something-I-know-not-what that underlies the appearances. The logical theories of Russell and Carnap are simply more elegant versions of Hume. These are spectatorial theories of perception. They ignore the perceptual field of the active body. They split the continuous act of perceiving into separate non-relational atoms, and leave out the revealing movements of the body which are essential. This, I believe, is a real insight which has recently emerged from the frontiers of phenomenology.

Let me now turn to a basic philosophical, or metaphysical, issue which is now emerging from this discovery of the active body and the human life-world. What is the relation between this horizon and the perspectives of objective reason, and the different natural or objective sciences? There is nothing, from the motions of the stars to those of the atomic nuclei, from plant growth to human behavior, that cannot be examined, measured, and analyzed from an objective point of view, and there can be no serious question that it has given us precious knowledge and power, without which our mass existence on the earth would now be impossible. The lives of all of us depend upon it. On the other hand, no one acquainted with the recent results of phenomenological research in philosophy, clinical psychology, psychiatry, anthropology, and other human disciplines, can seriously question the existence of another life-world, as we have been calling it, with which every living human being is directly familiar, and which is characterized by a different kind of fact (world-fact) as against scientific fact, a different kind of meaning, and a distinctive structure of its own. Psychiatrists now recognize that they must try to understand the disturbed world of the disturbed person, and there are now anthropologists who pursue a discipline known as ethno-philosophy which studies the different life-worlds of different peoples and cultures. On these points, there is widespread agreement among qualified investigators. But which of these horizons is prior to the other? Which is broader and more inclusive? Which will be able to find a place for the other with the least reduction and distortion?

These questions are by no means settled, and we find able thinkers on both sides. At the present time, positivistically and naturalistically oriented philosophers maintain that what we may call the objective scientific universe is the prior and wider horizon, and that what it calls subjective or immediate experience must ultimately be explained in terms of it. On the other side, almost all phenomenology-oriented thinkers, like William James in our own country and some recent analytic philosophers, hold that the life-world is the prior and wider perspective, and that the scientific universe can be understood without reduction or distortion as a set of abstract perspectives within it. This is a basic, philosophical question of our time, and the settlement of many other significant issues, such as the conflicting claims made by the sciences and the humanities in our colleges and universities, will depend upon the answer that is given.

I shall not have time here to develop fully the case that can be made for the scientific universe. But most of us are now familiar with arguments of this kind, which may be briefly summarized as follows. In the first place, there is no single life-world. What we are actually confronted with is, rather, a vast number of different world views, determined by the divergent prejudices and circumstances of individuals and groups scattered over the surface of the earth. Over against this multiplicity of conflicting, subjective views is the single system made up of the confirmed, objective results of the sciences. These results do not vary from group to group and from individual to individual. They are firmly established by the experimental verification of hypotheses, and are one and the same for all. This system is still in an early stage of its development. But eventually it will succeed in explaining and absorbing into itself the subjective opinions of different persons and peoples.

In the second place, the different human life-worlds are relative to the human body and to the perceptual powers of man. The natural sciences have opened up objective vistas that extend far beyond the limits of the natural powers of the human senses. Thus, astronomy has already succeeded in exploring galactic regions far beyond the limits of anything that can be perceived with the naked eye. Physics and chemistry have revealed sub-microscopic atomic structures that lie far below the threshold of vision. Not only have these sciences widened our spatial horizon into the supra- and sub-macroscopic, they have also extended our limited, normal perspective in time, revealing many facts about the physical universe as it was millions and even billions of years before man appeared on the scene, and as it will be long after the human species and its subjective versions of the world will have passed away. Since science has access to all that lies within the normal limits of perception, and to much that lies far beyond these limits in space, as well as in time, it is certainly the wider and more inclusive horizon.

In the third place, since it is better confirmed, and certainly the richer and more inclusive frame of reference, we may suppose that eventually it will be able to explain our subjective experiences, and to absorb them within itself without in any way reducing or distorting them. This explanation will no doubt take a causal form in which these private experiences, without alteration, will simply be correlated with their regular, objective antecedents, and, therefore, be comprehended.

Now let us turn to the other side. The following answer can be given. With respect to the first point, we must grant that, from an objectivistic, spectatorial point of view, interpretations do seem to be a scattered array of closed and conflicting systems, not one of which gives any real hope of being verified against the others. This is how it looks to a detached spectator. But in real life it is different. It is true that men are free to work out different accounts of the unfinished life-world, and its ambiguities and different ways of life, in accordance with these accounts. This freedom of interpretation lies at the very root of what we call human freedom. It is also true that many versions become fixed and closed, so that a given person or people may come to confuse its version of the world with the world itself. But fanaticism is not a necessary condition of human existence, and even the fanatic is dimly aware of the distinction between his version and the world itself, which he is trying to suppress.

In real life, I do not think of myself as living in one possible world frame that is closed against many others, standing by its side. I know that I am living the one and only life that is open to me, in accordance with the best version that I can work out, of the one and only world there is—and I am aware of other versions. Some of these I take to be sounder than others, and when questioned, I am prepared to give a verbal defense of my way of life. I never think of it as one finished possibility among many others on the same level, between which no comparative judgments of truth and value can be made. This is the view of a mere spectator who, as we have seen, can not make the distinction between reality and illusion.

Truth is never given to us in this way. It requires the action of the living body, which must bring it out of the shadows as it makes falsity and illusion disappear. Relativism is a disease of the inactive, theoretical attitude when it is absolutized. Hence, this disease will never be corrected by pure theory, but only by a deeper understanding of the world in which we actually exist, and on which phenomenology has at last begun to shed some light.

In answer to the second point about objective science having access to the field of our subjective experience as well as to much more, including the supra- and sub-macroscopic regions of space, and the vast intervals of prehuman and posthuman time, we must firmly deny the first part of this statement. Objective science does not have access to the field of our subjective experience. This is centered in the lived body that is not a pure object. Furthermore, this field is not enclosed within any mental, or subjective container.

My living body must act in order to perceive. But it does not perceive merely private impressions enclosed within a mind container. This living body is a real, active agency in the world, surrounded by other independent agencies, and perceiving is a mode of action that makes something happen—a revealing of the truth which would not otherwise exist. In perceiving an independent thing, or agency, I act upon it, gathering it together with other things to give it a place in the world field to which I am open and thus revealing it as it is. This is a real event which actually happens in the world. It is never complete and final, but always subject to revision and correction; for my revealing power is limited, and I cannot bring one thing into the light without concealing others. But in some region, to some degree, the truth is revealed. The living body of man is open to the whole life world of our primordial experience, which includes subjective, or intentional, as well as objective factors, and which is constituted by a different kind of fact, which has been called world-fact as against scientific fact.

The life-world and the abstract perspectives of objective science are constituted by different structures, and different kinds of fact. They are revealed in different ways. Hence, they cannot be adequately approached by the same attitudes and modes of understanding. Abstract, objective structures and facts that are not self-interpreted need to be studied by the methods of the special sciences. The more concrete and meaningful structures and facts of the life-world need to be approached by the methods of what has now come to be called phenomenology.

As to the range and inclusiveness of the life-world, we may first point out that all the basic data of the different sciences can be found in any given world fact, like our sitting here this afternoon. (The clock is ticking (astronomy), light is radiating from these bulbs (physics). Some of us are growing hungry (chemistry and physiology). This meeting has economic, sociological and psychological aspects which I need only to mention.) But in spite of its richness and complexity, historical facts of this kind are open to disciplined historical and phenomenological analysis by the humanistic disciplines. The concrete objects of the life-world, which we perceive only in profile, are indefinitely open, and beckon us on to further perspectives. Hence, there is room in them for all the results of confirmed, scientific analysis. The perceptual space of the life-world is ambiguous and open in both directions, toward the greater as well as the smaller. Hence, it is not closed to the supra- and the sub-macroscopic. This is also true of our lived time which is open both to the future and to the past. Hence, far from standing in the way of an extension of our probable knowledge in these directions, it beckons us on to just such extensions as astronomy and the physical sciences have achieved.

Not only space and time, but also other basic patterns, like being and non-being, knowledge and ignorance, which are involved in all our human activities, including those of the sciences, are primordially and directly revealed to us in the life-world. They are presupposed in all scientific investigation. Global religions and philosophical interpretations of this world as a whole are not required, as we should expect, of the more abstract investigations of the sciences. But as James pointed out, they are forced options in the actual living of life. No human person, and no human group has yet been found without such a global interpretation of the world as a whole that governs its way of life.

These facts point toward the conclusion that it is the horizon of the life-world that is the richer and more far ranging. Men lived for thousands of years without the sciences. But no science has yet been found which was not being carried on by living men, facing death in the world of history. The scientist may discount and ignore the life-world. But it is from this world that his thinking and his science take their origin. He may take it for granted. But he is nevertheless presupposing it in his researches. It is not the other way around.

Finally, in relation to the third argument, and in relation to the facts just considered, it looks as though we should have to deny that the objective frame of reference is the more inclusive frame. When the attempt is made to absolutize it in this way, several serious reductions occur. The living body becomes a mere complex object, and the world of which it is actively aware is reduced to a set of impressions, or representations, enclosed within a subjective container. The laws of science do, indeed, apply to certain abstract aspects of the world. They enable us to predict that will happen under certain conditions, and thus to intervene actively in the control of objective nature. But when they are regarded as the all-pervasive laws of the life-world and its history, there is no longer any room left for active human intervention and control. These laws control us, and the scientist, instead of predicting what may happen in a special field under variable conditions, becomes a seer who prophecies the inevitable course of events in world history. There is no place for the freedom and ambiguity which pervades our lived existence. These are all reductive distortions of the facts of our experience.

On the other hand, if we follow these facts more closely, we shall find that the active human body is neither a physical object nor a spiritual subject. As we are beginning to find and to see, this traditional dualism is avoidable. The lived body is the center of self-revealing intentions which open into the rich horizon of the life-world where there is room for both the so-called subjective and the objective, without reifying either. In this world-field, it is possible to find a place for all the specific objects and abstract laws discovered by the special sciences without reducing or distorting them. Does not the very existence of such a discipline as the philosophy of science show that we recognize the need for placing it in a wider world horizon?

I realize that much more needs to be said to support the conclusion I am suggesting here. I believe that the evidence now available points in this direction. But the issue is far from settled. The war of the worlds, as we may cal! it, is still proceeding in us and around us. It is, as I have said, a basic philosophic issue of our time. But now I must conclude.

I have tried to show you how recent phenomenology has opened up a structured world of experience, to which we have direct access, and which is far richer and more far-ranging than the restricted perspectives of British Empiricism and other traditional forms of empiricism. I think it is fair to say that since the time of William James, with what is called phenomenology, existential philosophy, and certain recent forms of linguistic analyses, a new style of empiricism is developing in our time. I have tried to give you a sense of current developments on the frontiers of this disciplined exploration of the life-world—new light on the lived body of man which may provide us with a way of overcoming psycho-physical dualism; and of explaining the a priori structure of the world in which we exist, on its acts as self-revealing, and on the role of this active body in making the distinction between appearance and reality.

These investigations are still in progress, and far from finished. The results that have been so far achieved may be interpreted in various ways, but there are firm results that have withstood searching criticisms and seem due to last. One of these is the fact that the human *Lebenswelt* is not a mere chaos of subjective impressions, that it has peculiar structures of its own, and is far richer and wider in range than has been generally supposed. I believe that the exploration of this world, now under way, should have a stimulating and stabilizing effect on the humanistic disciplines now suffering from the infiltration of attitudes and methods borrowed from the objective sciences, and from subjectivism and relativism which follow from this confusion of fields. When humanists become really convinced that they are concerned with an actual world horizon of their own not accessible to the methods standing, they may be able to approach their essential tasks with greater vigor and renewed confidence.

3

An Empirical Approach
to the A Priori

EXPLANATORY NOTE

One of Wild's most brilliant and original reflections is presented in the following essay, "An Empirical Approach to the A Priori." There is a great deal at stake here for the work and content of philosophy. Philosophy can lay claim to an autonomous domain of inquiry only if the a priori can be demonstrated to be already at work in the life-world prior to my entrance into it. Otherwise, philosophers are left to analyze the discoveries of the natural and social sciences, which claim direct access to that which can be known. The success in arguing for an empirical a priori is tied up, therefore, with the very independence of philosophy.

Wild initiates his discussion with a lucid historical reconstruction of the arguments of both the Rationalists and British Empiricists, and points out the limitations of each of these positions. He shows how Kant, though moving in the right direction in advancing the notion of the synthetic a priori, recoiled from treating the world of sensory experience as more than a disconnected sensory manifold. Wild argues that one of the genuine discoveries of phenomenology is the demonstration that there is a prereflective apprehension of the sensory world that informs our conceptual understanding. Wild argues that there are several criteria that must be met to qualify knowledge as a priori. The foundation for such knowledge is that it must be in the first instance "universal and in any sense necessary."

At the heart of his argument is the position that perception opens onto a variety of figure/ground relations that point toward and away from other experiences of the perceived world. There are, according to Wild, "implicit patterns of existence" to our being in the world. These include, but are not limited to, "the lived body . . . lived space . . . the continuous flow of lived time . . ." These structures are indispensable for navigating our life-world.

There is no manual that accompanies the operations of the preconceptual or oriented movement of time, space, the body and speech.

Wild then makes what is the beginning of a novel argument that has its precursor in the thought of William James. He acknowledges that our first registering of the patterns of the life-world are "vaguely felt and perceived." However, rather than finding vagueness as an objection to the empirical a priori, Wild states, "in my own experience, clarity and certainty vary inversely." The things about which I am most certain are vague, "not clear and distinct as Descartes thought." I am much more apt to be certain of what I do not understand and of the tentative character of my experience than I am of its clarity and distinctness. I know, for example, that I want to clearly restate the lineaments of Wild's position here, but I am quite vague about how to go about doing so. The empirical a priori makes it possible for us to understand the relation of reason to experience in a way that is closer to our originary sense of things. As Wild puts it, "reason does not appear on the scene as an alien intruder into an empirical chaos where order must be created *ex nihilo*. The way for clarification, further development of meaning and communication has already been prepared." In other words, reason is founded upon perception and has a provisional character to it that we recognize as we try to verbalize what it is that we know.

This essay represents an expanded and developed version of a talk Wild first gave in the spring of 1966 at Michigan State University. The title of the earlier publication appeared as "Is There an Existential A Priori?" in the Eisenberg Memorial Lecture Series (Michigan State University Press, 1969).

In my experience of teaching the history of Western philosophy, it has often happened to me after discussing some insight in a classic text that a student will say, "But I knew that already," and then he may add the significant qualification: "in a way." I believe that this sense of being in possession of an unexpressed and latent knowledge is not restricted to professional philosophers, but is far more widespread among reflective minds than is commonly supposed. Certainly the notion of an a priori knowledge conditioning the fragmentary results we can achieve by our finite consciousnesses has been a major theme of our Western philosophy ever since its beginnings.

Thus, in his doctrine of reminiscence Plato held that our knowledge of geometrical truths concerning straight lines, circles, and triangles, never observed in sense experience, and of moral norms, like justice, never achieved by any actions, must be a priori. Since it cannot be accounted for by any information coming through the senses, it must be due to glimmerings of a prior knowledge when the soul had access to the timeless and changeless ideas before it drank of the waters of Lethe, and entered into the confused and ever shifting realm of becoming.

Aristotle's views on this subject are less clear. But the Arabic commentators who read the obscure text of chapter one of the third book of *De Anima* arrived at an interpretation which has been widely influential. According to this reading, later challenged by Aquinas, the active reason (*nous poietikos*), which is separated from our bodily faculties, is one and the same for all men who, therefore, in their basic acts of understanding, share in these universal operations. The Averroists of the twelfth and thirteenth centuries adopted this interpretation, and used it to account for the universal agreement of all men on basic concepts and insights, an idea taken over later by different versions of objective idealism in the nineteenth century.

An analogous conception is found in the Augustinian tradition. But it is the Kantian formulation which has left the deepest mark on the tradition of modern philosophy in the West. According to Kant, there is no world of perception, for without concepts, percepts are blind. He speaks of sense data as a chaotic manifold. And without a transcendental synthesizing principle, holding these data together by the forms of intuition and the categories, no organized, objective experience would be possible. These ordering principles are, therefore, a priori in the sense that, even though they may never be clearly focused, they are presupposed by even the most rudimentary experience, and are, therefore, universally and necessarily operative in all men.

If we ask what these classical conceptions have in common, I believe that we shall find at least three features which can be distinguished. First, in all of its many versions, a priori knowledge is due to structures, or powers, innate in man which work themselves out spontaneously, without the need of any external support. These structures are common to all men, and they give rise to principles of knowledge which are not limited to any special situation or circumstance, but which hold for all men necessarily and universally. This is true not only of the Platonic view and its derivatives, but of the Kantian version as well.

In the second place, these a priori principles are either temporally and/or logically prior to the variable and particular facts of experience, and condition them in the sense of giving them a basic order and meaning. Thus, on the Platonic view, it is only by virtue of the a priori forms that the individual, flowing objects of experience become partially intelligible as plants, animals, beds, houses, and so forth. And on the Kantian view, it is only by virtue of the forms of intuition and the categories (in the second edition) that the manifold of sense, as he calls it, is ordered into an intelligible world of objects. In laying down these underlying patterns of experience, the a priori principles also condition intelligible discourse and science, which are necessarily concerned with empirical objects. Thus, common experience, discourse, and science all presuppose these principles which are a priori, or prior to them in a temporal and/or logical sense.

Finally, in the third place, these principles, though constantly at work, are nevertheless largely hidden from our waking consciousness. Thus the geometrical truths that lie ready in the mind of the slave boy in the Meno have to be elicited and made explicit by the skillful questioning of Socrates, and the Kantian transcendental unity of apperception and the categories are brought into the light only by an elaborate transcendental deduction. Of course, we are not completely ignorant of them. According to Plato, without some faint awareness of the pure forms, we would be unable to recognize and name the confused imitations that appear before us, and, according to Kant, without the transcendental unity of appercep- tion and its forms, no orderly objective phenomena would be possible. But on all these views, our a priori knowledge is very dim, and faint, and implicit, and lies on the fringes of our waking consciousness.

Now, as I see it, these three traits of a priori knowledge, as found in human existence as such are universal, and in some sense necessary. These traits as presupposed by concrete experience, ordinary discourse, science, and hiddenness, are recognized, with minor variations, in all the important versions that have so far appeared. As I see it, no version lack- ing any one of these could properly be called a priori or primary. So, these traits will appear in the empirical theory that I shall present. However, there are certain other traits which are also found in many traditional ver- sions. These intellectualistic traits, as I shall call them, are four or five in number, and I shall now try to characterize them briefly and to suggest certain criticisms.

The traditional tendency to discount and disparage the world of sense goes back to the Greeks and disqualifies this world (if it is a world at all) from being a priori or primary in the three essential senses just men- tioned. Thus, Plato compared the objects of sense to the fleeting shadows in his cave. Being in constant flux, and not remaining on hand long enough even to be mentioned without slipping away, it seemed clear to him that these particular, shifting data have only a minimum of stability and structure derived from an alien course. Hence, of themselves they fail to provide us with any adequate foundation for any universal knowledge, common to all men. Following the British Empiricists, Kant refers to this "world," in similarly disparaging terms, as a mere "manifold of sense." Such discrete particulars may give us material content. But they cannot provide us with the formal patterns which are clearly required not only for a priori knowledge in an eminent sense, but even for the most rudi- mentary awareness. They are, therefore, unable to qualify as the ground for an a priori knowledge that is universal and in any sense necessary.

Second, on the assumption that these units of perception are discrete particulars, there is no reason to suppose that there is any (necessary) experienced connection between them. After one has happened, any other might occur. Certain ones may occur before others in time. But to be sure of this, we must wait for them to happen. Such knowledge is a posteriori, even though the sequence may repeat itself indefinitely. In such a scheme there is no way in which any one impression, or set of impressions, may condition, or be presupposed by another set. Hence, such discrete sense data cannot meet the second criterion of a priori knowledge—conditioning a whole range of phenomena as logically prior.

In the third place, an impression may become faint. But as long as it exists at all, it is definite and distinct. As such, it must either be or not be. With this picture in mind, it is hard to see how any one of these, such as a sweet taste, can be semi-present, in a condition that is vague or half-concealed. It must either be there or not there. The notion of fringes and of a field of perception were not developed until the time of William James, Husserl and the Gestalt psychologists of the 1920s. But in the traditional conception of experience, shared by both rationalists and empiricists, there is no total background, no fringes in which objects may be first dimly felt, and then slowly clarified by a new concentration of attention. Hence, sense and feeling, as traditionally conceived, fail to meet the third criterion of the a priori—semi-consciousness and concealment.

Another major fourth intellectualistic factor that can be noted in traditional views of the a priori is the radical opposition between the empirical and the rational to which the discounting of sense and feeling must lead. On the one hand, we have the elements of sensation, like blue color, middle-C sound, and pain, which are discrete and unrelated; on the other hand, [we have] universal concepts which subsume these elements, and then subsume each other in an ordered hierarchy, thus relating them into a meaningful system. Hence, the perennial issues between rationalism and empiricism, each singling out one of these factors for special emphasis and subordinating the other. This radical separation has brought forth the famous theory of the two worlds; that of sense, where opinion alone (*doxa*) is possible, and the intelligible world of reason (*nous*), which is the a priori condition for the former.

In his "Transcendental Aesthetic," Kant recognized space and time as non-conceptual patterns conditioning experience. If he had developed this notion he might have overcome this dualism of sense versus reason. But his acceptance of the traditional theory of the mind as a transparent consciousness or subject stood in the way. Hence, in his theory of the categories, and the ideas of reason which transcend sense, he was forced back (in the second edition) into the familiar notion of a predominantly conceptual a priori, and the traditional dualism of the phenomenal versus the noumenal, the sensible versus the intelligible worlds. In the opinion of many critics, this dualism is responsible for the most serious weaknesses of the Kantian system.

This discounting of the world of sense, and the isolation of reason as a completely autonomous principle with a world of its own, ruled out the possibility of any empirical a priori. Sense alone is really not a world at all. Of itself, as a sheer manifold, it can provide us with no order and structure, which come from reason alone. This led to a one-sidedly intellectualistic conception (which ruled out the possibility of an empirical a priori) that was shared not only by so-called rationalists, but by empiricists as well, who have devoted their efforts not so much to developing any notion of an empirical a priori, as to destroying the whole notion of "innate ideas," etc. (the exception is William James).

This traditional intellectualism is confirmed, I think, if we look for a moment at the way in which traditional thought has regarded the process of gaining a clearer grasp of the half-hidden a priori patterns, and the consequences of ignoring them. Both of these are intellectualized to such a degree that the life of sense and feeling play only a very minor role.

Thus, according to Plato, sense experience has no intelligible patterns of its own. In *Theaetetus*, he goes so far as to say that sense has no access to number, sameness, difference, likeness, good, bad, right, wrong and even being. It is reason alone, using the body and the sense organs only as instruments, which perceives these formal patterns. Sensory images have no structure. They provide us merely with the occasions for the recollection of the ideas. Pre-conceptual experience, therefore, plays no essential role on bringing the a priori forms into the light. Once started, the logical process develops dialectically from one form to another, until the whole intelligible world is finally revealed. According to Kant, the impressions of sense carry a material content, but no relational structure or meaning. Hence, percepts without concepts, in the famous saying, are blind. Of themselves they understand nothing, and, as in Plato, give us only the starting point for a rational deduction of the categories. Once under way, this logical development proceeds autonomously, requiring no further aid or checking from sense and feeling.

Now a fifth intellectualistic trait in traditional theories can be mentioned. Similar remarks can be made about the consequences of neglecting or denying the rational a priori. In Plato the primary consequences take the form of either a vagueness that stands in the way of definite assertion, or of logical contradiction, both of these being closely linked. Thus in *Theaetetus*, the defender of the Heraclitean flux can say neither that the flow of any given moment is either A or not A, and that it is just as much one as the other (a contradiction). In Kant, the a priori is limited, at least partially, to the phenomenal realm. When these limits are neglected or denied, knowledge is left without any firm foundation, and falls into skepticism or dogmatic opinions which ceaselessly contradict each other, with no possible ground for a settlement one way or the other.

In neither position, Plato or Kant, is there any recognition of trustworthy belief grounded on a direct sense of human existence, or of any schism or contradiction, more deeply rooted than that which is expressed by contradictory presuppositions. Rational self-evidence and deduction are the only sources of sound knowledge, and without these belief is always untrustworthy. Hence, vagueness and logical contradiction are the most basic expressions of human error, for they affect the patterns of language and logic which are prior to experience, and condition it necessarily. So clarity is prior to vagueness, and logical disintegration to existential disintegration.

So much, then, for the general disparagement of sense, and the aspects of the traditional theory which, in my opinion, are subject to serious questioning, and have been questioned in recent times. In what follows, I shall try to suggest, in outline, the new conception of an empirical a priori which Kant might have worked out if he had connected the forms of space and time more closely with the manifold of sense, and if he had then dwelt longer with and further expanded his "Transcendental Aesthetic." Kant, of course, did not make these moves. But many suggestions of this kind are found in James's *Principles of Psychology*, and many further developments of these in later phenomenologists such as Husserl and Merleau-Ponty.

It is fair to say that one of the main achievements of recent phenomenology has been to reveal and to clarify many of the basic patterns of what Husserl called, at the end of his career, the *Lebenswelt*. In *Erfahrung und Urteil*, he speaks of pre-predicative experiences which are by no means to be discounted as a mere succession of discrete impressions. It is rather a world (*Lebenswelt*) with peculiar patterns of its own (cf. *Krisis*, pp. 105–51). According to Heidegger, human being (*Dasein*) cannot be separated from the world in which it exists, and in *Sein und Zeit* he is constantly concerned with our prethematic awareness of this world, and its basic structures. Similarly, Merleau-Ponty, in his *Phenomenology of Perception*, devotes himself to the task of revealing the primacy of this pre-reflective world and its patterns.

Preceding all these studies, James, in his *Principles of Psychology*, published in 1890, attacked the Kantian doctrine of empirical data as an unrelated "manifold," and adopted the opposed view that the relational parts of experience are perceived in the same way, and just as originally as its substantive parts (*Principles of Psychology* I, pp. 243–48). This became a cardinal principle of his radical empiricism which he defended against the empirical and Kantian schools of his time. The strongest part of this defense was his success in revealing certain relational patterns which remain constant as the particular concepts carry, and thus "always" hold as necessary, conditions for such experience. One of these is the continuity, or stream-like character, of the field of consciousness which he analyzed with great care (*Principles of Psychology* I, pp. 237–71), and which Husserl takes over. Today this would be called a penetrating example of phenomenological description and analysis. So, I think it may be worth a brief quotation and comment. Let us then take one of his examples, the hearing of a thunder clap. We have two words for thunder and silence. So it is easy for us to fall into the empiricist view, which is really a covert form of rationalism, and to think of these as two distinct impressions which follow each other—first silence, then thunder. But as James points out following Brentano, this is an oversimplified distortion of what we actually feel. "Our feeling of the same objective thunder . . . is quite different from what it would be were the thunder a continuation of previous thunder" (*Principles of Psychology* I, pp. 240–41), for this feeling bears within it something of the past. As James puts it: "Into the awareness of the thunder itself the awareness of the previous silence creeps and continues; for what we hear when the thunder crashes is not thunder pure but thunder-breaking-upon-silence-and-contrasting-with-it."

Hence, he refers to our experience as "a stream of thought," whose substantive parts are constantly related by feelings of transition. Here is a relational pattern which holds for all experience, and which seems to be prior to linguistic and conceptual formulations. For surely the young child hears thunder and is frightened before he knows the words. In fact, if James and the phenomenologists are right, this feeling of transition in the specious present is opposed to what the artificial separations of language would lead us to expect. But this and other patterns of our pre-reflective conceptual experience can be described and expressed by a disciplined use of language, as I believe this example shows. There are many other preconceptual patterns of this kind, which have now been at least partially brought into the light.

For example, there is the oriented lived space, or rather lived spaces, which are prior to the perceptual experiences of our waking life and condition them a priori. There is also the active living body, not as it is objectively observed, but as it is felt and lived from the inside. At the end of his career, in his *Essays in Radical Empiricism*, James speaks of this lived body as follows: "The world experienced (otherwise called the 'field of consciousness') comes at all times with our body as its center, center of vision, center of action, center of interest. Where the body is is 'here'; when the body sets is 'now'; what the body touches is 'this'; all other things are 'there,' and 'then,' and 'that.' These words of emphasized position imply a systematization of things which lies in the body . . . the body is the storm center, the origin of coordinates, the constant place of stress in all that experience-train. Everything circles around it and is felt from its point of view" (p. 170).

James then proceeds to identify this active living body with the self: "The word 'I'," he says, "is primarily a noun of position, like 'this' and 'here'." But while this 'I' is the source of subjectivity, it is not a transcendental ego separated from the world of meanings that it organizes around itself. It is in this world, and in this oriented space of which it is the active center, so that the very same activities which are lived and felt from the inside can, in part at least, be observed and measured from the outside. Later on Husserl also, near the end of his career, became deeply interested in this living body (cf. *Krisis*, pp.108–10), and notes its close connection (*liebliches Ichlichkeit*) with what we call the self. Still later Merleau-Ponty has developed these ideas in his phenomenology of perception (the phenomenological body, or *le corps vécu*). Of course, only a bare beginning has been made, but these investigations are still continuing, and the possibility of formulating a tenable identity-theory of a new kind is looming on the horizon.

If the world of direct perception, the world of sense, as James called it, can no longer be discounted as a mere sequence of discrete impressions; if it possesses stable structures which remain invariant as particular content changes, then the notion of an empirical primary knowledge becomes possible. We do not have to get outside the world and outside of our bodies to gain a transcendental position from which we can ask how this is possible. Perhaps we cannot gain such a position.

If there is an empirical a priori, we must gain access to it in another way. As we remain in the world with our bodies, we must catch these patterns of existence with the aid of memory, imagination, and feeling—in the very act as we live them through. These are not a priori structures of meaning, only pure possibilities that condition actual experience. They are, rather, implicit patterns of existence, necessary facts which are presupposed by the particular facts of which our human histories are constituted. Of course, these structural facts are not absolutely necessary since human existence is contingent. But they are bound up with existence so that we can say: As long as man factually exists, these structures—being in the world, the lived body and its basic patterns of behavior, lived space, the continuous flow of lived time, for example—will always necessarily be factually found.

It is true that these patterns are originally only vaguely felt and perceived, and that even after words have been found for them, the meanings of these words usually fade off into the dimness of the obvious, which is never clearly seen, but always taken for granted. I am not sure, however, that this vagueness should be taken as evidence against their a priori character, for, in my own experience, at least, clarity and certainty vary inversely. As long as I follow my lived perception and leave it vague, I am sure about time, that it is going on, and that I am involved in it. As soon as I look at it, however, in terms of a clear-cut theory that spells it out, I begin to doubt, not time itself, which is primary, but the way in which it is clearly and explicitly explained. Of course, we need clarification. But we also need to retain the original perceptual certainty of existence which should belong to what is truly primary.

The various lists of a priori concepts that have been worked out in our intellectual history overlap to some degree. Nevertheless, they show major differences, and every one is subject to serious doubt. Perhaps this is because not one of these has dug down far enough to discover the ultimate patterns of life which are found, prior to conceptual thought, in the world of feeling and perception. I believe that it would not be difficult to find tribes and peoples whose everyday speech departed markedly from any list of supposedly basic categories. But would it be easy to find any tribe, no matter how primitive and strange, which would not be vaguely familiar with the world in which it lives, with its oriented space, and its lived time? Would it be possible to find any representative of such a tribe or people, primitive or advanced, who would not be familiar with the human body as it is lived, who, apart from his language, would not perceive the vague sense of laughter and tears? This is the kind of empirical a priori I am suggesting. If William James and his successors, the radical empiricists and phenomenologists, are not mistaken, these patterns will be found universally and necessarily wherever man is found. Furthermore, these patterns lie at the ground of all the varying particular experiences which make up human history. Hence, our knowledge of them, so far as we possess it, meets the first two general criteria for the a priori. But how about the third? If there are necessary factual patterns of this kind, why should they be so extensively neglected and ignored? Why do they tend to remain half-concealed even though we have little difficulty in finding verbal ways of expressing them?

Here I must introduce the notion of another perceptual structure, first clearly focused by James, which had a basic influence on Husserl, Gestalt psychology, and the whole future development of phenomenology down to the present day. This is his notion of "fringes," or what he often referred to as "the field conception of consciousness." This conception can be summarized as follows. Our attention is ordinarily focused on specific objects of practical or theoretical interest. It is now recognized, however, that such definite figures never appear except on a vague field, or background, of fringes, fading off to a distant horizon. Language and conceptual thinking, in general, enable us to sharpen this focusing of attention by developing separate words for supposedly separate objects. But at the same time, they lead us to neglect the backgrounds and grounding patterns on which these figures appear. This tendency is strengthened by the fact that the boundaries of these fields are imprecise, and their patterns only dimly, vaguely and fleetingly grasped at the level of perception, whereas the major emphasis in sophisticated linguistic usage is on clarity and precision. Hence, the classical empiricists almost totally missed this field conception.

It is true that we have words in common usage for time, the world, and the self. But for the most part, the original meanings of these terms have slipped into the obscurity of the obvious, a form of the semi-conscious. Hence, when asked, we are apt to confuse the world with all the things in the world, time with the various things that occur in time, and the self, with an identical thing or subject, separated from all other things, and perhaps outside the world altogether. But then we forget the empirical a priori, that without a world horizon there can be no things in the world, that without time itself, there can be no succession of things in time, and that without a prior field, there can be no development of the self at its center.

This now offers us a way of accounting for the partial concealment of this empirical a priori. With our basic tendency to focus on specific objects, the world horizon and the subordinate fields of space, time, and self are shoved off into the fringes where they lapse into a dormant, semi-conscious or "obvious" condition, from which they can be rescued only by the arduous techniques of phenomenology. It will also serve to explain a remark of James on his whole procedure for which he has sometimes been taken to task by his more logically and intellectualistically oriented critics. "It is," he says, "the re-instatement of the vague to its proper place in our mental life which I am so anxious to press on the attention" (*Principles of Psychology* I, p. 254).

If this is true, pre-reflective experience is not a chaotic manifold of discrete impressions, but a vast world horizon including many sub-worlds and regions. I believe that phenomenology has now shown that such basic characteristics of linguistic consciousness as intentionality, meaning, temporality, retention, protention, understanding, in a broad sense of this term, and purposive striving are all present at the level of perception where objects are presented to us in their original bodily presence. This world is pervaded by ambiguity (vagueness), for perception is dominated by its object, and the fringes are always vague. The non-reflective agent can gain little distance from the situations into which he has been thrown, and his responses are readily dominated and enslaved. His meanings are individual, relative to the situation, and, therefore, incommunicable. But similarities and differences are recognized. Order and meaning are present in a confused way, and are ready to be linguistically clarified, fixed, and communicated. Hence, reason does not appear on the scene as an alien intruder into an empirical chaos where order must be created ex nihilo. The way for clarification, further development of meaning, and communication has already been prepared.

Furthermore, this perceptual world is not subjective, for in it things are presented in their actual bodily presence (cf. Merleau-Ponty). So, there is no need for any dualism of the sensible versus the intelligible, as disorder versus order, or as the subjective and relative is opposed to that which exists in itself. Perception already begins, in its limited way, to reveal things as they really are, and language goes on with the task. There is no essential discontinuity between the sensory and the intelligible words. Reason, as it has been called, is founded on perception. It needs perception for a sure grasp of being in its corporeal presence, and a dim apprehension of its basic structures like figure and ground, space, time, and the living body. Perception (the founding), on the other hand, needs reason and language (the founded) for clarification, the completion and fixation of partial, floating meanings, and finally for communication.

Once language is established, it is easy for us to become lost in it, and to regard it as a separate world or universe of discourse. This can happen. But from an empirical point of view, this is a serious mistake which ignores the founded character of speech. It is through language that we see things and patterns in a distinctive way and with a distinctive clarity. (It is often necessary to wipe the glass, but to become absorbed in the spots for their own sake is an obsession that does not help our vision.) Language has arisen in the *Lebenswelt* and is founded on it. Indeed, though it presupposes other patterns, like world and the living body, it is a necessary structure; for wherever man and the world are found, language of some kind, though not any one language or system of categories, is also found. But this founding world requires language and reflection (the founded) to be clearly known and communicated. To speak and to think are ways of being in the world, and perception is another. They represent two different levels of intentionality, each lacking something possessed by the other, and needing support. There is no need for two worlds. The one in which we live is rich, and far-ranging, and vast enough.

But if each supplies something lacking in the other, how, more exactly, are language and perception related? Which one is prior to the other? Are we then in a position to turn the tables on the traditional view? Can we defend the notion of a primacy of experience which is before language and conceptual discourse? As my whole argument has been trying to suggest, I believe that we can. There is evidence which tends to show that instead of experience being originally conditioned by language and its structures, it is the other way round. Language and reason are incomplete, and are originally conditioned and limited by structures of experience and perception. I have already indicated the general nature of this evidence. But let me now try to break it down into four lines of argument which I shall now suggest, in each case with a brief comment.

Let me begin with another example taken from James (*Principles of Psychology* I, pp. 221–22). This is concerned with references to unverbalized perception which are expressed by articles, pronouns, and the grammatical "subject" of any meaningful sentences or discourse. Such discourse takes place in a total situation which is already known directly, to some degree, by feeling and perception. This knowledge by direct acquaintance, as James calls it, is presupposed. Thus, as he says (p. 222), "the minimum of grammatical subject, of objective presence, . . . the mere beginning of knowledge must be named by the world that says the least (conceptually). Such a word is the interjection, as lo! there! *ecco*! *voilà*! or the article or demonstrative pronoun introducing the sentence as The, it, that." If this reference to the un-verbalized is lost, we fail to see what the discourse is about, and it sinks away towards mere verbalism. Does this not indicate that language rests on a prior kind of knowledge which it presupposes? Does it not always occur in a situation that is somehow already understood? Is it not surrounded by fringes of meaning that are never fully expressed but have to be read, as we say, between the lines? In speaking of a life situation, can everything ever be said? Is there not always something left over which, to use current phrases, is beyond all words, or even inexpressible? But in saying this, do we not show that we are aware of it in a non-linguistic way?

A second line of investigation is concerned with the a priori structures of the world of perception to which we have referred, such as lived space, lived time, and the living human body. Is it possible to clarify these structures by language and reason alone without constantly referring back to the perspectives of perception according to the methods of phenomenology? Is it not true that language presupposes these structures? Is not speaking (thinking) a way of being in the world? Would language be possible without a world that is already present, and without things and persons in the world to talk about? Does it not require an active, living body that is able to move in the fields of time and space? In order to suggest a justification for an affirmative answer to these questions, I shall mention only those recent studies of perceptual space by Merleau-Ponty and others which show its close relation to bodily motions and its pre-conceptual origin. This suggests a third line of argument concerned with the dangers which arise when language and thinking lose real contact with the world of sense that is prior to them. Any concept or theory or speculative system which fails to take account of this primary world and its structures, and passes beyond the limits they impose, cannot be taken seriously as a real possibility. It may be an empty conjoining of words with no real meaning.

So the Kantian work of criticism needs to be constantly resumed and sharpened, though in a different and wider context.

But even if there is a primordial world of perception that is always present on the fringes of our discourse, and presupposed by it, we may still raise questions as to how it is known. We may still argue that while this world and its structures are there, it cannot be known and accepted until it is expressed in propositions, and, therefore, subjected to the patterns of language. An a priori that is completely unknown certainly cannot qualify for what has been meant by this term. Is there any evidence to show that there is a primordial awareness of the whole perceptual world and its structures? I believe that there is such evidence, though I have time here only for a brief comment on this fourth line of argument. During his symbolic calculations the calculator may, of course, and should, doubt his projected proof and its special evidence. But should he entertain any serious existential doubt, as we may call it, concerning the whole world in which it is taking place and his existence in it, the demonstrative action would be interrupted. For this world background is presupposed.

James referred to this primordial acceptance of the world by the term belief. Husserl, in his *Erfahrung und Urteil*, used the term *Urdoxa*. We have used the word "feeling," but it seems also to involve an element of trust in the world as we engage ourselves into it, and a hope to be sustained. Back of the special noetic attitudes involved in the use of language: doubt, uncertainty, inquiry, probability, certainty, and so forth, there seems to be a more primordial belief in the real world as a whole which is non-linguistic in origin, but which is still maintained with the coming of language, and is presupposed by its special manifestation. Thus, just as there is an all-encompassing world horizon with its stable patterns that are prior to language and discourse, so there seems to be a prior kind of belief, an *Urdoxa*, which is prior to more special forms of knowledge. Hence, seriously to doubt the whole world which includes the doubter, or any of its basic patterns, is something more than a logical contradiction. As psychiatrists, the human sense of reality is involved. It is not merely discourse, but also its existential foundations that are affected. We might call this, for want of a better term, an existential contradiction.

This pre-verbal, pre-thematic awareness of the world is vague and unanalyzed. But in this very sentence we have verbalized it, and we have constantly stressed the need for conceptualizing and clarifying if it is to be fully understood. This raises a basic question. Can the pre-linguistic patterns of which we have been speaking be linguistically expressed without fundamental alteration? If not, this pre-verbal a priori can never be clearly expressed, and the whole conception I have been trying to express in words will be basically undermined. Is there any example of pre-linguistic meaning, at first vaguely grasped, which is then clearly expressed in words without serious distortion? I cannot argue the issues in detail. But I shall offer an example taken again from James's *Principles of Psychology.* He speaks here of the intention to say something before we have said it.

We are apt to dismiss this transitional state as one of complete ignorance, but this is far from the truth. We can reject the wrong words and feel the rightness of others. But this feeling is still in an indefinite and unformed state. As James says: "Linger and the words and things come into the mind; the anticipatory intention, the divination is there no more. But as the words that replace it arrive, it welcomes them successively and calls them right if they agree with it, rejects them and calls them wrong if they do not. It has, therefore, a nature of its own of the most positive sort, and yet what can we say about it without using words that belong to the later mental facts that replace it? The intention-to-say-so-and-so is the only name it can receive" (*Principles of Psychology* I, p. 253).

Here is a meaning first known directly by direct acquaintance. We must first feel what we want to say. In order to say anything clear and communicable about this feeling we must use words. But this does not mean that it is verbal. It is a distinct condition that is definitely pre-verbal. Furthermore, it is a noetic condition, which knows something before it is said. Otherwise, it could not select the right phrases and reject the wrong. When a right step is taken, it reverberates and answers back. So, by following these answers, we may be led to the right expression. Of course, a change has occurred—·the meaning has become analyzed, clarified, and communicated. But it is the same meaning that is expressed.

The status of what I am calling the empirical a priori is similar. It is first known by what James called "the way of direct acquaintance" (*Principles of Psychology* I, p. 221). This is irreplaceable, and presupposed by language. It must first be lived through to be verbally expressed. But its meaning can be clarified and communicated, for, if we are ready to listen, it will respond to our attempts at verbal formulation. In this way, the primary patterns of our lived experience can verbally be revealed, and, as I believe, some of them have been revealed.

These patterns do not come from another intelligible realm. They are not imposed on the world of sense by a separate worldless mind—they are found in the pre-thematic world of perception ingrained in it. Hence, we do not arrive at a clear formulation of them by any purely logical deduction which uses perception only as a starting point, but only by a careful dwelling on the phenomena in the dialectical process of reverberation we have just described. Here logos and language do not act alone but only together with the lived phenomena to find their logos, inherent in them.

Furthermore when these a priori conditions of human existence are doubted (and the vague acceptance of them which he called *Urdoxa*) something more than logical contradiction is involved as we have noted.

Here, also, the empirical a priori differs from traditional versions. Such doubt is concerned with the a priori conditions not only of reason and discourse but of human life. Such statements as, "I am asleep," being made by a waking man, and, "I am not sure that I exist," belong to this order. Such propositions are self-contradictory in the sense that they contradict a priori conditions without which their actual assertion would be impossible. For want of a better name we have called them existential contradictions, for when seriously meant, they manifest a disintegration of existence. In this way, what we are calling the empirical a priori differs from traditional versions, for violations, or denials, of these lead only to logical contradictions which leave our existence intact.

This, then, is the empirical a priori which I am suggesting, and the existential antinomies into which we fall if it is seriously denied. It meets the criteria for a priori knowledge which I have stated. Nevertheless, it differs, in certain ways I have tried to indicate, from traditional, rationalistic versions. I believe that instead of abandoning the notion of the a priori as they have tended to do in the past, empirically oriented philosophers should work out further and defend the empirical a priori to which their own empiricism should lead them, that is, if like that of James, it is an empiricism that is really radical.

4

The Perceptual Time-lag
and Lived Time

EXPLANATORY NOTE

In recent years, the phenomenological study of human time has produced novel insights in regard to a subject that has occupied a central position throughout the history of philosophy. In "The Perceptual Time-lag and Lived Time," John Wild presents a lucid and polished defense of essential phenomenological discoveries, and goes on to make important contributions of his own regarding this same subject.

Wild is concerned here with validating and illuminating existential time in the face of scientific criticism that finds our experience of time to be merely subjective, arbitrary and hence indefensible. What is unique about living time, we learn from reading Wild's essay, is that such time is interpreted as it is lived. In this way, it is always subject to being reinterpreted as it faces the radically contingent and unexpected future found in human experience. According to Wild, the paradox posed by the perceptual time-lag derives from causal and physiological analyses of perception. For example, we now know that the light that we perceive from the sun takes approximately eight minutes to travel to the earth where its illumination can be observed. Yet we still talk about the present as if there were no "lag" in time. According to Wild, the reason for this is that lived time is anterior to mathematical time and dependent upon experienced time for its own philosophical intelligibility. Through his phenomenological description of time, Wild explores the ethical, epistemological and metaphysical implications of the relationship "lived time" and the time demarcated by the mathematical, physical sciences. Here we can see him responding to a question asked of him by Herbert Spiegelberg some years before in *Philosophical Interrogations*, "What are the precise implications of the time-lag in sense perception for the epistemology of direct realism?" (p. 138). Wild's first response to

Spiegelberg points to the need for an extended answer that could not be given at the time and must "be prepared to recognize the ambiguities of sense perception" (*Philosophical Interrogations*, p. 142). A fuller response to Spiegelberg's question is presented here in the essay before us.

Wild argues passionately and precisely, in a style refreshingly free of technical jargon, that perceptual simultaneity between subject and object does exist, and that the paradox posed by the perceptual time-lag dissolves if we look more carefully at the phenomenon and use philosophical language with greater rigor.

It is in his description of the lived present that Wild makes his most novel phenomenological contribution to the study of time. In keeping with his position that we have a direct awareness of primary experience, Wild argues against the notion that the present is only a fleeting or "fugitive" moment. Such an analysis superimposes the mathematical model of time upon lived time, with its various phases of past, present and future. Unlike Heidegger and Sartre, who emphasize the importance of future over the present and past, and closer to Merleau-Ponty, Wild describes how I am aware of the present as an on-going phase of time, which is measured by meaning rather than number.

In this paper, I wish to examine certain temporal paradoxes of perception in the light of what is now known phenomenologically about lived time. These paradoxes result from physiological and casual analyses of perception based on the observations of a detached spectator. On this view, the process of perception begins with some change, like the ringing of a bell or the blowing of a whistle, in the external environment. This sets up disturbances in a surrounding medium, in this case the air, which are transmitted to the receiving sense organ, the ear. Changes in the ear then lead to vibrations of the nerves which are transmitted to the brain, where consciousness of the external event arises. These processes of transmission, of course, take a certain amount of time measured by the clock, which brings about what we shall call the perceptual time-lag. No human perceiver can sense an external event as it is going on, but only after it has happened.

This is a paradox, for there is no question that we feel ourselves to be coexistent and contemporaneous with the objects of our concern. But from a scientific or objective point of view, this feeling must be regarded as a subjective illusion. In the case of objects near at hand, the time required for the transmission of light or sound waves to the eye or ear may be very small. Nevertheless, there is always some time-lag, so that what the brain perceives as present is always really in the past. This is true even of touch, since after an object has made contact with the skin, a certain time is required for the transmission of the nerve impulse to the brain.

Only then do we become conscious of the contact which has already happened, and, as measured exactly by physical time, lies in the past.

My feeling that I am co-present with an external thing, or event, is, therefore, a delusion. Perceptual simultaneity is impossible. This conclusion becomes even more paradoxical when it is applied to our supposed perception of very distant bodies, like the stars. The transmission of light from such objects requires very long periods of astronomical time. Hence it is certainly reasonable to believe, at least in certain cases, that by the time the light reaches a human brain, the star itself, which we are supposedly seeing, is either radically transformed or no longer in existence.

In our lived experience, as we may call it, we feel that we are co-present with the objects which we see and hear. The train is now standing at the station, and remains there while I run towards it from a block away. As I hear it whistling now, at this time I run faster in order to catch it before it leaves. This is certainly true of the objects near at hand in the room where I am working. The chair is now present before me as I move to it, and get ready to sit down. The table is supporting me here and now while I lean upon it. These objects are not in the past—even one that is just past, for this past is closed and finished. But these things are open to my manipulation. I do not have to remember them. They are present as I deal with them. They support me or frustrate me in the present, here and now.

This is also true of persons with whom I interact and communicate. The friend with whom I am playing tennis is playing with me now. I am not aware of his stroke a little after he has made it. If this were so, I would always be behind the game. I am aware of him simultaneously as he makes it, and as I prepare for its reception. This is also true as I speak with him after the game. I do not receive what he has said after he has spoken, in the past. I follow him in the present, as he is speaking. I am with him here and now, as he is with me. We are coexistent and co-present both together during the same time.

In this paper, I propose to show that this paradox of the time-lag arises from a reductive misunderstanding of lived time and that it may be avoided by a non-reductive understanding of human temporality as we actually live it through. What I have to say, therefore, will fall into four parts:

1) the reductive view of time, and the time-lag paradox;
2) phenomenology and lived existence;
3) a phenomenological approach to the time-lag; and
4) an answer to some questions.

Where we have no time for detailed exposition we shall refer to the relevant phenomenological literature in the writings of James, Husserl, Gusdorf and Merleau-Ponty.

1. THE ABSOLUTIZING OF CLOCK TIME
AND THE TIME-LAG

The reduction of lived time to clock time is part of a larger strategy, characteristic of "objective" thought, by which the human life-world, or *Lebenswelt*, is discounted as "subjective," and supposedly assimilated into an objective frame which we may call the universe of science. From this point of view, which, of course, has its legitimate uses, the existing person is viewed as an object, or organism, interacting with other things in regular or irregular ways that may be externally observed and measured. This organism has no horizon, or world, of its own. It is an object, placed with other objects in the observer's frame. His consciousness, so far as it is recognized at all, is not intentionally stretched out towards a world-field to which it is open. Even though it cannot be observed and measured, it is correlated with certain events that occur inside the organism, especially in the central nervous system. Whatever these internal occurrences may seem to be to the subject experiencing them, they are, in reality, powerless epiphenomena, which have no effect on the real things of the world. These objective realities and their movements proceed just as they are whatever we may subjectively think them to be. They are simply what the detached objective observer observes, though this observation, of course, is a special mode of conscious perception.

From this point of view, time is conceived as an aspect of physical motion through space, both of which can be objectively observed. Thus, as a body moves from A to D, it must pass through points B and C. Corresponding to the indivisible points are the instants on the line of time. This line is like a spatial dimension, except for the fact that it passes. Thus, when the body has arrived at point B, the spatial point A remains, and the body can return. But if we regard the motion temporally, when the body is at instant B, instant A has vanished into the past, and no return can be made. Similarly, at the instant C, B has vanished. So time becomes a succession of nows, one replacing the other, or, in other words, a moving line, adding to itself at one end while it vanishes at the other end we call the past.

By the use of certain devices, like dials and watches, however, the passage of time over certain regular spatial intervals may be marked off and recorded. Thus, in spite of the embarrassing fact that it constantly passes, time may be correlated with space, and the lengths of different changes may be measured, compared and correlated with each other. I worked four hours yesterday, and my friends worked five; then we met together at the restaurant for supper at the same temporal now, that is, at 6:00 p.m. Without such an objective recording and measuring of time, the scientific study of natural change, and also cooperation in the subjective tasks of social life, would be impossible. So there is good reason for the attempt to generalize this system of objective time, and to assimilate our lived experience into it without remainder. But this attempt, when it is carried through consistently, leads to many paradoxes, including that of the time-lag.

Our lived time refuses to be squeezed into an instantaneous now or even into a succession of these. We are really recognizing this whenever we speak, with understanding, of what we call the present, the past, and the future, the ecstasies, or outstretchings, of time as they have been called. My lived time may certainly be passing. But it passes from a future towards which it is moving now, into a past that is left behind, but still remains in a peculiar manner of its own. Though they cannot be objectively observed and measured, we all know that our present, future and past make a difference here and now. Without a future and a past, the present would lose its meaning.

But even more embarrassing questions may be asked of this reductionist view. Can it make sense out of objective observation and measurement? Can such operations be performed in an instantaneous now? As we have seen, they cannot be. The transmission of light and sound takes time. Hence anything that I see, or hear, or observe, by the time I observe it, lies in the past. As we have noted, this also holds true of touch, for the transmission of nerve currents to the brain takes time. So even the object that I am aware of touching is already past and gone by the time I feel it. But the present alone is real, and this I can never observe. What I observe and measure is non-existent. What is presently real and active—this I cannot ever observe. Such a view would seem to be self-destructive. Its conclusions are inconsistent with its basic assumptions.

2. PHENOMENOLOGY AND LIVED EXISTENCE

I believe that these difficulties make it worthwhile to adopt another approach. Let us now try to shift our point of view and follow phenomenology in its attempt to bracket a priori theories, and to explore the world of our lived existence as we live it. Let us first consider the general nature of this exploration, and then apply a few of its results to our perception of time and to the paradox of the time-lag.

From this standpoint, no reduction is attempted. The task of the phenomenologist is not to explain, but simply to describe patterns of the life-world as they are directly lived or experienced. Of course, the living human body exists in the world, and it may be regarded objectively by a detached observer as it casually interacts with other things and agencies. This is not denied. Many noteworthy facts and laws of sequence may be found in the clock time that governs this point of view. The medical and human sciences have already progressed far enough to assure us of this. These facts and laws are of great importance. This is not in question. But in back of these facts and laws, prior to them and to the horizon in which they are observed, there is another, more primordial horizon of the living body as it is lived. Ex post facto, after it has acted; this is a subjective body, aware of what it is doing, never wholly observed, but always present in the background of whatever we say or do.

This living, conscious body is not an isolated subject, or substance, enclosed within itself. It is stretched out into a spatio-temporal world-field from which it cannot be separated. Wherever man is found, this world is found with him, and wherever a world of this kind is found, there is man at its center. This conscious body is not a powerless epiphenomenon. It is actively engaged in projects of its own, and in organizing meaningful regions around these projects. In terms of this world or meaning, it takes over the raw facts and casual sequences into which it has been thrown, and tries to give them a certain sense. Hence, it is not completely determined by them, and possesses a certain autonomy of its own. It may let itself go, and allow itself to be determined exclusively by objective, casual agencies. But if this happens it is due to choice, not necessity. This world autonomy is presupposed in all meaningful discourse and action. If it were determined by external, unconscious agencies, it would cease to be responsible and would lose any claim to truth.

The life-world temporalizes itself through its own mode of time, which we shall call the lived time, and which is quite distinct from the clock time that is ordinarily but not necessarily used as its measure. Since the patterns of the life-world are neither exclusively subjective nor exclusively objective, but both together in one, they are not open to the objective methods of the natural sciences. When approached in this way, reductions and paradoxes of the sort we have noted are bound to occur. These patterns require other phenomenological methods of exploration. We shall now try to use this method in examining lived time, and in seeking for a resolution of the paradoxes with which we have been concerned.

3. A PHENOMENOLOGICAL APPROACH TO THE TIME-LAG

With these factors of the human situation in mind, let us now approach the paradox of the time-lag. From what has been said, we should be able to see that this arises from the absolutizing of an objective analysis of perception that leaves out man and his projects as he lives them. The lived present is not a mere limiting knife-edge between the past and the future, nor is it a smallest interval that can be correlated only with ticks of the clock or metronome beats. The least unit of lived time is a human project of the living, conscious body, which has emerged from the past and is moving towards the future. Perception, as we live it, is not the mere reception of transmissions by a recording instrument, though such reception can always be found. Many other aspects of the project can be analyzed out of it. But in this case the whole cannot be understood as a mere summation of the parts. It is rather the other way around, as is always true when questions of meaning are involved. The parts are a function of the whole, and they can be understood only in the light of the total meaning.

Perception itself belongs to the project, as, for example, a guiding gaze, a sense of smooth flowing action or opposition, and a feeling of satisfaction or frustration at the end. Present perception, therefore, is always in a situation including independent agencies as well as the self. To exist and to perceive in this present involves both self-presence, the presence of the self in the present, and the presence of independent things. This present need not be accepted. To reject it—to escape from it into the past, or the future, or both—are possible ways of existing in the world. To be present in the present is not the same as immediate action which gives itself over to the situation, as always in the animal, and sometimes in the child. It is to return with some meaning, wrung from these realms of absence, to be inserted into the alien beings inside us and around us, which are themselves present to us in the flesh.

This project transcends the situation into which it has been thrown and does not let itself be taken over, unless it gives way, which is always possible. As long as it endures, however, it strives to take over the various facts and casual laws which constitute the situation, and to give them some further meaning of its own. To watch or observe some project is a project. The project is present, or going on now, as long as it is under way, and this always occupies an interval of objective time as measured by the clock. But while the clock can measure the length of this time, it cannot measure the meaning of this length. This is measured by another measure that lived time gives itself. There is no least unit, nor any greatest unit of lived time. The magnitude of the present as we live it depends on the project itself and its meaning. But it always has some temporal duration.

In ordinary language, we may refer to this living, moving present by the use of the present participle. Thus, I say I am not reading, or mowing the lawn, or writing a book. Since the ending of a project belongs to the project itself, this ending, or finishing, also can be expressed by the use of the present participle. But once it has reached its end, the project is over and passed, so that the past participle, or the past tense is used, and we say it is finished, or the lease expired on July 18. We sometimes use the future or perfect tenses in referring to the lived present in order to indicate its expanse, as when we say, I will be working until 5:00 p.m., or, I have been working for three hours. Nevertheless the fact that this whole expanse is embraced by the lived present is indicated by the fact that we can express the same meaning by using the present participle—I am working until 5:00 p.m.—or even the adverb—I have now been working for three hours.

The expanse of this living present has no fixed quantity, and is wholly indeterminate from the objective point of view. It depends on the meaning of the project for the agent, and the existential integrity of his history. Thus, the life of a disintegrated personality, like Kierkegaard's aesthetic man, has little continuity. It is lived in separate chunks which merely succeed one another, and require some external synthesis, like the results of an objective analysis of human existence. For him, the reading of a book for two days might be a long present. For another, who is now engaged in writing a book, this present might last two years as measured by clock time. And for someone engaged in long-range research, it might last through a whole career. The fluidity of the specious present, as James called it, is indicated by the way in which it can be divided into sub-presents. Thus, if I take note of myself on the journey to my office, I may say, now I am crossing the threshold, now I am walking to the station, now I am on the subway, and now in the ante-chamber. But during any of these sub-presents I might have said, I am now on my way to the office.

Of course, the only check on this description is the examination of our lived experience. If it is essentially true, we may give the following answer to the paradox of the time-lag: It arises from an effort of objectivist thought to take over the lived experience of the life-world together with its lived time, and to assimilate this into the special horizon of detached observation and its spatialized clock time. One result of this is the reduction and distortion of the living present to an instant correlated with a point in space, or to a least unit of time correlated with a small and meaningless extension of space. This leads to the confusion of lived time with clock time, and to the paradox which rests on this confusion.

As a matter of fact, the living present can never, even ideally, be reduced to a knife-edge. It is a project, pervaded and surrounded by meaning, which always endures through some interval of time as measured by the clock. In ordinary perception, which belongs to every project, it may take an interval of clock time for light and sound to be transmitted to the eyes and ears. But there is plenty of time in the expanse of the living present for these transmissions, and, indeed, for all those facts and sequences, which that effective project must take over and fill with meaning. A project is under way; for two hours, two months, two years, these external facts and sequences are experiences as going on now in the living present, now in a knife-edge of clock time. Now, while I am riding on the subway, the electric current is passing from the generators, the wheels on my car are turning, and my watch is ticking off the sounds with their regular spatial intervals.

But in my lived time, these regular intervals, each exactly like all the rest, are filled with a different content. Some are more significant than the others and dominate over the rest. Instead of lived time being taken over by clock time and reduced to similar atomic units, it is this regular clock time which is taken over exactly as it is, and filled with a differentiated meaning. While the present project is on its way, it is, of course, possible for me to perceive as present the work that I have now been doing, which is past according to clock time. The presence of what is future by clock time can also be felt in the living present, as the work that I now will be doing. But though mistakes are always possible, I do not perceive the living past (what happened before the project began) or the living future (what will be after the project has ended) with the living present. There is no time-lag, no confusion of the present with the past, if we remain within a single mode of time, and do not mix it with another. This, I believe, is the basic answer to the time-lag.

But it is important to dwell further on this capacity of lived time to reach back into the clock time past and forward into the clock time of the future. They involve not only the intentional objects of our present acts but the acts themselves. Thus, the writing I am now doing, and have been doing for the last hour, covers both my struggles and experiments with words, and the motions of the pencil by which the final words are expressed. I am well aware of the fact that the now of this lived time can be subdivided into a succession of smaller nows. In general, it is fair to say that lived time always has a place for clock time, though the reverse is not true. But it is worth noticing that the succession of subdivisions applies rather to the objects, whereas the overall unity is found rather in the acts. Thus, I may be legitimately asked as to precisely when a certain paragraph was written on the sheet, and I may say, upon reflection, that this was about fifteen minutes ago. But if someone says, when did you do this, I may answer, it is not finished; I am doing it now. If I abstract from my meanings and intentions, I can readily break down the whole project into a succession of objects in clock time. It is the unity of a meaningful experience, in this case an active project, which holds them together in a living present time.

With this in mind, let us now approach the question of the distant stars. Even in an adventitious experience of hearing, this flexible, living present may reach back into a past clock time and make it contemporaneous. Thus, if I am waiting at a small country station for a train which I cannot see, and I suddenly hear a distant whistle, I may say: There it is coming now, even though I know that the transmission of sound takes time and that the whistle took place in the clock time past. I may even use the intensity of the sound, which is quite loud, as a means of estimating its distance in terms of clock time, as when I say: It is now quite near, or, it is now only three minutes away. The first statement reaches into the past, the second into the future of clock time, i.e., it will be here now in three minutes. In both cases, the living present (now) covers an expanse of objective time.

With these facts in mind, let us approach the problem of the distant stars, beginning with our own particular star, the sun. Suppose at the end of a troublesome day I step out for a walk, and climb the bluff overlooking the lake to the west. The distant clouds in front of me are tinged with orange and pink, fading off into lavender and yellow where the light is less intense to the north and south. The whole landscape and the blue waters of the lake are bathed in this eerie light. Then through a thin layer of cloud I see the red ball of the sun itself on the horizon. I see it before me, and I feel its presence in the flesh. But then I meet my scientifically oriented friend, and in talking of the sunset, he reminds me that this so-called sun is an object ninety-two million miles away, and that its light takes eight minutes to reach my eyes. This object, therefore, that I think I see is not really present. What I see has now vanished into the past. It is not now there at all. In fact it has been past and gone for eight minutes, and what is now really there I will not see, unless I wait for eight minutes. But then this sun also will have vanished into the past.

But now suppose that after dinner I walk out again, weary of the monotony of my evening tasks. Glancing upward through the trees, I notice that the sky has completely cleared, and I catch a few glimpses of the stars. In order to get a better view, I climb up the bluff once more. Then in this open space, I raise my head and stare at the vast firmament of the summer sky. As my eye slowly moves from one direction to another, I feel enveloped by an expanse of incredible magnitude, and by countless luminous presences. My gaze then dwells on one in the constellation of Orion, which I recognize from the past. After a moment of contemplation, I think of what my friend would say.

He would tell me, of course, that this star is so many light years away, that what I think I am now seeing is something that did exist millions of years ago in the past, but is now completely transformed or probably no longer in existence. My subjective perceptions are the late effects in my brain of complex nuclear and transmissive processes, which cannot be trusted. They must be replaced by the objective facts of physics and astronomy. Apart from these, taken by themselves, they are subjective delusions. Here is the time-lag with vengeance.

The living present is being reduced to a mere moment of clock time, and the world in which I perceive and exist is being absorbed into the astronomical universe as a tiny sequence of subjective delusions. But is this radical conclusion sound? Is not the astronomer perceiving in the usual way when he looks through his telescope, and when he reads the numbers on his spectroscopic instruments? In discounting the direct evidence or perception, is he not undermining his own procedures? Perhaps this interpretation needs further examination. Let us now examine it in the light of the facts we have noted, in particular those which indicate the need for distinguishing between lived time on the one and clock time on the other.

Let us remember that these two times are quite distinct and that both are involved in this perception. What we call the present (now), future and past are ambiguous. Each of them bears a different meaning on these two modes of time. What is present in objective time, as, for example, the present state of the sun in astronomical usage, may not be present to me at all in my lived time, since this state can be experienced by me only in my lived future. Furthermore, as we have noted, what is past in clock time may be perceived by me in a lived present. Can we apply this distinction to our perception of the sun and the stars in such a way as to eliminate the paradoxes we have been considering? Let us try.

If the setting sun that I see in the evening were both the sun of eight minutes ago as well as the present sun either in clock time or in lived time, this would be a contradiction. But that I now see the sun, my present lived time as it was eight minutes ago in clock time is not a paradox, just as it is not a paradox that I now hear the train whistle of a few seconds ago in my lived present at the station. This, I believe, is a sound analysis of the situation that is non-reductive, and discounts nothing directly perceived nor any astronomical fact as a delusion.

The case of the distant star is more complex, since I do not directly perceive the object which the astronomer calls by this name. This object is a construction, built up on the basis of special observations made with the aid of instruments. What I directly perceive is a point of light coming from some source at a vast distance from me. But there is no inconsistency between this perception, as I experience it, and what the astronomer says. There is no reason why I should not now, in my living present, see a distant source of light that is thousands of light years away in clock time, just as I now hear the whistle of the distant train that is a few seconds away in the past by clock time. It is important to recognize in this connection that it is not a mere sound in my ear that I hear, but the train itself coming around the bend. It is this train, with its whistle of a few seconds ago in clock time, which I now hear. In the same way, it is the real sun of eight minutes ago clock time which I now see in my lived present, as I watch it setting. Similarly, it is the distant source of light, or more exactly the light coming from a vast distance many light years in the subjective past, that is now present to me on the summer night.

4. AN ANSWER TO SOME QUESTIONS

The view we are defending may perhaps be clarified if we now turn to certain questions that may have occurred to the reader. A first question is as follows. The extended present, of which you have been speaking, is a wholly subjective phenomenon which you then read into independent objects like the sun, or the train on the rails. But it means nothing to the sun to be setting. It is simply proceeding on its natural path, and the earth is rotating on its axis. Also it is only in relation to us that the train is coming. Apart from us and our subjective purposes, it is simply being impelled by its engines to move along the rails. These physical changes are adequately measured by clock time, where there is no need to suppose a specious present.

In answer to this, we say that of course the world of the lived present is relative to the conscious existence of human beings. While our human existence may seem small and unimportant when measured by astronomical space and time, nevertheless it cannot be denied that, such as we are, we do exist as conscious beings. Hence, the various relations of physical things to us cannot be denied as unreal. Furthermore, it is only confusing to refer to these relations as subjective, for this suggests that they depend exclusively on us. But this is clearly not so. The setting of the sun is a human experience. But the sun could not set without the sun, nor could the train approach us around the bend without any real train. The present is that phase of time when, if we are present, we feel the presence of alien, independent beings, like suns and trains, and encounter them.

This present is always an interval as measured by clock time, and this interval varies in accordance with the different character of our projects, and the different positions of the objects with which we are concerned. But this does not mean that the sun as an independent body is not moving in its path, and that the earth is not rotating on its axis. These facts belong to the whole situation. They are required. But we also, such as we are, are there perceiving this sun through the clouds as it was eight minutes ago by clock time, and are feeling its very presence in the flesh as we temporalize the time of our lived existence.

But this may lead to another question. The only way we become related to the past is through memory. You see the sun at a certain moment on the bluff. The sun as it was eight minutes before must either refer to some experience you had at that past time, or to an astronomical theory concerned not with your subjective experience of a round object, but with its supposed external cause. Immediate experience has no meaning. This is imposed on it by the mind. You are confusing the two.

This question is the expression of an influential type of objectivist thought, which is at many points false to our lived experience. When I first see the sun from the bluff, I am looking at something present to me, not remembering another experience of the past. Furthermore, even if my astronomical knowledge be minimal, this direct seeing of the sun has a meaning. I am looking at an object that is not only round, but bright, and very distant, far beyond the distant clouds. This much meaning is directly perceived, and was perceived by men long before there was any science of astronomy. But the meanings of perception are always filled with vagueness and ambiguity. Thus, "very distant" can mean many things, which can be more exactly determined and developed only by further investigation of the discipline known as astronomy.

This science, however, is not dealing with another sun in back of, or behind, the one that we see. It is dealing precisely with the visible sun of the life-world with which all men, not blind, are to some degree familiar. It has been discovered that this sun is approximately ninety-two million miles away, and from another allied science we may learn the velocity of light. From these facts, it follows that the sun I see before me now in the flesh, as it sinks below the horizon, is the sun of eight minutes before as measured by clock time. Both facts are true. One is a fact of my direct experience, than which, in spite of its vagueness and ambiguity, nothing can be better known; the other is a fact of confirmed scientific theory. They are inconsistent only if clock time, with its momentary instants, is the only time that there is. But it is not in this time, at such a moment, that I see the sun slowly sinking below the distant horizon. It is in the fluid, expansive present of my living time that I watch this setting sun.

But this may lead to a further question. You are making a mountain out of a molehill! There is nothing amazing about the transmission through time of messages by which something in the past may be made present to you. Thus, by radio you may learn of the death of our friend on a ship at sea two hours ago. As you recognize the meaning of the message, and grief overwhelms you, the very scene will rise up before your eyes, and become present to you. But there is no need of inventing a new kind of time to explain such familiar facts.

But the facts are very different! Irrespective of my grief, and no matter how vivid my imagination may be, I was not present at the death of my friend. I did not witness it in the flesh. It is true that it now becomes present in my lived time, but present only as something that happened in my absence. This is very different from the sunset where I witness the sun itself (not a message from it) before me in my living present. Or to shift to the example of the train, it is nothing else that I hear but the train itself now only two seconds away in the past. It is this presence of something in the clock time past that requires us to distinguish another mode of time with a different present.

At this point, the following question may be asked. You have admitted that clock time does measure what you call lived time. But that which measures must be like what is measured, as the measuring rod and the lengths that are measured both share in spatial extension. Hence, what you call our lived existence and the clocks that measure it must share in the same kind of time.

There is some truth in these abstract principles. But they require serious qualification. Jewels of very different quality may turn out to have the same weight when balanced on a scale. With the lead which balances them they may have weight in common. But other qualities, like radiance and transparency, which have great "value" to us, they may not share either with each other or with the lead. These qualities must be measured in a different way. Similarly, we may say that both lived time and clock time share in something we may call mobility, that is, they both move on and pass away during intervals that can be correlated and measured by regular intervals of space. But this does not mean that the future, towards which they are moving, and the past from which they are departing, nor the intervals through which they pass, are similar. As a matter of fact, the past of lived time is not a mere set of no-longer-nows over and gone. This past is not now over, because it was never all there. It is still going on. Hence, it can be taken over by the present. The future of lived time is not a mere set of not-yet-nows. It is actually present before me, and is now at stake. Also, while lived time may be divided into periods of equal length, like hours and days and years having equal value, this does not take account of the meanings which pervade this lived time, and which demand a different kind of division, and a different kind of measure. Hence, different intervals of the same length in clock time may have very different magnitudes or meaning.

But if this is so, different individuals will measure their lived times in different ways, and cooperation will become impossible. Even the same individual may think that two intervals of time the same in length, say a week, that one is longer than the other. But then he will become chronologically confused and sink into a subjective world of his own.

As a matter of fact, this kind of "confusion" does constantly occur. In a free society, different individuals can work out different time schemes and, indeed, different worlds of their own. In fact, this is the essence of what we mean by freedom. But this does not mean that they become unable to use the common measure of clock time in their objective tasks. If they become free, and not insane, they must do this. In spite of a certain tension, they must learn to take over interval and measures of clock time, and fill them with new meanings of their own which they measure in a different way. If the individual achieves some degree of this freedom, he does not have to understand his life as divided into equal intervals of clock time, each of which is the same in value. He divides it rather into intervals of meaning—the time before he learned a certain truth, for example, then the critical period, and now the time when he is working.

Even in primitive societies we find that the crucial intervals of life—childhood, youth, maturity, and old age—are recognized by the group, marked off by festivals and celebrations, and thus endowed with meaning. With the rule of clock time in our industrial civilization, little attention is paid to these critical ceremonies, and they tend to disappear. Time is divided into equal intervals that are all alike, and one passes through them in a cyclic routine, like the hand of a clock. This leveling down of the qualitative differences that may be found in lived time has contributed to that growing sense of meaninglessness which is characteristic of contemporary culture. Lived time has lost its own measure, and is being taken over by clock time.

It may be asked what kind of a measure this would be, and if there is any real evidence for such a measure. As we have suggested, this would be a way of organizing history which, though still roughly chronological, would judge the importance, and even the length, of time intervals in terms of their meaningful content. There is such a measure, and all individuals who have achieved any degree of autonomy are familiar with it, both in understanding their own existence and that of others. In his text on psychology, *Principles of Psychology* I (pp. 624–27), William James calls attention to the fact that of two intervals which are the same by clock time, the one that is filled with interesting experiences appears to be shorter as we live it through, but longer in retrospect. The other, which is empty and devoid of meaning, appears to be longer and to pass more slowly as we live it, but shorter in retrospect.

This reordering of time in retrospect is only roughly chronological, for it attends not only to the calendar and to the clock, but also to the meaningful content. It divides time into intervals, and times of transition, which carry a certain sense that affects the length of the different times, and even the rate of flow. To the objectively minded, this will seem to be a mere "subjective" distortion of the one and only true and objective time. Others, I think more correctly, will see it as a manifestation of the freedom of the individual person who is able, by such reinterpretation, to take up clock time into a lived time which makes some sense to him, and for which he is to some degree responsible.

We will conclude with a summary statement of the chief differences between these two modes of time, which have emerged from this discussion. Clock time is divided into equal intervals, correlated with equal lengths of space covered by a constant motion. These intervals, or lengths of time, are all alike. They are separated and terminated by instants, or beats, that are correlated with points in space. The present is conceived as such an instant, or very brief extent of time, which separates the past from the future. This indivisible present is the only real phase of time. The past is regarded as a set of successive no-longer-nows which is over and gone, and the future as a set of successive not-yet-nows that is now non-existent.

The instruments which measure this time (clocks, watches, etc.) are objects, and their measuring motions can be objectively observed. The length of the duration of any observable thing, or event in the world, can be correlated with these regular motions, and measured in this way. Even human existence and the world itself, though they involve non-objective factors, can be measured in this way. In so far as they are subject to this kind of measurement, all these things and objects, including our subjective existence, are said to be in time, the form of objective experience.

Lived time, on the other hand, which in modern culture has to take account of clock time and its divisions, is ordered into intervals bearing certain meanings which may differ radically in content and style. The present time, which separates the future from the past, may also join them, and, in any case, it is never an indivisible instant. As we have tried to show, it is flexible and varies in length when measured by clock time, depending on the situation. It is in this fluid, living present that we confront independent things and agencies, and insert our own being into the world. Nevertheless, it is impossible to dismiss the lived future and the lived past as non-existent nows. Each has a distinctive being, and is involved in the flow of lived time in its own peculiar way.

Neither the past which I have enacted nor the future I project ahead of me can be objectively observed—hence the tendency to think of them as "subjective" and unreal. Nevertheless, the past is ever-present to me in the mode of absence, and, whether I remember it or forget it, I must endow it with a meaning of some kind. I cannot escape from it, for it belongs to me. So I speak of it as my past. The future also is present as absent, and it is from this projected future that the basic meanings of the past and present are derived. It, too, belongs to me. So I speak of it in a familiar way as my future. But the present does not belong to me in this way, and I do not normally speak of it as mine, though I may be present in it. This present is rather the present where I face the independent, alien beings of the world, and strive to find in them and to give to them a meaning, in so far as I make myself present among them. In so far as I manage to take them over, my present expands; in so far as they take me over, it contracts.

But whatever happens, I am this living time in which, through the present, the future merely lapses into a senseless past, or takes it over to give it a real sense. Since this temporalizing existence involves not only a mere succession of objects, but a becoming (or passing) or meaning as well, it cannot be adequately measured by the counting of clocks or other instruments. It demands, and, as we have seen, it sometimes receives another measure of its own from within. Perhaps the most significant aspect of living time is the way in which it measures itself, or, as we sometimes put it, "fights the clock." I am not something in this living time. I am it.

5

A Phenomenological Approach to Relativism

EXPLANATORY NOTE

This is arguably one of Wild's most important unpublished essays. The reader will notice that it is also one of the least polished essays found in this volume. It appears, like a number of his posthumous writings, to have been given as a public talk. Wild, more than most phenomenologists of his generation, was keenly aware of the charge of moral relativism that extended to both existential philosophy and phenomenology. In this essay, Wild discusses how the discoveries of the social sciences, history and anthropology in particular, have opened new cultural horizons that have made us aware that the patterns and practices of important elements of human conduct differ from one society to another. He argues that even the history of philosophy cannot completely escape the prejudices of the era in which the historian of philosophy was thinking and writing. He presents, in a dispassionate way, some of the key findings and arguments set forth by positions in philosophy usually associated with relativism and historicism.

At the same time, Wild does not subscribe either to relativism or historicism. Moreover, he subsequently takes note of both egocentric and anthropocentric tendencies within existential phenomenology that must be faced and augmented with alternatives that do not fall into any of these forms of reductionism.

Wild perceptively notes here that "in real life, we have a strong tendency to absolutize our own way of life and to regard all others as deviant variations." At the same time, Wild points out the way that cultural relativism can give way to political and religious absolutisms. This, in turn, leads to the very kind of soulless objectivism that pluralism abhors: "So far as men participate in living their ways of life, they have no access to culture, but only to an array of conflicting cultures, no access to the world as it is, but only to distorted, subjective worlds. Here, all is externally determined, biased, and relative." Wild is very much aware of the way that cultural excesses tend to leave a vacuum that are filled by totalitarian regimes.

He goes on to reiterate his important distinction between "versions of the world" and "the world." It is the task of philosophy to describe not only versions of the world, but also our access to the world beyond our versions of it. This distinction is one that would remain important to Wild throughout his career and is most prominently elaborated in his book *Existence and the World of Freedom* (Prentice-Hall, 1963).

Wild goes on to argue that there are certain invariant patterns of cross-cultural conduct that remain to be elaborated. In all societies, human beings struggle to find meaning in a finite world marked by anguish, guilt, freedom and responsibility. However, different cultures make differing responses and present different versions of the world to these vital patterns of existence.

Wild makes a distinction, increasingly important for our own time, between what he calls "devotion" and "fanaticism." Devotion and fanaticism correspond to "open and closed systems of interpretation, conduct, and versions of the world." These insights of Wild's on devotion and fanaticism, open and closed systems, remain to be elaborated.

Wild's essay will benefit students interested in philosophy and phenomenology at virtually every level. While the essay does not resolve the problem of moral relativism, it sketches a novel approach, providing clarification and direction concerning this issue, vital to our own times. We believe that Wild's essay is also important for the way that it challenges other philosophers to take up an issue that deserves further exploration.

Throughout much of our history it has been believed by theologians, philosophers, and students of the humanities that an objective system of the world, including a pattern of objective values, could be clearly demonstrated by reason as true for all men at all times and places, and in every possible circumstance. It has been commonly held in the past, and is still widely held by many, that without such an absolute system of truth, human life would be cast adrift without stable moral guidance, and would soon fall into anarchy, confusion, and despair. Several important thinkers in our history, beginning with the Greek philosopher Protagoras, have challenged this belief, but on the whole they failed to gain widespread support. In recent times, however, owing to the closer contacts between alien cultures, and to the scientific investigation by historians, philosophers, and anthropologists of radically different ways of life and variant cultural patterns, it has been adopted by many able thinkers, and has become so widely disseminated that it now constitutes a dominant current of contemporary thought. Those, like us, who are concerned with education, are acquainted with that widespread sense of meaninglessness in our students, which is also confirmed by the statistics on mental disturbance and breakdown.

The more traditionally minded among us attribute this disorientation to the influence of historicism and relativism, which, they say, have broken down all respect for objective moral standards, and have brought us to the verge of cultural collapse. As we all know, these two opposed parties are now engaged in a vigorous combat, the one favoring objective standards that hold good for all men, and the other denying them. Since this is certainly a basic issue in which philosophers are involved, I thought that it might be of some interest to you at this time to hear someone approach this issue from a standpoint, the phenomenological, which is, as yet, not too widely known in the Anglo-Saxon world. I believe that it offers us a new approach quite different from that of either objectivism or relativism, and, in the time at my disposal, I shall try to explain it as clearly as I can by way of a criticism of the latter point of view, since, in my opinion, the viewpoint of traditional rationalism is more familiar to all of us.

What then is relativism? In brief, it may be summarized as follows. In the first place, the disciplined, objective study of man always confronts us with radically different patterns and points of view. Thus, the historian shows us such differences in the ways of life, which happen to prevail at two different periods in the history of a culture that is often supposed to be the same, such as the time of the Cluniac movement in the twelfth century when thousands of adults sought refuge from life in the monasteries and convents of Europe, as over against the sixteenth-century Renaissance, when men were concerned with escaping from these prisons and with the active exploration of the world. The philosopher, in the aspect of history with which he is concerned, shows us individual thinkers whose mental worlds are totally distinct. What, for example, does the world of Pascal have in common with that of Feuerbach? Finally, and most devastatingly of all, the anthropologist shows us living patterns of culture that are literally worlds apart, like that of modern nationalism since the French Revolution, where war is an accepted manner of settling social disputes, and that of the Eskimo, let us say, where social war is unheard of and impossible. Each one of these divergent patterns of life has developed norms of its own. Any attempt to judge between them in terms of value must come from a source that is extraneous and irrelevant. We are left with a sheer set of complex objects lying before us that is simply diverse, each being a response to different circumstances and conditions.

We must now turn to a second step which is crucial for the relativist argument. It is interesting because it recognizes a difference between existence as it is lived and the objective perspectives of the scientist, of course greatly to the advantage of the latter. In real life, so the relativist argues, there is a strong tendency towards provincialism, that is, towards absolutizing the patterns and standards of one's own culture as though it were the culture from which all the rest are deviations. Objective science frees us from the dangers of this egocentrism and culture-centrism. Instead of actually making judgments of the living culture and pursuing its norms, we simply describe these aspirations objectively from a detached point of view. In this way, we can lay bare the patterns of many different cultures without becoming trapped by any one. Then we can examine them as objects lying side by side without any arbitrary judgment or bias. This view has much to be said in its favor, for there is no difficulty in finding examples of cultural fanaticism and bigotry in real life. Indeed, there can be no question that the relativist has here hit upon a most important difference between actual existence and objective analysis. But, as we shall see, there is some question as to whether this difference has been truly and integrally interpreted.

The next step spells out the meaning of this objective analysis, and makes the claim that it offers us the only way of escape from subjective bias. Each particular individual and culture develops values and norms in response to the peculiar conditions of its history, and any attempt of an outsider to judge one form of life as better than another would simply express a determinate aspect of his culture, of course quite different from those he is judging, and, therefore, irrelevant to them. Even if the scientist is prepared to admit some element of free choice in such preferences, the net result is the same. A large element of social determinism plus a small element of arbitrary preference does not add up to an objective norm valid for all mankind. In the end, we are left with a vast array of divergent styles and patterns, which are simply lying out there, or succeeding each other in history. These objective facts can be shown and analyzed. Objective contrasts and comparisons can be made. But any judgment of value is the mere expression of a bias, whether it be culturally determined or an arbitrary choice. Thus, the only way to avoid a biased value judgment is to make no value judgment at all.

A fourth step is needed to point out the meaning of the term "relative" and to rule out any objective absolute. Since this whole current of thought has arisen in opposition to traditional absolutes of this kind, it is important to get a clear conception of what it is opposing under such epithets. The absolute is what is absolved from all particular restrictions and qualifications. Thus, an absolute decree holds good for everyone, under all conditions, without exception; an absolute norm is valid for all men everywhere without qualification. The relativist rejects all values and norms of which this can be said. His intellectual background lies in empiricism, and can be traced back to the nominalism of the later Middle

Ages. Hence, he also rejects what he calls universal abstractions of any kind, such as the categorical imperative, the order of human culture as such, the world, etc. For him, there are only the particular demands that are found in the six of seven hundred cultural patterns that have been discovered up to date, and the different worlds belonging to them. As he sees it, these are all relative to the particular conditions or preferences determining them. There is no absolute cultural order in itself. This would not be found in the particular cultures. It would be something in itself found elsewhere, possibly in the mind of God, in paradise, or in some other mythical locale for which there is no available evidence. All such abstractions are projections of wishful thinking which do not actually exist anywhere. In fact, there are only the definite individuals and cultures which are all relative and restricted to the particular circumstances of their unique histories.

There is a fifth and more hidden element in the relativist case which is worthy of attention. This is the way in which each cultural pattern is regarded as closed within itself. Once under way, a culture seems to live a life of its own, until it is destroyed or assimilated into another civilization. When externally regarded as an object, its intrinsic structure can be contrasted with that of other similar complexes. It has its own intrinsic pattern, and its own way of responding to every object. It is, therefore, a world within itself, possessing a unity of its own. Inter-cultural communication, if it occurs at all, is radically restricted. These cultures do not seem to be open to anything beyond. They are separate, insular structures, closed within themselves. We shall refer to this as the atomism of relativistic analysis.

In conclusion, we may summarize the above five aspects of the relativistic argument as follows: Empirical research is confronted with a vast array of radically different ways of life and cultural patterns. In real life, we have a strong tendency to absolutize our own cultural order, and to regard all others as deviant variations. The only way to avoid this distorting bias is to adopt the detached attitude of scientific observation, which compares and contrasts these different cultural forms as objects before the mind. As a result of such objective analysis, each culture then turns out to be relative to the particular circumstances of its history, and, therefore, incapable of working out a true version of the things as they really and objectively are. In and between these different cultural types there is no overarching unity. Each is a world enclosed within itself. Science alone can discover the objective truth about things as they really are. So far as men participate in living their ways of life, they have no access to culture, but only to an array of conflicting cultures; no access to value but only to relative values; no access to the world as it is, but only to distorted, subjective worlds. Here, all is externally determined, biased, and relative.

This, in brief, is the position now widely known as historicism and relativism. As we have said, it has not only won widespread, popular support, but has also appealed to many penetrating and well-trained minds. There is, no doubt, much truth on its side. Let us now examine it critically from a phenomenological point of view.

First of all, in connection with the radical diversity of different worlds which lies at the foundation of the relativist argument, we may note an important qualification that is demanded by the evidence. In real life, while we are at least dimly aware of cultural differences, we nevertheless continue to recognize what we call the world as one. Thus, in our ordinary discourse we speak of x's conception of the world, y's view of the world, and even of z's world. This implies a significant distinction between a limited version of the world and the world itself. There is also no doubt that when we speak elliptically of the Greek world as over against the Roman and German worlds, and of the Western as against the Eastern world, we have the same distinction in mind. These are different perspectives on the world, not completely closed systems.

It is true, of course, that this distinction is often minimized, and even suppressed, in the interpretations of dogmatic individuals and frozen cultures. But it is never entirely eliminated. World solipsism is a position that may be approximated in real life, but never actually reached. The ways of life of alien tribes and peoples may be dismissed as wholly false, or mythically interpreted as forces of evil and error. But they are always recognized in a way that implies at least some limits on our own perspective. If we ask, what are the experiences which lead to this recognition of limitation, I believe that we may be aided by recent phenomenological studies of our perspectival perception of external objects. Such perception never gives us the whole object all at once, only limited versions. What then do we mean by a version, and how do we become aware of its limits? *Versio* means a change, a turning. In order to get a better grasp of an object, I hold it in my hands, if it is small enough, and turn it around so that I can see it from different angles. It is through such change that I become aware of the limited nature of a single perspective, and gather some sense of the whole. There is something analogous to this in our world understanding. In so far as I remember different ways of grasping the world in the past, I become aware of the limits of my present perspective as against different perspectives that lie beyond. In the second place, I am constantly checking my perceptions with those of others who may have keener insight, or a more inclusive point of view. In a similar way, I get a sense of the limits of my world perspective by communication with members of my own tradition, or with representatives of alien cultures.

Finally, phenomenological investigation has now greatly clarified the manner in which a single perspective of a given object points beyond to the whole of which it directly presents only an aspect. Thus, as I look down upon this table in front of me, the surface which I see directly cuts off my view of the top of the left front leg. But I see the bottom part directly, and also the leg's full shadow on the floor. It is not that what I see suggests something entirely separate that is not given in any way whatsoever. It is rather that what I see in perspective actually involves something further, which is actually seen, but only in part, or perhaps vaguely and dimly, as the fine vein structure of the wood involves a background of still finer structure which can be brought out with a magnifying glass.

No single perspective, nor any set of them, can ever be exhaustive. No matter how many of them I may achieve and hold in memory, they are still incomplete and point beyond to an inexhaustible, total being, that I know I do not know in its entirety. In an analogous fashion, every living version of the world points beyond and actually involves backgrounds and mysteries which are actually known to be not known. This is something which all life-worlds share in common. Each horizon involves, and is known to involve something more, and, thus, by its very nature, reveals the distinction between our perspective, and that of which it is a perspective. In these three ways, then, through change, communication, and mystery, we grasp our human worlds as versions of the world beyond.

It is important to note here that the world is not another world that might be apprehended in another way. Just as the whole table appears to us only through our partial perspectives, so the world appears to us only through our versions, and is inseparable from them. We can say that it is a common style running through them. Gathering them together in some total meaning accounts for every version, as the whole table enables us to account for our partial perspectives, even those that are distorted and untrue. And yet the world is radically distinct from any particular version. It is not a world in itself, lying back of these versions, and differing from them in certain respects. This would be just another version lying over against the rest. The world is involved in its versions and cannot be separated from them any more than the table can be separated from the upper surface that we see. Yet it is not the sum total of these versions. It lies beyond them and yet in them. It includes them, and yet at the same time makes them possible.

This distinction between versions of the world and the world itself is totally missing in the relativistic analysis. This detached and objective approach sees only separate, closed systems which it calls worlds. It takes no account of the openness of a life-world which enables it to change continuously into others, and to communicate with them, and most important of all, to be open to the world which both encompasses and yet transcends them all. Hence, as objects lying out there before the mind, each is fixed, separate from all the rest, incommunicable, and closed to anything beyond. And yet, while the distinction between version and total world is suppressed and ignored, it nevertheless appears, though in a distorted and contradictory form. In so far as it is recognized that these systems are inadequate and exclude each other, they are held to be relative to certain conditions which determine them from the outside, though nothing is outside the world. But then in so far as each is seen to be an inclusive system of meaning with a place for every conceivable event, it is called a world, though this is incompatible with its being excluded from other all-inclusive systems. These inconsistencies are evident in the whole relativist analysis. They arise from a failure to make the distinction between version and world, a distinction which lies in the phenomena themselves, and, therefore, cannot be neglected except at the price of incoherence and distortion.

Let us now confront the next step in the relativist argument. This is its claim to greater scope and comprehensiveness, based on a certain understanding of the difference between real life and the results of objective analysis. In real life, it is said, there is a tendency towards provincialism, which imprisons each culture within its own boundaries, and prevents it from really understanding the rest. This solipsism and ethnocentrism can be corrected by an objective approach, which will enable us to compare and contrast different systems objectively without distorting value judgments. Is this claim really justified?

We can certainly agree that there is an important difference between our lived existence in the world, and the results of objective analysis. But if there is such a difference, the question is raised as to how far such results really apply to existence in the concrete? Hence, instead of jumping at once to the conclusion that this approach is superior, let us dwell for a moment on the difference. What does it involve? And what does it mean?

The main difference can be stated in terms of concern or engagement. To be actually engaged in the world is not the same as to observe or describe this engagement objectively from the outside. Of course, abstractly speaking, it is the same phenomenon. But in the two cases, it is understood (and we do understand our projects from the inside as we are engaged in them) in a different way, and placed in a different horizon. Let us now spell out this difference in two distinct respects.

In the first place, for the detached observer, the project that he examines is one possibility among many others, each with its own surrounding field of meaning and with no one enjoying a privileged status. In real life, on the other hand, my chosen project becomes an actuality with privileged status around which all other meanings are organized, and at this point, the single world comes into view. As I become actually engaged, I am no longer existing in one possible world among many others. I am existing in the one and only world there is for me. The other possibilities cease to be world islands, each anatomically enclosed within itself, and each with equal status. Instead of separate worlds, they become versions, which are now ordered in a single all-encompassing horizon. With some of them that are friendly, I can cooperate. With others, opposed to my way of existing in the world, I must struggle and compete. But I now exist together with them in a single world that embraces us all.

The same basic difference can also be developed in terms of abstraction. The observer can regard different aspects of the life-world abstractly, and separate them from each other. Thus, the relativistic analyst can focus on certain objective features of differing cultural patterns or ways of life, and as he does this, he may abstract from (i.e., forget) the actual existence of those who are living in these ways, from the existence of others with whom he communicates, and finally from the overarching horizon which embraces them all in real life. In this way, as we have seen, different versions, different ways of life in the world, become frozen into closed patterns, atomic worlds in themselves, which may then be contrasted and compared. But in real life, as we sometimes say, everything happens together—striving, sickness, science, war, and competition—all at once in the same single world-horizon. In this world I am existing and facing death in my own way, or the way of my culture, together with others existing and facing death in different ways. If I am to understand my situation, I must work out a version in terms of which I can make some sense out of everything, my own existence, that of others opposed to me, and most of all, of the mysteries in the overarching world-horizon around me which I know that I do know. My interpretation may be crude, oversimplified, and inadequate. But in order to live, I must have a global interpretation of this kind.

If this is the nature of the difference, we may now raise a serious question as to whether relativistic analysis offers us the wider view, and as to whether it can exert the liberating influence that is claimed for it. To bring different cultural patterns before the mind in this way is useful for certain purposes. But they are not worlds. They are not even living versions of the world, for they lack existence, intercommunication, and the overarching world-horizon. They are abstract patterns, the skeletons of lived existence placed in an alien, objective frame which is not the wider horizon, for this way of observing and analyzing is itself a way of being-in-the-world. This life-world, if it is not closed arbitrarily by fanaticism, is the broader and richer horizon. We cannot get outside to observe it in an objective manner. We grasp it only from the inside by a mode of awareness that attends our acts, or that is able to follow these acts imaginatively, and to grasp their sense. It is not through abstract observation of objects, no matter how sweeping this may seem to be, that we gain access to this all-inclusive horizon, but through our lived existence. It is here that it comes into view and actually envelops us.

The relativists are, of course, right in pointing out that our human versions of this world often become rigid and closed by dogmatism and fanaticism. It is easy to confuse our versions of the world with the world itself. But the way to correct this tendency is not to reduce these versions to abstract objects, which are atomic and self-enclosed. This, in fact, will turn out in the end to have an opposite effect, for both relativism and fanaticism involve us in systems that are fixed and closed. The only difference is that fanaticism commits itself to such a system, whereas relativism, while it tells us that such atomic systems are all that there are, claims to remain uncommitted. But the way to avoid making fanatical value judgments is not to make no judgments at all.

As long as we live, we are engaged in the pursuit of some values. We cannot avoid engagement. Hence, the net upshot of relativism is to guide living men towards that despair-free and open interpretation, which merely fans the coals of a fanaticism that is simmering in all of us. Relativism and static skepticism are a fertile ground for dogmatism and tyranny. As the history of the Nazi Revolution in Germany shows quite clearly, this is not the way in which humanistic research can effectively promote freedom and develop its own proper concerns. The only way in which it can do this is by following a mode of investigation that will keep it in closer touch with lived existence, and then, by revealing the artificialities and inadequacies of the dogmatism into which it is constantly falling, to keep it open to the overarching structures and mysteries of the *Lebenswelt*.

Can we not see, in fact, that the dogmatic rationalism of traditional systems of philosophy and modern scientific relativism has certain assumptions in common? Do they not both disparage the immediate data of consciousness as self-enclosed, subjective, and incapable of yielding any universal truth which is valid for all mankind? As a result of this, do they not both make a radical separation of pure meaning from the contingent facts of history? It is only by accident that these meanings are connected with historical world facts, and we cannot get to the former by dwelling on the latter. This will only lead us astray. To get an understanding of pure form and structure, another, quite different approach is required. Is this not in both cases a method of objective observation, which gives us access to such universal truth? In the one case, it is reason and logic; in the other, it is the scientist who detaches himself from the world of his culture and then, as a pure spectator, observes this world and compares and contrasts it with others. Do they not hold that our lived experience is externally determined and caused on the one hand by a system of fixed essences, on the other by physical, biological, and other environmental agencies?

Are these systems of explanations not already fixed and determined? If they were not already in existence, how could they yield a causal explanation? Both views, then, look back to meanings already established rather than to those which originate, grow, and decline in history. Finally, as we have seen in the case of relativism, do they not both fall back on systems of meaning that are finished and closed, as the divine first cause of Aristotelian philosophy is complete and fully in act, and the cultural patterns of the scientific anthropologist are closed to each other as well as to any world beyond?

It is true, of course, that there are differences. The traditional rationalistic claims that his system of meaning will justify certain objective value judgments that are valid for all mankind, whereas the relativist denies any such claim. With respect to values, we are culture-bound. The truth to which we have access will concern only the relative comparing and contrasting of these different value systems. Here we are left with a plurality of worlds. The rationalist, on the other hand, believes that he has access to a single explanatory system of meaning that can bring not only the facts of nature but also those of human culture into an all-embracing unity. But in spite of such differences, the common assumptions remain. Both the relativist and the rationalist discount the world of our lived existence in favor of a purely objective method of observation and abstraction. Both separate a system of pure meaning from the chaotic facts of history, and insist that it requires a distinctive, objective mode of approach, if it is to be understood. Both agree that the world of our lived existence can be causally explained, and thus assimilated into a system of meaning which is already fixed and closed.

In the light of these common assumptions, we can see the continuity between modern scientific relativism and the classical philosophy from which it has developed. Indeed, it is fair to say that the relativist is a chastened or disillusioned rationalist still in the Greek tradition, but more modest in his claims. This is often concealed by his polemics against traditional philosophers who pretend to be able to think and to evaluate for all mankind. But we must not forget that in a more restricted area, apart from value, he is making the very same claim. His science also has its history, and, at its foundations, is also culture-bound. Neither position offers us any real escape from dogmatism and fanaticism in real life where foundational meanings and values are always at stake. Here, the rationalist offers us a great plurality of philosophic systems not one of which can be demonstrated, and not all of which can be true; and the relativist offers us a great plurality of cultural patterns of which the same may be said. So, since we must live in some way, we can make an arbitrary preference. But this is hardly an escape from dogmatism, unless we do it all cynically and half-heartedly, in which case we hardly live.

Is there any escape from these dilemmas into which our traditional rationalism has plunged us? If so, it must avoid those common assumptions which we have just examined, and have found to underlie both relativism and rationalism. I believe that in phenomenology, and in certain types of current analytical philosophy, we now find such an approach.

Let us think of phenomenology in relation to these assumptions, considering them one by one. If I can show how it has really broken down with them, I may be able to suggest to you how it offers us a viable alternative to rationalism and relativism, and, therefore, a way of philosophizing, not mere verbal play, that is neither trivial nor fanatical and dogmatic. Phenomenology, as the word implies, is a return to the phenomena of our lived existence. It has already shown, I believe, that these phenomena, so long disparaged and discounted in our tradition, are not locked up in any subjective mind container. Rather, they constitute a cast world which includes objective as well as subjective factors, and many regions, like those of mining, transportation, manufacture, business, politics, and that of education and leaning, for well or ill, about a critical question of our time.

This world has a structure, a freedom, and a truth of its own, which is now beginning to be explored in a disciplined way by the methods of phenomenology. It has been found that such global meanings cannot be separated from the particular, contingent events of human history. For example, history itself is a meaning of this kind. We can abstract it from this occurrence or from that. But it is not an essence which can be separated from all concrete occurrences. We try to achieve such a separation; it becomes empty and meaningless. It is a flowing form, a way of existing that pervades the events it characterizes, and cannot be understood apart from them. Furthermore, meanings of this kind cannot be observed from the outside as objects, and placed in the frame of the spectator. They must be understood, first of all, in the world-horizon of those who are actually engaged in the situation. Thus, before the historian can inquire into the real meaning of an event, he must first use his imagination to gain as adequate an understanding as he can of this event as it was lived through from the inside, and as it can be placed in the world-horizon of those who were actually involved.

Turning now to the assumption that our lived experience is externally caused, we reach a controversial topic which we cannot argue out here in detail. We shall simply indicate a few of the major reasons which have led phenomenology to reject this traditional notion. First of all, a cause is a particular activity or agency, a specific thing, in the world (minimally) which influences something else in the world. But meaning is not a specific thing of this kind. Such things are already surrounded and pervaded by meaning. They have a sense (causation), or they would not be what they are. Meaning is the world background on which they appear. Causes may occur and act in this world. They cannot cause what they presuppose. Furthermore, we can ask what meaning can be given to that which lies totally beyond this world of our lived experience. It is true that science can give us information concerning the stars and the earth before man appeared. But stars, earth, and time (before and after) are not totally beyond our lived experience. We know what they mean precisely from our life experience.

Hence, while the astronomer expands the range of our temporal knowledge, he does not get us beyond the basic meanings of the life-world. He merely extends its limits. The fact that the world of meaning is not a thing in the world that can be caused by other things is well attested by evidence often noted in the history of Western philosophy. Thus, as the Stoics maintained, while human resistance can be easily overcome, there always remains a certain freedom of interpretation concerning its meaning. No cause can tell us what it finally means. It operates; it does not signify. World meanings are not caused; they are constituted with a certain degree of freedom.

Furthermore, they are never fully determined and fixed. They are made ready, originate, and then grow or decline in history, like freedom, for example. This meaning of freedom remained latent, and was never fully developed in the Greek tradition. It was more at home in the Jewish-Christian life and thought, but remained inactive and half-suppressed in the high Middle Ages. Then, with the coming of nominalism and the Protestant Reformation, it sprang into life, and became a dominant theme in art, literature and philosophic speculation. In the seventeenth and eighteenth centuries, attention was first focused on the social and political aspects of this theme. It was only later on in the nineteenth and twentieth centuries that personal freedom attracted much attention, so that it has now become a topic of central importance, and even a political issue. And who will say that its final meaning is as yet definitely fixed and clearly determined? Basic meanings of this sort, like the world to which they belong, seem to have inexhaustible depths which are only partially expressed in a history that constantly points beyond to further possibilities.

It is true that, when regarded from the outside objectively, this world disintegrates into a number of different worlds, each self-enclosed and separate from the rest. Relativism takes this point of view as final. But as we have pointed out, this is not true of the horizon of our lived existence. We never think of this as merely one possibility among many. We exist in the one and only world there is, which includes ours as well as any other versions of which we may be aware. In this world, there are mysteries and vast regions of ignorance, which we know that we do not know, and which we share with other cultures. We are unusually aware of dubious choices that have been made in the past, and of many other imperfections in our culture, such as poverty, self-centeredness, stupidity, and injustice. We know of its limitations even though we may never have studied anthropology. When pressed, we are ready to grant that it is only one version of the world among other versions, not the world itself. And yet we never think of it as closed. In spite of many difficulties, we feel that we can communicate with other different versions, and that our culture, in spite of its limitations, is open to a transcendent horizon, the world, which in some sense embraces our own as well as all other versions.

Thus, when we witness a deed or an act of thought which carries with it the ring of authenticity, we feel that it transcends the limits of its cultural situation, that it would be respected by any man anywhere who could understand its nature and its circumstances, and that it, therefore, bears a lasting meaning, not merely for this world or for that, but for the world itself. It is when we become disoriented in our way of life that we begin to look at it objectively as one infinite form among many, and then fall into a fanaticism which freezes it into a fixed pattern. But then our culture is in transition. An age of criticism is at hand. If we are to face such an age with understanding and courage, we will not be helped greatly by the dogmatism of a classical system of philosophy, nor by the related detachment of a scientific relativism. We need a new mode of approach that may give us some understanding of the actual situation in which we are existing, and of the world, which is in crisis. I believe that phenomenological thinking offers us such a new approach, which is radically different from any traditional closed system as well as from any form of scientific relativism, though it has something in common with both. Let us now try to gather together the strands of our preceding argument in order to [demonstrate] that this is so.

With the relativist, the phenomenologist will agree that the world is manifested only in radically different cultural worlds; each is determined in various, objective respects by different climatic and other environmental conditions. He will also agree that each of these cultures is a total horizon with its own way of taking account of anything that may happen. However, he will deny the relativistic doctrine that this whole world of meaning has been determined by external causes. One thing in the world can exert its causal influence on another thing. But the world of meaning is not a thing that can be produced by any external cause or causes. It develops not through any causal interaction, but rather through something more resembling a dialogue between man and the independent things and agencies around him. Man's life-world is an answer that he has worked out to the situation into which he has been thrown, and this answer involves some freedom of choice. The phenomenologist will also disagree with the relativist thesis that each cultural pattern is a complete world enclosed within itself. Instead of this, he will follow the evidence which indicates that these are not separate worlds, but rather versions of the all-encompassing world beyond. Every cultural version, even the most fanatical, opens into this world, and is at least dimly conscious of it. The world appears not through a relativistic disengagement, and a closing of the version into a frozen "world," but rather through a more intensive engagement, and an opening of the version towards what lies beyond.

With traditional forms of rationalism, the phenomenologist will agree that man is not locked up in a number of frozen, cultural patterns, and that we have access to a single world with stable structures of meaning and value, such as oriented space, lived time, freedom and history. He will also agree that the perspectives of science, as well as those of different cultures, are ultimately to be placed within this global horizon of meaning. But he will deny that this is a different world in itself, apart from these human versions, to which we have access only through the methods of objective reason and logic. He will also deny that these human versions are to be dismissed as mere subjective distortions or accidental variations of a real, subjective world. The real world has a place for the "subjective" and the human, as well as for the objective and the non-human. It appears, or fails to appear, precisely in and through these human versions and must be understood, if it is to be understood, in the same way as we understood our own existence-in-the-world as we live it from the inside. This all-encompassing world-horizon is not a system of essences already fixed, finished, and ready to be copied down. It is in becoming, a still unfinished history, ready to be reinterpreted and redirected by responsible thinking and acting. Values are not separate from lived existence. They do not dwell in any special realm or region. As ordinary language clearly indicates, they pervade the whole *Lebenswelt*, for the independent things and persons around us are either friendly or unfriendly to our projects.

These projects cannot be adequately judged in terms of virtues objectively defined in terms of the realization of a fixed human nature. In this sense, the relativist is right. There are no abstract moral principles valid for all mankind apart from the culture in which we exist. They should be judged rather as ways of existing which either face up to, and meet the conditions of life in the *Lebenswelt*, or do not face and meet them. Ways of thinking and acting which, in addition to meeting the special conditions of a given culture, meet these conditions with freedom and integrity are authentic. Those which do not are unauthentic. This difference can be recognized by other individuals living in radically different ways, and even by alien cultures. In this sense, value judgments can be made that are valid for all mankind at a given juncture in history. But we must also recognize that even the most stable world structures are subject to reinterpretation and change.

Such, then, is the way of the phenomenologist, which, as we have interpreted it, divides into two distinct tasks. The first is to explore his own world version, that of his own culture in all are various manifestations, and that of other cultures to which he has some access. In this task, he will always be concerned with the actual usages of ordinary language, the language of the *Lebenswelt*, through which we express and understand, to some degree of clarity, our existence in the world. But he will not be bound by the forms of this language, and will never be content merely to repeat such usages as they stand. His hope will be to shed further light on the usage by clarifying the situation to which it belongs. No phenomenon will be too small or too remote to attract his attention. He will be concerned with the clarification of any manifestation of life in the *Lebenswelt* whether or not it has already achieved a distinct linguistic expression. But he will be particularly interested in such basic structures as human space, human time, history, freedom, responsibility and anxiety, which seem to have a universal world significance. I believe that some progress has already been made in this part of the task, though one often finds, as in Heidegger, the confusion of an aspect of a particular culture with a structure of world significance. One should also mention the fields of psychiatry and anthropology where noteworthy progress has already been made by the use of phenomenological methods of gaining a better understanding of the life-worlds of disturbed persons, and those of primitive peoples.

After we have gained some insight into an experience of a person or a people as they themselves interpret it, a second question arises. What is its general significance? What does this really mean for the world at large? This, of course, raises ultimate philosophical questions, but in a new context, quite different from traditional modes of approach, where new evidence is now available. Many traditional conceptions which, like the dualism of mind and body, have entered into our common speech have been critically analyzed and found wanting (cf. Merleau-Ponty, *Phenomenology of Perception*). Other novel conceptions, like that of the lived body (*corps vécu*), are being developed to take their place. Some oversimplified world constructions have been attempted. But here the situation remains confused and incipient. Perhaps it will always be. One can say, however, that the foundations have been laid for a new approach to what has traditionally been called ontology or metaphysics.

I have now tried to give you a sense of the phenomenological method, and of some of its more basic results. I believe that they give us a new approach to the traditional conflict between absolutism and relativism which should be of interest to living philosophers, whatever their point of view may be.

Part II

Conversations, Reflections and Beliefs

6

Conversations and Reflections: The Guggenheim Journal

INTRODUCTION

In 1957–1958, John Wild traveled to England and Europe under the sponsorship of his second Guggenheim Fellowship. During this time he met with some of the most important philosophers of the Anglo-Saxon and Continental philosophical traditions. His carefully kept account of these conversations is published here for the first time. The recollections appear to have been written down shortly after his encounters with each of the persons with whom he spoke. Recognizing that Wild speaks more freely in the semi-journalistic style he adopts here, we have eliminated only the most highly personal notes and characterizations.

Wild's journal proves fascinating and illuminating in several respects. We see him recording his encounters with such luminaries as Gilbert Ryle and J. L. Austin in England, and Karl Barth, Karl Jaspers, Georges Gusdorf and Eugen Fink on the continent. The Guggenheim Journal, as we have called it, shows Wild in dialogue with important analytic philosophers. He attempts to convince these philosophers of the importance of phenomenology, the life-world in particular, and the converging aims between the two schools of philosophy. Trying to forge common tasks for phenomenology and analytic philosophy would remain a preoccupation for Wild for the next ten to twelve years. As *Time* magazine noted, "Yale's John Wild recently published an article suggesting that the lebenswelt, the 'lifeworld' of experience, that phenomenology investigates is the world of 'ordinary language' that the linguistic philosophers are studying" (*Time*, Jan. 7, 1966). Perhaps it might be more precise to say that we find Wild, here, arguing that linguistic analysis presupposes and relies upon the world of "ordinary experience" that phenomenology rigorously explores.

For the most part, Wild's concern is with the burning issues of contemporary philosophy, and he only secondarily concerns himself with personalities. At times, such as in his moving descriptions of Barth and Jaspers, we see how Wild regards the philosophers he has encountered as embodying the philosophical positions that they represented.

Although he had already reached a position of philosophical eminence, Wild never ceased to think of himself as a student of philosophy. He is constantly asking questions, even of men of lesser stature, not as an occasion for speaking himself but in the genuine expectation of modifying his own previously held positions. The discussions with Gusdorf and Roger Mehl are particularly instructive here. Wild's passionate relation to philosophy, and the fervor of his expression, have led some to think of him as a polemical thinker; the evidence here is of a genuine openness to points of view different from his own.

It is worth noting the degree to which even figures cited by Wild's interlocutors were to be entertained seriously by him. For example, when Pierre Thévenaz, a Swiss philosopher who died at the age of 42, had published *An Introduction to Phenomenology*, it was Wild who would later write the forward to the English translation of this book. Another example of Wild's follow-through concerns Mikel Dufrenne. Dufrenne's book *The Notion of the A Priori* made a deep impression upon Wild, and Wild subsequently devoted an entire course to this subject emphasizing Dufrenne at Yale in 1968. The figure of Dufrenne is important in his own essay included earlier, "Is There an Empirical A Priori?" Hermann Wein, whom Wild met on this trip, would serve as one of the major questioners of John Wild in *Philosophical Interrogations*. When he notes in his diary that "I must buy all of Gusdorf's books," he in fact did so, and later often praised him as contributing original phenomenological insights.

The lively portrait of Wild at work as a philosopher engaged in dialogue with some of the most significant thinkers of both the analytic and phenomenological traditions more than compensates for the episodic nature of his journal entries. It should in fact serve as a model for expanded philosophic projects of exactly the kind that Wild was undertaking.

Appended to the end of this section is a brief description of Wild's interlocutors as well as notations indicating names referred to by him in his journal. In several instances we were unable to identify the figures with whom he was speaking. The readers should note that we have left Wild's own parentheses intact and have added brackets in places we felt needed clarification.

JOURNAL FROM GREAT BRITAIN

Explanatory Note

When John Wild visited analytic philosophy's sanctuaries in Great Britain, it had come a long way since the logical positivism of the early part of the century. Under the influence of Ludwig Wittgenstein's *Philosophical Investigations*, British philosophers turned from the attempt to reconstruct the world as an assemblage of hard and finished facts reflected in a tenseless ideal language (an attempt which Wild in his realist period had criticized roundly and incisively) to the sifting of ordinary language. They had seen that language is rich and irreducible to a single "ideal" language. We are thoroughly in it, one might say, and we cannot get out of it completely to look at it. But we can explore language, feel its nuances and sensitize ourselves to its distinctions and to the differences between the broad types of language games into which it is ramified. In the process we may find, and frequently do find, certain philosophical problems getting set up in a very different way or in some cases dissolving altogether.

John Wild saw in this term the hope for a new style of philosophical investigation, less dogmatic and less reductionistic than earlier British philosophy. Indeed, one could hope for a philosophy much more truly empirical than traditional "empiricism" had been (see *The Radical Empiricism of William James*, Doubleday and Co., NY, 1969).

It is interesting to see Wild gratified that ordinary language philosophy had not lost its sense of continuity with a broader philosophical tradition. We find him raising the question of primary and secondary qualities with a young Charles Taylor. And he is able to voice his own special concerns—"True authority is for free men"—with some of these British philosophers.

Earlier in his career, Wild had argued forcefully against the commonly held assumption of an absolute separation between fact and value. Now, however, a certain more sophisticated version of that distinction was forcing itself upon him, namely, the distinction between scientific fact and what he would later call "world facts." Regardless of whether the classical tradition is right in claiming that objective factual being carries with it a hierarchy of fixed values (and at this point Wild was inclined to think that it was not), there seems to be a distinction between objective fact and the richly textured and complex world of meanings that we intersubjectively and creatively give to what otherwise would be bare facts. The chief merit of ordinary language philosophy is that it seems to implicitly recognize this world between objective fact and the merely "subjective"; a world where meaning is not fixed and unalterable, but which is nevertheless a world I do not just dream up or call into play out of nothing. From this point of view, the ordinary language philosophers are saying: Language is the key to, and the articulation of, this world. To study language is to study the real world, the place where we start from before the subject-object split, the *Lebenswelt.*

But the British philosophers do not seem to want to talk this way. They wanted to avoid all reference to larger ontological issues, with the consequence that their discussions often appear clever but trivial. Wild located one of the most important reasons for this deficiency succinctly: They are overly "impressed" with logic.

The careful reader will note that Wild, trying to find common ground with these philosophers, remarks after speaking with Austin: "Perhaps I am doing a kind of linguistic phenomenology." This is consistent with Wild's sense that the work of philosophy was too important to allow itself to be diverted by sectarian differences, except when philosophically unavoidable and consequential.

To understand what Wild means by this, it is necessary to realize first that he has nothing against philosophers being either logical or clear; Wild was surely himself a rigorous thinker. But there are two things that always need to be said about the role of logic in philosophy. First, for the philosopher logic is a tool, not an end. Making perfectly clear logical distinctions and drawing conclusions, disengaged from the interest that leads us to make these clarifications in the first place, is just game playing. But in order to keep our logic-chopping in touch with the matrix of our search we must not be afraid to continually attempt to articulate that pervasive philosophic concern. Sometimes this articulation will be at least temporarily paradoxical, and it will always carry with it a certain vagueness, an ambiguity. Second, the most widely venerated system of symbolic logic used by the moderns, like any such system that departs from classical logic by disengaging itself from the explicit aim of sorting out what the Medievals called intentional objects, will harbor epistemological and ontological prejudices all the same. In the contemporary case, the system developed by the earlier analytic philosophers is still uncritically accepted by the contemporary analysts, with at least one drastic consequence: Statements about existence, or which predicate existence of something, are ruled out of court. Obviously such a system is unacceptable to anyone who takes either of the positions John Wild has been known to champion, which are neo-Aristotelian philosophy or existential phenomenology.

Faculty Meeting, University of London, November 5

A professor at Birkbeck (University of London), Peters, read a paper on authority. It was fairly adequate and filled with good references to Hobbes, Max Weber and others. He also raised some good questions such as: de facto authority. For example, when in a theatre, a man suddenly directs people how to get out in the case of an incipient fire. He has no right according to Peters. Sheer de facto authority. Also, charismatic authority from Weber. A leader just has this kind of personality, influences people. (Is this authority or merely influence?) The distinction between authority and having authority? (It is traditional rather than functional. May happen in outworn group structures.) He said that scientific authority, like Einstein, is a mere channel. Other forms of authority are more creative. I question this very much.

In the discussion, I raised a point about authority always implying capacity to rebel. Otherwise we have mere power which Peters wants to distinguish from authority. Then the discussion finally turned into this channel and the argument seemed to go my way. They agreed authority was for free men. But I do not think they saw the mediating function of authority, which means that all authority really is a kind of channel. Can we have authority without a feeling of awe? I say yes. Cf. scientific authority. I think that authority can always be misused, and therefore is always de jure in some sense. Otherwise a man could not misuse or betray his authority. They referred to Wittgenstein's distinction of use of language as the ultimate criterion. Also, Peters sharply distinguished between the a priori meaning of authority, which cannot be decided on any factual grounds, and the empirical conditions for authority, which might be some feeling of reverence, etc. But this is only an empirical condition, not part of its a priori meaning. This is important for me now that I wish to distinguish fact from meaning, demonstrating [this distinction] from intentional words. These linguistic people are right on this. There is always a flexible and ambiguous structure of meanings, which are ready in our minds. We would like to prove this in the facts as realists. But we can never do this. But we can do phenomenology and become acutely conscious of their meanings, which these English certainly are now. Language helps this. It is part of an intentional phenomenology—very concrete. By such phenomenological study, we can never hope to get our meanings out of the facts. But we may hope to make them more sensitive to the facts, more self-conscious, more global, more coherent, and closer to the global world structure culminating in transcendence.

Visit to Oxford, November 12–14, 1957: Charles Taylor, All Souls

Had lunch with him Nov. 13 and talked for two hours about Oxford and phenomenology. He spent a year in Paris listening at the feet of Merleau-Ponty, but according to Austin, had very little personal discussion with him, as I can well understand. But he still respects him. The Oxford attitude is that he is O.K. to read. But Taylor goes much further than this. He has a high opinion of phenomenology, but thinks there are difficulties, and that the method is not sufficiently rigorous. Of Husserl, he said that he rejected

Kant's 'thing-in-itself' and devoted himself to an eidetic description of objects. Merleau-Ponty, he said, tries to describe the pre-categorical, pre-objective world. But he has to use ordinary language or language of some kind to do this. Hence there are difficulties. These people are acutely self-conscious about language and rightly so; they are very much aware of its conditions, necessary objectivity, etc. I argued that language was sufficiently flexible to describe intentional situations and even pure self-consciousness. But he did not seem convinced, though he was willing to listen, and seemed to grant that phenomenology of the *Lebenswelt* was possible, and that some inter-subjective verification was possible. He has tried to present some phenomenological ideas to groups in Oxford but without any great success so far, because of insufficient cogency and rigor. These people have to have a logical argument. They are terribly impressed with deduction and logic. They feel that pure description is apt to be mixed with subjectivity and is apt to be personal and naïve. He sees the problem of the scientific vs. the phenomenological (description) of a given object like a chair. Molecules do not have color; the concrete thing does. He even granted that two worlds are involved. Has discussed this with Hampshire whom he knows well. His difficulty now is in showing that these two objects are the same. Since the chair is inexhaustibly rich, why not both the scientific analysis and the phenomenological? There is room for both. (I think this is right.) The problem arises when we generalize the two and arrive at two worlds. It is these two worlds, each with comprehensive claims which clash. Otherwise, the scientist and the phenomenologist may be talking about different phases (of the same) and therefore different objects. (I think, however, that they are aspects of the same thing because of same position in space and time. Science has to start with the colored chair, and must connect its analyses with this finally, and must return to it or it loses all perceptual existence.) He is now working on this problem of sameness.

I discussed the column on metaphysics with him. He claims that there is a genuine movement among the younger men towards metaphysics, mentioning especially Hampshire and Strawson. Miss Murdoch is not very active now. He says that Strawson in lectures two years ago showed that ordinary language cannot be explained by a pure mind or a pure body or a mere combination of the two. The person is strictly and logically implied by the ways in which we talk. This is typical Oxford analysis now. I asked how he then went on to deal with the person. But he did not know. They seem in general to prefer any kind of deduction from concrete language to an attempt to describe. He thinks many of them realize that a choice between sets of basic categories must be made. This is metaphysics. Cf. the volume *Nature of Metaphysics*. I pressed him on a pervasive metaphysics data capable of verifying such a set. He would not grant this, but agreed that the choice need not be completely arbitrary; a founded choice can be made, but not ruling out other sets of categories. He liked Murdoch and her ideas on ethics. I asked him about the scientific dogma that all facts belong to science and he admitted that it was a widespread presupposition. He certainly does not accept this. Also, there is a strong trend towards objectivity here which comes out at the end of Hampshire's article in *Metaphysics*. Taylor read *Sein und Zeit* some time ago in part only, but has not been able to withstand the bitter prejudice here against him (Cf. Ryle and Austin).

Taylor is a Canadian and may be returning soon to Canada. According to Ryle and Austin he is one of their brightest young men. He is pleasant, serious and knows Merleau-Ponty very well. He is also deeply sympathetic with phenomenology in general and the idea of the *Lebenswelt*, though he has not yet found his own ground. There is a chance that a real linguistic phenomenology may develop slowly here. But they desperately need the idea of the *Lebenswelt* so that they can focus more on the actual phenomena.

J. L. Austin

I went to his lecture where he is using Ayer as a basic text, the last book, I gather. He was talking about reality and the real, a word that causes philosophical suspicion. He claims that reality is a mere hypostatization. When used sensibly, real is an incomplete or hungry word that requires something else to modify. (But Cf. *Hamlet*, "To be or not to be.") Also death— non-being. He claims that real is approximately synonymous with genuine, natural, proper and other words of this sort. He would say that being is an hypostatization, I think. He also thinks the negative use of real is prior to the positive. We say this is a real X when there is doubt, when evidence points to its being unreal. Also he stated that real must not be confused with existence and exist. 'This', he says, is a demonstrative or referential word—about something, points to something, like the term 'same'. This is clearly demonstrative (I believe that he is right here). As over against 'this', real, like, and similar are formal or signifying terms which do not necessarily point. All language can be divided into these two types. 'This' is like a division into fact words and meaning words. The idea seems to be that we have these meaning words already prepared. With them we classify, relate to us, grade and interpret what exists, and to which we refer by demonstrative words like 'this', pronounce, proper names, pointers, etc. 'This' is like the distinction between essence and existence, except that essence is also referential. But perhaps he would admit that the interpretive words do also refer through the demonstratives. I hope so. If so, I think I can agree to this. These are intentional words which express our own intentions coming from us in response to what confronts us. First there are the demonstrative 'existentials' which we grasp through feeling and action and other sub-rational sources. Then there are the interpretations which we can show or prove by observations, etc. These are facts. It is so that it is a fact, that A is like B, etc. Finally, there are the pure intentions and basic intentions which underlie all our interpretations, and which we hold always ready within us. Realism believes that intentional words can be reduced to demonstratives and facts. Idealism believes that facts and demonstratives are forms of meaning. Both are impossible extremes. Language shows there is a reception in response. Phenomenology is the attempt to describe this whole intentional structure—intention together with object which runs through all our language. It is also interested in *Sinn* genesis, showing how new facts can elicit new meanings and new meanings also new facts. The Oxford people are not sufficiently aware of the purely conscious and the subjective. The basic intentions, like being, pervade both subject and object, also consciousness, meaning, etc. Being is more like fact; meaning and consciousness more like intentions. But they pervade the whole. Metaphysics is the attempt to clarify these pervasive intentions and also the highest categories. But being fades into the transcendent. Something can be known here. Certainly we can see that there are alternative categorical systems. But such knowledge is strictly limited because of transcendence.

Austin then gave some comments on Ermson [Flew volume] and his theory of grading. Good and other value terms are grading words. We rank in an order of grades: good, better, best. According to Ermson, there are different criteria for grading different objects. Also we can give different reasons in these different cases. We grade tools in one way, personal acts in another. (A good family is neither.) He sees no argument for thinking that these must all have something in common. Austin here disagrees. Real also is a grading word, but another kind of grading as over against the artificial, the improper, etc. Austin thinks that in order to distinguish these two we must find something that good criteria have in common and also real terms have in common. (I think Murdoch is right in suggesting that terms like good and right are not now the real value bearing words they used to be, but have grown worn and hackneyed. They have passed away with the other absolutes of rationalism. Authentic and real are now more appropriate for human values. This refers to a standard not absolute and outside of man, but an intrinsic human standard we can know about in ourselves and in the *Lebenswelt*.) Austin then went into an acute phenomenology of the unreal, unauthentic, improper, etc. Talked about false pearls. True and false are like real and unreal. They are intentional, hungry, with a prior negative. Also do deep-sea fish have real colors? What is the real color of a chameleon? Probably we would say: that which it has in its natural habitat. Can't apply this to the color of a wall. She dyed her hair; so is unreal. But of a rug. Each hair is dyed. We would not say that it was artificial (because it is an artificial thing). Also toy is very interesting. What is a toy bicycle? If it is for a child, and tiny. But what if it works? We do not say an exact model of ship or building is a toy. (Idea of play should come in here.) Cf. electronic knife, slices 100 in a second hair thin. Is this a real knife? No, too good, super-knife. This was interesting phenomenology, but with no conclusions. He merely brings up the cases. Does not dwell on them long enough to extract the basic meanings. Never answers what is "toy"; what is "play" in terms of a general theory. This would be going beyond ordinary language. So he distrusts it. This in incipient linguistic phenomenology could easily grow into a genuine phenomenology with less emphasis on language.

Ryle and Austin in Magdalen Common Room

After lunch Ryle joined us and we talked for an hour. I asked Austin about phenomenology and he said he would not object to this term. I suppose I am doing a sort of linguistic phenomenology. But he does not like Marcel. Used the term "nasty" of him, perhaps because he referred to Bugbee at Oxford. Ryle and Austin dislike Heidegger, Ryle especially. Austin thinks that he will soon explode in Germany, but he has perhaps performed a service in getting them into something new, and away from Kant. According to Ryle his terminology will be harder to remember. This is carrying progress too far, I think. They hate Heidegger's Nazi record and kept bringing it up in its worst possible interpretations. He was responsible for Husserl's not being able to walk on university ground, etc. This is going too far. French never read English books. Their history of English philosophy stops with H. Spencer. They never even read German which is certainly wrong. So I challenged it. Ryle is very cocksure, dogmatic and extremely provincial, much more so than Austin.

BETWEEN THOMISM AND
EXISTENTIAL PHENOMENOLOGY

Explanatory Note

The following brief reminiscence is the only example we have from the last stage of his philosophical career of an exchange between Wild and a representative of that classical tradition he had championed for many years before the turn to existential phenomenology.

Contemporary Thomism underwent a revival in the late twentieth century largely, at least on its popular side, through the agency of the French philosopher Jacques Maritain and Etienne Gilson, who was one of Wild's teachers at Harvard. They disavowed what had been known as neo-Thomism, condemning it for being little more than a Kantian or Cartesian compromise emptied of all the dynamic thought of Thomas Aquinas. Understanding itself instead as simply an extension and development of Thomism, this spirited movement headed by a couple of French laymen developed out of contact with many of the same historical pressures that had called forth existentialism. It stressed the embodied condition of human and the priority of existence over essence, and had found itself insisting, particularly in a work like Maritain's *Degrees of Knowledge*, on the special epistemological availability of the human essence to philosophical inquiry.

De Raeymaeker, despite his advanced age, represented this new wave. We find him expressing the expected Thomist caution against reducing philosophy to philosophical anthropology. The deeper issue, which we do not find Wild raising here, is the question of identification of being per se with being in time, as Gilson puts it in a discussion of the limitations of the thought of Kierkegaard. We suspect that it is around this Heideggerian issue of the relation between being and time (which should appeal as well to "process philosophers") that future discussions between Thomists and heirs of the existential phenomenological school will have to center if they are to be productive.

Conversation with Louis de Raeymaeker, Louvain, May 18, 1957

The old man talks too much and is regarded as something of a nuisance by his colleagues, but he knows Thomas and gave a good idea of the defensive attitude of Thomism to the new philosophy. This was an illuminating conversation.

He was especially strong on the mind-body issue. He said that the Neo-Thomist psychologies are all wrong, beginning with a discussion of thought and the soul proving its immateriality, etc. and then in a final chapter speaking of the union of the soul and body which already in this language implies a separate subsistence of soul, and is really Augustinian. Marcel is speaking of incarnation of soul and is also subject to this criticism. This is dualistic language that implies a separate non-physical subsistence of soul. The whole Thomistic tradition according to Raeymaeker has misinterpreted the radical view of Thomas himself and has relapsed back into Augustinianism.

Thomas says, he claims, that the soul as a spiritual principle requires a body. It is bodily from the very beginning and exists only as a necessary relation to a body. I must look this up—I think he is right. If so, most Thomistic treatises on psychology are definitely wrong and very misleading. He admits that this gets Aquinas into difficulty with respect to immortality, but he works out his own answer. Even the separated soul is relative to a body. Note that the body is the source of individuation. So as individual, the soul, whether separate or not, is in a necessary relation to its body. Hence he is quite sympathetic with the new line on man as a bodily being, and thinks it is in accord with the basic trend of Thomas himself. I pressed him on existentialist themes in Aquinas, and though at first hesitant, he finally agreed that there were a good many themes of this kind. There is a sense in which the new phenomenology is developing in the spirit of Aquinas.

I asked him about the priority of existence in Thomas over essence. He said that Gilson had at first talked in this way, but had later stopped. This is because for the new philosophers existence is *ex esse*, ecstatic being which is peculiar to man. To say that everything is relative to existence therefore means that everything is relative to man. Gilson and Thomas certainly do not mean this. Existence here means the act of being, independence, outside of its causes—that is spontaneous and can autonomously initiate acts of its own. *Ex esse* means acting outside of its causes. This conception is very general, and not just restricted to man.

I then asked him if he did not think that at least in the case of man, the new existence philosophy was not carrying out certain implications of Thomist thought implicit in Aquinas himself? He finally agreed to this, and said that a thesis along this line, on existentialist themes in Aquinas, was being written at Louvain. He was sympathetic with this and thought that this student might really be finding many such motives. Aquinas is not exactly a phenomenologist, but he does his own phenomenological descriptions in his own condensed way.

He is critical of Marcel as being too dualistic, and also of Strasser, who though very clever, in his doctrine of the pure self in thinking and willing, also falls into a kind of Augustinianism. Human thinking and willing absolutely requires the body. There can be no pure thought without any relation to an object, to perception and therefore the body. He is trying to "out-Merleau" Merleau here. And there is some ground for this. He picks out Sartre of course as an example of the irresponsibility and irrationalism of the new thought—a childish and emotional phenomenon of our time that appeals to youth but will soon pass away.

At first he held that man is a metaphysical being (cf. Heidegger) and that any real light on man must require metaphysics. He is doubtful about any philosophy of nature, because he holds that man is the only being we can define. Other beings are too far from us. We have no access to their inner being, and can only read ourselves into them in various degrees. The old idea that we can know natural things better than ourselves is all wrong. When I asked him if this was not precisely what Heidegger was saying he admitted this, but felt that his philosophy was too anthropomorphic and anthropocentric. His metaphysics is a mystic hope with no real content as yet.

The task of metaphysics is not a fact that can be established by science, but rather meaning, and especially necessary relations of meaning. Science just tells us the facts that happen to be so. It cannot enlighten us on what these facts mean. The task of philosophy is to discover meaning, and necessary connections of meaning. Cf. Husserl here.

This is as cogent a statement of the Thomistic reaction as I have yet found. But it shows the way in which the classical tradition is now on the defensive. The best it can do is to claim that many of the new motives are implicit in Thomas. Something can be said for this. Cf. the human essence is now being studied in act. Before Aquinas analyzed the essence and faculties one by one, in a state of potency.

BETWEEN PHILOSOPHY AND THEOLOGY

Explanatory Note

The next few reflections and recollections are characterized by an emphasis on theological or religious questions that were later to become largely submerged in Wild's thinking, at least on its public side. He is thinking hard about the idea of a Christian philosophy, an idea he expanded on at some length in *Human Freedom and the Social Order*. He is concerned with the creative dialectic between philosophy and theology, as the carefully recorded conversation with Van Peursen shows.

But already there is the idea, even as he listens to theologians, that perhaps what we are after is a philosophy that in no sense depends on any particular dogmas or theological claims about historical events. He was not ready to say this here, but he finds himself alone in feeling that existential phenomenology could be employed to elaborate a truly Christian philosophy. These religiously oriented thinkers seem insufficiently acquainted with Heidegger, always raising Sartre to illustrate the way philosophy without God, particularly existential phenomenology, only etches the confines of a hopeless world devoid of the redeeming message. More and more the idea that Heidegger might be the thinker through whom one must pass to encounter transcendence is making itself felt in Wild's thinking.

There is another hint that Wild is beginning to feel that even demythologized theological concepts stand in the way of the development of a philosophy for our time. Wild notes that Brunner's insistence on a stable human essence is buttressed theologically. We can speculate that Wild's old, intense concern with human freedom found itself threatened here. Could it be that Sartre is correct on this point at least, that all God talk inevitably closes off human possibilities?

There is a certain irony in Wild's reaction to a lecture by Jaspers. Jaspers the pure philosopher "open to transcendence," eschewing all particular theological concepts, lacks a kind of excitement that Wild finds in Barth. We have included the notes on Barth's lecture despite their extremely fragmented condition because they show something that must have impressed Wild. The old patron of continental neo-orthodox theology was not giving abstract lectures on Hegel; he was doing the work of exploring and articulating the structures of the *Lebenswelt*. Ironically, in this most anti-philosophical of theologians, "the job of the philosopher is being done."

Conversations with Van Peursen, The Hague, May 25, 1957

This was very illuminating as he was willing to talk to me and to give his own views on some fundamental problems that bother me.

On idealism and realism he sympathizes with the De Waelhens line trying to go beyond, but does not think that Husserl really said this clearly,
though he hinted at it and was moving in this direction. He does not want
to attribute meaning to the mind and facticity to the non-human factor. This
will be only a confusion of idealism and realism. But he sympathizes with
what De Waelhens is getting at in his dialogue metaphor. As suggested in
his paper, from one point of view—or on one level the transcendental ego
does constitute the meanings of experience. But constitution is itself a real
fact. There is an idealist as well as a realistic perspective on experience.

He thinks that the most realistic trend is Husserl in his constant emphasis on the infinity of the concrete. Wahl has also seen this—the concrete is inexhaustible. (But we are finite, and our meanings are therefore
fixed and determinate. But reality is infinitely rich as Husserl constantly
emphasized. This infinity cannot come from us, but must come from another source non-human.) Is this the key to Husserl's creative intuition? If
we can only open our reception to the concrete as it is, we are led on and
on into new vistas because of the infinite richness of the concrete. It is becoming closed within our own limited perspectives that freezes us and
fixes us in what is ever the same!!!

He is deeply concerned with ontology and has thought about my problem of meaning. His book on reality will soon appear. *Soul and Body* has
appeared and he is trying to publish it in English. He is a young and active man and will be heard from I think. I shall try to do what I can. I told
him to get it published in English and to get out articles in *Philosophy and
Phenomenology.* He sees my point that the *Lebenswelt* must come first and
that science and other special levels are only abstractions from this concrete *Lebenswelt.* The world as it is given is beautiful and good. It does not
first exist and then have value predicates added to it. Heidegger is right
here. The main problem of ontology now is to formulate this priority of
the concrete. Theology is perhaps necessary to do this (cf. God is both being and meaning). Objectivity and science are derived from this initial
concrete world. The new ontology must formulate this clearly and coherently.

On this meaning problem he thinks that both meaning and pure being
are derived from a richer being—in which both are fused. Cf. the mar-
velous Dutch word *ansein*—being present before. Ultimately meaning is
being and being is meaning. The two are fused. Being is an abstraction,
just being there—Cf. Mehl—indifferent. Thus my razor exists. Meaning
by itself is a sheer relation of this to the mind or rather to man. But in fact
these are only derived abstractions from an original *ansein* that includes
both. Being in the concrete both exists and exists before the mind of God.
Teleology does not have to be added on to being. It is originally and primordially before God, or under the Presence.

Plato says this often implicitly. Thus, cf. Rep. 509, the good is *upekeina tex ousias*, beyond mere being, and now Glaucon's response, what a divine exaggeration!!!! So it is. Each *eidos* not only is as an essence. It also shines forth with a light, and gleams with its own intelligibility. The idea of the good is the source both of being and intelligibility. Here is a sense of the union of being with meaning, and of their transcendental source in a transcendent which unifies both in an eminent way. (I think Heidegger is too harsh on Plato!!) His sense of transcendence was perhaps inadequate but he had it to some degree. He may have confused presence as such, the presence with essences which are present. But he at least saw that in these *eide* there is a union of being with meaning which points to a transcendent source in which both are one. Thus he glimpsed the relational character of being as goodness and truth which are relational. The new ontology must see this clearly and express it coherently. In Aristotle and his tradition substance comes first, *pros ti* afterwards. Relation is subordinated. But the truth is that relation comes first. Substance is a later abstraction from it. But we must be on guard against the danger of dissolving all genuine plurality into an idealist system of relations. (The present emphasis on truth is recognition of the fact that being from the beginning is relational, a being before, not mere indifference, an existence to which value is then added as tends to happen even in the Thomist tradition.) This comes out clearly in the Christian notion of creation. God created finite being and saw that it was good, very good. There is a Hebrew word for being which also means beautiful. He is going to show this is an article. Being and meaning are united in the Christian conception.

On philosophical anthropology he agrees with me that it can be distinguished from pure philosophy though not separated from it. Soul and body are of course one. He shows this in his book. Also seems to agree with Strasser that there is a pure active self that leaves a trail of objectivity behind it. This objectivity can be conceived either as body or as soul. But the two are held together in the pure activity of the original self. He speaks highly of R. Guardini and G. Marcel, also I must get Gusdorf *Myth et Metaphysique*. This is very interesting. Also get Swede Thorleif Boman, *Griechisch und Hebraisches Denken*. Also books of Eliade on the phenomenology of religion. He is the best authority at present. Finally recommends G. Van der Leeuw, *Der Mensch u. die Religion*. Get this in Germany.

Finally he is very interesting on theology and philosophy, was just going to lecture on this at Nijmegen, for a meeting of philosophers and theologians. There is a dialectical tension between the two, not a fixed and final harmony as in the mediaeval tradition. This is certainly the line I must now take. Philosophy tries to be scientific and empirical, a discipline, but necessarily seeks for salvation. Thus, even the analysts are trying to free us from illusions, and false use of language. All philosophy has this tendency to religion. But it also tends to construct absolutes of various kinds like that of Spinoza. This has something in common with the Christian God but not very much. When confronted by these philosophic absolutes the theologian rightly criticizes them as pseudo-religious concepts. They are too abstract and theoretical. This critique is sound and very good for philosophy. But the theologian also in expounding the word of God has to use the philosophic concepts of his time, Greek thought, etc. He does this semi-consciously. Here the philosopher (Cf. Tillich) has a right to criticize and to show the relativity of this language. What then is the remedy?

We must have an open philosophy that does not fix itself in finitude or some artificial absolute. We must strive for a philosophy like that of Jaspers which is open to transcendence. Such a philosophy will not be subject to this criticism. Theology on the other hand must give up trying to get at the pure abstract word of God. There is no such thing. The word of God must be a word in relation to human thought and language. This is what the theologian must expound, the living word in the language of his time, which he must clarify and refine as much as possible, looking for assistance here on the human side from the philosopher. As knowledge grows, and as philosophy develops this must change. It must never be frozen as in the tradition. Van Peursen is skeptical of natural theology. He must be a Protestant.

But questions: How then avoid philosophical relativity? Also can God be being? Cf. Heidegger. I should have asked him this.

Brunner, Peter, Heidelberg, June 27, Lecture

Christology: He gives an interesting defense of essence (*Wesen*) against existential criticism. Physis, nature in Christian dogma *Gefüge* (flexible structure—joints) of the concrete. The nature of God is the being (*Sein*) by which He is God. The essence of man is the being by which we are man. This is the human world frame which we cannot break without ceasing to be men. (Not just properties—but existential world structures.) God expresses man in His creative word once and for all. (Note this theological ground of a stable essence.) God does not take his Word back. [He] creates man and sustains man in all of his phases, innocence, sin, salvation, kingdom. Essence remains but undergoes a history. (Note growing historical essence! My idea!) [He] doesn't take his word back even in Hell. Man remains man. This has basis not in Platonic or Aristotelian philosophy but in [the] Bible. (Compare Brunner's statement with mine that without ontology theology can't go on!)

Now we are man in sinful condition through a history. Christ enters man, assumes our human flesh in this historical condition of sin. Barth is right here. (Must take sin and human corruption seriously.)

[The] Son assumes our essence in the flesh. But this essence has a history. [It] goes through a real history with real historical changes. He takes over the sinful flesh in (the) condition of sin. He is tempted like us. He is under the Law—in our place. It comes under the charge and condemnation of God. He bears our sin. (He) lets sin become sin through Him. Sin rolls over Him. If in living this human life He merely restored old Adam as in Roman doctrine He would merely give us . . . But he does more than really restore our lost nature. He comes into the very depths of sin. He takes over the sinfulness into Himself. He becomes weak with our sin—yours and mine. In this sense He is like us —in our sinful state. Romans 8:3 (He) takes over our sins. He comes into our human corruption. Here he is with us—like us.

But we are slaves of sin. [We] cannot not sin, Augustine: But He is free. He freely takes over our sin. This freedom is His sinlessness. He is utterly empty of sin. So He can take our sins over—yours and mine. He is empty of sin—like *nous poietikos*. So there is room in Him for your sin and even for mine. These sins are all strange to Him, as each form is strange to the empty *nous*. These sins are not strange to us. We are these sins by very being. He freely takes them over as [the] pure Lamb of God. He can be wholly for us because [he is] wholly for God. He can love God—does love God with His whole heart and mind. He can make our sins His because of his emptiness—His sinlessness. We are broken by sin. He [is] free from sin. He is completely for us because he is completely for God, loving Him with pure heart and mind. He gives up his very humanity; *in forma servi* means sin. He takes over the sinful condition.

No adoptionism. He takes over the corrupt human essence, not an individual man. His human individuality (is) in virtue of his act of becoming man. He takes over *menschsein* not an individual man here and now. His individual existence is from the act of Incarnation. (This is deep Protestant spirit here.)

Brunner Conversation, Lunch

Theology needs ontology. He studied with Brightman at Boston University. Got his Th.D. at Harvard. Has sound systematic sense. Very Lutheran. Does not like Bultmann. This is what "they" mean (Dillenberger and Welch) by saying he is conservative. He is sympathetic to my ideas of trying to do a Christian philosophy. He admitted, when I pressed him, that existential phenomenology is favorable to, near to Christianity. Best matter for Christian interpretation that has yet appeared. Is bored with Bultmann. It is like a mill that turns out what is ever the same.

I asked him if it was not strange in Heidegger's existentialism to find such a separation of message from the personal life. He said there was this truth in it: Without the message, details of the Christian biography have little significance. But when I pressed him on the possibility of separating [the] human word from [the] human person he agreed.

(Sees American weakness—religion is mental healing. But admitted our revival was not all this.)

Roger Mehl, Strasbourg, July 3

He was genial and pleasant but had an engagement in preparation for the visit of the president of France so our contact was somewhat brief.

I said I was especially interested in his idea of the revival of, or rather the inauguration of, a truly Christian philosophy. He thought that much more needed to be done in this direction and agreed that existential phenomenology is a favorable starting point. But he did not seem to think that this could be understood as already the beginning of a Christian philosophy. As in the case of Brunner, Sartre seems to stand in the way of his interpretation. I asked about his notion of significance as always value. Is this not value in a very broad sense? And does he (like Heidegger) think of value as synonymous with being? He said no! Values to him are creative—timeless aspects of the created world, he said, timeless invisible aspects.

But do they not point to God? And I referred to the indirect arguments from value in his book. He did not seem to want to develop these and said he had become more cautious since writing that. He will be tough on this in his new book soon to appear.

I then switched to the subject of signs and meaning which he has said will be the great contribution of pure philosophy to the new Christian thought. Has anything worthwhile been done along this line? He did not speak of Heidegger but mentioned some passages in Sartre, and Merleau-Ponty's *Sense and Nonsense*.

I asked what he thought of Bultmann—not much, for he at once distinguished his work as an exegete from his systematic thought. He thought that he had used Heidegger uncritically in a field with which he was not sufficiently familiar. I asked about demythologizing and he admitted that it was important, but that it had come to the attention of French Protestants only through Catholic books on Bultmann and was only beginning to be discussed.

He asked about America, and I spoke of the religious "revival." To my surprise he said there was something of this sort in French Protestantism but not so impressive because of the small number. He has ten students in the theology faculty.

He spoke lightly of Lehmann and without enthusiasm of Tillich. Then we got on the track of his book and I said I would write Harpers. He called Gusdorf.

Mehl recommended Thévenaz. (Swiss, died at 42. Brilliant young thinker. Plans a complete Protestant philosophy.) Two volumes. This is the French title, *L'Homme et la Raison*, Neuchâtel.

La Baconisiére (sp?). Must buy. Barth respects this very much. His student. Now less anti-philosophical. (Also not Mehl. Get Gurvitch: *La Vocation Actuelle de la Sociologie*. Paris 1950–52.)

On Saturday I then met R. P. Florkowski—a Polish Catholic priest with whom I talked about French philosophy. He did not know Ingarden. Ethics is his special field.

Did not seem too much influenced by phenomenology. Skeptical about Louvain.

Georges Gusdorf

A very lively and brilliant person. He was most friendly, and I had a most moving and exciting conversation with him for more than two hours until 1:30 on European philosophy and the whole situation in America. I asked him point blank at the beginning whether he was a relativist. He seemed to like this, and realized that I had read his metaphysics. He developed his ideas about God and said he believed in God. I pointed out that this conception was rather indeterminate, it seemed to me. He said one question at a time! He was not a relativist—though our investigations are always relative to an historical setting. Whether he was a determinist was another matter.

I then asked if in spite of his acute sense of historical relativism, his writings did not imply a certain universal, existential structure—true for all human existence, like temporality, human spatiality, choice, etc. He finally agreed that he did hold this, though philosophy was a constant human need that each generation must approach in its own way and freely work out for itself.

I said I admired his radically modern tone and his new apologetic à la Tillich, that all, even atheists and agnostics, believe in God—though not the orthodox rationalist approach and intellectualist conception. He developed this for me, emphasizing that modern men are groping in their own way for religion, a way very different from past ways. He mentioned the Lisbon earthquake [1755], and how this had bothered religions more before our time. God must hate us to inflict such miseries, or [be] indifferent. But now we experience the atom bomb, really much worse than any earthquake, but no one now blames God for this. Curious! A vast change. Religion must now be approached in an entirely new way if a modern mind is to be touched. He thinks Bultmann has raised an extremely important issue—demythologizing—but [he] has confused this with other issues also. He does not care for Heidegger. He was derisive of a magazine picture he showed me. [He said] that Heidegger's world was closed. Obviously does not like the grand manner. [He said] it may be a matter of temperament after admitting the insights of *Sein und Zeit*.

[He] is a friend of Merleau-Ponty and thinks he is the greatest French philosopher. De Wahlens is not even in the same class. [He says that] Merleau-Ponty was angry when de Wahlens's books appeared. [He] says that Merleau-Ponty has not written very much (certainly not, if he [Gusdorf] is a standard). They were in the same class, trained together, and [are] real friends. [He] has read very widely in English, though he cannot speak a word. Knows Dufrenne and Luiton. [He] thinks that philosophy should now work in close cooperation with certain sorts of scientists. He knows Dufrenne and thinks well of him.

[He] believes that phenomenology is very important but (we) need more than phenomenology. Cf. Fink. Recommends strongly Maurice Leenhardt, Dokamo, a missionary who lives for years with this tribe and really comes to know them. Must get this (Gallimard).

[He] gave an illuminating account of de Chardin—reconciles evolution with Catholic dogma. Jesuit. Can't publish this while alive. Church opposed. But now very popular after his death. Not too important to read. Desan wrong.

On English philosophy I told him Wittgenstein was better than Quine. He was interested. Said he knows Ayer, charming person, but has nothing—absolutely nothing to say. I told him about Arne Ness and he seemed interested. Knew that Scandinavia was full of tension.

[He] wondered whether there were any philosophers in the U.S.A.? I told him at [the] end that there were some people there now who were trying to be!

(Translation of his article in *Philosophy Today*. Indiana. Did I know? European philosophy. I did not. Ask H.)

A very bright and radically modern mind. I must buy all his books. He gave me several pamphlets.

Barth, July 9

Reconciliation. Situates God. Creator God. Christ comes. Seeks truth. Turns it into untruth. Then contradicts truth. Distorted picture. Right and left—over equals under. Error has reality. My point. Characterizes us. Bewitched man and bewitched world. Punish—against created order. Early pre-punishment. Man of sin exists as though Christ never existed. False picture grounded in truth. Falsity has no power. Lives off truth. Restless, endless search. Yesterday one thing—tomorrow another. Winds blow here and there. No boundary (historicisms). Confusion. Open on all sides. Inner arbitrary—external accident. Parallel—word? No fellowship bounds. Only wants other for help—use. Infinite pleasure, etc. Strangeness of other. Then sudden realization—others closed. Then resignation. Or despair. Other erring ways. Deep falsity. No consistency. Life like butterfly— endless dialectic. Relativity lonely against each other. Pharisees to gypsies. Is there an Ernst without envy—a smile. Religion without worldliness? Revelation → reaction → revelation. Where is standard? Is one. A price. Individual freedom vs. common good. Is there stability. Seriousness without boredom.

Pilate—last word! What is truth! All comes to it . And problems of human speech. Human—must talk. Must listen. Express—reveal human reality. Communion the end. Can and should happen but—untruth. Concealment. Can't express, can't reveal. Can't communicate. The use of *Sein* is epoche. Dwellers widely around. Always begin again. Can't talk to selves even. Comic and tragic misunderstandings. Truth inexpressible. Silence the best (Heidegger). Speech makes us (very) lonely—more apart (Heidegger).

(Damned—deeper and deeper in this. Far from God. Let man do what he wishes with self.) Truth around.

Phenomenologists appear to be talking about a very man-centered world—the *Lebenswelt* in fact.

The problem of the place of nature within a phenomenological-oriented philosophy remains a great one. In an age when an objective scientific view of nature has secured itself so firmly in the imagination it is a problem for any philosophy. Indeed, it is one of our central questions. We do not find the problem resolved here but we do find it raised into articulation. The job of the philosopher is being done.

CONVERSATIONS AND REFLECTIONS
ON PHENOMENOLOGY

Explanatory Note

In this next group of entries, where we find Wild meeting with serious phenomenologists, Heidegger is at the center of the stage. Heidegger is the
philosopher par excellence for most of these thinkers, as he is becoming for
Wild. The question seems to be, however, whether Heidegger is too anthropocentric. There are two closely related attempts to vindicate Heidegger
from this accusation. One is to insist via the later Heidegger that his thought
was Being centered not man centered: Being throws us, gives itself to us,
etc. The other is to distinguish philosophical anthropology from philosophy
pure and simple, and to say that *Sein und Zeit* (*Being and Time*) represents
the former. However, this was not Heidegger's view of his own work.

There is a difficulty these accommodations do not solve. There is a problem that bothers Wild. Nature is not *Sein* (Being) and it is not merely something relative to *Dasein* (Being-There). Can we say anything about it? The analytic philosophers abandon it to the scientists. Thomists like de Raeymaeker
say that there could be a philosophy of nature only if the essences of things
below us in the scale of being were more intelligible—but they are not. So
we have to settle for science that gives up essential knowledge for calculations upon the surfaces of things.

However, Wild clearly cannot accept this analytic view that surrenders
an autonomous domain of inquiry for philosophy and would leave the
great questions of human existence outside of the scope of philosophy
proper. The major discussions that he enters into involve well-known figures in the German philosophical world. These include, but are not limited
to, Walter Biemel, Hermann Wein, and most important, a conversation
with Eugen Fink, an important student and expositor of both Husserl and
Heidegger. Subsequently, we find Wein, as one as Wild's interlocuters, in
the interview given in *Philosophical Interrogations*. Wein served as professor of philosophy and lecturer on philosophical anthropology at the University of Göttingen.

Here, Wild recognizes the need for a new elaboration of metaphysics
founded on a more adequate understanding of philosophical anthropology.
Wild, both in his discussion with Wein and even more so in his conversations with Fink, focuses on the relation of meaning to being and to world.
The involved conversation with Fink appears to demonstrate to Wild that,
despite Fink's attempts to exonerate Heidegger from the charge of anthropocentrism, Fink himself is very close to Wild's substitution of "world for being." Wild, here, already expresses his reluctance to go along with the direction of Heidegger's "later thought," and while he commends Fink on his

own phenomenological investigations, particularly of play, he appears to reach, at least for himself, a philosophical position that refuses the reduction of meaning to being and of being to meaning. Here, we see the precursor to Wild's important distinction, prevalent in so much of his later writings, between the world and its multiple versions. The tenacity of Wild, in holding out for a position of his own that can reconcile what he believes to be some of the deficiencies in Heidegger's work, is visible in his conversations with Biemel, Wein and Fink. The exchange between Wild and Fink, while somewhat episodic, helps to link American and Continental phenomenology and will be of interest to historians of the phenomenological movement.

Visit to Göttingen—Wein, Lectures on Descartes, Three Seminars, Philosophy and Medicine

I heard a two-hour lecture on Descartes and the current problem of rationalism and irrationalism.

Wein is basically interested in philosophical anthropology but thinks, in his sense, it is neglected in Germany. Only two people outside Germany are doing it. One a Turk, and one me. This is true. Same impression in Köln [Cologne]. Falls between. The philosophers say it is science; scientists say it is mere philosophy. Many philosophers do it and lecture on it here. Cf. Fink.

Wein's book on Real-dialectic is interesting. Purify Hegel of speculative, constructive side. He does in the *Phenomenology des Geistes* especially describe certain real dialectics as master-slave. (This discussion led me to see that Aristotle's theory of change is too passive. Has to be produced by an external cause already in act. Matter and nature as such cannot move selves. This is against modern science as I have seen. Man moves self and even subhuman nature to some degree. Aristotle analyzes change as from privation to 'form'. One form replaces other. This other merely disappears. But this is usually not so. There is antinomy, struggle ending in the emergence of a new form with these opposed moments. Process is full of this creative tension which Aristotle misses. Perhaps I should teach Hegel again. He is involved in these new movements.) Wein is anti-Heidegger. But he has to admit that the first part of *Sein und Zeit* is O.K. *In der Welt Sein* [*Being in the World*]. Death and time he does not like. He wants me to see Bollnow at Tubingen. Philosophical anthropology is done here, he says. Phenomenology is traditional at Göttingen. Husserl was there. But there are many different interpretations of it. Not really active. Wein strengthened my desire to study recent American social psychology and anthropology.

Wein and his students read G. H. Mead. I must read this. He is phenomenological, really, and advances beyond behaviorism at the end of his life. All but *The Philosophy of the Present* [ed. 1932] is *Nachlass*. This did me good at Göttingen. I must read Mead again. Perhaps I can use some of his ideas. In his Descartes lecture, Wein showed a good knowledge of original French terms. He also stressed Cartesian opposition of opinion vs. knowledge based on Plato, *doxa* vs. *episteme*. Descartes admits of no middle ground. All opinion must be rejected as false. No place for the probable—or for any gradual advance from opinion to knowledge of the clear and self-evident (idea).

By new philosophy, Wein means also Heidegger's general revival of metaphysics. Not just Whitehead and Hartmann.

Asemussen

Asked me to lunch with his wife. Very pleasant. Book on perception will appear soon. Will send me a copy. Should be interesting. He lectures on philosophical anthropology at Hannover Techn. Hochschule. He worked with Plessner. Says Merleau-Ponty's psychology is now out of date—also Wein's students say this. [He] has picture of Husserl in library, but says Husserl talked always about phenomenological (philosophical) method—method—method. But never really applied it to do phenomenology. Work on details. Yes! Thinks philosophical anthropology is possible as a discipline. Can cooperate with psychology and sociology. Talked politics also. They are social democrats. Don't think Adenauer really wants unity. Germans do want unity. Distrust Adenauer.

Duikler, Cologne

Gave us pamphlets. Stimulating discussion on theology. There is no doubt that Heidegger is the philosopher. Older students about 50, like Gadamer, are respectful. Realized what Heidegger has. But are independent. Heidegger is the center of theological and philosophical criticism. Biemel worships him but edits Husserl! Heidegger and Bultmann attend each other's seminars at Marburg.

He says Barth, Bultmann, Gogarten and Brunner belong in the '20s to a small theological circle—edited *Zwiszhen den Zeiten*. Very close. Broke up in '33 on National Socialism. Gogarten went along. Brunner then with him. Bultmann and Barth would not. Duikler was also Bekenithms's man. In 50 years, Barth will simply be a historical figure. But Bultmann issues will still be discussed. Especially demythologizing. He is a student of Bultmann but I think he is right that Bultmann is by far the more profound and important. As against Barth, Bultmann has opened up discussion with philosophers and Christian vs. philosophical faith as in book, Jaspers and Bultmann essays, 1954, which I must buy. Barth says such discussion with a neutral philosophy is impossible because it means abandoning the Faith and its perspective. I must read Bultmann more. Gifford lectures are now out in England. Worked very hard on this—problems beyond his capacity. Strained himself. Last book—should be a masterpiece. (Cf. my situation now).

What is Heidegger's attitude toward Bultmann? Would say his philosophical language is clear (as Bultmann claims) and is philosophically consistent. But he goes beyond what he can say as a phenomenological philosopher. Gets into fields and questions beyond philosophy. A philosopher must retain his autonomy—he must be on the borderline, open to religion, but always questioning (can I do both religion and philosophy?) (Cf. Mehl.) Heidegger has a religious mysticism (like Tillich) but not faith—not Christianity. Duikler says he never was anti-religions—not in *Sein und Zeit*. Heidegger, good in classical philosophy, has finished a 800-page text on the pre-Socratics. Has reduced to 400 pgs. But publishers make difficulty. At home in Augustine —really at home—moves freely in Aquinas and Scotus. Rejects all this metaphysics. But it may be coming back again.

Thinks highly of Löwith and Bleuler also. Just heard him in lecture criticize Heidegger as too anthropocentric. No place for cosmos. Only man has history. History requires self-consciousness. For science and for theology, also rest of world—nonhuman world does have a history. This is basic criticism of Heidegger now—too anthropocentric. (Compare Van Peursen here. God—before God—cosmos can have a history!)

Bultmann thinks the theological language (in philosophical areas) is soft and fuzzy. Must be clarified. For this he takes over Heidegger's language as a clarification of the human situation and human history. But Bultmann has not taken over the whole Heidegerrian view. Is independent even in philosophical development and uses this language in his own way.

In West Germany there is constant dialogue with Marxism, looking forward to ultimate union. Must distinguish authentic Marxism from inauthentic communism. This is his line. (Cf. Goldenwasser.) Now translated in English and used at Yale. I must get this. Duikler and he were both captured by Russians. (Goldenwasser was worked on—tried to convert him. He writes about this in his book. Duikler got out in 1948. Not such a bad time.) He just lectured on demythologizing. I asked him to summarize!

World view of Bible is not Christian but pagan. Must separate out the pure Christian kerygma. Then, in the light of this, interpret old cosmology as myth. What is its truth—its relation to human existence before God. Bultmann is right in all this. Modern mind cannot accept the old views literally. But Bultmann goes too far. He gives us only man before God, and history of kerygma. Too humanistic. Rest of cosmos is unimportant for Christianity. Bible said something about rest of world also. This cannot be eliminated from Christianity and left to science. Bultmann is too anthropocentric. Cosmos has a history.

Books: Van der Leeuw [1890–1950]. *Phenomenology der Religion* II and III, 1955, can't go beyond this in phenomenology of religions. Has left a vacuum. I must get this.

He thinks that philosophy of religion has disappeared in Germany, owing to Barth, though the Jaspers-Bultmann book is an exception. We must go on with this. Keep up debates between philosophy and religion. But natural theology is gone. It cannot be revived. But must discuss religion constantly in relation to the human situation as revealed by phenomenology.

See Löwith at Heidelberg. Also Claude Welch is there, can help me!! Duikler and whole evening—with wife who dislikes America.

Says Merleau-Ponty psychology is out of date. Philosophical anthropology is dangerous because between. Philosophers are psychologists scorning, but he is a phenomenological psychiatrist, I think. Tries to find examples for philosophical insights of *Sein und Zeit*—empirical evidence a matter of emphasis. As he sees it, phenomenology is the science of meaning. Psychology gets facts. It needs to know, in general, the phenomenon. He thinks many psychologists who use the word "phenomenology" do not really know what it means—don't know Husserl really well. I think he does. He came to Royaumont and also knows McCloud, Allport, and others in America. Believes philosophers and psychologists can cooperate, and should, in developing philosophical anthropology.

Philosophy is compulsory for all psychology candidates. The two are not as separate as with us, even now. He has great respect for Buytendijk (1887–1974).

Psychiatrists are declared enemies of psychology. Use their old tests which psychologists have shown up. Not many jobs available for young graduates 23 and 24 in psychology. Parents won't accept their useful advice on children.

Had long discussion of American conformism, etc. Said it was a problem of technologists—now universal. America simply first and in a higher degree. He and his wife have great respect for Heidegger. They seem to agree on America. Showed me Roman wall in parts of old city.

Brunner studies perception—how it is immersed in cultural background. Work on theory. American psychologists work on theory—interpretation. Europeans more casual on facts and experiments.

Wife thinks Heidegger is against science and technique.

Heidegger's View

Volkmann Schluck teaches in Volkshochschule [continuing education]. Is expanding like our adult education. Interesting phenomenon. Psychologists seem to meet with philosophers and to be quite close.

James Field raises questions about adult life. Raises philosophical questions. Widely played in Germany. He thinks they see many good American films. Also Miller—they know. Existential themes in American literature.

Biemel, June 21

Afternoon on Rhine with student. Asked him about his book. Relation of cultural world and individual world? He rather evaded this and talked about art. Philosophy should have dialogue with art and the world of the artist. Begins now with Heidegger.

We discussed art. Then got on sense! From here it follows relevant to our primary project. Is this the same as value? Compare Mehl. They criticized the notion of value à la Heidegger but admitted that being and value (in the broad sense—primordial sense) are close.

Then they distinguished *Sinn* vs. *Bedeuteng*. Compared our sense vs. meaning. *Sinn* is more basic and primordial. Meaning is the attempt to work out clearly and logically and articulately but meaning (*Bedeuteng*) is grounded on sense (*Sinn*). Does this make sense? What is the sense of it? (Perhaps being is the ground of value.) What we call value (*Gelten*), is the attempt to logically work out a theory of being! Finally, I asked if *Sinn* and *Sein* are synonymous for Heidegger. Biemel said he would have to think about this. Admitted they are very close. (I think they are since being is the revelation of beings. Perhaps *Sinn* is signified thought in abstraction from the beings which are illuminated.) I asked about Merleau-Ponty's critique of Heidegger as anti-scientific. They thought this was a misunderstanding. Heidegger is against only a science which is unaware of its foundations and therefore capable of undergoing a crisis. They think Heidegger is not against a psychology or sociology aware of its fundamental problems, and proceeding on a philosophical basis. Thus, they played down Heidegger's anti-science and anti-technological bias.

But can philosophical anthropology be pursued as a distinct discipline, apart from pure philosophy?

They seem to agree that my kind of cooperation is possible. We must discuss this further.

They think de Wahlens oversimplifies in his *Phenom. de la Verité*, jumps over the hard places.

Evening of June 23, Biemel

(These people certainly do not agree that Heidegger is only a negative break, a vast set of wholly unanswered questions.)

They have a great enthusiasm, an underlying reverence for him as a great creative thinker. All his thoughts are subtle, and they will accept no criticism without careful distinctions and qualifications. Thus, he is not against science, but only science which is incapable of a crisis, with respect to underlying presuppositions. Heidegger is creative: He has answers! For example, he inaugurates a real philosophical *Auseizandersetzung* [argument] with art, something very new and important.

After Reading Wein, Criticism

Has good points on avoiding abstract identity (contradiction): true is the whole: out of moments and tension, a new whole develops: '*objectiver geist*' a vast realm—real phenomenology here: sheds light on man. I can use these ideas. Man is dialectical—grows from opposition. Needs dynamic synthesis but:

1. Is philosophy to be restricted to man? Things are moving this way. But compare being and sense which Wein says belong to many regions. Cf. Heidegger—*Sein*, but not tradition. These are general problems of first philosophy.
2. Dialectic is sometimes over-simple. Is a good first step but needs further and more careful analysis. My own—common (world). Yes. Need both. But what is self? Can say more about this. Opposition only a first step.
3. Subject-Object must be transcended. But how? Need new concepts which are closer to subjective and objective. He admits Heidegger's analysis in *Sein und Zeit* is more important. Not just dialectic.
4. Evades: what is *Sein*?
5. Anti-religious? This transcendence is more than just man transcending self. Cf. Gusdorf!!

Fink, Conversation, July 5, afternoon in Restaurant

He was very kind after his lecture on *Spiel* (play). Said he had read a good deal of anthropology for the facts about magic, cult and totemism but he was interested in a more basic point—the way in which these phenomena express a sense of the whole of existence—a philosophical point. Will publish fairly soon. He did make these phenomena very vital and meaningful, especially the mask as not a plaything, but the gateway into the world of play, and the cult in its primordial form, as a mode of action, a bringing of existence into contact with the whole. Also, [he clarified] the way in which primitive life was, and is, filled with anxieties about sicknesses and constant threats of destruction and the need of warding off these demonic forces.

He also said he was working on an alternative to the classical view of play (in Plato) as imitation—mere preparation for reality—mirroring it, imitating it. Thus, in his lecture he stressed that the symbol of the demonic cannot be similar. It means rather an elimination of the purely human—combining it with a leopard for example, leaving the way ambiguous, and open to the more than human.

The classics student who was with us then asked about Aristotle. Fink admitted this was different, but my German broke down and I missed a good deal of this.

They got into the *noesis* as pure act and the importance of *energeia* which I brought in. It is clear that Fink is following Heidegger in reacting against pure *schauen* (seeing) and the intellectualism of the tradition. Then I raised basic questions on Heidegger: Can't the Thomistic distinction between essence and existence in a wide sense be found in Heidegger? Cf. the existentialists, true for all men (essence) and the act of existing—widened to include man's openness to being (*intellectus* in 'act')!

I. In answering, he stressed the way in which the tradition took *Sein* (Being) to be *Vorhandensein*, that is, in other words, some thing objectively present in these entities out there (a form of objectivism). Its existence is this kind of being, essence is a set of properties in a substance there. In Heidegger all this is changed. The essence of man is to be and to be (*existenz*) is to be open 'to be', to be concerned with (his) own being and the being of all beings—to be in the world. This is very different. Especially the transcending of the idea of substance.

But can't the traditional notion of existence, *esse*, be widened to include this understanding act, and the notion of essence to include the *existentialen*? I gather that the answer is that such a widening means a complete transformation. Perhaps so. He gave me a long review of Heidegger's notions that was illuminating. I think now that the notion of essence is in Heidegger but the classical view of existence of the act of an essence (preexisting) is quite different. The two are now fused. This is, perhaps, the real gist of Heidegger's statement that [the] essence of man is to exist. The two are dialectically fused and interdependent. One can't distinguish them without uniting them in an historic act, dynamic, full of growth, open to being, not God, or rather to God only through its relation to being.

II. Then I asked him about the relation of *Sinn* (Meaning) to *Sein* (Being) which worries me very much. He gave a long list of interpretations of *Sein* as power, as essence existing as God. These are senses of *Sein*. In back of them is an unformulated understanding not expressed. Heidegger has abandoned all of these because of their tendency to confuse *Sein* (Being) with '*seiendes*' (beings). *Sein* is certainly not to be equated with any such sense (the interpretation by man). Man is necessarily concerned with *Sinn des Sein* (the meaning of Being), and has a preontological understanding of it. But [he] also [has] a readiness to work this out in terms of what is thematically before us—*vorhandensein*.

But these are false senses of *Sein*. What of the real authentic *Sinn* of *Sein* (meaning of Being)? Is this not *Sein* itself? I refer to *Sinn* and *Zeit* (*Meaning and Time*) where any reification of *Sinn* apart from *Sein* is rejected.

Fink answered that for Heidegger *Sein* gives itself to man (in his later thought), in the form of a human history. Truth has a history. It is not timeless. Cf. Merleau-Ponty, but in correlation with that there is a *Sein an sich* (being as such) that is always withheld from us, unrevealed. This is not covered, nor can it ever be adequately covered by any human *Sinn des Sein* (meaning of being). This is the transcendence of *Sein* over I (being over meaning). On this view, *Sinn* is the human grasp of *Sein* (meaning as the human grasp of being). If it ever could become adequate it would be *Sein* itself—identical with *Sein*. But this can never be because of the finitude of man. I was not satisfied with this answer. But it was fairly clear and needs to be thought about.

The discussion then focused on *Sein* and *Sinn* with '*Seiendes*' (a terrible Anglo-Saxon habit). Fink pointed out very cogently how the tradition had substantialized *Sein*, and how Spinoza had gone to the greatest extreme in identifying substance with the world itself—turning of the world itself into a vast thing, 'thingizing' being. This continued in the West in German idealism and Hegel. Kant is the only exception. Must remember this!!

Fink noted in his remarks how *Sein und Zeit* was clearly an attempt to work out a philosophy of Augustinian, Pascalian and Kierkegaardian lines. Apparently [Heidegger's] last work is not so much this.

III. Finally, I asked about the anthropocentric critique à la Löwith. Fink said he could not answer for Heidegger, of course, but then referred to Being which transcends men. Heidegger is 'being-centric', not anthropocentric. Man is thrown. [He] has no control of his (ontological) grounding. Sense for Heidegger (Cf. II) is the relation to the direction of human life—is a formula in *Sein und Zeit*, but the meaning of *Sein* (is) more basic. This question is necessarily raised by man. So basically [there is] no control of the sense [of being]. The real sense of his life is given by being. This is not anthropomorphism! Fink gave a long, interesting discourse on Heidegger's notions here.

But then we interrupted and pointed out that nature is only a region of the world which is related to man. Is this not too anthropocentric. Regions from Husserl, regional ontology, and world perhaps are incorrect, but world does not equal *Sein*. Fink answered that Heidegger accepted the idea of regional ontology from Husserl—phenomenology of reasons (Cf. philosophical anthropology!), but originally admitted that the world conception of *S. u. Z* [Being and Time] is rather anthropocentric (there may be something in Löwith's critique). Nevertheless, he insisted that though these matters now stand in need of a more exact formulation, world is not the same as *Sein*, and *Sein* is transcended. (Cf. my ideas about the possibility of a purely theoretical correction of the first, subjective, and pragmatic world we are first given.) There is something in this anthropocentric critique.

I then walked awhile with the classics student after Fink left asking him about Heidegger's interpretation of the pre-Socratics. He admitted this was very stimulating but had strong doubts about it especially on two points:

1. *Aletheia*, in Greek *onta* (beings), means concealed only from memory, in relation to man: not absolutely hidden as such, in Heidegger's sense. He is doubtful about this.
2. Also doubts Heidegger's view that the logical view of truth begins only with Plato and Aristotle. This is found in early literature and in pre-Socratic philosophy.

Jaspers, July 9, Basel

His face was much the same but not his manner—now very formalized. Dressed in perfect conventional manner with pressed summer suit and broad summer tie. The very opposite of Barth who came slouching in with his hair standing up and without a coat. Jaspers' age showed in his conventional style and manner. He lectured sitting down and followed his notes very closely, again the opposite of Barth who was quite spontaneous, and thought right there on his feet. Jaspers on the other hand seemed to be summarizing from an already written manuscript.

He was talking about Hegel, the philosopher of ordered movement. All is ever in motion. The truth can never be obtained, the hermeneutic truth from a single statement or proposition but only through the movement through many. The smallest gesture or statement is a symbol of the whole. Everything moves in a circle. Each bears negativity within it, every love is at the same time a struggle. Understanding gets only abstractions, never the whole. Hegel's mind is never satisfied with 'constation' (finding), with the direct and the immediate, always reflects upon what is already before, and something is always already a priori. He penetrates into things, and deepens them. He is the hermeneutic thinker par excellence. The absolute for him really means such penetration. He is not interested in facts, 'constations' (findings), but rather understanding. This is the method of the *Geistenswissenschaften* [human sciences]. Even his enemies, like Ranke, learn from him. He is the final philosopher brooding over a phase of western history and ending this phase, as a last reflection over it, extracting its last drop of meaning. He says it as a whole and gives a final interpretation of it from a sympathetic point of view.

7

The Things I Am Clear About in Philosophy

EXPLANATORY NOTE

John Wild's previously unpublished philosophical credo, "Things I Am Clear About in Philosophy," was likely written within a relatively short period of time after his visit to England and the continent in 1957–1958. There are internal indications from the text that support the dating of this personal reflection. For example, Wild mentions his conversations with Hermann Wein, whom he had recently met and who would later serve as one of Wild's primary interlocutors in *Philosophical Interrogations*. The attentive reader will notice that in addition to stating some of his well-known views on phenomenology, this piece also suggests further reasons for his break with the realistic movement that he helped to found.

Wild affirms and fortifies his view that exploring the life-world is the major task for phenomenological inquiry. Wild argues that there are stable truths that can be discovered, although the means of discovering them differ for different generations of inquirers. It is for this reason that philosophy does not advance "automatically," as Wild puts it, but grows in history. This is interwoven with Wild's two-fold view that human freedom governs our capacity to discover stable truths and to elaborate meanings of the life-world, although not in a finished or closed system. These themes, among others found in his philosophical credo, would be amplified, developed and modified in *Existence and the World of Freedom* as well as in *The Radical Empiricism of William James* and in articles that he would continue to write throughout the 1960s. We are by no means suggesting that this philosophical credo, however instructive regarding Wild's philosophic direction, is exhaustive or even a summary of his philosophical beliefs. However, it does give us a clear overview of Wild's personal engagement with the great theoretical issues that concern him and that remain to be worked out.

(1) I am sure about the *Lebenswelt*, and have defended it for a long time. This is the source of all abstraction where the basic experiences occur all together without abstraction. This world has a subjective factor and is thoroughly relative and practical. This is subject to an existential analysis, the task of philosophical anthropology. One can call this the general condition of man; dialectic, anxiety, impersonality, human time and space.

(2) What is called common sense of the philosopher, the broader perspectives, the insight that suddenly clarifies is not common sense at all. It is a sense that is bathed in the *Lebenswelt*, and comes from it. This is the source of those broad and homely truths that are the life of philosophy and which have always been its peculiar contribution, the evidence and simplicity that mark its contributions. This is worth developing.

(3) Aristotle defined nature as having a source of motion within itself. But then he compromised this by his theory of act preceding potency, and his view of causation that seems to dictate motion from outside. But whether he believed in self-motion or not, this is true. The whole of nature is in change. I have held this for a long time and have criticized the tradition here. Motion is a primary fact. New things come into being. Being is act.

(4) I am convinced that Wein is right. In man this creative motion takes a dialectical form. Out of opposed tensions and phases, new developments occur. These creative wholes are more than the moments out of which they come. There is this real dialectic in man which cannot be understood without dialectical reflection. Contradiction and identity express an abstract partial type of thought which cannot understand and oversimplifies the processes and dynamism of human development.

(5) I am absolutely convinced that each generation must work out its own philosophy in freedom. This does not mean that stable truths cannot be discovered which will be true for all men. They are very precious when discovered. But they must be constantly questioned and resubjected to tests. Philosophy is not like science which grows automatically from age to age. It is essentially connected with human freedom. This thought is worth developing. Philosophy can never be fixed in a finished system.

(6) Even though truths may be stable, the approach to truth is always relative and variable from generation to generation. Also the only truth we have must emerge out of history. It does not dwell in a timeless realm beyond history. We must develop the idea of a growing truth that has a history. Philosophy must be possible but never finished.

(7) Man is not a substance but a field, ecstatic both in space and in time. The whole category of substance is indefensible, and inapplicable even to inorganic nature. Cf. Hartmann's *Gefüge*, balanced forces, tensions of opposed vectors. Even the traditional notion of essence and existence is dialectical. Each exists only by virtue of the other. Each is different, and yet the two constitute a whole which is more than the mere sum of the two. This is dialectical.

(8) When philosophical anthropology is everything we fall into relativism and historicism. When it is neglected we fall into rationalism and dogmatism. This is my idea! In my Royaumont paper. The conclusion is that it is an essential part of the philosophic enterprise, but not all. In addition there is pure philosophy or first philosophy, the clarification of basic terms like change, meaning, being, and truth. The meaning of these terms is not restricted to the *Lebenswelt*. This world is constantly changing into another, not itself. It grows in history. Also, being and truth are not necessarily restricted to the limits of our finite world. But is there any evidence available to us in the world which shows that it is not constituted by us? Yes, there are three kinds of evidence of this sort: first, the inexhaustibility of the concrete (Wahl); second, the fluidity of the world horizon which grows, and its opposition to other such horizons; and third, the experience of transcendence which points beyond. Hence, it is necessary in first philosophy to go beyond the human world and its horizons. Without revelation this is the last horizon open to us. But there is insufficient evidence to finally justify any fixed point of view as is shown by the history of philosophy. Here all is unfinished, and an element of risk cannot be excluded. To deny this is a danger to human freedom. The chief dangers to be avoided are, first, a form of objectivism, either scientific or realistic, which leaves out existence and the *Lebenswelt*, and second, idealism which absolutizes the *Lebenswelt*. We are now ready for less abstract attempts beyond both idealism and realism. But these can never hope to be proved with apodictic certainty. They must include a speculative element and be subject to choice. They can range all the way from Sartrian nihilism to the spiritualism of Marcel. To do this a pure theoretical epoche is necessary which tries to reduce the arbitrary as far as possible in interpreting the meaning of such evidence as is available to us.

(9) I believe in a sharp distinction between a being and being present; or between something having meaning and meaning. There is a dialectic here. It is easy to see a meaning in the most rudimentary fact. This leads to a constitutive idealism for which everything is meaning. On the other hand we can also see that the most highly developed system of meaning is itself a fact. This leads to an objective realism. These are two distinguishable

moments in the life of thought. But each (in mind) exists only by virtue of the other. Realism and idealism as such are mere abstractions. Consciousness is neither wholly one nor the other, but something new emerging out of these moments.

Science is concerned primarily with facts that can be determined, definite, and fixed. Philosophy and phenomenology are concerned primarily with meaning.

Facts have their source outside of us; meanings come from us. What we call experience is a dialogue between the non-human and ourselves. Though this dialogue is absolutely *sui generis*.

Facts (Strasser) are atomic, fixed and objective. Meaning is always relational, developing, and all enveloping.

Meaning is a special symbolic form of consciousness, and what we call fact is a special scientific form of meaning, though it also contains a distinctive factual element.

Both being and meaning are abstractions from a richer idea that emerges from these moments—presence or being before. This is a presence which brings itself and other things into its presence, making them present. It is in these things but yet radically distinct from them. The classical conception according to which being is literally in these things, and exhausted by them is a form of essentialism, a confusion of being with beings, of meaning with what has meaning. If consciousness is not being it must either be a certain kind of being (tradition) or nothing (Sartre). Neither of these alternatives is satisfactory. The first is a form of essentialism identifying consciousness with something of which we are aware. If consciousness has a certain determination of this sort as Aristotle pointed out, it could not know everything. But we can know everything. The second is unacceptable for nothing does not act, or grow. But thought is active and develops. We must therefore conclude that what we call consciousness is being itself.

Like being, consciousness is no thing. In this sense, but in this sense only, it is indeed no-thing.

Like being it is a priori to everything we know.

To understand a thing, to become fully aware of it, is to being it into relation with being.

Consciousness, like being, is a relational net that binds all things together, making them, present with one another.

This is not idealism because being is also the creative act of existing. In its pure form, or in any existent appearance sharing in this, it is also a form of presence that makes present around a center, assembling beings, by revealing the being. This being is not the things revealed but a presence that brings out their meaning. It is a presence that radiates in and from an existential center. The consciousness of a human person is the being in which he participates, which illumines himself and all the beings around him. But in man this is only a finite and participated light. The light is vague and confused and what it illumines is always filled with shadow. Hence our notion of being is dim and confused. Also it cannot be separated from the things that are. In the same way it is hard for us to focus consciousness. Our notion of it is not clear, and it is hard for us to separate it from things or objects of which we are conscious.

From this analysis it is clear that this being cannot be identified with God. It is only a participated light that hardly apprehends itself, to say nothing of a pure awareness. Hence it stands between us and God like a dense curtain. But for us it is an ultimate. We cannot know more than our knowing; we cannot penetrate any further than the floor of being. These two are the same. Our awareness is the pure being in which we share. This being is the presence that reveals a pure act of bringing before. To bring before is to first win detachment from things and then to unite with them all the while remaining detached. To be detached and then to unite with them all the while remaining detached is to create. Knowing is a lesser degree of creating. They possess an ecstatic structure in common, a passing outside while remaining within, the structure of transcendence. There are two ways therefore in which an entity may lack transcendence. First, it may go beyond itself but not remain the same. This is seen in all the processes of nature which constantly advance into something different. Second, it may remain the same, but never go beyond. This form of inflexibility is found in obsession, delusion, prejudice, and evil in general.

For evil is an incapacity for transcendence, a clinging to what has been thought now unfit and regressive. In knowing, both of these privations are to some degree overcome. I unite with the object in a persistent detachment which remains intact and does not mix with the object so far as it is known, though of course I am changed in the knowing, and advance to a new condition. Also this is a genuine transcendence in which the act of knowing passes to something genuinely other than itself. But not completely other, for the object of knowledge already shares existence with itself. Hence it is not completely other. The most perfect act of self-transcendence would be a pure creation *ex nihilo*. Here, being passes into something wholly other than itself (nothing) and unites with it to bring it into being, without mixing with it, remaining detached. Hence, Husserl was right in seeing a connection between knowing and creating, like other idealists. The most perfect knowing would be a creating constitution of an independent entity. But this is an idealist fantasy, beyond our finitude. But knowing is always a passing beyond to give sense to presence and meaning. In this sense all intuition, as Husserl maintained, is definitely creative.

(10) The things that we know are known as revealed as in the world, not as unknown things. Why do we ignore this? This is because we confuse intentional transcendence, as otherness beyond my act of knowing, with a real transcendence, an otherness beyond my being and out of the world.

(11) To think of meaning as Morris does, as a certain kind of response, to A as if to B when B is absent, is to confuse it with something having meaning. It is to confuse an a priori with what a posteriori to it, the *hysteron proteron*. Other examples of this are the confusion of consciousness with objects of consciousness, of lived space with geometrical space, of being with beings, of time with the flux of things in time.

(12) Animal consciousness is pre-reflexive, wholly given to the object with which it unites. It is wholly immersed in the situation from which it never gains detachment. Hence it is in a constant blurred flux with no stable resting places. It has to take whatever comes as exactly what it is. In the constant flux of nature, the only constant factors are derived from its inherited responses, common to the species. It can become aware of the way in which certain experiences are really connected with others, as the scent of the prey with the prey, and can come to learn to respond to the former as a sign of the latter in accordance with its basic needs. It is these particular needs and urges, and cannot become detached from the environmental field which they determine. It is swept along with the shifts of this field like a cork in moving water.

The human person is also a determinate entity with a pragmatic animal awareness. But it belongs to the being of this entity to be concerned with its own being as such. This means that beyond its nature and its flowing awareness, it has access to being as such. This capacity for a pure act of being is what we call consciousness, or rational awareness. This is not a particular kind of thing that exists, but an act of existence as such which is empty of all determination. It is not something that is present, but a pure presence detached from all things and capable of bringing such things into presence before it. How does this operation work in the concrete? The phenomenology of symbols and language has not provided us with an answer to this question.

Pure consciousness arises with the word or arbitrary symbol, which is an element of experience, any element in fact, taken to refer to something other than it is. In this symbolic act man is able to say NO to the concrete situations in which he falls. He does not have to take each thing as just what it is and to respond to it as hidden desires dictate. He cannot indeed reject it altogether. But he can relate it to anything other than itself, and thus take it as something other than it is. In this way he ceases to be lost in the situation and can bring it before him as an object which he can interpret as he sees fit, relating it to other objects in the world.

The two phases of this activity, detachment and interpretation, are worthy of special comment.

The pure being that says NO to the fleeting experiences as they pass is not nothing (as Sartre says). After all, particular determinations have been removed, something remains—an act of indeterminate being centered in the human body. But though detached from them it still remains projected spatially and temporally into the entities of its environmental field. As pure being it is indeed ready to take on any determination whatsoever. This combination of union with and detachment from it is what we mean by an object—something present before the mind. This mind can become detached from itself and regard itself as an object. It can even negate this whole bipolar structure and bring it into an objective presence. The word which names an object is always at our disposal. This enables us to bring the object before us whether it is physically present or absent. Thus, certain stable points emerge in the flux of experience. The flowing field becomes a world with structure. As the child begins to learn his language he spells out the structure of his world sentence by sentence. This brings us to the second factor of interpretation.

Meaning is the connection of things before the mind. The objects of nature are really connected. Thus, clouds are a natural sign of rain, the footprint a sign of the tiger. Through the medium of human action, technical objects are also really connected. Thus the chair is for sitting and the hammer for hammering. These meanings are simply found in experience and presented to the child. They found a relatively stable core of meaning in the structure of the world. The 'value,' that for the sake of which objects and activities exist, here plays the decisive role. It is in the light of a final value that we interpret the meaning of objects and acts to perform. But the horizon of being is infinite. Hence, there is no limit to the objects and values that imagination and experience can bring before the mind. This gives room for creative originality in ordering a world in the light of divergent ultimate objects of concern. Different cultures choose different ultimate values, and therefore interpret all objects in different ways. Even within a single culture different individuals are constantly discovering new values, making different choices and thus giving new meanings to things and events. A great man is one who can create and radiate a new meaning to his fellow men.

Being is ever self-diffusive. Hence, even particular entities project themselves into a field, and radiate by physical motion and change. Pure being (consciousness) radiates itself by communication. All language is not only interpretation but communication to others as well. Even when I think by myself I am talking to myself as an other. Hence, in our language the most important conversations which I have with myself about the most important matters come to result which in our language is called conscience—the knowledge that I work out with myself concerning human values. It is now clear in fact that the human person and his consciousness work themselves out only through communication with others. I am myself only over against them and with them. Hence, all consciousness as the word itself indicates is a knowing with and through others.

Communication is of course a bipolar process involving both expression on the part of the speaker and understanding on the part of the human or those who hear. To be able to listen is just as important as to be able to speak. As the beginning of this complex enterprise it is the expressive factor which predominates. The child of course is aware of others, but he is primarily intent on expressing his own needs and desires. It is only later when he has learned to play the role of the other within himself by games and other social enterprises, that what we may call the communicative factor becomes prominent. Then he thinks not only of expressing himself but also of expressing himself in such a lucid and objective way that he may be understood.

Nevertheless, these two factors are in an uneasy and dialectical tension with each other. Each individual has his own world, his own interpretations and his own particular needs. What we call a language is only a fixed set of open possibilities. Each act of speech is a free and novel contribution. The way a person expresses himself and his world in spoken or written language is his style. But the more marked the individual features of a given style the harder it is to understand. What is easiest to communicate are general ideas and objective facts which have little expressive value. Hence communicative power and individual creativeness vary inversely. Most of us, after passing through a period of youthful egotism, try to be clear and objective, stressing the communicative power of our language, with a result that is banal and impersonal. Everything sinks to the level of an objective thing. Even personal matters become universal and objective. The linguistic master, the person who really knows how to communicate, is one who can express his own self, and the world in which he lives, and still be understood.

8

Editors' Appendix to Conversations, Reflections and Beliefs

NOTE TO THE READER

We have included brief biographies of persons whom Wild encounters or mentions in his Guggenheim Journal, along with people who are referenced by some of his interlocutors. In the case of the better known public speakers, we have simply emphasized Wild's relation to them. We could not identify several of the figures mentioned by Wild, and we were not able to find dates for all of them.

IMPORTANT FIGURES MENTIONED OR CITED IN WILD'S GUGGENHEIM JOURNAL AND IN HIS PHILOSOPHICAL CREDO

ALLPORT, Gordon, 1897–1967
An American humanistic psychologist who was a close colleague and personal friend of Wild's at Harvard. He influenced Wild to study James's *Principles of Psychology* (1890).

AUSTIN, J. L., 1911–1960
British philosopher. Austin was a formative influence on analytic philosophy. Austin was known for his subtle analyses of ordinary language and is particularly remembered for what he called "performative utterances," or speech acts. White's professor of moral philosophy at Oxford, 1952–1960.

AYER, A. J., 1910–1989
British philosopher. Author of *Language, Truth, and Logic* (1936), one of the best known expressions of logical positivism.

BARTH, Karl, 1886–1968
Swiss theologian and professor. A formative figure in twentieth-century Protestant theology. Barth was a prolific writer and a signatory of the "Barmen Declaration," of which he was the principle author. This was a Protestant organization that resisted the Third Reich. Author of *Church Dogmatics*.

BIEMEL, Walter
German philosopher. Student of Heidegger at Freiburg. Biemel is perhaps best known for being one of the group of workers at the Husserl archives, devoted to preserving and disseminating the work of Husserl. Biemel wrote on Kant and also on the philosophy of aesthetics. His approach is existential and phenomenological, with a special emphasis on aesthetics.

BULTMANN, Rudolph, 1884–1976
German theologian and biblical scholar. Best known for his call to "de-mythologize" Christian scripture. His influence on Wild is apparent in "The Death of God and the Life of Man."

BUYTENDIJK, F. J. J., 1887–1974
Dutch phenomenologist. A major contributor to phenomenological psychology and psychiatry. Made significant contributions to the phenomenology of the lived body.

DE CHARDIN, Pierre Teilhard, 1881–1955
French philosopher and paleontologist.

DE RAEYMAEKER, Louis
A Thomist who was concerned about the new direction in Continental philosophy (that is, phenomenology), particularly Heidegger, whose works caused him grave concern. De Raeymaeker had strong ties to the Louvain. Author of the *Philosophy of Being: A Synthesis of Metaphysics and an Introduction to Philosophy*.

DE WAELHENS, Alphonse, 1911–1981
Belgian philosopher and phenomenologist. He was an interpreter of Husserl, Heidegger and Merleau-Ponty.

FINK, Eugen, 1905–1975
German philosopher and phenomenologist. Fink occupies an important historical role in the development of phenomenology. As Husserl's primary assistant from 1928 to 1938, Fink collaborated with Husserl on his research and was a significant thinker in his own right. He was also very

much aware of Heidegger's adaptation of Husserl's thought, and is in turn influenced by it, especially with respect to Heidegger's views of finitude in Being and Time. For Fink, the problem of the world that he distinguished from being remains an important issue. For Fink, "Death, work, conflict, love, and play represent the five fundamental reference points" demonstrating a "common reference corporeity with different pattern and emphases" (Anna-Teresa Tymieniecka, ed., *Phenomenology Worldwide: A Handbook for Research and Study of Phenomenology* [Boston: Kluwer Academic Publishers, 2002], 256–58).

GUARDINI, R., 1885–1968
Italian phenomenologist and Catholic theologian. Guardini was known as a prime architect of Vatican II. As a phenomenologist, he helped to contextualize existential phases of human development, growth and crisis.

GUSDORF, Georges
French philosopher and phenomenologist. "Gusdorf's philosophy developed parallel to the existentially oriented phenomenologies of Sartre, Merleau-Ponty, and Paul Ricouer" (see introduction to *Speaking*, xxii, translated by Paul T. Brockelman [Evanston, IL: Northwestern University Press, 1965]). He was a professor at the University of Strasbourg. He wrote numerous books implying the phenomenological approach, the best known of which is *La Parole* (1965).

HAMPSHIRE, Stuart, 1914–2004
British philosopher. An analytical philosopher, Hampshire appeared to Wild and others to have a more active view of the human agent than most of his British contemporaries. In terms of his philosophy of mind, Hampshire may have been influenced by the phenomenological doctrine of intentionality. Wild taught material of Hampshire's in some of his courses. Perhaps Hampshire's best known book was *Thought and Action* (1959).

HEIDEGGER, Martin, 1889–1976
Student of Edmund Husserl, to whom he dedicated his major work, *Being and Time* (1927). Wild studied with Heidegger in 1931 at the University of Freiburg. Wild would later prove sympathetic to Heidegger's directing of phenomenology to the patterns of human existence. Heidegger figures prominently in Wild's journal, both in England and on the continent. Heidegger's Nazism from 1933 on is incontestable. Wild was critical not only of Heidegger's political views but also of the obscurity of his later writings devoted to thinking about being. Wild urged the substitution of the notion of 'world' for 'being' in his own advocacy of existential phenomenology.

HUSSERL, Edmund, 1859–1938
Husserl is regarded as the founder of modern phenomenology. He wrote numerous books on phenomenology and in addition, left over 50,000 pages of posthumous papers. His better known books include *Ideas*, *The Phenomenology of Internal Time Consciousness* and *The Crisis of the European Sciences*. John Wild personally met Husserl in 1931 at the University of Freiburg. Wild was deeply impressed by Husserl's methodological rigor, and his subsequent discovery of the life-world (*Lebenswelt*) would play a major role in shaping Wild's thinking.

INGARDEN, Roman, 1893–1970
Polish phenomenologist. Ingarden was a student of Edmund Husserl and was best known for his work in aesthetics. He authored *Controversy About the Existence of the World*. His work was interpreted and advanced by his student Anna-Teresa Tymieniecka.

JAMES, William, 1842–1910
One of America's most original thinkers, James influenced philosophers as diverse as Edmund Husserl and Bertrand Russell. Wild devoted whole courses to James's philosophy for graduate students at Yale. Wild's book *The Radical Empiricism of William James* (New York: Doubleday, 1969) explores the thought of James systematically, especially in terms of its phenomenological implications.

JASPERS, Karl, 1883–1969
German philosopher and psychiatrist. Jaspers explored the ways that human beings confront suffering, guilt, conflict and death. He introduced the term "the encompassing," substituting for his earlier use of "transcendence," to indicate that his was a thoroughly worldly kind of humanism. Distanced himself from Heidegger due to Heidegger's association with the Nazis. Students of Jaspers include Paul Ricoeur and Hannah Arendt. Also influenced Gadamer, who succeeded Jaspers at Heidelberg. Associated with the approach of what Jaspers called *Existenz Philosophie*, or philosophy of existence. A major contributor to both philosophy and psychiatry.

MARCEL, Gabriel, 1889–1973
French philosopher. Crdited along with Buber for stressing the importance of the I-Thou relation. Arguably the best known Catholic existential thinker. Author of *The Mystery of Being*.

MEAD, George Herbert, 1863–1931
American philosopher. John Wild's teacher at the University of Chicago. Wild stated, "Of my teachers at the University of Chicago, it was certainly G. H. Mead who was the most profound, and who left the deepest im-

pression on me, especially his notions of the control of meanings by controllable symbols, of otherness, implying the role of the other in relation to consciousness" (William E. Kaufman, *John Wild: From Realism to Phenomenology* [New York: Peter Lang, 1996], 213). Mead is regarded as one of the founders of American pragmatism, and exerted a major influence on twentieth-century social theory. Mead published numerous papers. His books are taken from his manuscripts and notes as well as from the notes of his students.

MEHL, Roger, 1913–1997
French theologian and philosopher. Deeply influenced Wild's search in the late 1950s for a Christian philosophy. Mehl left more room for philosophy than did Barth, although he did not seem to think that the goal of a Christian philosophy was possible as such.

MERLEAU-PONTY, Maurice, 1908–1961
Merleau-Ponty authored *Signs*, *The Phenomenology of Perception* and *The Primacy of Perception*. John Wild regarded *The Phenomenology of Perception* to be one of the most important works in the field of existential phenomenology. Wild devoted entire seminars to Merleau-Ponty and placed considerable emphasis upon Merleau-Ponty's argument that the phenomenological reduction, in Husserl's sense, could not be carried out from a standpoint of transcendental consciousness. Perception, the lived body, temporality, spatiality and other people were always presupposed in the phenomenological reduction. Wild translated "Phenomenology and the Sciences of Man" (cf. *Primacy of Perception*, 43–95 [Evanston, IL: Northwestern University Press, 1964]).

MORRIS, Charles, 1901–1979
A friend and fellow student of Wild at the University of Chicago under George Herbert Mead. He is best known for his monograph *Foundations of the Theory of Signs* (1938), a foundational work in the modern field of philosophical semiotics. Morris was reunited with Wild in Wild's last year of teaching at the University of Florida, 1969–1970.

MURDOCH, Iris, 1919–1999
Murdoch was an Irish-born novelist, essayist and philosopher. She authored *Sartre, Romantic Rationalist* (1953).

RYLE, Gilbert, 1900–1976
British philosopher. Ryle became interested in phenomenology in the late 1920s and reviewed Heidegger's *Being and Time* in 1929. He is remembered for advancing the notion of the "category mistake," where two things are mistakenly treated as logically equivalent to categories because of their

grammatical equivalence. Ryle was known for his anti-Cartesianism, arguing that the mind is not a non-physical substance in the body, "a ghost in a machine," but intelligible only in terms of corporeal capacities.

SARTRE, Jean-Paul, 1905–1980
Wild believed that Sartre's *Being and Nothingness* (1943) constituted a major advance in existential phenomenology. Wild was sympathetic to Sartre's notion of radical human freedom but believed that it needed to be complemented by a more adequate notion of responsibility. Wild was one of the first American academics to teach Sartre's *Search for a Method*. Wild found Sartre's specific phenomenological descriptions more compelling than his ontological framework.

STRASSER, Stephan, 1905–1991
Dutch philosopher and phenomenologist. Strasser helped to transcribe a significant portion of Husserl's shorthand, working in 1942–1943. Strasser's influence was international. Wild was influenced by Strasser's views on phenomenology. Interestingly, both moved toward the thinking of Levinas in the last phase of their careers. His works include, among many others, *The Soul in Metaphysical and Empirical Psychology* (1963), *Phenomenology and the Human Sciences* (1963), *The Idea of Dialogical Phenomenology* (1969) and *Understanding an Explanation* (1985).

TAYLOR, Charles, 1931–
Canadian philosopher. Studied at Oxford. Later professor of moral philosophy at Oxford University. Well known for his work on morality, the problem of identity and political philosophy. Taylor is often associated with communitarianism and with his series of public talks on the Canadian Broadcasting Company.

TILLICH, Paul, 1886–1965
Philosopher and Protestant theologian. Born and educated in Germany. Taught theology in various German universities and philosophy at the University of Frankfurt. In 1933, he was dismissed because of his opposition to the Nazis. Taught at Union Theological Seminary in New York from 1933 to 1953. Professor at Harvard from 1954 to 1961. Tillich incorporated existential and ontological themes into his theological reflections. Tillich was the author of many books, including the three-volume *Systematic Theology*.

VAN DER LEEUW, Gerardus, 1890–1950
Received doctoral degree from the University of Leiden in 1916 with dissertation on Egyptian religion. Appointed to a chair at the University of

Gröningen. Influenced by Husserl, as partly shown in his focus on the mutually constitutive power of object and subject in religion. Emphasized *Verstehen* rather than explanation. For a period, he served as minister of education in Holland. His most famous work was translated into English as *Religion in Essence and Manifestation: A Study in Phenomenology* (1938).

VAN PEURSEN, C. A., 1920–1996
Dutch philosopher and phenomenologist. Shared important interests with Wild, including phenomenological anthropology and the pursuit of a dialogue between ordinary language philosophy and phenomenology. He was deeply influenced by Merleau-Ponty. His books include *Body, Soul, and Spirit: Introduction to a Phenomenological Anthropology* and *Phenomenology and Analytical Philosophy*.

WEIN, Herman
Professor of philosophy and lecturer on philosophical anthropology at the University of Göttingen, Germany. Author of *The Problem of Relativism*, among other works.

WEISS, Paul, 1901–2002
America's most original, systematic metaphysician. Colleague and friend of John Wild. Author of thirty books, including *Reality*, *Modes of Being* and, more recently, *Emphatics and Surrogates*.

Part III

Toward a Phenomenology of Transcendence

9

The Death of God and the Life of Man

EXPLANATORY NOTE

Philosophy in the twentieth century saw a collapse of the ontological categories, which through the periods of scholasticism and rationalism had reigned, even when witnessed to by their empiricist detractors, from Plato to Hegel. God had been thought of as the highest exemplification of metaphysical categories. When Nietzsche announced that "God is dead," the phrase meant at least this to many thinkers: "Onto-theology" had played itself out.

In the tradition of existential phenomenology Wild was happy to overcome Onto-theological theism; but in this engaging lecture he cautions against a sanguine jettisoning of all God talk, lest we throw the proverbial baby out with the bathwater. Socrates emerges as the hero who allows the light of a barely glimpsed divine fullness to show up the limitations of our philosophical and political formulations.

The issue here is the danger of killing that dimension of human self-transcendence that stretches toward an infinite and dares to name the holy, if only indirectly. To celebrate the death of this God might entail the murder of man himself. The fact that some contemporary post-modern philosophers have reveled in this death, in an academic environment known for its increasing spiritual irrelevance, only underscores the importance of the issue to which Wild calls our attention and the decision to which he summons us.

Philosophers have long been warned that if they will stretch up their necks to reach for the sweet fruits of theology, they will get their heads chopped off. I am aware of the fact that something like this has happened to more than one philosopher in modern times, and so the force of this warning is not lost on me. Let me try to take account of it, by saying at the very beginning that I shall be speaking only as a philosopher and dealing, therefore, with philosophical issues rather than theological issues, in so far as these can be distinguished. But if my argument leads me into areas that some may say belong to theology, then neck or no neck, I must take the risk.

What I wish to examine with you this evening are certain implications of the slogan "God is dead" for the life of man. This slogan is usually traced back to the well-known passage in Nietzsche's *Joyful Wisdom* published in 1882 where the mad man, Nietzsche's mouthpiece, ". . . on a sunny morning lit a lantern and went about the marketplace ceaselessly crying 'Where is God!' Then many of those standing around who had no belief in God began to laugh. 'Has He got lost?' said one. 'Has He run away like a child?' said another. Or has He hidden Himself? Is He afraid of us? Is He traveling or on voyage? So they cried out and laughed with one another. The mad man sprang into the midst of them boring through them with his gaze. 'Where is God?' he cried. 'I will tell you! We have killed Him, you and I! We are all his murderers. But how have we done this?'" (*The Mad Man*, no. 125). However as Heidegger has pointed out in his interesting discussion of Nietzsche's saying (*Holzwege*, pp. 193–248) it is found in Hegel's youthful work *Glauben und Wissen*, written in 1802, though in a different context. (Perhaps after a certain time we will not have to be reminded that everything can be found in Hegel, though in a somewhat different sense.) In Nietzsche, I think, the sense is fairly clear. The God of the Judaeo-Christian tradition, as we now call it (which may be an aftermath of this demise), is dead, together with the whole Platonic other world of ideal norms and values with which He became involved in the early post-Christian centuries. As Nietzsche's mad man puts it: "Is not the greatness of this act too great for us? Must we not ourselves become Gods in order to seem worthy of them? There was never a greater deed." Then the mad man grew silent and looked again at these listeners who were now also silent and staring at him in a strange way. Finally he threw his lantern to the ground, shattering it into pieces and extinguishing its light. "I have come too soon," he said. "The time has not yet come. This happening is still going on and has not yet penetrated into the ears of men . . ." But since then the proclamation of this *Joyful Wisdom* has glimmered with increasing intensity, like an approaching comet through the atmosphere of Western culture, until, in the America of our time, it has certainly reached the ears of men and has emerged into public view in the form of scholarly publications, magazine articles, and recently, broadcasts in the mass media.

A very vocal group of theologians and New Testament critics have now taken over this saying of Nietzsche. They are telling us not that certain gods or images of God have passed away; this, of course, is a familiar phenomenon. They are informing us in no uncertain terms that God! is dead. The divine names a dimension of human history, a way of existing. This is an indisputable fact which is open to empirical investigation and interpretation. Man is here trying, now and then with some success, to transcend himself. But when the aim of this human process is objectified and turned into a transcendent object in the sky, a God-thing beyond all human existence, it degenerates into a myth, which is open to criticism, and must be finally eliminated in the light of the verifiable truth.

According to Bultmann, the great New Testament critic, this arduous process of demythologizing began in the New Testament itself, and has been developing as a half-suppressed underground movement ever since. According to some of his followers now, this critical process will not be finished until the idea of God as a great external power, forcing His way upon us, is eliminated. Man exists freely in the factual universe which the sciences have partially revealed to us. If he is to achieve what has been called salvation, he must achieve it by his own efforts. God is dead.

This striking statement is of concern to every thinking man, for its acceptance or rejection will have a profound effect not only on his individual way of life but upon the life of our Western culture as a whole. There are philosophers of our time who say that philosophy should not deal with substantive questions of this kind to which demonstrable final answers cannot be expected. Such questions should be left to each individual to decide for himself, apparently in an arbitrary manner without disciplined reflection. Philosophy, on the other hand, should rather follow science in restricting itself to problems concerning minor matters (one is tempted say matters which do not matter) that can be solved by conclusive demonstrations. The English philosopher Berkeley had a good name for little thinkers of this kind. He called them "minute philosophers," and argued for a different way which he himself pursued.

In facing the ultimate question of life, we find ourselves involved in mysteries that may be deepened rather than in problems that can be solved and then forgotten. But even though mathematical demonstration is impossible, and computers will not help us, a disciplined approach is still possible. Different approaches may be contrasted and compared in the light of relevant evidence, and there is such evidence—too much, perhaps, rather than too little. The answers we give to such questions are found not so much in speculative theories as in our ways of life. But as Socrates said in his *Apology* these ways of life can be examined and criticized. Certain answers may be found to be over-simple and out of line with facts or experience. Others may be able to withstand such criticism.

They may be shown to be in line with wide patterns of experience, and open to further deepening and development. Let me, then, in the time at my disposal, try to approach the questions of that problem in this way. Of course, I shall be speaking only for myself. But here and there, perhaps, what I have to say may find some answering reverberation in the minds of some of you.

Let me begin by saying that I find many reasons for the doubts that underlie this question concerning God in the world situation we now confront. Let us look for a moment at some of these doubts. They are certainly relevant. They should be raised. But do they say the last word? Do they rule out the possibility of any further affirmative answer? Or should the dialogue continue? Let us see!

First of all, let us grant that in the world of science, as it is now being presented to us, there seems to be no place for any great emperor of the universe, nor, indeed for any transcendence. Wherever science looks, it finds things related in singular ways. These may be called "laws." But there is no evidence in these perspectives to support the theory of a divine law-giver. With the coming of space travel, the Copernican Revolution has at last really struck home to us. Our earth is a minor planet of a solar system that is not peculiarly distinctive in any way. There is a strong probability that among the millions of galaxies there are many other planets with conditions equally favorable for the development of intelligent life. From this point of view, the notion that our earth should have been singled out for a special revelation from a divine King seems implausible and even fantastic.

But we need to remember that this scientific perspective is not the only horizon to which we have access and that it is highly abstract. Most of our experiences as we live them through, and many of their objects are simply left out. There is, for example, the experience of ultimate concern, as Tillich called it, that of choice and responsibility, the mystical experience, and many others which find no place in the realms of science. There is another whole horizon recently focused by the new disciplines of phenomenology, which is broader and richer in scope. This is the historical world in which we exist, grow up from infancy, pursue our chosen projects and face death. There is room in this life-world, as Husserl called it, for all the vast spaces and galaxies of recent astronomy, for the experiences we have mentioned, and for myriad others as well.

It is true that this life-world is physically centered in our planet, which may be only one among millions of others. But from this we cannot infer that the real meanings emerging in human history must be centered there. For this world including its astronomical spaces, is pervaded by ambiguity, and surrounded by mysteries to which science has no access. If we are to gain some inkling of their meaning, we must turn to other experiences which may be relevant, and to other methods, like those of phenomenology, which may enable us to get a bit closer to their sense. The argument from the magnitude of astronomical space and the probability of non-human forms of intelligent life may tell against anthropomorphic conceptions of a divine emperor, or *pantokrator*. But against the possibility of something transcending not only our notions of space, but all our human ideas and categories, and touching our lives with a sense of ultimate ambiguity and mystery, it carries little weight. And the same may be said of the other arguments that underlie our present questions about the death of God.

One of these, we may call a moral argument which follows the philosopher Feuerbach in holding that instead of man being made in the image of God, it is really God who has been made in the image of man. According to this view, man has projected his highest qualities such as foresight, sacrifice, forgiveness, and love, and alienated himself from them as a corrupted mass of sin, selfishness, and pride who can do nothing worthwhile on his own. In this life there is only misery and evil; in heaven only good. Such traditional doctrines lead to moral lethargy and to an undue tolerance of social injustice. We are familiar, for instance, with Marx's saying that "religion is the opiate of the people."

Another anthropomorphic feature of traditional theology is the notion of a divine Providence which dilutes the whole notion of human freedom, and makes the divine ruler responsible for Auschwitz, Belsen and all the great human conquests and tortures of history. According to St. Augustine, these agonies are like the dark shadows on a picture which the Divine artist uses to bring out the noble pattern of the lighted whole. This doctrine is now very hard for us to take, for we know, and I think many Germans now know who was responsible for Auschwitz. How can we worship a ruthless God-king of this kind? For many of us this God is dead. At its best, of course, the tradition has recognized that this talk of divine law-givers, kings, and artists using human symbols for a divine transcendence to which they do not literally apply and to which they only point. But we are now aware of the terrible dangers that arise from confusing the two. If our faith is not to wither away, we need to think more carefully about the notion of transcendence and how it is experienced. Then, if necessary, in the light of this reflection, we must find less inappropriate symbols that do not eliminate the element of mystery nor dilute our sense of human freedom and responsibility.

Having considered a physical and a moral argument raising serious doubts concerning the existence of Gods conceived along traditional lines, let us mention a third rational doubt which has carried and still carries a certain weight. This is the criticism of those causal arguments which, since the time of Aristotle, have been defended as proving the existence of a necessary first cause, endowed with the attributes of perfection, omniscience, omnipotence etc. I have no time to go into the details of this abundant literature; I will only state my own opinion which is based on a reading of significant portions of it, and is by no means exceptional amongst philosophers. To one already convinced on other grounds, these demonstrations may be convincing. But to one approaching them in an impartial way they raise more questions than they can answer. At most they are able to show a certain inadequacy in the finite universe, an incapacity to explain itself, a sense in which it points to something beyond. But they are unable to demonstrate to a critical mind the existence of a necessary being, whatever this phrase may mean, endowed with the whole array of traditional attributes. The traditional notion of cause as containing its effect within itself is a dubious metaphysical construction which is open to serious question. We are now living in a post-Kantian age, and most of us see that reason has empirical limits. Instead of inventing pure concepts of this kind, its proper function is rather to clarify and to bring out the implicit meaning of certain basic experiences.

Do such processes of clarification deserve to be called arguments? The intellectualist assumptions that have played a dominant role in our history, and have tended to be disparage perception and direct experiences of every kind, still lead many of us to deny this. But there are strong reasons for questioning this negative answer. We speak of a lawyer as arguing for his client against the prosecution, and of a doctor as arguing for his diagnosis of a case against professional criticism. But in neither case are they merely logical conclusions from clearly stated premises. The premises here are a complex and confused array of empirical facts and symptoms. The question at issue is how to fit these empirical data together in such a way as to make sense out of them and to reconcile them with other well-known facts.

The American logician Charles Sanders Peirce called this logical process abduction, and sharply distinguished it from induction and deduction. The serious disputes that arise between living individuals and groups involve issues of this kind. This is also true of major issues in philosophy. Thus the dispute between the determinists and those who defend free-will concerns different interpretations of the facts; it is an issue of abduction. Each tries to show that the other is failing to recognize certain facts as they are, or that its interpretation is confused and inconsistent. Arguments concerning the existence of God are disputes of this kind. They involve the meaning of certain experiences. Do they or do they not point to something transcending man? In what follows, I shall try to suggest a few points on the affirmative side.

The first experiences that come to mind in this connection are those called mystical. In his classical text on *The Varieties of Religious Experience*,

William James devotes a long chapter to this theme, and defines a mystical experience in terms of three primary traits. First of all, it is "directly experienced" as an imposed condition that "defies description," so that "no adequate report of its contents can be given in words." In the second place, it has a "noetic quality." That is, it seems to be a state of "insight into depths of truth unplumbed by the discursive intellect" (Modern Libr., p. 371). Such insights are remembered and "carry with them a curious sense of authority for after time." Finally, as James says, though the oncoming of these states "may be facilitated by preliminary voluntary operations," once it has set in, the subject usually feels "as if he were grasped and held by a superior power" of some kind (p. 372).

After examining many different concrete experiences of this kind, from both Eastern and Western traditions, James concludes that, as an empiricist, he cannot dismiss them all as manifestations of mental derangement or delusion. In any case, they need to be examined and interpreted in a careful and disciplined way. From the little we now know of them, I believe that James's conclusion is not unreasonable. These experiences, when taken together with other evidence of the same kind, point towards the presence of a mystery transcending the powers of our understanding but with which some minds are able to establish fleeting, conscious contacts.

The other evidence of which I have spoken comprises in large part minor mysteries, as we may call them, when at unforeseen junctures—it may be in watching the ocean at night, in making a critical choice affecting ourselves and the lives of others, or in the presence of death, we find the experience opening up, and in it we suddenly feel the presence of mystery. Many of us, I believe, even in this technological age, have experiences of minor mysteries of this kind. As our knowledge grows, this transcendence may recede from the areas we think we have covered. But it is always there on the boundaries, and when the last man dies, I believe he will die with a sense of the presence of mystery.

However it is with another kind of evidence that I am primarily concerned, and to which I shall now turn. This evidence comes from a certain insatiable restlessness in man which St. Augustine expressed at the beginning of his *Confessions* in his well-known saying: *Cor meum inqueatum est donec requiescat in Te*. Its meaning is harder to decipher, but its presence in all men, at least to some degree, is far more widely recognized than that of the mystical experiences we have just considered. Let us now ask what is the meaning of this peculiar restlessness that makes us eventually dissatisfied with our human accomplishments, and that has so far kept our history moving? Perhaps we may get at the meaning of this restlessness more directly if we ask what would have happened, or what might happen without it? Men seek for meaning and order in their existence. For this they must find a center in their world, an ultimate object of concern.

What is to be the ultimate reality around which my world is to be ordered?

We are all aware of the strong tendency to identify this with a human individual or a human group of some kind. Thus I may make myself the center of an ultimate concern to which everything else is subordinated. Most of us have lived through patterns of this kind. But if we were fortunate enough to be moved by a disquiet that enabled us to transcend this self-centeredness, we also know the prisons of egotism and self-righteousness to which it leads. Or we may center our life on that of another person dear to us. But can any human person, no matter how strong he or she may be, bear such strain? Such idolatrous love is damaging to both parties. Is there not a certain benignity in the disquiet that leads us towards something beyond? What is this to be?

It may be a larger human group like the family, the community, or the people to whom we belong. To become attached to such objects is certainly an advance, for they are larger than us. But they are also finite, fragile and ephemeral. They also pass away. Can they, therefore, stand the strain of an ultimate devotion? Does this not necessarily lead to nepotism, parochialism and a one-sided xenophobia? Is it not well for us to be touched by that restlessness which can lead us beyond? Where then shall we turn?

Many think that they find an ultimate peace of mind in attaching themselves to those seemingly more stable patterns of meanings and ideals which form the collective lives of larger groups. Hence they have devoted themselves to socialism, the free-enterprise system, baroque art or the structures of life and administration that are embodied in great historical empires, or in the modern nation-state. But can any of these patterns stand the strain of being absolutized in this way? Does this not bring about the distortions or a restrictive fanaticism that finally breaks into pieces from the internal pressures it is trying to enclose? The absolute state, absolute sex, even absolute freedom—are they not like deep-sea fish which become distorted and explode when they are lifted to the surface and artificially freed from the external pressures to which they are normally subjected at the bottom of the sea?

Can any human being, or pattern, be lifted into a supreme position where it can dominate the whole life of man without becoming a ruinous tyranny which needs to be destroyed not only for the sake of the others but for its own sake as well? Are we not grateful to the critics and rebels who have always appeared in the past to lead us on beyond? Will the whole of mankind not be grateful to them in the future if they help to dispose of the even more subtle and formidable tyrannies, say the world of 1984, which may appear in the future?

Do we not now hope that they will be able to pray for the strength and courage to fight against these coming world Leviathans and to destroy them? But if God is really dead, no undeluded man will ever pray. Do we look forward to this? In this connection, it is interesting to note how great empires in the past have usually tried to win the support of established religious institutions, for this indicates recognition on their own part of a weakness and fragility which is inconsistent with their absolutist claims. Is it not significant that even these world dominions have felt the need of transcendence? But they were profoundly mistaken in thinking that it could be identified with any world empire or any human system of any kind. It transcends every one of these infinitely, and lies beyond them, infinitely far. It was only in virtue of anthropomorphic elements read into it by faulty interpreters that it could be lastingly captured and placed within a human system. Hence wherever the sense of this transcendence was alive, the union dissolved, and in the West, at least, the Church was finally separated from the state.

But how about religion itself? Has it not often tried to identify the divine transcendence with fixed systems of dogma and institutional practice? The answer is, of course, yes. But where the sense of transcendence, the peculiarly religious sense, has remained alive, critics and rebels have again been at work to lead us beyond fixed patterns and formulations. It is because of this that all world religions, including our own Western Faith, have had a history. Without the sense of transcendence this history would become bogged down in a morass of habits and customs which would hold us fast and prevent our freedom of motion. Should we not then be grateful to those critics and innovators who have pulled us out of these swamps and have helped us to move again on our way?

This is an important part of the argument we are suggesting. Why is it that, after such experiences of breakdown, recognizing that there is little or no hope of reaching a final end, men still go on struggling for the establishment of institutions and political systems which are, on the one hand, unified and orderly, and yet on the other hand, open to further development and free? In the past, we find these two directions incompatible, for in their human manifestations, order suppresses freedom and freedom disintegrates order. What is luring us into these recurrent inconsistencies? What then are we moving towards? Is it not some source of freedom and order transcending all possibilities of realization, but enabling us to recognize genuine advances and declines?

What kind of an argument is this? From a philosophical point of view, it is a hypothesis for which the claim can be made that it takes account of a variety of disparate facts more adequately than other alternatives. These facts are mystical experiences of manifold kinds, criticisms of absolute systems, the constantly renewed attempts to create new and better systems, and the recognition of genuine advances and declines. What are their meanings? Of course in most men we can find traces of two general urges, one towards freedom and another towards order. This certainly must be admitted. Is the argument, then, a mere case of wishful thinking which asserts that, as a matter of fact, we are seeking to satisfy two incompatible desires? I think not, for the argument also refers to other facts. It attempts to show that these different types of fact cannot be fitted together within a pattern of a certain sort. We may now state it in the form of a dilemma.

Without the recognition of that element of transcendence which can be found in traditional conceptions of the divine, we are left with two alternatives. We may give our ultimate allegiance either to some faulty human being or system, which means idolatry and tyranny of some kind, or we must recognize an ultimate chaos in which neither free criticism nor that any serious struggle for order and freedom has any lasting ground. Of course it may have a temporary ground in human desires. But these are unstable and conflicting, and some kind of order is necessary for life. It is not hard to see that in the fluctuations of history this will end and in an order without freedom, which means tyranny again. To those who are not impressed by the role of freedom in human history, this abductive argument may have little appeal. But if they are still seeking an impartial judgment, they should raise the following question: Does either of these interpretations (the absolutizing of a human pattern or pure relativism) adequately account for all the facts we have considered? More especially does it do justice to the apparently unlimited capacity for self-transcendence that is found in man?

This argument is based on the endless self-questioning and restlessness that moves our human history. Most of us have participated in this vital motion in some area of our culture, at least to some degree. Have you ever lived through one of those arduous times of trouble and questions when you doubted some fixed structure or pattern of meaning to which you had become closely attached? Has such doubt ever led you to move towards new attitudes that were wider and more open, and even towards new ways of life? If so, you may be able to see the meaning in an existential argument of this kind. It is not based on fixed concepts and categories in the mind, though these are certainly involved. It is based rather on questions than on answers and on motions rather than on notions.

Perhaps I can clarify the argument for you by speaking of my own discipline, philosophy, and of its history, which now seems strange when we compare it with that of the different special sciences. We still tend to think of philosophy in terms of regions in our libraries, and of great systems written in books. All of this, indeed, is important and needs to be taken into account. But it does not take us to the first roots. We need to remember that those of us who are teachers and, as we say, professors of this ancient discipline, still hold up as our patron a man who never occupied a chair in an official institution, nor even wrote a single book. We need to remember Socrates.

Having no official standing, he went about talking to anyone he met on the streets of Athens, questioning artisans, poets and politicians about what they thought they knew . . . When it dawned on many of them that they did not know, they attributed such knowledge to him. But over and over again he says that he does not possess such knowledge, for in questioning others, he is also questioning himself. The ironic distance from which he speaks, makes his audience restless and uncomfortable. So at last he is brought on trial for corrupting the youth. But here again, his attitude is puzzling and disquieting for he seems to be neither for the 500 jurors who are judging him nor against them. He is not a rebel, for he might have run away, but he does not do so. He respects the laws of Athens and submits to the trial and condemnation. But there is something strange about this respect.

He seems to be accepting the laws only with a view toward changing them. As he proceeds with his defense, he explains to them what the City is, as if they were not the City—as if they did not know! As he goes on, it seems that instead of their judging him from an objective point of view, it is rather he who is judging them on the basis of standards to which he has access from within. He accepts nothing uncriticized as it stands. He seeks to know the meanings and the reasons for what is going on. What is the harm in this? Why should we not search for an interpretation? But the matter is not as innocent as it sounds. As soon as one set of reasons is formulated, other opposed reasons can be found, and we are plunged into the confusion of controversy. Why will he not accept the laws and the religion of Athens as they stand? This is what a majority of his fellow citizens expected. But this was precisely what he would not do. And so he was put to death.

What is the ground of this endless questioning? From whence does it proceed? On this point, both the reports of his friends and Socrates himself are in profound agreement. There is a mystery brooding over our human history and its seemingly routine events. Thus in *The Symposium*, Alcibiades tells us of how one day on the expedition to Potidaea Socrates fell into a rapt state of concentration, which held him standing through the whole night, and then "with the return of light he offered up a prayer to the sun, and went on his way" (p. 220). The wisdom Socrates is seeking is grounded in a mystery that is luring him on and giving him glimpses not only of lasting truths here and there but of something transcendent, radically beyond anything he, or his questions, can ever clearly see. Thus, in

The Apology, he speaks of his questioning mission as a divine gift to the state (p. 30).

Once embarked on this quest, men may find out that the care of the soul, the moving principle of life, is more important than the care for material things, and that injustice, the corruption of this moving principle, is worse than death. But precious as these grains of knowledge may be, it is only in the light, or darkness, of a deeper mystery that they can be properly understood. For in the end, as Socrates specifically says, "human knowledge is worthy of little or nothing" and "God alone is wise" (*Apology*, p. 23). The failure of Socrates' strange defense and the imposition of the death penalty have been duly inscribed on the scrolls of history, and in our time, we tend to take it for granted as a manifestation of the mediocre political judgment of the time.

But this should not blind us to the surprising support it elicited from more than 200 of the jurymen. A change of only thirty cotes, as Socrates points out, would have reversed the sentence and subjected his accusers to a fine. It is clear that the Socratic mission of restless questioning, while it antagonized the majority as dangerous and subversive to the established order, also had its attractive side. It was not a mere carping criticism. It pointed beyond to a ground of mystery. To those who felt this, it therefore had a strange appeal, awakening the hope for deeper and unprecedented levels of life and understanding.

Do we not find a constant reawakening of this hope in the history of philosophy and in other histories since the Socratic time? In its broad outlines, does it not suggest an endless continuation of his quest? Has any final solution yet been found? As soon as a great system has been formulated which welds together theories of man, the world, and God into a final unity, has it not always been subjected to criticism which has always found and always will find weaknesses, mistakes and ambiguities? This has sometimes led to disillusionment with the whole enterprise and to carping questions with no ground more basic than a subjective sense of failure. But is it not true that, in spite of all these failures and vicissitudes of our history, the search still goes on? What has inspired this constant renewal of hope? Is it not the transcendent truth still beyond us that can be further explored and have we not made real advances in its direction? Have we not seen that certain positions have been ruled out as inadequate, and that lasting insights of limited scope have actually been achieved?

There is a certain kind of skepticism which is an essential moment in all genuine philosophizing. It enables us to gain a distance from any attitude or point of view that we are criticizing. It is only by transcending this point of view that we may cease to be either for it or against it, that we may really examine it, and try to find its meaning. To transcend our own views in this way is even more important. When this moment of transcendence is lost, philosophy will lose its critical mobility and will also die. This happens to our positive affirmations when they take possession of us, and we lose all distance from them. It also happens to our questioning attitude when it loses all sense of direction and freezes into a negative attitude that is closed to any possible further manifestations of the truth.

Philosophers learn to distinguish between these two types of skepticism, the one that is open, at least vaguely aware of its transcendent ground and ready for the true as well as the false, and the other that is groundless, closed, and ready only for the false. In the latter, we are no longer seeking for an answer not yet given. We are merely expressing a negative answer that has already been given. No lasting meanings are to be found. So our questions become captious and quibbling. They no longer express a will to seek but only a will to negate and destroy. Such a position may be negative. But it is no longer moving. It is as fixed and frozen as any dogmatism that may happen to be affirmative in form.

I can summarize the existential argument I am trying to present in the form of two questions, addressed to those who now wish to celebrate, I think somewhat prematurely, the death of divine transcendence. Are they really asserting that human life is meaningless and that all interpretations are equally absurd? Then they are saying that no meanings have really deepened, nothing has been shown to be either false or true, that the whole search for reality and meaning has been in vain. But does an extreme view of this kind really fit the facts of history? Even though we do not find in the extensive literature of philosophy any all-encompassing system which finally satisfies our craving for truth, do we not here and there, often in the most unexpected places, find grains of truth and partial insights that arouse our hopes and lure us on? Finally if this human restlessness lacks any ground, beyond us, what real motive is there for continuing this futile search? If we do not now and then catch glimpses, which enable us to see the inadequacy of our past achievements, why should we go on? Why should we not rather accept some dogmatic system, that happens to prevail at a given time, and the institutions associated with it? Why should we not freeze them into a changeless absolute that is good enough for us, abandon our ungrounded criticism, and rest content? Do you choose to have this happen? If so, it may happen, and the restless Eros that has kept our history moving will be stilled. We may then come to rest in peace with a God who is also dead. Such an interpretation is possible and appeals to many who long for rest. The situation, as always, is ambiguous. Does the overall evidence point in this direction? Is this Eros only a human, mortal restlessness that can be made to die away? Or as Socrates suggests is it not at least, in part, immortal?

10

Guilt

EXPLANATORY NOTE

Wild's unfinished essay on guilt begins with a characteristically cooperative declaration. "We now recognize," he says, "three types of guilt, legal, moral, and religious (sin)." Wild saw himself as a partner in a project; he was involved in a hopeful new phenomenological effort that was beginning to pile up solid results.

Perhaps he is very American in this earnest optimism. However that may be, his co-workers at this point hail from the Continent. In the present case we may helpfully single out Martin Buber who comes to mind when we ask: Who are these others with whom Wild shares this threefold division? In "Guilt and Guilt Feelings" Buber distinguishes three "spheres" of guilt: the law of society, conscience and faith.

It is when we contrast the perspectives expressed in these essays, however, that we sharpen our sense of what Wild the philosopher was about. Buber, writing for psychologists, focuses on the second level in order to secure a dimension of healing that takes guilt seriously as an indication of objective disorder. Wild, dealing with all three and treating them as a kind of ladder of existential ascent, can be seen in implicit and explicit dialogue with other philosophers. For instance, while he chides Heidegger for ignoring transcendence in his account of guilt, when Wild turns to the second level he interprets moral guilt in terms congenial to Heidegger, that is, rather than open the question of relationship to others he focuses on the standpoint of the individual faced with the task of giving sense to his own world. Moral guilt, which admits of more and less, results from the contrast of fragmentary personal achievement and the infinity of the task. At the same time, Wild uses this topic as an occasion to challenge an apparent Heideggerian failure to distinguish personal from collective guilt, to say nothing of authentic guilt from mere pathological guilt feelings.

Buber's profound development of the second level cannot concern us here. It is significant, though, that he leaves the third level to the authority of religious traditions for which he has great reverence, and which are not in any case, he argues, the proper province of the psychological practice he is attempting to influence. Wild by contrast is the relentlessly Protestant thinker here, accusing the traditions of a conflation of religious guilt with legal guilt, and of failing (yet) to properly found the third level by ignoring the integrity of the first two.

Wild's notion of absolute transcendence (there is an oblique reference to Otto's *Tremens et Fascinans*) protects that integrity. Beyond the dialectic of legal and personal guilt lies a reference to an otherness, recasting without essentially disturbing the first two levels. Wild's incomplete development of this religious level affords a most important glimpse into the direction his thinking was taking at this point. Quite beyond Buber's particular relationships, the existential subject "before transcendence" is now "responsible for all men, and shares their guilt." The manuscript breaks off with a reference to the *Brothers Karamazov*, and, in recalling that "we are each of us guilty before all and I more than the rest," we cannot help but think of the philosopher whose favorite ethical maxim it is, Emmanuel Levinas.

We now distinguish between three types of guilt, legal, moral, and religious (sin). The last two are not clearly distinguished, and the relation of the three to each other is generally left unclear. It is very seldom that these three types are all recognized in a meaningful pattern. Usually moralists dismiss sin as a purely authoritarian religious conception, and theologians dismiss moral guilt as a more secularized version of sin.

What is guilt in general? It is failure to do something for which I am responsible to an authority of some kind, and which I could have done. As long as I am simply responding to stimuli, I am not capable of guilt. I must be responsible, that is, take over my situation, all my environment and my responses, and place them in an ordered world of meaning. In such a world I can become guilty in various ways, that is, by failing to do what I am responsible for to something or to someone.

Criticism of legal and social theories of responsibility and guilt. This is certainly a level of human behavior, but it cannot be generalized. If so, bad confusions and mistakes occur. Nevertheless the accepted theory and vocabulary of guilt is largely taken from this field. Every individual belongs to a society. In belonging to it, he must accept its authorities and norms, which make cooperative action possible. Thus the child is responsible to his parents for the performance of certain works or things to do (duties). If he fails to perform them, he is held responsible by this external authority and punished by certain sanctions. Similarly, every citizen of a state is responsible to the state for certain duties, paying the taxes and obeying the laws of the community. If he fails, he is guilty, and is punished. In this case, he is not himself guilty, in the sense that he is himself wrong or depraved in the totality of his being and his world. He has no world of his own in this context. He is guilty only in the sense that he has caused a wrong product, an evil work for which he is responsible, i.e., the cause. In this context, the word "responsible" has come to mean merely being the cause of. Thus we say x was the guilty party. He went to sleep at the wheel and ran into the child at the side of the road. In this case, he is not himself to blame. He is rather to blame because of the work that he did, or failed to do; he is to blame for the effect that he caused.

When this social level of behavior is generalized, then these objective concepts gain a universal range. Responsibility is identified merely with being the cause of, and guilt with being the cause of anti-social or harmful work. Furthermore, all authority is identified with external authority, and the scope of human freedom is gravely reduced. All men are put into the position of children under some external authority or control, and responsibility is reduced to the level of obeying external commands. Guilt is reduced to disobedience. The person himself in his entirety together with his whole world of meaning is neither responsible nor guilty. Social change is evil and revolutionaries are always wrong. The notion of being responsible to oneself, personal freedom, is absent. This level of behavior is certainly existent, and this kind of legal thinking has its legitimate place. We can say, on the whole, that laws that tend to the welfare of all mankind, and to the preservation and realization of man are justified. Works that are done in accordance with law to achieve self-realization are good and deserve to be praised. Those that do not are evil, and should be blamed and, if necessary, deterred by sanctions. This is the field of natural law thinking, and it certainly has its place. There are adequate and inadequate modes of legal philosophy and legislation. But when generalized, this mode of approach fails to recognize the freedom of the individual person, and his wider range of responsibility and guilt.

For moralistic philosophers another type of behavior has been the object of attention. This is the free action of the individual person existing in a free society where individual freedom is respected. Heidegger is a moralistic philosopher of this kind, and he has given so far the profoundest analysis of the free existence of the individual person.

Heidegger's view, while existentially profound, and far surpassing past moralistic treatises in subtlety and depth is nevertheless deficient for the following reasons. In the first place, there is no adequate treatment of legal and social guilt. One gets the impression from *Sein und Zeit* that the whole social realm is anonymous, impersonal (*das man*) and therefore unauthentic. There is no consideration of the early guilt-feelings of the child, nor of the breaking of laws. This may not be the most basic type of guilt. But it exists, and certainly has some importance. In the second place, there is no discussion of the difference between authentic as over against pathological guilt. After reading Heidegger's discussion, one gets the feeling that every human guilt feeling is authentic, and that to avoid it or to get beyond it is always a matter of pathological forgetting, philistinism. But surely a distinction must be made between unfounded, imaginary guilt and authentic guilt. Third, there is no consideration of transcendence. So far as Heidegger is concerned, one is guilty only before oneself. This is no doubt an important type. But surely there are deep and poignant manifestations of guilt to someone else or to something else outside of me to whom I am responsible, and who brings me to feel guilty. This is absent from Heidegger's moralistic discussion. Finally, fourth, there is no consideration of expiation, forgiveness, and repentance that, at least, should be examined as possible ways of overcoming guilt. The absence of any treatment of these phenomena gives the whole discussion its unduly somber and pessimistic tone.

Religious guilt is called sin, and is usually interpreted as breaking the commands of a supreme judge or lawgiver. But usually in such discussion not enough attention is paid to legal and personal guilt, which leads to serious confusions and mistakes. Sometimes in theological discussions, sin is regarded as simply replacing guilt with no remainder, since the latter is conceived merely as a secularized version of sin. But this is false to the phenomenon, for at least, in its purer forms, the sense of sin involves not only condemnation by the divine power but also a sense of personal responsibility and guilt. When this is not recognized, another serious confusion is likely. Sin is reduced to a special form of legalistic guilt. The sinner is thought of as being responsible to a supreme lawgiver in the same way that a citizen is responsible to the laws of his state and its supreme authority. The only difference is that the one authority is finite whereas the other is omnipotent and omniscient. But this is subject to many objections. It reduces the phenomenon of sin, and unduly restricts the freedom of the religious agent. It plays into the hands of dogmatism and authoritarianism. It leads to the view that religion can directly take over social forms and institutions without having any access to the free individual person. (Cf. *Human Freedom and Social Order.*)

Since these interpretations are inadequate, let us now see if we can work out one that is less inadequate. We shall connect guilt with responsibility on the ground that a guilty act is always one for which the agent is responsible. It is also true that one cannot be responsible without running the risk of falling into guilt. Hence each of these meanings involves the other. So we shall think of guilt as an irresponsible action or thought, and shall begin our analysis with a brief examination of the concept of responsibility.

We may summarize this examination by saying that responsibility involves getting a distance from the situations into which we are thrown, and then working out a way of life, or a course of action, which will not only do justice to the facts but will also make sense to the agent. A responsible act (or thought) will then be one that is able to take over the whole situation, and to lift it up into this free world of meaning. An irresponsible act (or thought) is one which either slips back to the level of a mere blind response, as in the case of childish guilt, or which fails to take over a situation in such a way as to give it meaning. (This may be broken down into two subordinate types. In the first, which is less serious, the meaning is adequate but the act is deficient. The agent knows what he should do, but fails to do it. In the second, which is more serious, the agent does what he means to do. But since both the meaning and the act are deficient, the situation fails to be taken over.) As we have suggested, meanings may be deficient in two ways. Either they fail to do justice to the facts, and are therefore, out of the key with the situation, or they are in touch with the given facts but fail to bring them into a unified pattern of meaning which exerts a genuine appeal. For these several types of action we are both responsible and guilty. We have acted in a meaningless and irresponsible manner for which we are responsible. Let us now examine the three different levels of responsibility and guilt to which we have just referred.

At the first level, the child is responsible for certain duties to an external, human authority. The citizen and, indeed, the member of any corporate institution, like a university or a business company, is responsible in the same way to his institution for the production of certain works. If he fails in this, he is guilty in the eyes of the authority and is punished. Here the world of meaning is already in existence, and the child, or the citizen, is not responsible for thinking through on his own. He is understanding of its norms and what they require him to do. Those who set up the institution in the first place and who govern it are responsible for maintaining the institution, which includes keeping its structure of meaning intact, and presenting this structure in an appealing way. If they fail, they become irresponsible and guilty.

Such guilt is on both sides inevitable. The native equipment of the child makes it impossible for him to take over the imperfect meanings and duties imposed on him without infractions and irregular responses that ring down punishments on his head. Hence the sense of infantile guilt (which is universal in almost all human cultures) [cf. Freud]. But the institutional authority is also guilty, for its structure of meaning is imperfect, that is, it fails to take account of all the facts, and is administered arbitrarily and often tyrannically with insufficient appeal. This social guilt may be reduced by intelligence and tact. But it can never be entirely eliminated.

When the child is able to choose for himself, he then becomes responsible for ordering a world and a way of life that will give meaning to the situation into which he has been thrown. Here also guilt is inevitable, as can be shown in one way by referring to the dialectic of freedom and order, both of which are essential to authentic human existence. If he simply accepts things as they are and fails to choose, this is a deficient mode of choice that leaves him guilty. He is supporting an established order that always involves certain injustices, as well as the suppression of freedom. On the other hand, if he chooses to choose, and to work out an independent way of his own, he will be working to destroy an existing order that, though imperfect, gives sense to many lives, and thus to bring forth new injustices. Freedom and order are both necessary for the human living of life. Yet in the imperfect manifestations that are open to us and that have appeared in history, one cannot be achieved without suppressing the other. So in either case, whatever we do, we are guilty, and our consciences tell us so.

We may fail to listen, or try to escape from this conscience. But this does not make us any the less guilty before ourselves in our moments of lucidity. It only increases our guilt. If we listen to our conscience, it tells us we are guilty; take over this guilt; become what we really are! This, in truth, is the way of freedom and responsibility. There is no use pretending against oneself. To overcome our guilt and to struggle against it, we must ourselves become guilty. This becoming guilty is a free act that may be avoided by flight and suppression. Thus there are two levels of guilt: one into which we necessarily fall, whether or not we choose, and another by which we become guilty by a free act of taking it over. Hence those who say that guilt is necessary and those who say that it is relative to choice are both right.

Each of these views, when isolated against the other, dilutes and finally destroys the sense of guilt. Thus when we hear that we are guilty from the very beginning, that all are equally guilty, and that we remain so whatever we do, any further effort would seem useless. And without any possibility of taking it over, this is true. All that is left is the making of further blind responses that only involve us more deeply in the same morass. If we simply confine ourselves to an analysis of the world into which we have been thrown, without recognizing that it is a free world with a future, struggle becomes meaningless. Furthermore, a guilt without responsibility would seem to lose its meaning. If this merely belongs to the human condition to which we have all equally been condemned, why should anyone take it seriously? This is associated with rigid theories of determinism and predestination that have no place for futurity and freedom. In such theories, guilt itself loses its meaning.

But the same is true of relativistic interpretations that pay no attention to what we may call original guilt. Here it loses all ground in the factual past and present. It is reduced to arbitrary decisions and interpretations that are relative to the "morbid" predilections of particular groups and individuals. Every conception of guilt is false to the facts and unauthentic. It is a pathological manifestation and should be removed, if possible, by objective reflection that never finds guilt in the observable facts, or by therapeutic treatment. Theories of this kind are also associated with psychological determinism. They fail to take account of the universality of the sense of guilt that is found everywhere among all tribes and peoples, and of the very existence of the *Lebenswelt* as a world of freedom.

Like responsibility itself with which it is essentially involved, guilt involves both of these factors together. On the one hand, there is a necessary guilt that belongs to the factual situation into which we have been thrown. This is not necessary, in the sense that it could not have been otherwise-absolute necessity (logical and apodictic necessity). It is necessary in the existential sense of facticity—this is as I am and have to be—this is just so, with a shrug of the shoulders. The situation I am in, and I myself am guilty; that is, I myself and my way of life are not meaningful. Either they are not in accord with the facts of the situation, or they do not make sense. And yet at the same time I have been, and now am able to respond. I am responsible. So I simply am guilty here and now in the world where I am. This is so whether or not I recognize it, for I am factually and existentially responsible, whether I like it or not.

I have been thrown into the world as a responsible being. This belongs to my thrown facticity, as does my guilt. Therefore I am called upon by a call that is bound up with my factual existence to take over the situation, including the guilt, and to lift it up into a world of meaning. It is my conscience that is calling me out of my real possibilities in the future where I really am, to take over the guilt and the meaningless which I have been, and to become what I really am. I may forget this call and suppress it. Or I may listen and decide. This is a free choice that is in no sense compelled. But neither is it arbitrary or subjective. It is founded on the necessary facticity of my existence. Guilt is neither an irredeemable necessity, nor an arbitrary relative choice. It is a choice to take over a world without meaning—the eruption of freedom and responsibility into regions of casual sequence and necessary response.

As over against the level of social and legal responsibility previously discussed, this level is restricted to the individual person. Only the person is capable of a pure responsibility of this kind. By taking over his guilt, i.e., himself and the whole meaningless world into which he has been thrown, the individual person becomes responsible to himself for himself and the world in which he lives. Here responsibility becomes complete and self-enclosed. This is never true of group action. Here an officer is responsible to his superiors, and they are responsible to the legislative authority, which is responsible to the people, etc. At this level, the emphasis is on action rather than on meaning, for the public world of ordinary language is accepted as it is given and never questioned (cf. *Human Freedom and Social Order*). In this frame, the individual never becomes responsible for the whole of himself and his world. He is responsible to some human authority outside himself for the production of a work, a function, or a task. He does not ask; he works. He is judged as a person only in terms of these works. Hence as we have said, he is not himself wholly guilty, but only in a qualified sense. He is guilty of such and such a failure, or guilty because of failing to do this or that. He himself and his whole world are never at stake. He is thinking and acting within an established frame.

Free, personal action is human responsibility pushed to a higher point. Here, as we have said, I am responsible to myself for myself and the world into which I exist. The emphasis now is not exclusively on action but on meaning as well. Here I become responsible not only for my deeds but also for my thoughts. Here I sin not only through my will but through my mind (cf. the New Testament). Most Western ethics, including utilitarianism, has been concerned primarily with social action and self-realization. As over against this, there is much truth in the intentional ethics of the Kantian tradition which holds us responsible for our intentional irrespective of their actual results. But these intentions are not mere subjective thoughts contained within the mind of the subject. They constitute a whole world of meaning which is the actual horizon of everything we say and do. The free individual can become responsible for this world of meaning, by either accepting as it stands, or by reconstituting it in his own way on his own. If he does not make sense out of his existence, then he is responsible to himself and guilty before his conscience. Such a responsible person does not merely perform works and functions which are subject to social judgment. He takes over these works and places them in a life-world for which he is now responsible. He now thinks through and acts out his version of the existence not in any accepted frame that is taken for granted, but in the world itself, which transcends and human version. Before transcendence both he himself and his version of the world are now at stake. Once this level of responsibility has been attained it can never be eliminated except by as self-imposed slavery.

But now let us ask: What is the issue of this struggle to become responsible and to make sense of our history? Has it succeeded or has it failed? After the excesses of the nineteenth century, there are few who will try to defend the notion of constant progress. On the other hand, it would be futile to deny, it seems to me, that the experiment of what we rightly call advanced civilizations in encouraging personal freedom is justified. This experiment has given us technical control over nature, extraordinary individuals capable of heroic and sacrificial action, and, in the arts, flashes of revealing insight and worlds of meaning that here and there achieve lasting truth. That these gifts are not to be rightly scorned is shown by the fact that many primitive and underdeveloped societies are now actively seeking for them. This experiment has not been an abject failure. Responsible men can do something in struggling to overcome their guilt. But in an age of mass conformity and tyranny when the cultures in which some remnant of freedom has been preserved are pervaded by a sense of the meaningless of life, it would be fatuous to judge this experiment as an unqualified success. The history of human thought is pervaded by dialectical tensions which reveal a basic instability and imperfection in any system of human meaning. We have already mentioned the dialectic of freedom and order which will never be resolved in purely human terms, and which points beyond to something further. We may now mention another, which we have already suggested, between fact and meaning, and which is even more basic. Structures of meaning which do some justice to the known facts, like unified systems of science, fail to take account of our human aspirations for freedom and justice, etc. On the other hand, idealistic systems, which make sense to us, are not in accord with the known facts. There is a basic tension between the is and the ought that man, himself, by his own efforts, will never overcome. The brute given is pervaded by an opaqueness and mystery which resists every responsible effort to take it over, and to give it sense. In the end, man cannot become the responsible being he is. The last word man must pronounce on his own efforts before himself is: I am guilty. But this is not the end.

The dialectical tensions to which we have referred point beyond to something transcendent. They are not proofs; they are suggestions, indications. It is only by recognizing the absolute transcendence to which they point that we can finally make a certain sense out of our existence. But there is always the possibility that it is ultimately meaningless and absurd. This cannot be disproved or abruptly ushered off the scene. It remains as a real possibility that must be taken over and recognized by all responsible agents. The recognition of transcendence is a free choice that, like any free act, involves fundamental and inescapable risk. As Kierkegaard pointed out, it opens up a new way of existing to those who make this choice. But as he also indicated, it cannot replace the other modes which lead up to it. This choice must be made by a responsible person in a responsible way and, as we have shown, this means a taking over of the actual situation exactly as it was. Hence after making this choice to transcendence, the free person remains responsible for himself and his version of the world to himself. He also remains guilty before himself. The whole situation of self-responsibility is taken over intact. But it is now reinterpreted and lifted up into a new world of meaning much broader and more mysterious than that which preceded it.

If this does not happen, if personal responsibility is abandoned, instead of advancing into a new level of responsible existence, we have merely slipped back into the level of external authority and irresponsibility. Religion then becomes, as it has been for the most part in our history, an imperial form of social control, a reinforcement of the status quo by a few new mysteries and threats. If it is not this, the personal responsibility for the self and his world to the self must remain intact. This means that the term "transcendence" must be taken seriously, and must not be merged with any anthropomorphic or human elements. The slightest admixture of these will compromise religious existence.

Transcendence is beyond all meaning and being which are only the broadest of human concepts. I is the fascinating and tremendous, beyond all human morality which Otto describes in this first part of his book *The Idea of the Holy*. It is not any absolute whole which can take the finite up into itself. Any form of pantheism or panentheism, even that of Spinoza, makes too many concessions to anthropomorphism. At their worst they end in a sentimental absolutizing of human ideals. It is not a philosophical absolute of any kind. As Pascal saw, these are only pale, theoretical reflections of transcendence in the mind of man. They are fixed and frozen versions of the living God, which quenches the fire of its living presence in us, and conceals its creative lure. This transcendence is not pure being. It leads us ever beyond. It is not a first cause that produces finite things analogically like itself. It creates only beings that are radically different. It is not a transcending substance possessing entitative and voluntary attributes in which we can participate in various degrees. We cannot participate in it at all, at least in the Greek sense of participation. Indeed, this whole conception of participation needs to be rethought.

We participate in this transcendence not by accepting any fixed articles of faith but by creative love and trust, not by copying divine meanings that are already present in the facts but by a creative finding of meaning, not by the realization of a given nature but by our free existence. It is by a free decision that must be constantly repeated that we may communicate with this transcendent life which remains wholly other, as in the case of a trusted friend whom we know and wish to be wholly different from ourselves. We share in life not so much through what we think as how we think it, not so much through what we do as how we do it. Transcendence is a purely free and creative unity that is beyond all orders and systems and syntheses. There are always only a one-in-many and never purely one. These are human necessities. So these are left to us. Every one of them is finite, imperfect, and unstable. But if we establish them and ourselves in them with a touch of skepticism, and with a profound sense of what lies beyond all of them, in this way of thinking and existing, we may be touched by the divine. But this comes to us in the acts of existing, not in any of its fixed results. Responsibility is the human ability always to give a further meaningful answer, no matter what has been done or said. It is the endless capacity for self-transcendence which is the image of God in man.

The sense of the absolutely transcendent to which this capacity leads opens up a new way of existing and a new type of responsibility beyond both the legal and the personal. All known cultures, even the most primitive, have been touched by this, including our own. Just as the responsible person takes over his social tasks and duties intact, performing them scrupulously in the new world of meaning where they have been placed, so the devoted person takes over his self-responsibility intact, and goes on freely acting and freely ordering his version of meaning in the wider version of the world where they have now been placed. But this will lead to a different way of existing which now bears a different sense. We can here only briefly consider some of the most significant of these differences.

In the first place, he will become responsible for maintaining the search for further meaning, now lured on by transcendence. He will recognize that the world is not absurd; it is rather a mystery and that while these two phenomena are superficially similar, they are nevertheless radically distinct. This does not mean, however, that he will never fall into despair, and the deepest level of guilt. *Corruptio melioris pejor*, as the ancient saying has it. Furthermore, the range of his responsibility has now been vastly extended. He is now not only responsible to himself for his own version of the world. He is responsible before transcendence for making some sense out of the world itself. Hence before transcendence he becomes responsible for all men, and shares their guilt. As Fr. Zossima says in the *Brothers Karamazov*:

1. Repentance
2. Sacrifice
3. Creativity
4. Forgiveness
5. Caritas

Part IV

New Directions,
A Philosopher at Work:
Toward a Phenomenology
of the Other

11

The Rights of the Other as Other

EXPLANATORY NOTE

The two essays included here, "The Rights of the Other as Other" and "The Other Person: Some Phenomenological Reflections," form a suitable introduction to Wild's masterful commentary on *Totality and Infinity* that we have entitled "Speaking Philosophy." The first, "The Rights of the Other as Other," appears to date from 1967–1968, amid the continuing turmoil in the civil rights movement in the United States. However, it also bears the trace of Wild's earlier concern with a philosophy adequate to describe and explain a basis for human rights. Here it is important for the reader to keep in mind that Wild had, in his Realistic period, been an ardent defender of the doctrine of inherent right. Wild's defense of the doctrine of inherent right had an applied dimension as well. His reference to the United Nations Charter on Human Rights is especially noteworthy. A former student and colleague of his, Dr. Charles Malik, had been a member of the American Realistic Association founded by Wild and, furthermore, had gone on to draft the U.N. Charter on Human Rights.

Wild's turn toward existential phenomenology is accompanied by a change in language and emphasis. For example, he speaks of existential right as opposed to natural right. In fact, Wild is somewhat critical of what he regards to be the overly formalistic character of the U.N. Charter on Human Rights. He argues that it does not do full justice to the variety of human societies and cultures and suffers, therefore, from a certain societal egocentrism. Wild argues that human rights and obligations must be viewed in a more embodied manner and in a way that is more open to "the rights of the other as other."

In order to achieve this objective, Wild now believes that we must become more aware of the claims that arise concerning human rights from

159

different cultures and societies. The only way to do this is by beginning with the other rather than the self. He is preoccupied with demonstrating the importance of the other and otherness. William E. Kaufman has correctly observed that Wild's concern with the other is more a matter of emphasizing and focusing on a subject that has been with him throughout his philosophical career (John Wild, *From Realism to Phenomenology*, 168). As Wild says, "In serious ethical dialogue, we must remember the otherness even in the similarities of the other person to myself." He reflects on the universality of language and its normative implications. Wild stresses that the phenomenon of difference does not arise from the concept of "same." On the contrary, he argues that, "Group egocentrism is not a problem addressed by natural right theory." Wild states that, "Ethics arise when I confront the other with his divergent meanings and claims." He believes that this might help to explain the great difficulty of coming to grips with the increasing turmoil and dissatisfaction experienced by minority groups in the United States. In other words, such restlessness and upheaval may very well derive, as Wild puts it, "from overlooking the otherness of the other." He emphasizes the importance of the face-to-face relation and the phenomenon of expression that precedes thematic discourse. For example, "The gaze of the other does not arise from the alter-ego." He specifically credits an essay by William James, "On a Certain Blindness in Human Beings," with opening the door for further exploration on this subject.

While he does not mention Emmanuel Levinas specifically by name in the first essay, he does make some points that appear to indicate that he was already familiar with Levinas's great work *Totality and Infinity*, to which he would author the introduction to the English edition published in 1969. For example, his remarks on the face-to-face and expression in particular appear to bear the influence of Levinas. He says about expression something very close to what Levinas himself says: "The expression is what expresses." In other words expression is not reducible to the level of meaning and may, in fact, found the origin of meaning itself. Furthermore, Wild argues that at the ethical level there is a very close relation between justification and explanation. He concludes his reflection, perhaps in anticipation, of a criticism that can be leveled at Levinas by distinguishing between "open-systems" and "closed-systems" of explanation. For Levinas, it appears that all systems must be considered closed.

I shall try to reflect with you this afternoon about the nature of man, the various declarations of human rights, especially in France and the United States, which have played such a prominent role in our modern history, and finally about the United Nations Declaration of Human Rights accepted by a majority of the member nations in 1948, though the United

States and Russia abstained. It is very fitting, I believe, that a period has been set aside for serious reflections on the nature of man, the notion of human rights, and the various ethical issues in which this conception involves us. So I am very glad to be here this afternoon to speak to you about these issues—especially about a certain misinterpretation of the notion of human rights, which is rather widespread, and about a missing conception which, I think, needs to be clarified and reemphasized.

Now first of all, on the positive side, let us turn to the American Bill of Rights and the corresponding attitudes embodied in the British and French traditions. These are basically concerned with the weak and fragile human individual. First, they try to protect him in his weakness against the paralyzing effects of uncontrolled group power, against arbitrary arrest, seizure, and torture. Then, in an affirmative way, they aim at fostering and promoting the free and responsible activities of thinking and choosing, which he alone can perform. If in his weakness, his opinions are indoctrinated and manipulated by alien forces much stronger than himself, he will lose his autonomy and the system will break down. Hence, the basic need for the Bill of Rights.

In the United Nations Declaration, these rights of the individual are further extended. He has a right to domicile in a country where he may be supported by the powers of a full community, so that he may live his own life and pursue his own projects without arbitrary deprivation or restraint. He has a right, furthermore, to periods of rest and leisure, and to adequate medical care to protect him in his weakness against the constant dangers of physical breakdown. Finally, since he is born in abysmal ignorance, he has the right, not specifically recognized in the American Constitution, to an education, so that he may learn to think and to choose responsibly without avoidable impediments.

From these articles and declarations, we may certainly infer that a primary concern for the peculiar powers and dignity of the fragile and ephemeral human individual belongs essentially to the meaning of democracy in our time. But if we now turn to certain specific ways in which the notion of human rights has been interpreted, especially in our own Western tradition, some basic questions need to be raised. In the central portion of this paper I shall raise these questions, and attempt to show that a certain conception has been missing, and that this neglect has brought forth certain misconceptions. At the end I shall try to suggest an approach through which they might be corrected.

Like others concerned with racial problems in America, I have been moved by the remarkable transformation that has occurred in the so-called civil rights movement of the recent past. In the early days, liberals in the North and in the South were inspired by the traditional ideals of the rights of man that we have been considering. Because of poverty and racial discrimination, a black minority had been deprived of its rights, which should be restored.

But this picture has now almost completely broken down. The earlier enthusiasm for civil rights seems to have largely faded away, and the phrase at present seems to suggest abstract and legalistic aspects of prevailing institutions, rather than anything close to the roots of the struggle now going on. Why did the notion of civil rights and the "rights of man" tradition break down in the case of this living movement of our time? What is missing in this great tradition which made it seem to be finally abstract, and even irrelevant, in a vital struggle of our time? As I thought about this question, I went over the various historical objections to the theory of human rights with which I was familiar. Some of these traditional objections seemed relevant to the theory of rights as it stands today. But other new objections, and a new center of focus occurred to me as I thought of our present situation. Let us now turn to certain objections.

In the first place, there is a basic objection to the priority assigned to rights over duties in the "rights of man" tradition. Why does it not refer to the obligations of man instead of the rights of man, since the two are correlative, or to the obligations and rights of man? There is no doubt that the term "right" has a greater appeal than the term "duty," which no doubt explains the selection of the former. But what is the reason for this appeal? A right is a moral claim made by a conscious self on other selves for something that will satisfy a felt need of some kind. Thus, a child has a right to food for the satisfaction of his natural (normal) hunger. On the other hand, an obligation is felt by me as an urge to satisfy an alien claim, which usually involves some sacrifice. Hence, duties are felt primarily as a burden, while rights are originally felt as derived from self-interest and as leading to self-satisfaction. Hence, the choice of the term "rights" over "duties" is connected with self-interest. Let me now develop this thought by a further consideration.

We may notice also that a right depends on a need or felt lack of something required for the realization of some legitimate tendency in the active agent. It thus has a subjective origin, and proceeds from an inner felt lack of the object that will fulfill it or satisfy it. An obligation, on the other hand, proceeds from an opposite direction. It is imposed on the individual subject from something external that makes a claim upon him. Even when my conscience imposes an obligation on myself, this comes from an ideal self that is divided from, or other than, my present condition. But rights come from felt needs and self-interest.

A second objection can be made against the indiscriminant use of abstract universals, and the resulting tendency to emphasize human similarities and to slur over differences, which has been so characteristic of this school of thought. Thus, in spite of the different cultures in which they have lived, and the historical intervals separating these cultures, all human individuals are said to share in the same human nature. In spite of certain similarities which may justify such statements in a carefully restricted sense, they ignore certain basic differences which are always ethically relevant. We need to recognize now that the great mediaeval controversy over universals ended in nominalism. In serious ethical dialogue, we must remember the otherness that is found even in the similarities of the other person to myself. As an individual, he is unique, and exists always in a situation different from my own. In so far as he has made choices in such situations, they have been different from mine. In so far as he has thought for himself, the order of the world in which he lives is different, and even the similar words that he uses will have diverse shades of meaning and fringes.

We must also remember that though we cannot speak without using universal terms, they cover not only all past, actual examples, but all future ones as well. Thus, when I use the term "man," it covers not only all past individuals, but all future possible men as well. Thus, there is a normative element in our use of such terms by which we express our different hopes, fears, and aspirations (these differences affect the meanings of universal terms, which we think of as the same). The philosophy of natural law and the rights of man has seen many similarities in the diverse, but it has often neglected the basically divergent in what it has called the same.

We are thus led towards a point of view which minimizes the factor of otherness in human experience. Each member of the community is regarded as an isolated self, a center of similar needs and rights. Now, insofar as the emphasis is placed on rights over against duties, these claims are not mutual. It is not that I myself, or the group with which I identify, is making certain claims on another person and a group with which he identifies, and that he, from his divergent point of view, is making different claims on me. This would involve us at once in the confused and difficult problems of ethics, for ethics arise when I confront the other with his divergent meanings and claims.

The natural rights way of thinking tends to avoid this reciprocal situation. It leaves us with a set of claims that are basically similar. Everyone has these abstract rights, and expects them to be satisfied, not necessarily by this person or group that is confronted in the concrete, but by something that is highly impersonal—the economic system, the welfare state, or the community conceived as something quite distinct from the concrete individuals making it up. Many individuals are forced by economic pressure to work in the system and to contribute, thereby, to the goods and services it provides.

This leads to a third objection that can be raised and has been raised against the human rights conception, its tendency to crystallize into an ego-centric drift. We seem to be dominated not by individual tyrants—elections might get rid of them—but rather by a vast scientific and technological system that is drifting, without adequate human control, into a serious waste of life and resources, towards, finally, ultimate self-destruction. Why is this now happening?

The human individual is of course a creature of habit and there is always a tendency for his responses to congeal into routine reactions, which proceed automatically without clear conscious control. Now, the self that I already am is readily identified with these congealed patterns of thought and action. It is through dialogue with the other that I am aroused from my lethargy, self-consciousness is awakened, and I am aroused from my dogmatic and egocentric slumber. In large groups of individuals who share similar thoughts and needs, the tendency to identify with prevailing customs and institutions is greatly strengthened. The interest in self-preservation and self-satisfaction become national policy to maintain and expand the nation and its institutions as they already are. Individual rights, when thus reinforced, become national rights and national interests, and work against needed growth and change. This form of group egocentrism is now known as nationalism, and has become an increasingly dominant force in our present-day world (apparently not diminished by the rights of man tradition).

I have no time to dwell here on this special topic, but it must be noted that this new form of social egocentric drift became highly accentuated at the time of the American and French Revolutions, which were both motivated by the modern conception of human rights. As we might expect, the egocentric interpretation of individual rights has brought forth the socio-centric notion of national rights, and the drift of nationalism has not decreased. The principle of self-preference which underlies the utilitarian ethic privileges for the self as it already is, and loyalty to the interest of the institution, means loyalty to this institution as it already is, no matter how anachronistic this condition may be. Egocentrism leads to unconscious drift, and in the case of customary group organizations, these forces of social drift are very strong.

In order to change such power systems, a show of force, or the threat of force, is necessary. This is why sit-ins, boycotts, demonstrations, strikes, and picketing, for a long time regarded as illegal in democratic nations, have now become legalized and accepted as a legitimate part of the democratic process. The liberal tradition has not seen that there are factors constantly at work in human history that are other than the conscious intentions of large groups and even of majorities. Voting is not enough. The notion that the basic needs of all individuals are similar does not foster recognition of the peculiar needs of minority groups. It also makes it difficult to find serious fault with a growing national technological system that has already raised the general standard of living, and is now satisfying certain vital needs of man more fully than ever before. Utilitarian philosophy is basically egocentric. Hence, it has never been overly sensitive to the distinctive needs of special groups. They are outbalanced by those of the majority.

The other loses his uniqueness, and is absorbed into an encompassing egocentric system which is everywhere and nowhere, but always essentially the same. This system is becoming increasingly mechanized and efficient, and satisfies the vital needs and rights of the majority as this majority wishes. Concessions are constantly made to voting procedure, but whoever is elected, the system goes on, and ever more effectively dominates public life and thought. Its ideology does not have to be overtly spelled out and defended. Hence, it has been seriously argued that the day of ideologies is over. But without open explanation, this ideology pervades every field of technical endeavor, and is ingrained in the very facts of life.

If put into words, it might be stated as follows: It, the system in general, is sound and good. It is constantly growing in productive efficiency, and is, therefore, satisfying more effectively the basic rights of man. The standard of living and the life expectation of the majority have been raised. Hence, the system is supported by a majority in free elections, and protected by freedom of thought, freedom of speech and the other provisions of the Bill of Rights. All this is morally sound and rational. If any of these statements is questioned, a positive answer can be found in statistical facts. The system verifies itself as it goes along.

At a time of positive scientific thinking, when reference to the facts is supposed to give us the answer to all soluble questions, it is extremely difficult for others to challenge this ruling point of view by cogent argument. Any other alternative is bound to seem odd, and metaphysical, and out of line with the existing facts. And yet the nation is torn by violent dissension on the part of minority groups, rebellion on the part of large sections of the youth, and widespread fear and dissatisfaction with present conditions. Why is this happening? What misunderstanding, what mistaken shade of emphasis, has crept into our conception of our human rights?

So far I have shown how the doctrine of human rights can be taken in an egocentric manner with the view of others as similar to the self, and with the absorption of the other into an encompassing system that is everywhere self-same. Can it be that in these prevalent misinterpretations we have slurred over the otherness of the other in trying mistakenly to assimilate him into the system of the self or a majority of selves? Have we forgotten the right of the other to be other, and confused it with my right to be myself? [By responding to these questions] we may bring out a neglected, but essential aspect of the Declaration of Human Rights.

It is his actual or possible questions I am trying to answer; it is before him that I am trying to justify myself. Now I can think for myself and make choices. It is because of these capacities that I need protection and encouragement. But whether I am acting on behalf of a group, or for myself, this freedom is originally flawed by imperfection. Since I have grown out of a particular culture, I have been conditioned in certain ways. Hence, my outlook will be biased. Since the world in which I live has been organized around my own projects or those of my people, my outlook will be egocentric. When opened to the critical thought of the other, these flaws of special bias and egocentrism are apt to be revealed. It is in living dialogue with the other that my errors are brought into the light and possibly corrected. Our serious thinking is always done before an Other of this kind, who may be physically present or absent. But he is always lurking in the vicinity. Every monologue, no matter how lengthy it may be (ten volumes!), is an interrupted dialogue. Every system is an attempted escape from such personal bias, a justification of myself before the other.

Now the system of rights and obligations is a system of this kind. Protecting all individuals equally in their weakness from hunger, sickness, and seizure; and assuring to all men, including myself, the possibility to assemble, speak freely and engage in dialogue with others; is to escape, at least in thought, from special bias and egocentricity. But surely, you may say, this system comes from reason. How else is personal bias to be eliminated? How else is justice to be achieved? Are you telling us not to think? Are you saying we should not think?

I am not saying this, nor am I denying that the system of rights and obligations has expressed a lofty ideal, and that it still may be performing a worthy instrumental function. But something is missing—the ethical! What are these rights and obligations ultimately ordered to? What are they for? Let us suppose some small area where all the rights mentioned in the United Nations Declaration are realized. All the children have food and medical care. There is a guaranteed minimal income to assure comforts for all, though the lives of most inhabitants are largely meaningless. The U.N. right to education is achieved. But no one knows why he is educating, nor what he is being educated for, aside from the further proliferation of machines, and greater technological proficiency. Freedom of speech and the press is enjoyed by all the public media. But nothing of importance is said. No basic questions are raised. These media, subject to what are called "stabilizing pressures," censor themselves, though official censorship is publicly abhorred. Open authority and domination are also out of the question. But, in fact, everything is dominated by the pressures of the technological system and its ingrained values, as it drifts on towards further waste and violence. One may, of course, say that with a Bill of Rights still in force there is always the chance of something happening that is novel and creative. But suppose that, as technology advances and habits grow firmer, this chance grows even more remote, as, in fact, everything is increasingly dominated by "the drift." All our human rights, that is, possibilities for freedom, would be present. But would this in fact be a free community? Or one of slaves?

We should not confuse the realization of rights with the achievement of individual freedom or of a free world. We should regard it as the removal of certain obstacles to responsible thought and action. But to remove the obstacles is not to attain the goal. To suppose that it is, as Marxist critics have shown, is apt to be a mere disguise for the uncontrolled drift of dominating forces.

Let me conclude, then, by contrasting two different ways of interpreting human rights with which I have been concerned in this paper—first the self-centered way, as I shall call it, and then the other-directed, non-systematic way.

The self-centered way starts from the point of view of the person who possesses, or receives, the rights rather than that of him who recognizes, or actively bestows, them. It therefore stresses rights rather than obligations and responsibilities in accordance with those usages, which speak of "having my rights," "asserting my rights," "claiming my rights," "enjoying my rights," "violating my rights," or "losing my rights." This egocentric way of reflection thinks of a right as an actual entity or property of some kind possessed by the infant or person having the right. In order to justify the fair treatment of all men, it prepares elaborate and dubious arguments to show that all individuals have such value properties in equal degrees in order to deserve beneficent treatment. This treatment is exclusively concerned with the satisfaction of felt lacks or need in the individual subject. It is good to maximize the satisfaction of these needs, and the recognition of human rights can, therefore, be justified on utilitarian grounds. To satisfy the common needs of men will reduce the risk of rebelling and lead to social stability. Openness to change and freedom are justified in so far as they lead to a more effective satisfaction of human needs. They have no intrinsic value of their own. The other person is an alter ego with needs and lacks like my own. This is an egocentric system.

The other-directed interpretation, on the other hand, starts from the position of the person or community, which actively recognizes and bestows the rights on others. It stresses obligation and responsibilities rather than rights already possessed, in accordance with those usages, which speak of the giving, granting, bestowing of rights, and even of the creating and working out of new rights. We have briefly tried to describe what we go through when we meet the other person, the stranger, face to face, and with him also the basic problems of ethics. Am I ready to give something of myself and my world to him in the form of words? Or shall I ignore him and pass him by? The community in which a negative answer tends to be given becomes enclosed within itself, a closed society. That in which a generous affirmative answer is given tends to become open. Now the other-directed interpretation regards the granting of rights and privileges as a further development of this original act of generosity, which underlies all unrestricted dialogue and social life. Rights are regarded not as actual properties or worths residing in the individuals possessing them, but rather as opportunities (possibilities) for further growth towards something not now actual, but other than what is. Hence, the notion of an equal, factual worth of all men does not have to be defended. What needs to be defended is, rather, the offering of equal opportunities to all, and the removing of obstacles standing in the way of this in any given case. Those who believe in generous actions of this kind do not worry about the desserts of the recipients any more than a doctor worries as to whether his patients deserve proper treatment. They have embarked on a moral project, which is grounded on hope and aspiration for the future of mankind, not on some theory about the closed nature of existent facts. In the light of this aspiration, other men deserve such treatment. Their vital need and lacks should be satisfied. Any failure to do this is an avoidable obstacle to the autonomy of the other person. But this is only one part of a larger project. In addition to their needs for self, existence and survival, men also have desires, as we may call them, for what is other than themselves and beyond all need. To give rights to others, and to work for their autonomy, does not come from any lack, or scarcity, on the part of the giver. It comes from fullness and abundance. In order to be generous, I must have something to give. On this interpretation, the granting of rights is not grounded exclusively on utility, though it may have uses, but mainly on respect and hope. Freedom and responsibility may lead to certain satisfactions. But they also have an intrinsic value of their own. The other person, in his otherness, is not an alter ego. He may inhabit his own world in his own way. This is the other-regarding point of view.

This interpretation of human rights is not overly attached to the status quo nor to any fixed system, and is open for change and advance. In general, we may say that it is oriented not to the self-same self or selves as they already are, but to the other and his otherness. I believe that this is a fuller and richer and sounder interpretation, more fitting for our time.

12

The Other Person:
Some Phenomenological Reflections

EXPLANATORY NOTE

Wild considered "The Other Person: Some Phenomenological Reflections" completely finished and ready for publication. Wild again acknowledges an indebtedness to James's essay on "A Certain Blindness in Human Beings,"as he says, a "blindness to others." He acknowledges a certain force in Sartre's description of the other as menacing; however, he objects that Sartre's account is "an oversimplification." He proceeds to introduce the important description of the handshake and what it implies in Ortega's description of the greeting.

"The Other Person: Some Phenomenological Reflections" much more clearly demonstrates the influence of Levinas. The reader familiar with Levinas will already see his influence at work in Wild's description of the face-to-face encounter. While the work surely appears to be written after reading Levinas, Wild has already introduced some of his own distinctive emphases. Note Wild's description of the face, the source of all expression, and therefore signification for Levinas: "The strangeness of the other is expressed in his bearing, especially in his countenance—the way he-holds-himself-together." Wild stresses the importance that rests on a genuine description of otherness for both religion and political life. He argues that group egocentrism is at the heart of tyranny and fanaticism. In short, Wild's essay is a clear, imaginative work that inserts the discussion into the history of Western philosophy while seeking to free the tradition from dangerous biases and presuppositions.

Wild was clearly searching for an existential phenomenological approach to ethics that could not be charged with anthropocentrism, moral relativism or, above all, nihilism. As Kaufman correctly notes, Wild's concern with the other and otherness is an elaboration of his long-standing preoccupation with openness to different cultural moral and religious points of view (p. 158). In fact, this takes Wild back to the very formative years of his philosophic education under George Herbert Mead, "whose conception of the 'generalized other' first impressed Wild with the importance of 'otherness'" (from *Realism to Phenomenology*, p. 68).

These reflections on the other person began some years ago when I was listening to a friend's talk on "Social Experience" in which he presented and defended Husserl's interpretation in his Fifth Cartesian Meditation of how we experience the other person. Analogical argument played a large role in his interpretation, as in Husserl's, and at one point in the discussion he remarked, "I can hope to gain knowledge of the other's mind only in so far as it resembles mine." This called forth some hot discussion, and I shall not forget how one student suddenly arose and said: "This one you call the other is not really other at all, he is simply another version of yourself. Your view is nothing but a semi-social solipsism." This toned up the discussion and made me think of the traditional theories I was familiar with, and of my own in particular. All of them, of course, accepted the other on the basis of some original experience. But then, instead of dwelling on the original experience, and reflecting on it as it comes to us, they at once proceeded to reduce it to intelligible or egocentric terms. Thus, analogical theories reduce this other to an alter ego, as Aristotle called him, or another version of the self. The Sartrian theory in *Being and Nothingness* reduces the other to an object of my stare, which necessarily leads to conflict since he does the same to me. The Hegelian theory reduces him to the opposite of me, or negation of me, which is still correlative to me, and finally gives us both a place in an encompassing rational system with which the ego readily identifies.

Has traditional thought ever done full justice to this otherness of the other? By our many attempts to include this otherness in a system that is always and everywhere one and the same, as I am, do we not perhaps show a certain fear of this otherness, an attempt to escape from it so that we can go along as we already are? Is there not a sense in which all explanation is an absorption of otherness into a system of self-identity, all synthesis, a joining with myself? As I studied many past theories of our knowledge of other minds as we call it, I became more critical of these theories. I have referred to some of these criticisms in the first part of this paper, which I shall not read here since it would take too long. I shall turn rather to some reflections on the original experience of meeting the other person, which I think has been neglected in the past. After this, I shall try to bring this experience into relations with other aspects of our experience, and make some suggestions, which grow out of recent phenomenology, about its general significance. Throughout this study I have been moved by William James's essay "On a Certain Blindness in Human Beings" (that is, blindness to otherness), and his statement in this essay (*Essays on Faith and Morals*, Meridian, p. 260) "how insensible, each of us, to all that makes life significant for the other!" [Wild continues,] "Hands off: neither the whole of truth nor the whole of good is revealed to any single observer, although each observer gains a partial superiority of insight from the peculiar position in which he stands. Even prisons and sickrooms have their special revelations. It is enough to ask of each of us that he should be faithful to his own opportunities and make the most of his own blessings without presuming to regulate the rest of the vast field" (*Essays on Faith and Morals*, p. 284).

MEETING

We have not met before. I am confronting him for the first time. It matters not whether the meeting has been arranged or has come by chance. We have been thrown together, and he is present before me in the flesh. What is he really like? And how shall I approach him? I believe that the thinking or living through of such questions is our first response to one who is strange to us, and whom we, therefore, call a stranger. He is extraneous. He comes from the outside and lives in another world of his own that is unfamiliar to me. The unknown is fearful to some degree, and so my response is tinged with hesitation. I may try to remember what I have been told about this stranger, or if I have heard nothing, I may try to size him up by gazing at him to size him up. To this extent, Sartre's analysis of the other's gaze is true.

I seek to categorize him as an object, and to find a place for him in my world and sometimes this is largely successful. But Sartre's claim (*Being and Nothingness*) that this always happens in both parties is an oversimplification. The stranger is never completely transparent to me. His questioning glance never quite accepts my categories. I can never be sure of what may lie hidden in the background. There is always a chance of surprises and shocks. This is a chief source of the "fascination" of meeting and talking to other people. It is originally rooted in a sense of uncertainty and danger, which is missing from Sartre's account. In different persons, it takes on many different forms and degrees. But there is a constant element, a seeking to protect ourselves against the hidden possibilities of the other. This widespread reaction of hesitation and fear has now been brought into the light.

Thus, there is Ortega's penetrating study of the handshake in *Man and People*. As he points out, there was in early times no more dangerous being to man than the human stranger. Hence, there is the need for modes of greeting to show shared loyalties and friendly intentions. The stranger may be carrying concealed weapons ready for use, especially in his hands. Hence, the need for opening the hands, coming open handed in our tradition to a meeting, and the touching of the two right hands holding no knife as a mode of greeting. This being open handed is probably the origin of the handshake.

Why is it that in cultures which are supposedly more civilized and in which physical danger has largely passed, we still feel the need of formal introductions and the giving of names by third parties? Why do strangers need to be introduced, and why is a third party needed? Is it not to mediate the distance which lies between them, to ease the way towards genuine communication which can never be taken for granted, and always carries a risk of psychical shock and injury? Hence, friendly gestures and smiles are needed.

This strangeness of the other is expressed in his bearing, especially in his countenance—the way he-holds-himself-together. This face is present before me in the flesh. In the case of written words and the other works of man, the author is not himself fully present in this way. To some degree, he is always separated from them. They are only signs from which his original intentions must be inferred (Plato, *Phaedrus*, Epistle VII). What is put forth is different from its inner meaning. But in the expressions of another in a face-to-face encounter, this distinction cannot be made. The expression is what is expressed. It is impossible for me to understand the sign but mistake the meaning. So far as I misunderstand one, I also misunderstand the other. The mistake is total. So far as I grasp the expression, I also grasp its meaning. In human relations, this is a completely unique situation where the other is totally present face to face.

This face is constantly in motion, and takes on many forms of sorrow, joy, anger, and sympathy. But in the very assumption of these forms, it is already beyond them, and beyond what I do and say. We can see this vitality of the living countenance if we contrast it with the fixed and frozen masks which are worn at carnivals, and which are imposed on it after death. But in and through all the forms taken on during life is the initial asking which is constantly maintained. This returns again and again in the glance of the other, to place me in question. It does not come from an alter ego. I am in no sense questioning myself. The gaze comes from a source altogether independent of me. After all my explanations and justifications, after the last word has been said, the look is still there as if waiting unfinished, expecting more.

I may regard the other as an obscure object that is waiting to be disclosed and clarified by me in the light of my understanding. But this turns out to be an error. He is the source of his own light, which shines forth in his glance. He does not have to be disclosed by me. He reveals himself by his own expressions. He refuses to be assimilated into my world, and speaks for himself! I cannot read my own meanings into what he expresses if I am to understand him. I must wait, and listen, and follow him as we say. New meanings may be conveyed that are foreign to me. In this way, the event of teaching, and learning what I do not know from another who knows, may take place. But whether or not this occurs, as soon as I meet the other he is there facing me, revealing himself in his own style of light and questioning me. Every question is a seeking, and it is directed by the other to me. He is waiting, asking for an answer from me. And this appeal is also expressed in the face of the other. Shall I answer or not?

Who am I? First of all, I am the incarnate center of a perceived world made up of many regions, together with the persons, places, and objects contained in each of them. This body is exposed to the view of the other—its motions and expressions as I engage it in the pursuit of my various projects, and also the objects around us which we can perceive in common. All these are accessible from the outside, and can be perceived. But there is a vital aspect of these which cannot be directly perceived—these bodily motions, objects, and projects as they are lived through by me, the inner life, my lived existence, as we sometimes call it. This includes my dreams so far as I am aware of them, my imaginings and illusions, my memories of the past, my hopes and intentions for the future, my image of what I call myself and of the world that I inhabit.

To these experiences as I live them through, the external observer has no access apart from language. They are in constant flux, and the image of myself, for example, is filled with ambiguity, ever breaking down and reforming. But with all of these processes of my own inner life I am directly familiar. They may be well ordered or relatively informed and chaotic. But in any case, they constitute my version of the world which I am living through, my own existence. In all of this, from the future through the present and into the past which has been passed by, there is a thread of identity that I call myself. It is to this self that the questioning glance of the other is addressed. So certain assumptions are being made. The glance is assuming that my face is expressing a version of the whole world, and an inner life that is invisible. Furthermore, it is assuming that this world is at my disposal, that I have some understanding of its meaning, that I can put it in words and answer for it, that I am able to respond—to be responsible.

All these assumptions are contained in the glance, for there is no point in asking a question if no one is present to give a meaningful answer. There is no part of my world that is immune to this questioning of the other, no object that I think I perceive, no dream or illusion to which I have yielded, no friend or enemy, no meaning to which I have become attached, no past memory or future project, nor I myself, the agent of all these lived activities. Am I to respond or not? In one sense, this appeal is irresistible. A word must be spoken, but it may take on an indefinite number of variations. Back of these, however, the basic anti-thesis between response or no response remains. With words of no moment I may pass the other by and evade his question. Or I may really speak and give an answer.

Of course, I may use violence or the threat of violence, which also have their words. But then the stranger loses his autonomy, and becomes a passive object or an instrument in my world. The way in which I can become related to him as other intact is by speaking to him, and by letting him speak for himself in dialogue. I do not have to engage in such an interchange. As we have indicated, words may be found to avoid him. This is also a way of relating to the other in the mode of indifference. But as soon as he confronts me, I am confronted with a decision. Shall I remain enclosed within myself and my dwelling, or shall I expose myself and my world to the other and his questions?

This ethical decision has to be made before any exchange may take place, and must be repeated throughout its whole course, for a dialogue can be broken off at any point. Language, therefore, in its primordial form, rests on the decision of an autonomous self. I say "primordial" because the face-to-face encounter is the basic social relation which lies at the root of all the rest. Hence, the character of the society will depend on the answer that is given to this question, and the type of language that prevails among the members. The decision to give my world to the other in words, to open myself to his question, is a basic kind of giving or generosity. This readiness to open the self to the other's questions, when it prevails, leads to an open society. Those in which the individual locks all the doors and windows to remain within himself, like a Leibnitzian monad, become closed.

But if I become related to the other through language, and we remain on speaking terms, does this not mean that we are taken up into a neutral system which assigns to each of us his place, and, therefore, destroys our uniqueness and autonomy? There is no doubt that language is often used in this way, in the third person, for the conveying of the information and the articulating of panoramic views of objects and objective structures, which are thus encompassed in a total system. It is possible to regard the personal self in this manner as a peculiar kind of object, and to dismiss what we have called the inner life and the inner world as lived as a subjective illusion. In this history of Western philosophy, this attitude has been predominant.

According to the traditional view, the arbitrary prejudices of the individual subject can be corrected only by detachment from all practical urges and impulses. From this impartial point of view, we can see all things, including the personal self, as they really are in the light of Being. When we think objectively and impersonally in this way, subjective differences can be overcome. I no longer see things from my own special point of view, determined by accidental choices and prejudices, but as all men must see it so far as they can become detached. Thus, the universal concept appears on the scene; agreement and objective truth become possible. This rational truth will then offer us the only reliable guide to rational moral action. Just as I see what all men can see, I will what all men can will, and common action is in sight.

Thus, the global system will take precedence over the partial and fragmentary, the universal over the individual and unique, the detached and impersonal over the concerned, and rational thinking will come before ethics and action. Men are properly understood not in terms of their own thoughts and feelings, but in terms of their observable works, which determine the course of history.

This history is to be understood as a general rational advance in which subjective myths have been replaced by rational thought, and capricious and biased action by rational freedom. The inner life, the existence, of the individual is recognized as an arbitrary factor which interrupts the objective events of world history. But on the whole, they are directed and controlled by what Hegel called "the cunning of reason" (*Der List der Vernunft*). Thus, the individual self and the unique other confronting me are discounted and supposedly absorbed into an impersonal system that is gradually developing in the observable works and events of world history.

These traditional attitudes are now dominant in the East, and in many parts of the Western world. They have proven to be fruitful in the natural sciences. But when generalized and applied in the human disciplines and in the philosophy of man, as in the twentieth century, it seems to be highly abstract and reductive. Human egotism, though apparently discredited, seems to be nevertheless intensely active even in those whose overt thinking is highly objective and rational. Individual, and especially social, egotism certainly need to be corrected. But instead of being corrected, they apparently flourish by being passed over and ignored.

It has even been pointed out, as we have indicated, that impersonal thinking, which sees a thing or a person in its own neutral light, is the first step in gaining control over it, and, therefore, is itself an expression of egotism. This is not an egotism of the individual person. It is, rather, the egotism of a general attitude which lies very close to the person, and which it is very easy for him to take since it frees him from the troublesome questions of the other. It assimilates him as a finite object into a global system with a transcendental center of pure light, often called reason, with which the individual ego readily identifies. The tradition of rational thought has also been shown to be subject to other criticisms. We shall now briefly summarize them so far as they bear on the major priorities of objectivism, which we have just outlined.

In traditional rationalism, the global system takes precedence over the concrete other confronting me as only partial and fragmentary. He is one object among others which have been given a place in a larger englobing totality. This is true, but only with a certain reduction, for he is also a self with a world version of his own. This version no doubt includes arbitrary and eccentric features. Many facts and regions known to others are absent from it. But within it there is a possible place for all of them, including the system that tries to include it. His world may be further refined and corrected, but not included, for it is already an inclusive world with a system, or lack of system, of its own. In the second place, this world of the other has an active, moving center—the other himself, who has access to this world and can enjoy it. This other can also reject or ignore any neutral system that claims to include it, and, in the choice of suicide, can reject even his own world and everything in it. This evidence is sufficient to show that the other is not an object that can be taken up without reduction into an external system, brought together under an alien light. He has a light of his own.

Now, let us look at the other traditional priorities. Does the universal take precedence over the individual and the unique? We find that the great medieval controversy on this problem ended in nominalism. Two conclusions, also strongly supported by other sources, seem to be well-established: Only individual persons and things first exist in the world—universal concepts and propositions are derived; and there is no science of the individual as such. Is it not clear to us that the universal comes only with language, and that language grows out of the face-to-face encounter? What is the very first step? Is it not an act of generosity? Is it not a readiness on the part of the self to put its world into words, and to offer it with all its various things and regions to the stranger? The rationalist tradition has maintained that it is only by giving themselves to a system of universal concepts that men become social. But do we not need to reverse this priority? Must not men first become social, and ready to share with the other, before the universal concept and system become possible?

There are those who say that the impersonal and detached must take precedence over the personal and the concerned. It is only by abandoning our biased and egotistical interests that the objective truth becomes accessible to us. It is only then that we may see other things and also our interests as they really are in the light of Being, and operate in the cold logic of the facts. It is only in this light that a third party may impartially judge between our rival claims, and give to each of us his proper position in an enveloping system. Much has been said, and much more can be said, in favor of this familiar position. But an essential correction must be made. This is not the sudden shining of a translucent light in which there is no interest, nor any support, from the desires of men.

This mode of understanding does not grow from any egotistical interest, but it is not disinterested. It grows from a desire for the truth, as we call it, which is strange to me and my self-interests. It comes from beyond me, like the questions of the other. And like that strange desire for the other that is not a need which leads me to speak to him in the first place, it leads me beyond myself and my personal concerns. The desire for truth is closely related to my desire for the other. This is shown by the fact that when a third person intervenes, and begins to adjudicate our dispute as if impersonally and directly from on high, we see through his pretentious claims and join together against him. Unless he can appeal to us as a finite person, with a real desire for the truth in which we can join with our persons intact, he will become a third party to the argument. The impartial and the unbiased truth comes to us only from a desire for what I do not possess, have never possessed, and will never possess—for otherness of a radical kind.

Let us now turn to the last priority to which the others lead, that of rational thought over ethical choice and action. Until very recent times, the dominant traditions of Western thought have spoken unambiguously on this theme. The rational system (ontology) must come before sound action (ethics). Before men can act effectively, they must have put together a set of ideas in an orderly and harmonious way. Otherwise, their action will disintegrate and achieve nothing for themselves. Intelligent purpose must precede action, as lightning must precede thunder. If the purpose is to be achieved, it must be known and articulated in advance. Those who have opposed this dominant thesis have been called irrationalists, subjectivists, voluntarists, haters of science, and even enemies of man.

But now, instead of calling names, let us try to think phenomenologically or empirically about some facts. Is it not true that thinking is speaking, and that the primary mode of speaking, as we can see it in the child, is dialogue with the other? Does monologue precede dialogue? Is it not true that dialogue requires an active response to the appeal of the other which, in adults, takes the form of an ethical decision—to speak or not to speak? Must this decision not be made and remade as long as the dialogue goes on? Is it not true that monologue is the possibly lengthy interruption of a dialogue, and that the most voluminous literary and technical works are always addressed to an other who is either present or absent, but always lurking in the background, ready to come forth with those pressing questions which I do not want to have asked? Is it not true as we have suggested, that our serious thinking, as opposed to daydreaming, is carried on before an other of this kind?

If the dialogue is really sustained, can I ever precisely anticipate what this other is going to say? Is this not responsible for the remarkable fact that our everyday dialogues, when we really meet, in spite of the pretentious claims that are often made, proceed towards a strange and distant goal that is chaotic and unplanned? Is it not for this reason that even in planned debates those who tend to come out ahead can meet the unexpected and think more readily on their feet? Does all of this not indicate that because of the depths and mysteries in the other, meeting him is an adventurous act that rests on an ethical choice? It is not that the social comes from the rational, but rather, as I have indicated, that the rational comes from the social! True dialogue rests on a prior ethical choice.

JUSTIFICATION

In much of our conversation, each individual has agreed to play a certain role in a common endeavor whose principles he has accepted. His expressions, then, make a special contribution to the developing system in which he has a place. But as we have seen, before this can happen, he must decide to accept this system as a free person inhabiting a world of his own. He may maintain this decision and become more subservient to it as the system grows. But this is not necessary. In his existence, he retains his otherness, and to some degree his freedom remains intact. He can always doubt the steps that are taken, and can question even the basic principles he has accepted in the past. In spite of the general attributes that are attached to his works as scholarly, practical, medical, historical, constructive, or indifferent, he remains individual and unique. If his desire for the truth ebbs away, or it is surpassed by other interests, his activities may fall into a sterile routine, or he may abandon the whole enterprise. Underlying all purposive systems, whether they be theoretical or practical in nature, is there not an ethical area where individual decisions are made? I wish now, finally, to say something more about this ethical area and its patterns.

The individual person, in what we call a free society, is living through his own version of the common world of his people, which has been built up by the choices of individuals through longer intervals of time. Now, with a world at his disposal that he can enjoy in his own way, the choices he makes are bound to include arbitrary and eccentric factors. Since his version of the world is centered in himself, his choices will also be egocentric, especially when they are backed up by the powers of a state with members, and are affected by the drift of these powers. Because of the very freedom that has constituted them, the primary worlds of states and of individuals are egocentric and include arbitrary factors. They are, therefore, always open to criticism.

Now let us return to the original face-to-face situation. We have already spoken of the initial choice for generosity which opens my world to the other in words, and lies at the root of every human society. But as soon as my world is expressed to him, then, whether I am speaking for myself alone or on behalf of others, its egocentric and peculiar features are revealed. Now at this point, the other may regard me simply as an alien object to be dominated or dispensed with as soon as possible, in which case violence of some kind will ensue. But as we have seen, this is not necessary as Sartre supposed in *Being and Nothingness*, part III.

A decision is made. The other may decide to give me an answer and to raise his questions, for he is also free and lives in an egocentric world of his own. These are related alternatives, violence and dialogue, since warfare is carried on only by separated, egocentric beings between whom dialogue and argument is possible. Rhetoric is a kind of force. But if mesmerism and the charm of words is left behind, and the choice is finally made for genuine dialogue in prose, violence is abandoned. By his most harping, searching questions, the other is then not seeking to obliterate me. He is concerned with vagueness and uncertainties in an unfinished position that I also should understand. He is looking again at my words, as we say, with respect, which leaves my self-identity intact.

In following my words, he finds arbitrary biases in them that have been hidden to me. How can a free being, not forced into warped intentions, inhabit a distorted world of this kind? He is not disputing my right to express my attitudes and thoughts, for he seeks an answer from me. He is not merely trying to dispense with my words. He has listened to them, and, at least in part, from his own point of view, has followed their meaning. He is not asking me for a recantation of the words, but for an explanation, a justification. In the light of our Western history, this is usually understood as a request for reasons in terms of some neutral system in which his reasons and arguments also have a place. But this holds only in so far as we both have freely accepted the principles of this system, which (as we are now painfully discovering with some of our so-called fellow citizens) need not be the case.

In back of this secondary meaning (in terms of system), which often has its place, there is another meaning which is evident in the original sense of the word "justify," that is, to make just. In back of all rational argument, there are ethical issues and ethical choices to be made. The other is asking me to do justly, to justify myself to him. What right have I, in his presence, to proceed in my egocentric way, unfolding my supposedly neutral systems and my own idiosyncrasies without taking account of him and the other world in which he lives? The dialogue now clearly shows its primary ethical character, which is also revealed in the appeal for a response. Am I able to respond, to become responsible? Here another ethical choice must be made. If I choose to answer, what kind of answer should be given?

The thinkers of our Western tradition have long known of the endless eccentricities and the basic egocentricity that are always found in the lived existence of the free individual. Unless some correction can be found, they have seen that this must lead to anarchy. So apart from rebels, especially in modern times, they have in general agreed on a systematic answer to these problems, which has been, perhaps, best stated by the German philosopher, Hegel—still, perhaps, the most influential philosopher of our time. Heidegger also has taken this general way, especially in *Sein und Zeit*, his most important work. According to this way of thinking, the essence of man is to be found in comprehending all things in a total system that is being realized in world history (Being).

The egocentric freedom of the individual will lead only to willful dreams and illusions unless it is fitted into this system, and realized in the public world by the rational planning and organizing of men. The individual must be judged by his works and their consequences in world history. Only that which is successful and realized is rationally justified. *Die Weltgeschichte ist die Weltgericht*. There is no appeal from this judgment. Thus, the personal self and the other confronting him are taken up into this englobing system. Both of us are only serving the course of history. If I refuse to perform the functions allotted to me, I will come to nothing. All the legitimate questions the other can ask me will be answered by the system that englobes us both.

In this way, a kind of answer is given to the problems of eccentricity and egocentricity, and many similar answers have been given. Those who are able to identify themselves with the functions they perform in a larger whole have accepted an answer of this kind. I do not deny the profundity of this doctrine, nor that many answers to egocentric problems can be found in this way. But as I have tried to argue in this paper, I do not believe that this is the final answer. In addition to the arguments I have given, I will only now add that many of the most subtle and grievous forms of intellectual tyranny and political despotism have resulted from this point of view. It has been called a gigantic egocentrism, and a breeding ground for dogmatism and fanaticism. But surely some answer to egocentrism must be given. If this is not to be found in eliminating the troublesome other, what kind of answer is to be found?

Order of some kind, even if it comes with tyranny, is preferable to chaos. When we are confronted with the dilemma, either chaos or force, we must choose order and the force that comes with it, including certain restrictions on our personal integrity and freedom. This is the kind of answer that lies at the back of the great systems that have been constructed in our Western intellectual history. Either system or chaos, and system is better.

In this paper, I have argued along existential and phenomenological lines that we do not need to accept this dilemma (either chaos or tyranny). There is a third way between its horns, something that is properly described neither as tyranny nor as chaos. This comes from a recognition of the radical otherness of the other, and from dialogue with him. I have tried to show that the independent person can participate in such dialogue without sacrificing himself to any finished system, and with his autonomy intact. This peculiar relation with the other through language does not require that he let himself be subsumed under universal categories, or that his unique identity be diluted. Furthermore, in the third place he does not have to detach himself from his active interests and concerns. In fact, this moving away from the ego towards the other expresses a particular type of interest that cannot be identified with a selfish need. To move in this way does not demand the acceptance of any system. Rather, all systematic thinking rests on an ethical decision of this kind. It leads to a mode of thought and action which can achieve justice and peace without theoretical or systematic agreement. It can lead to a judgment on history that will not coincide with the results of stronger forces at work in the course of world history. For this judgment comes not from systems of power but rather from the inner life, the existence, of free and independent individuals in dialogue. So this judgment is not an imposed order. But neither is it an arbitrary fiat laid down by an isolated individual, and, therefore, filled with eccentricities. It has faced the searching questions and criticisms of the other. In so far as this occurs, we do not have to accept the course of history as the final judgment of history. There is another free and independent judgment to which we may appeal, the judgment of free persons in dialogue. Perhaps the real aim of philosophy, and of a discussion like this, is not to merely reiterate the decrees of history, and to judge men according to their works, but rather to work out a free existential judgment from a dialogue of independent persons.

13

Speaking Philosophy: John Wild's Commentary on *Totality and Infinity*

EXPLANATORY NOTE

In his last, untitled work, John Wild devotes his attention to the thought of Emmanuel Levinas. It was John Wild who discovered the work of Levinas for an American philosophic readership, encouraged the translation of *Totality and Infinity* and authored the introduction to the English edition of that work. The original French edition appeared in 1961, the English translation by Alphonso Lingis in 1969. Wild's original manuscript references both the English and French editions of *Totality and Infinity*. Where there is only one citation, I have included the English page reference. The subtitles as well as the chronological format of the text are Wild's own, and can be read quite fluidly in conjunction with *Totality and Infinity*. It should be noted, however, that Wild's text stands on its own and can be read apart from *Totality and Infinity*.

The animated conversation that Wild is carrying on with Levinas and others has inspired us to call Wild's untitled commentary *Speaking Philosophy*. The original manuscript found among Wild's posthumous papers contains seventy-nine typed pages along with a number of penciled comments and asides. These marginal asides and reflections are marked off in our text as a running commentary at the bottom of their respective pages.

While undated, the manuscript almost certainly derives from the last creative phase of Wild's career, 1968–1970. During this time Wild taught seminars for graduate students and interested faculty at Yale University, and subsequently taught a course on Levinas at the University of Florida in 1970. It must be stressed that Wild's text, while forming a coherent whole, remains unfinished. At various times, it is fragmentary, tentative and occasionally paraphrastic, hence the special need for expository endnotes appended to this manuscript. At times, in the endnotes, we have taken the original thrust of Levinas's meditation and asked how Wild might speak philosophy with him. In other instances, we have ventured editorial observations in order to clarify ambiguities in the manuscript or to place the comments of Wild and/or Levinas within the broader context of their respective reflections.

Wild believed that the future of phenomenology depended, in part, upon providing a serious critique and positive alternative to Heidegger's understanding of philosophy as fundamental ontology and the attendant conception of the project of phenomenology that follows from this view. Levinas presented for the first time in *Totality and Infinity*, in Wild's view, the first serious, systematic philosophical alternative in phenomenology to Heidegger's fundamental ontology. By beginning with ethics rather than ontology, the other rather than the self, Levinas was revisioning phenomenological philosophy in an original and positive direction. For Wild, it is very clear that all future phenomenology and, for that matter, philosophy cannot bypass *Totality and Infinity*. Wild's international stature as a philosopher, and acknowledged master of the tradition, made him uniquely able to introduce the writings of Levinas to an American philosophical readership. In this way, Wild was opening the Continental philosophic tradition for a new generation of American students of philosophy and securing a place for it within the American academic curriculum. There is little doubt that Wild was preparing to write a last book that would incorporate insights drawn from *Totality and Infinity*, as it was his belief that the future of phenomenology would depend upon the outcome of its encounter with the thought of Emmanuel Levinas.

As the reader can see, Wild's vast knowledge of the Western philosophical tradition continually reasserts itself as he compares the position of Levinas on a given issue with that of Plato or Aristotle or Kant and Hegel, as well as that of Heidegger and the contemporary existential, phenomenological thinkers. In addition to the direct comparison with Heidegger and the tradition, Wild introduces, on behalf of the tradition, questions which he believes have not been fully dealt with by Levinas. In this respect, *Speaking Philosophy* serves the vital task of embedding Levinas's investigations within the broader context of the history of philosophy as a whole as well as the phenomenological movement.

What we see above all here, in Wild's reflections on Levinas, is the mind of a singularly able and disciplined philosopher bringing to fruition the labor of his entire education. Wild speaks directly to thinkers he finds addressed by Levinas, alternatively raising questions to him on their behalf while calling for, through the mediating datum of the text, a response from the author. The passionate advocacy of existential phenomenology that dominates the last phase of Wild's career is not impervious to its deficiencies. It is in Wild's own sensitivity to the anthropocentricism that often accompanies phenomenology in its single-minded attempt to reposition man in the center of his own human life-world that makes Wild so receptive to Levinas's radical assertion that philosophy begins with ethics rather than ontology.

We can see from John Wild's commentary on *Totality and Infinity* how seriously he takes Levinas as a thinker. We find Wild expressing his agreements in many diverse ways. At the same time, readers familiar with Levinas will see Wild asking questions to Levinas that will be taken up in works that come after *Totality and Infinity*, especially *Otherwise than Being: Beyond Essence*. We have tried to point out in the endnotes the almost uncanny way that Wild anticipates Levinas's discussions of responsibility and sensory perception, in particular. Surely Wild is every bit as adamant as Levinas in resisting the idea advanced by Hegel and modified by Heidegger that the inner history of philosophy is capable of a univocal rendering, or able to be accurately presented under the rubric of a single dominating concept or idea. No more than Levinas is Wild willing to yield to a tyrannical concept of Being that would divest each being of its uniqueness and alterity.

Still, Wild remains a tenaciously independent thinker who poses serious questions to Levinas. Wild asks: Is it not possible to have an open system that will do justice to beings who inhabit an open society? Cannot the phenomenological discoveries pertaining to human temporality secure the basis for a living philosophy of history? What is the place for authentic acts of moral courage that are non-egocentric? Above all, cannot Levinas's original discoveries be augmented by an elaboration of the life-world?

Wild holds out for a strenuous view of embodied democracy. Unlike Levinas, he is not completely willing to give up on thinking dialectically. There is synthetic thinking that survives through negation without violence. Over and over again, Wild introduces the notion of one world with many versions as a way of describing what, for Levinas, remains resistant to description, that is, the relation of totality to infinity.

Wild adamantly insists that perception informs all discourse, and that we can and must be able to speak of pre-conceptual understanding, or to use James's term, "knowledge by acquaintance." There are places where Wild raises valuable questions, acknowledging that Levinas is suggestive, but he is always alert to the unintended consequences of adhering religiously to Levinas's philosophical position. Wild continues to believe that the task of true philosophy involves elaborating the contents of the human life-world that appears to be situated between totality and infinity. Here the reader is encouraged to see both the running commentary extracted from Wild's original text and the expository endnotes.

Levinas was appreciative of Wild's introduction to *Totality and Infinity* and admired *Speaking Philosophy*. In a letter to Wild from Nanterre, referring to Wild's introduction, Levinas writes, "Therefore, I have the opportunity before anything else to express my gratitude to you both for the intelligence that animates your text, and for the spirit that is ever present" (November 19, 1970). In a letter addressed to Richard Sugarman in regard to *Speaking Philosophy*, Levinas refers to Wild's manuscript as an "eloquent review devoted to my modest works . . . an excellent text on *Totality and Infinity*" (August 20, 1992).

Richard Sugarman would like to express his appreciation to Professor Anna-Teresa Tymieniecka, the editor of *Philosophical Inquiry*, for permitting us to reprint the annotated and edited text of Wild's commentary that first appeared in *Philosophical Inquiry* (October 24, 2000).

SECTION I. SPEAKING PHILOSOPHY

All this we are thinking in the twentieth century when acute minds have shown us that hunger and fear explain all the acts of man, that all comes from need, from lack. This misery of man cannot be doubted. But to be man is to know that this is so. It is to constantly postpone the moment of betrayal to the animal. This distinguishes man from the brutes, which presupposes the disinterestedness of benevolence (of the importance of generosity), the desire for the absolute other, nobility, grandeur, the theme of metaphysics.

The Rupture of Totality

This movement to the really other cannot be reduced to any internal presence of the self to the self. The claim for this is made, not demonstrated, by the word "transcendence." Wahl has called it *transcendance* in *Existence humaine et Transcendance* (Boconniere Neuchâtel 1944).[1] For Levinas, the metaphysician is absolutely separate from his object. The relation of the self, *le même*, to the other is irreversible, not reversible as left to right and right to left. There is no correlativity here. This would mean that someone might get outside the relation and include it in a system. One cannot get outside it to register this correspondence, or non-correspondence. If this were to happen, both the self and the absolute would be united in a common regard, and the distance between them would be run through. This relation must have its point of departure in a term (the self) which remains absolutely at its starting point, so as to enter into this relation. Only the self can do this. It remains self-identical through all the changes that happen to it, so, of course it changes. But it remains and maintains its identity in and through all these changes. Here Levinas quotes Hegel on self-identity as otherness, though Levinas does not accept Hegel's scorn for the immediate.[2] However, he does accept the notion that every self-rejection, boredom with myself, for example, is an identity in difference. Such expressions of identity-in-difference are, for Levinas, all modes of self-consciousness. Self-rejection is a mode of self-identity. We cannot grasp this formally merely as A is A.

We need to think this through concretely in terms of the self in the world, inhabiting it.[3] It is here that the identity of the self with the me is found. The world is from the first other than I—strange and hostile. But the I dwells in it, inhabits it. At every instant it is *chez soi* (at home) with itself. It holds itself, maintains itself as itself, while sojourning in the world. As the body remains and is able to stand, so the self holds to itself as against the world, in its very manner and style of being. All is at my disposal—I can do, make of all these things. We must note, if the self were related to the world merely by opposing it, then they would both be reduced to parts

of an englobing system. We must understand this in the concrete as egotism, all is at my disposal.

But how can I be related to the absolutely other without depriving it of
its alterity? The absolute other is not transcendentally constituted. This
would make it belong to the self. This other is not just in another place. As
Aristotle remarked of the Platonic ideas that they were in no place, so this
absolute other is not in any place or district. Alterity of myself and the
world with its neighborhoods is only formal. This world falls under my
egotistic powers as we have seen, but the absolute other of metaphysics is
anterior to all initiative on my part. This otherness does not limit me, for
a limit is held in common by the two. The community of the frontier
would make the two the same.

Now Levinas shifts to self and the other. The collectivity where I say you
or we is not a plurality of I's (Cf. my notion of democracy). I and you are
not the instances of a common concept (I question this, though it is a most
peculiar common concept).[4] I and you do not belong to a unity of possession, of number, or of concept. We lack a common fatherland. On him I
have no power as over things. He is free. Even if I dispose of him he is not
entirely in my world. This leads to a major thesis of Levinas; that the relation of the self and the other is language belongs to metaphysics. The relation of the self to the other, and this relation is first played out in language
where the self, without losing its uniqueness and particularity, goes out to
the other. We speak together. But in this neither is taken up into an englobing system. Each is able to maintain himself and his whole world.[5] In discourse I maintain my radical separation from the other, and my egotism.
But being in a discourse shows that I recognize that the other has a right
over this egotism and that I need to justify myself before the other. I need
to justify myself before a transcendence. Discourse leads to a benevolence
that involves this apologetic as one of its moments. There is a void which
ruptures any totality here. This is not merely an operation of thought
which cannot resist synthesis and totalizing, for it is only before the other
that I really speak and think. This other cannot be brought under a category. Together with an object I constitute a totality. But before the other I
must speak. The relation with the other that does not constitute a totality
(I shall call it religion).[6] The other retains his otherness and transcendence
at the heart of history. The same is identity in the diverse, whether this be
history or system. It is not the individual self that refuses the system as
Søren Kierkegaard thought, but it is the other—the self as other.[7]

Transcendence Is Not Negativity[8]

Negativity presupposes a being already installed in a place in the world.
Hegel said that work is the negation of the matter it transforms. But work

is rooted in the world that it remakes ("I think that remaking is a better term for this notion"). If I remake myself along my lines, I accept the world. Marx really does this. (I get a distance from what I am already, then I develop a new system of meaning. After that I take it over, and fill it with meaning that makes sense to me. I must rethink this in terms of transcendence.) The Hegelian dialectic is a piecemeal process: First my force negates the object I am against, and it is remade. But then my force is negated and I move towards a synthesis with the thing through a negation of myself—a double negation. And the synthetic negative process starts again. But in terms of transcendence the movement is in a vertical dimension, away from both myself and the world. It proceeds from a double negation of myself and the object.[a]

The negator and what is denied form a system. The poor want riches, the doctor wants to be an engineer in this world as it is. Even the suicide wants a dramatic death that will be seen; the believer wants another world like this. One wants what is here already with some changes. This is not the radical negativity of the stranger.

It is not true that we attain the idea of perfection by denying all imperfections. Descartes is right, Perfection is radically other. It draws us on high beyond all these to what is absolutely other, to the very limit which means transcendence. The idea of the perfect is the idea of the infinite. Here the distance does not destroy the relation, nor does the relation destroy the distance, as is true in the world. Here there is a relation to what is absolutely distant, and something at an absolute distance with which we are related. This relation is without mystique or ecstasy. So we still need apology, no matter how far we go.

Language comes before yes and no. These are not ultimate. They are in the system.

Metaphysics (Open System) Precedes Ontology (Closed)

Metaphysics prefers the form of theory to express itself. This is no accident since theory in its primordial essence knows the other in its full density without touching it or marking it, as itself, as other, as it is. (Cf. perception.)

---

a. "Both myself and the thing must be negated and transformed towards an ultimate transcendence. It is only in this way that a genuine synthesis may be achieved, looking down from above. Levinas does not have this. He rejects all synthesis and system. The world needs to be rethought and remade from above, in a vertical direction toward transcendence by an open dialectic. In Hegel the end must be present at the beginning, so there is only a gradual continuous development. In mine there can be creative leaps towards what is in no sense present, except as absent and beyond. Levinas sees this in part only. (Does Levinas think, as I do, that real advances and declines can be made though the distance still remains infinite. Can a direction be seen? Can the idea of the infinite be illumined at all and given positive content?)"

Does it do this? I guess I shall have to say no.[9] This knowledge through theory gets only the in-itself-for-us. It gives us a sense of the thing with its opaque depths, as a mystery. Then as in theory, understood as intelligence, it tries to place the thing in the world, or at least to struggle with it for the sake of its projects. At least it gives us the thing and the person as independent and full of obscure depths (the germs of this are in perception). After this initial movement the way divides.

One path that has dominated our Western history so far is theory as *nous*, as intelligence which to absorb the independent thing, brings it into the world of the self, to achieve a complete union with it where being and meaning coincide. Intelligence in this sense becomes logos, the pure light of being, where all is transparent and translucent. Being here does not express itself as a being with depths. This leads to ontology which promises a complete liberty of the self to master all alienation of otherness. All will be known and the other established in a system established by the liberty of the knower.

But there is another way of criticism which puts in question this spontaneous liberty of the knower, and its free spontaneity. The Kantian way of criticism discovers dogmatism, and arbitrariness at the heart of this spontaneity. In each moment of thought it looks for dogmatism, which leads to an infinite regress and therefore to transcendence.[b]

The criticism of spontaneity is ethics, which is beyond ontology. This shows the strangeness of the other. It puts my spontaneous thoughts, my egotism in question, and comes ultimately from the other. Ethics is the reception of the other by the self. It accomplishes the critical essence of knowledge. This is the strongest part of philosophy, leading beyond pure theory to ethics, self-criticism by the other. But it leads to wholeness also which Levinas rejects.[10]

Western philosophy in general has been ontology which is an embracing of the other into the self by means of a translucent middle term like *nous*, the ideas of Plato, God, intuition, Heidegger's Being and so forth.[11] This middle term is neutral—not the self-same, not the other. It absorbs the shock of what is really other, and takes all into a system. This is the lesson of Socrates; not to receive anything passively, as if from all eternity I have possessed all that is strange to me. To receive nothing—to be free, this is not the capricious spontaneity of free will. It is to hold that permanence in the self that is called reason. This reason is the manifestation of a pure liberty, neutralizing the other by mediating it, englobing it. Neutralized in this way, the other becomes an object before me, englobed by an empty space, a horizon of nothingness. To know a being in this way is to

---

b. "Does an infinite regress always lead beyond to transcendence? I think so. The infinite regress of causes shows the limits of this category, leading to transcendence."

take it into a horizon of nothingness where it appears and becomes a concept. To clarify the thing means to take away its otherness in the light of nothing. This self-reason knows only itself and has no limits to its enlightening power. It looks at the other as an object, neutralizes it, and takes its otherness away from it in the light of nothingness. To clarify a thing means to take away its resistance from it. Mediation reduces all distances. A great betrayal must somehow take place in order that the external other utterly independent of me, should give way to intermediaries and give itself up to my thought. The external thing is reduced by being made into the instance of a concept. It is only the individual who exists. But there is no science of the individual.[12] He has to be placed under a concept. The humane individual, apart from me, is reduced by terror (Cf. Sartre)[13] abandoning his freedom to be dominated by another. In the West philosophy has become an egology, a way of reducing all things to the self-same, to the ego. This is ontology. Thus Berkeley wants to overcome the distance separating the subject from the object.[14] They must be taken into the mind. The peculiar quality that makes them independent of us is seen in terms of its lived essence. Sensible qualities are my feelings. The coincidence of being with meaning is turned into the coincidence of the lived with itself.

Ontological imperialism appears even more clearly in phenomenological mediation. Here, to know a being depends on a previous knowledge of being. To know this being is not to coincide with it but to be included within the horizon in which it is placed, where we can find its profile. From the beginning, phenomenology has been dominated by this notion of the horizon. Cf. James.[15]

This horizon plays the same role as the concept in classical idealism. Being is phosphorescence and luminosity. The being of this being is reduced to intelligibility. Being for Heidegger is both the source of meaning and of independence. For Heidegger, to approach a being from the point of view of being is both to let it be and to understand it. (This is certainly wrong.)[16]

But Levinas writes: To let it be means in its otherness, in its depths and obscurity—not to understand it. One thesis is under the whole of Heidegger—Being is inseparable from the understanding of being. This is already an appeal to subjectivity.[c]

The Heideggerian ontology subordinates this being to Being, which is detached and impersonal. Liberty means here to remain myself at the

---

c. "I must stress my idea of Being, not as light, but as opaque depths, independence, obscurity, transcendence. It elicits understanding but does not achieve it—surely it is not subjectivity. The priority of responsibility over freedom which is egotism. Responsbility is always to something beyond. It is intellectual only in second sense. Primarily, responsibility is active and ethical—realistic."[17]

heart of the other. Ethics is subordinated to knowing. For Heidegger, liberty is not capricious free will. Being is to be obeyed. Liberty and obedience are dialectically synthesized in the notion of truth, but this is the primacy of the same.[d] For Heidegger, instead of being related to someone in an ethical manner, trying to achieve justice we are related to Being, which is impersonal and inhuman. Thus we can dominate the other, know him and possess him. This means that liberty is conceived as opposing the other, remaining yourself against all otherness and mystery. There is no responsibility here to what lies beyond. Justice gives a place to the other we do not comprehend.[e] Ontology is a neutralizing of the other so that anonymous reason can know him and possess him. It is liberty in the sense of maintaining myself against the other. The *je pense* of Descartes is turned into a *je peux*, domination, power over him.[20] It leads to the violent non-violence of the totality. It leads to Hitler and the tyranny of the state, in spite of Heidegger's polemics against the authority of techne.[21]

Heidegger says that we are in the power of techne and only the state can freely master it. Is not this for a final obedience to a personal self? Heidegger denounces Socratic philosophy as forgetful of Being, but he goes back to the pre-Socratics who express the obedience of possession, building, and cultivating. All through Western history this has been the attitude of the sedentary building peoples who, near to the things they cultivate, wait for the coming of the gods and the company of men which never comes. This becomes an ontology of nature, impersonal fecundity, generous mother without a face, Mother of particular being. This is the inexhaustible matter of a "thing." This is a philosophy of power which never places the same in question. It means obedience to anonymous being, to the being hidden in this being. It leads not to the tyranny of techne over reified men (not to this directly) but to the tyranny of pagan states of soul, of the soil, to the adoration of masters by their slaves. It means Being before this individual being, ontology before metaphysics, liberty before justice and responsibility. According to this tradition, conflict between the self and the other is solved by theory, where the other is reduced to the same, and by the state, where warfare becomes the oppression of the anonymous state.

In ethics the self takes account of the other, and power; the natural murderer of the other feels desire, and instead of murder, against all good sense, finds murder impossible and considers the other as such. In this relation with a being infinitely distant we invoke his authority on every question we raise concerning his Being. Instead of asking ourselves ques-

---

d. "In my book I have also accused Heidegger of intellectualism in relation to James. Cf. Heidegger's basic ontologism over the ontic."[18]

e. "I must defend the priority of the ethical over the ontological, the basic importance of ethical, moral categories."[19]

tions about him, we ask him. It is in this relation with the other that language and benevolence arise. This relation wants more than opinion (i.e., it wants grounded opinion that he (the other) also can agree to). It works out the intention that animates the effort for the truth. Unlike Heidegger's conceptualized Being, this social relation with a being precedes all ontology and underlies it.

Transcendence as Idea of the Infinite

The Greeks glimpsed this radical separation from the infinite other. Thus Socrates at the beginning of *The Phaedo* compares us to soldiers who must stay at their posts no matter what happens. Any ecstatic merging with the infinite is a desertion. The way is hard. We do not already participate in it. To hold this is to do violence with the infinite.

At this point Levinas takes over some arguments of Descartes in the *Meditations*. All our other ideas might have been caused by us because their formal reality is less than ours. But the idea of the infinite is utterly unique in this respect. We cannot account for its being which transcends all that we know and are. It must be real—the ontological argument. The content of this idea is the very distance between the idea and the ideatum. It is possible to have only one idea of the infinite in us. This is the only idea of this kind. But Levinas does not accept the rest of the arguments, for the existence of external things, etc.

Pascal also argued that any explication of Being must presuppose already the existence of this being. Heidegger tries to refute this in the first pages of *Being and Time*, but does he? This thinking of an ideatum radically separate from the thinker goes back to the active reason of Aristotle and to certain conceptions of Plato. The difference between the infinite and the objective underlies all that Levinas argues for in *Totality and Infinity*. Plato's theory of the divine madness is relevant here, the poet being divinely possessed. These examples do not express the irrational (but the super-rational which is essential to genuine rationality).

The Cartesian notion of the infinite expresses not an object appearing relative to us, but an infinite that maintains itself intact in this relation which seems like a contradiction. How can the absolute be thought by us without being relativized? This is to touch the untouchable, but this is exactly what happens. The infinite is absolved from this relation which cannot be abstractly understood. It must be described. Levinas gives concrete description of this relation in terms of discourse and the way the other expresses himself to me. First of all he must have the desire—not a desire that can ever be satisfied but of something beyond—the desire of the infinite. This presupposes a possession of a world understood, for the other cannot be approached with empty hands. But in approaching the other, this possession of a world at his disposal must be ready to be given in a disinterested generosity. I understand this approach in the visage—which at every moment destroys every plastic image that I make of it. This visage expresses itself, and this expression is beyond the distinction of form and content, for what is expressed is its expression. In receiving this, I learn what was never known to me. New truths come from the master who teaches me. It is not maieutic which already contains all and is never surprised.[f]

At last the infinite which surpasses its idea will lead us beyond the subjective (towards realism). Levinas claims that his notion of visage is behind most of what he will say. It originates in the pre-philosophical, before any giving of sense. This visage is received without any damage to the self that receives it. It does not depend on the interiority of Platonic recollection.[g] It shows the priority of this being to being in general—a direct familiarity with particular being not mediated, but direct.[h]

Levinas says that the immediate is not contact, it is face to face. *Totality and Infinity* describes an immanent economic history broken at crucial points by transcendence and communication with the other, that cannot be synthesized and englobed.[i]

Separation and Discourse: Atheism or the Will

The Hegelian antithesis in rejecting the thesis appeals to the thesis. They already form a totality that embraces them, but an absolute transcendence cannot be integrated in this way. A negation is correlative to what it negates. But the separation we are speaking of is accomplished by the infinite passing beyond our idea of it. As against Hegel this must not be a negative but a positive movement. The category of correlation does not

---

f. "This suggests another answer to the learning paradox not [along] maieutic lines. Here I do not know in part already. I have to *begin with only the desire of the infinite and an acquaintance with what I already am.* But I am seeking for what is absolutely other, so I can learn what is radically new and different from the other. Teaching is possible. This is more realistic than the Platonic view."[22]

g. "It will open up a real philosophy of the immediate which has not yet been written. (This is very important to me after James. But I do not agree with what he says here.)"

h. "But then Levinas says that this is an imperative of language??? I can say much about this. Language presupposes this face to face. Language requires it to have something to speak of and express. This is not mediated by being and nothingness. This is always familiarity with my very existence or that of an other—not first of being. Then with language we may be able to express the Being of these beings are as they are. Such a philosophy, like that of James, must be primarily ontic rather than ontological. It is a direct acquaintance, face to face with beings."[23]

i. "Is the infinite already present in the world of perception? Perhaps this is what Merleau-Ponty means. Transcendence. I must say again that the world itself points beyond. Being does not."[24]

suffice for transcendence. A non-reciprocal transcendence of the other cannot be grasped through abstraction and through essences. It is imposed on us by the concrete realities of our moral experience. (Phenomenology is here—a phenomenology of ethics.) That which I require of myself does not compare with what I can demand of the other. We are incommensurable. This banal asymmetry of moral responsibilities is metaphysically significant. It shows the impossibility of understanding ourselves from the outside. I cannot get into the other and absorb him into a system. He has to speak for himself. We can grasp him only through discourse, by talking to him. This direct experience of confrontation that is based on the face to face underlies all social experience. This must first be directly understood and analyzed before science can be understood in its meaning. The separation of the self manifests itself under the form of interior psychic life. This psychism is not a reflection of external beings. It is based on a resistance to a system; it is a way of being.

Now Levinas returns to Descartes; the *cogito* leads to the infinite, to God in Descartes' language. But this is only a second step in the movement; the first involves time. There is an inner temporal order distinct from the common public time. By time we maintain a distance from ourselves, though this does not involve a nothingness. (Against Sartre here).[25] The cause of time, more ancient than itself, is still to come. The cause is known as if it were posterior to its effect. The positivist speaks of this "as if" as if it were an illusion. The future here precedes the past (final causation).[j] This is brought forth by memory and by thought—it is logically absurd but constitutes a revolution in being. That which comes after (the effect) conditions what comes before (the cause). Similarly, the particular being which is placed in a region is going elsewhere. The present of the *cogito*, though later it will find itself in relation to the infinite, now finds itself absolutely alone. In this instant of full youth (the present) where it cares not about its gliding into the past or its coming again in the future finds the separation of metaphysics and of the metaphysician. It is a mistake to introduce the unconscious and the implicit here; it is wrong to bring this under a totality of determinism. The ignorance here is a detachment, nothing like the ignorance of things. It is founded on an internal psychic life; it is a positive enjoyment (*jouissance*) of self. The imprisoned being, ignoring its prison, is at home with itself. (Is this a pure moment of play?)

Its power of illusion, if it is to be illusion, constitutes its separation. Note that Levinas agrees here that the source of freedom lies in detachment, which is not the same as negation.[27] It does not simply say 'no' to

---

j. "Final causation as I have said is a new way of being."[26]

this situation. It is a positive event. It moves to something. Nor does it negate all to which it remains attached. It indulges in projects or illusions which are its own. The thinking being at first seems to be already integrated in a whole. As a matter of fact he is not so integrated until he is dead. Life gives him a holiday, a vacation, a postponement which is precisely the interior life where that which is objectively impossible becomes possible. For the historiographer this place where all things are possible is the realm of madness. As a matter of fact this internal life is a possible break with the continuity of world history, and of a death which is just an impact on those who survive.

The internal life may have a direction of another kind in the child. The separation of a being means that he may set up a destiny of its own which is more than a mere interval between two points in world history. This means a new time which is always open and pending. This being, who comes out of nothing, can make a radical new beginning—on his own. This new beginning is a break, an absurdity from the standpoint of the historiographer. It can live an interior time of its own.

By memory I return to the past and suspend what is already accomplished there. By memory I can found myself from the beginning after it has happened. (This shows how I can overcome clock time). Today, I can assume and take over this past, floating free from its origin, which with no subject to take it over, just weighs on us like a burden. By memory I can now take it over, and place it in question (at least its meaning).[28] In separation I can take it over. As the inversion of historic time this memory is the very essence of the interior life.

In the totality of historiography the death of the other is the point where a being is thrown into the totality of history, and continues only through the heritage that his existence has amassed behind itself. But the interior life can open up a mode of existence which resists this turning into an existence that is nothing but the past. The internal life resists this pure passivity which takes over in the strange order of objective time. The anguish of death is the tension between these two times, the one projects out of himself. For one to whom everything happens in accord with his projects, death comes as an absolute event, absolutely a posteriori and new, not giving itself over to any power, even that of negation. Death is anguish because in terminating it does not terminate. In death one goes where one is unable to go, suffocated, but until when? There is no reference to the objective time of history. Is it an utter end? This indifference of death to historic time shows that it is proceeding in another dimension that is not parallel to the common time. In this dimension life can have a sense that triumphs over death. This is not a new possibility that comes at the end of all possibilities. It is resurrection in the child where the rupture of death is surrounded and encompassed.[29] There is suffocation in the impossibility of the possible. But a passage is made to the descendants. This fecundity is a very personal relation, though it is not offered to the I as a possibility. As the personal life cannot be absorbed, so the interior personal time that is lived cannot be taken over by the life of another survivor. Internal time cannot be absorbed into the time of history. Our mortal existence is unable to pass. But this does not mean that it will be present after his death which the common clock chimes. Husserl tries to absorb interior time into objective time and to prove immortality in this way. But he is wrong.

Birth and death as commonly understood are seen in the third person from the outside. We need a phenomenology of beginnings and ends.[30] This is death seen from the external point of view of the survivor. Internal life is lived only by the first person. Here, the being refuses to be absorbed. Each being has his own time, his own way of existing internal to himself. This active refusal is necessary to the idea of the infinite, which does not produce it.[31]

The discontinuity of the internal life interrupts historic time, which sees only groups. The primacy of history constitutes a choice where internal life is sacrificed. Levinas proposes another choice which cannot be demonstrated. Can it then be made probable and grounded?[32] The real must not be identified exclusively with history but also with the internal life that breaks it. Only this makes social pluralism possible. It is really impossible to make an idea of the whole of humanity.[k] This should be qualified. My experience of the other as a separated being is the source of the meaning of totalities, as lived experience is the source of sense for the sciences. The interval of separation or death is a third notion between being and nothing.

This interval between birth and death is not to life as potency is to act. Levinas will call it a dimension of being, dead time or time of death, which ruptures the totalized time of history. He says the discontinuity of Cartesian time saw something of this dispersion into the plural, separated existence of many creatures. This is the time of creative voluntary action, not of works. We shall study later this separation of selfhood. In this separated condition the self is alone, isolated and atheistic. He has broken with participation in Being, though he may rejoin it and God through belief. This inner life of the separated soul is naturally atheistic.[l] This atheism is anterior to the negation and the assertion of the divine. It is a glory to the creator of setting up beings capable of atheism, who are not *causa sui* but nevertheless have an independent point of view of their own and an independent world. Without being *causa sui*, they can become anterior to their cause (and build a new world).

---

k. ("Cf. mankind. I think that this needs to be qualified.")[33]

l. Wild asks: "Are we returning to this condition now?" He suggests: "[We] could build a theory of belief into this."

Psychism taken more precisely is sensibility. Sense is the basis of the internal life. It lies at the root of egotism and the self. Greek theory of individuation, the *tode ti*, cannot prevent these "individuals" from being actualized and totalized in a whole wherever they disappear. If they fall under a concept, they fall under a genus, or being. No special attribute or quality, like that of Leibniz, can separate them. Attributes and concepts form a hierarchy and constitute a whole. The plurality of discourse requires that each term is endowed with psychism which has a direct sensual awareness, i.e., self-awareness. (This is the preconceptual source of individuation; man is measure of all things. He cannot be measured; he does not fall under a concept or a genus.) Sensibility constitutes the separate egotism of the self. Sensing as opposed to what is sensed is active. This active self-grasp in sensing ruins all systems, including that of Hegel. Hegel places the origin of his dialectic in the sensed, not in the unity of sensing and sensed in sensation. The start of his phenomenology is inadequate. It is no accident that in the *Theaetetus* the thesis of Protagoras is dependent on Heraclitus or involves it. It is only through the sensuous egotism of Protagoras that the Parmenidean whole can be split up and decomposed into the flux, which never turns on itself. (Physical things are constant and maintain themselves under concepts and laws. So in this way, becoming is a category radically independent and opposed to Being.) This depends ultimately on singularity of sensation.

We shall show later how selfhood, ipseity, emerges from enjoyment (*jouissance*) of welfare or happiness. This owes nothing to the other logically or dialectically, who remains transcendent. The atheistic independence of this enjoyment is without opposition to the infinite but it makes this relation possible, and is not annulled by it.

Without separation there would be no truth, only the being. Truth is tangency rather than contact. It rests on distance which brings with it the risk of error and illusion. As against existential philosophy Levinas says the truth is not rooted in a previous union with existence.[m]

The search for truth is a search for forms which involves distance.[35] Participation does not lead to truth. Participation is a mode of being. It is to develop my being without in any way losing contact with him. Truth is the end of this stage, a breaking with all participation. Levinas admits that the truth maintains some contact but does not derive its being from such contact. For the truth, a being must exist in himself not from his frontiers, independently and separately. This is the point of the myth of Gyges in the Republic—to see without being seen.[36] This means to become uprooted, not to participate at the ambivalent risk of truth and error. To know something is not to be it. It does seem to involve distance. But Lev-

---

m. "I say this wrong."[34]

inas has no place for direct acquaintance, the *cogito* as involving a coincidence of being and knowing. He tears everything to parts that are unrelated. I suppose this is otherness and pluralism?[n]

The notion of externality which guides the search for truth is made possible only by the idea of the infinite connected with desire. The infinite is
not an object. It is desirable. The idea of the infinite reveals itself in the
strong sense of this term. It can be approached only by a thought that at
each instant "thinks more than it thinks." This measureless, measured by
desire is the visage.[38] This shows the difference between desire and need.
Desire is animated (Cf. eros) by its object, the desirable. It comes from the
object. Whereas need arises from a lack, from the subject.

In truth, a being seeks the other from a distance which is both overcome and not overcome. It does not bury itself in what it seeks, i.e., the
other. It arises in a being who lacks nothing, needs nothing. This is the
situation of language, which is always at a distance which it is overcoming.[39] Language is never touched by the other. Separation, interiority,
truth and language, these are the categories of the infinite and of metaphysics.

Desire is the misery of the happy, the going beyond of a being who does
not need the other in a happiness he already possesses. In this enjoyment
he is already above being. But in desire he can sacrifice this being. This desire of the infinite is insatiable not because of our finitude; it is already satisfied but desires more. Not nostalgia, a desire for what we have lost, but
it is a desire for richness itself. In rejecting the half-man myth of Aristophanes in the Symposium, does not Plato see the possibility of this positive affirmative desire? But the first object of desire is not immortality;
here Plato is wrong. It is simply for the other, the stranger. Its name is justice. It is absolutely non-egotist, for the other. And this is connected with
the idea of creation *ex nihilo*, which means the creation of what is absolutely other, not partaking of the father. So happiness is separate from
desire, as politics is separate from religion. Politics is based upon equality.[40] It achieves happiness. Religion is pure desire, not a struggle for
recognition. It comes as a surplus in a society of equals. It means a glori-
ous humility, responsibility and sacrifice, which are also the real conditions for equality itself.

Discourse

In knowing the claim is that the knower does not participate nor unite
with what is known. Thus truth involves a dimension of interiority where

---

n. "I must defend a direct self-knowledge (i.e., the existence of not-positional knowledge)."[37]

the metaphysician and metaphysics itself hold back and from which they seek the truth. This relation of truth both overcomes and does not overcome the distance; it forms no totality with it. Levinas says that it rests on language, a relation where the terms absolve from their relation. Language is essentially intentional. The word cannot be a word without intending. Even if we say that the words vanish in fulfilling their function, they disappear; they are not absolved. (They remain what they are—independent—in the relation? This is true of what is known, but it is not true of the knowing language.)[o]

This absolution that Levinas speaks of does not pertain to objective thematized knowledge. Here we do not know the thing *kath auto*. In uncovering as in Heidegger we take the thing up into our own horizon. On the classic view experience of it cannot be attained until it has been modeled by the intellect. We know the object only in relation to us. (Sartre tries to answer this by his notion of nothingness . . .) Now we say it is known in relation to our projects—not *kath auto*.

To know objectively is to know what is now passed, the fact, what has been done (fait accompli). Objective knowledge thematizes since the facts are no longer really present and do not speak. This world of facts or phenomena is neither real or unreal. It is an anarchic world without a principle of the infinite. This is the world of enjoyment, insufficient for the search for truth, to be found in metaphysics only. Levinas contrasts this partial truth of uncovering with the real truth that is expressed. Here the other confronts us with its visage without being uncovered in an alien light. Absolute experience is not uncovering but revealing, where he who expresses is one with the expression. This expression is its own. It does not come from an alien light. This visage always goes beyond the form that is acceptable to the knower. This is to signify or to have a sense. Against all existential philosophy Levinas asserts that to signify is not to be given?[p] He de-emphasizes intuition which is a solitary thinking. Meaning is said and is taught by a presence. This is the overcoming presence of an Other who can lie because he is free. The act does not express, for example, the acts of history which indicate their authors indirectly in the third person. One can conceive of language as behavior, as gesture, but this omits the essential coincidence of the revealer and the revealed in any

---

o. "Perhaps, I do not understand but I cannot agree with this. He gives no examples. It stands as a mere assertion."[41]

p. Wild asks here: "Is meaning the presence of externality?" Furthermore, he asks: "Is to give a sense as present an event irreducible to evidence?" Both questions derive from Levinas's assertion: "To give meaning to one's presence is an event irreducible to evidence" (*Totality and Infinity*, 66). Wild states, in opposition to Levinas, "this is against all existential philosophy."

expression, for example, teaching. We attain true objectivity only beyond objective thematized thinking, where the interlocutor questions us and talks to us independently of himself.

Levinas now inveighs against the primordial field of Husserl and Heidegger as the coupling of the body which can constitute an alter ego. We do not find the absolutely other here. (I can agree with this. Here, we need a phenomenology of discourse where the radical other is involved.)[42] Heidegger has an original "witness (*Mitsein*)," but it is impersonal and neutral. Being in general comes first, before being-with. This witness is neutral and previous to the genuine I and Thou. This face to face underlies a real society involving a separated other and a separated self. Levinas says that Durkheim surpasses this optic conception of my relation with the other. He bases it on a religious transcendence which at least does not deduce from and reduce the relation to a multiplicity of individual objects, examples of a concept. Then Levinas refers to the I and Thou of Buber which he says is very formal and is remote from the concrete. It is a sort of scornful spiritualism which makes the I-Thou a sudden eruption in a sick world of economics, unfriendliness, etc. Levinas is doing something else based on the idea of the infinite.

The claim of reaching the other as such is attained through language and especially speaking in the vocative, directly interpellating, speaking to him in the first person or second. You may be rejecting him, departing from him, condemning him to death here, but at least you respect the other. You are speaking to him, not absorbing him as an object in a system.[q] He is asked. He is called to the word. This is a call to the present. This present is not made up of a flow of frozen timeless instants. This is a presence which constantly, incessantly takes them up and masters them. This is the presentation—the life of the present. It maintains itself and goes beyond the time when it appears. It teaches new things and facts; it is magisterial. It is not a mere Platonic reawakening. In a dialogue the object offers itself to us through the master who is the oneness of the teaching and what is taught. Language is not a mere incarnation of thought as the Hegelians think; it is conditioned not by matter, but by otherness. It is essentially transcendence. (This is too radical but an extreme statement of a good point.)

Society does not flow from truth. It is rather truth that flows from genuine society. Rhetoric is dissimulation and deception. To overcome these is justice, the recognition of his privilege to be other, to be master.[44] Equality for Levinas means very little.

---

q. "This is good against Sartre."[43]

Discourse and Ethics

The traditional concept of reason makes real communication impossible, for reason is one. How can reason be other to reason? It is one and universal, not many and singular. How can reason be singular? The very essence of traditional reason is the renunciation of singularity. Reason speaking in the first person will not address the other; it will hold a monologue.[r] This traditional reason englobes the thinker. His own unique insights and attributes are all absorbed into the total system. Protagoras was really right: Man is the measure of all things.[45] He is independent, separated by his relation to the infinite. He cannot be absorbed into being.

The function of language is not to take over the unique thought and world of the other—to force his assent to an alien system, to destroy the other by taking him into the me. Language cannot be fitted into the subject-object pattern. The other with whom I speak is not an object, not a particular given to be subsumed under the universal of language. Language does not presuppose the universal; it makes the universal possible. It is communication with the other, leaving him intact. It represents an endless ethical approach to an infinite that can never be stopped by any system. The communication of the self with the other is ethics. (This is close to Marxism here.) Communication is a form of action in which the self and the other are left intact, but achieve an advance towards the infinite idea. Plato sees the difference between a fixed objective truth with which he is mainly concerned in his writings, and a living discourse which can defend itself and knows whom to address and when to keep silent (*Phaedo* 276 a [Cf. my point in Phaedrus and Epistle VII]). He knows the strangeness and wonder in which language begins. Only another man can be strange because he is free. Language depends on freedom. In speaking, Levinas says that it does not merely unroll an established plan, but it speaks in the lack of a plan, of common terms. It tries to link terms together where there are now only gaps. It is constantly, advancing ever-proceeding towards the infinite.

This is right, but where is the notion of common agreement?[46] There are facts shown, and insights that demand agreement. These need to be recognized. Levinas says that strangeness of the other which language always faces is his freedom. It is this that pervades the whole of discourse, but it is freedom that must be satisfied freely and still maintaining itself and its command—not the command of mere static fixed facts.

When we interpret discourse as a forcing of the unique other into the common meanings of an already coherent system, the other vanishes as a

---

r. "Cf. Whitehead—great philosophers who speak only for themselves. No real dialogue is possible here. We need a phenomenology of dialogue. Cf. Buber."

unique being *kath auto* and becomes neutral and nude, mere function in a constituted order. The same is true of Heidegger's analysis of tools, each of which performs its function for another and vanishes in this function. But such instruments as cities, highways, power plants, have a life of their own in themselves which cannot be reduced to these instrumental functions. Thus as we now know, waste appears; the cities degenerate into slums, the air and the streams are polluted. These things are always opaque and resistant. As Plato sees in *The Republic* these things must be seen by an eye in the light of a sun outside of them. They have no light of their own, and our light is inadequate to reveal the existence they have in themselves. Art uncovers new forms in this nude nature—to illuminate it by pure forms. But the work of language is quite different. It enters into relation with a nudity, lacking form, but having a sense of its own. It does not appear on an ambivalent background either good or bad, beautiful or ugly. It appears always as a positive value—as a visage which I do not have to uncover, which is not a thing offered to my powers to a light of mine that is external to it. It turns itself to me and expresses its own light. Bodily disrobing and nudity presuppose this nudity of the visage and extend it either with or without shame. My relation with a visage is never with an object. This visage is separate and absent from the world. Therefore do I not know it by some different kind of knowledge? The other reveals his transcendence, his absence from the world which he is constantly entering.[47] He is free and therefore strange. He is other than me and the world he is entering. He is other and strange, and this strangeness involves a misery. I also share this strangeness with him. The nudity of his body is revealed in coldness and shame. To exist *kath auto* in the world is a misery that we share. This sharing of misery is beyond all rhetoric. This nudity is denument . . . This look does not merely turn me into an object (Sartre); it requires from a height. It requires a recognition that is given, and in and through which all things are put into question. Levinas claims that generality and conceptualization appear here. The self gives his own joyous possession of all things to the other, and the general idea appears. He seems to imply that perceptual objects appear only with the concept.[s] The generality of the object is correlated with the generosity of the solitary self going towards the other. This makes possible the community of all goods of this world. Language is universal in the same way; it is the passage from the individual to the general.[48] It lays the basis for possession in common. It abolishes the inalienable property of the solitary self enjoying all. I give my world to the other in thought, communication, the universal. Heidegger is wrong when he speaks about things as the basis for all

---

s. "I doubt this. But he may be right that at this level of things of the world all sink to the level of merchandise. Money is made possible. This is rather sketchy."

the relations and for-structures of the world in its different regions. Prior to these there is my giving by generosity to the right of the stranger, the widow and the orphan. To them, I must either give all or refuse all things. I am not above these things as building with them but first of all as giving them to the stranger in generosity.

The Metaphysical and the Human

The atheist self receives transcendence without mystical merging or suffering the violence of the holy. So Levinas calls it atheism—this purity from all myth. He is open to the other and gives to him in all generosity. In the metaphysical relation we come to transcendence through the noumenon, not the numinous.[49] We are related to the other and at the same time absolved from this relation. There is no union, no participation. The idea of the infinite comes from a humanity without myth. Revelation is discourse. It therefore involves otherness. We are related to a real God *kath auto*, but this relation is neither to an object, or to the numinous. I am related here to a substance that is more than my idea of it, and I go on towards it. This metaphysical relation involves motion toward words. It is not theoretical but ethical. It is justice here that reveals the transcendent. Human relations are to the revealing of the transcendent as sense experience is to understanding in Kant. God is revealed in justice; in ethics, not in theology. Religion apart from our relations with other men is always primitive.[t]

We cannot be directly aware of God except through the word. But the other is no mediator. He is not God incarnate. But he reveals the direction, the height where God is revealed. First it is revealed in justice, in action with others, moving towards transcendence. God is revealed through meaning, teaching and justice.[u] Metaphysics is at work in all ethical relations, with the right of the stranger, the widow and orphan. In ethics I must act on my own, not in a drama imposed on me, where I play a role that I do not control. Obedience yes, but this is free, not a blind participation. (Cf. Primitive men participate in their worlds. When freedom comes this blind participation goes, though it may be replaced by choice and belief.) Spontaneous liberty is supposed to be admirable in recent existential thought. Any limits on it are supposed to be tragic. But it can be selfish and arbitrary unless it is checked and asked to justify itself through ethics. This comes from the other and the infinite. Criticism leads to this. To justify freedom is not to prove it but to make it just. Critical philosophy leads to desire. I feel murderous and ashamed in my arbitrary spontaneous

---

t. "Cf. Christianity here."
u. "This is Jewish. Cf. The Rabbi. God teaches."

freedom. In shame I come to desire the infinite (perfection). This leads to ethics. From Spinoza to Hegel, philosophy strives for absolute liberty of the self-grounded on a synthesis of pure reason. This is neutral and impersonal, so it appears as an escape from the arbitrariness of the spontaneous will. Justice is transcendental. Justice is the condition for knowing. It is not a noesis-noema—it is active, ethics and rests on a desire for the infinite—not a knowing of it.

He who offers the world to the other in language constantly maintains it in question and answer. He offers the world, interprets it, sustains its meaning. The word is the origin of all signification. I question this; my liberty is not the last word, and I am not alone. Moral conscience gets me outside of myself. Like desire it is insatiable. I can never satisfy it, for it has the infinite, perfection in it.

I think this is so. Conscience has something of the infinite in it. Also it is non-conceptual as Heidegger shows. The infinite appears here. I never have done enough. There is always more and more . . . Here is the infinite touching us. It comes to me from beyond, like teaching. Also this relation is irreversible. My conscience tells me. I shall say that the moral, the existential is prior to truth and to theory. Thus I take "the social is the place of truth" in this sense. Also, conscience does not arise from need. It speaks to a freedom that can possess a world and self beyond all need. Conscience does not tell me what I need. It tells me what I ought to do—beyond all needs. Also it is positive, not just negative.[50]

The infinite opens up the order of the good which is above the neutrality of being. It makes a society of strangers possible. In formal logic there is no distinction reflecting the difference between desire and need. Both are regarded merely as need. The creation from nothing breaks the system of being. From Parmenides to Plotinus the multiplicity of finite beings has been degraded to a status of appearance and discounted, together with time and change. The many have been synthesized into a system of being and thus reunited with the one does the notion of world fit with this? The world points beyond. Also it is temporal, and thus related to freedom.*

---

* Wild's reflection is so sustained that the argument does not indicate the closure of the first section of *Totality and Infinity*. "Interiority and Economy" begins on page 109 of the English edition.

SECTION II. INTERIORITY AND ECONOMY

Heidegger has left out enjoyment of living, etc. He is very weak on 'for the sake of *Dasein*'. On this point all becomes vague and relative in Heidegger's thought. To live on bread (*vivre de pain*) is not to perceive, to present it or represent it or to act on it, or to act by it. It is the content of my enjoyment that embraces them. These contents occupy me. They amuse me. I live in them. They nourish my existence. Note that food is omitted by Heidegger, and nourishment in general. My food is not a *Zeug*, an instrument. If I eat my bread to work and to live, I live in these and enjoy them autonomously.[v] Levinas says this is consciousness of consciousness, but is not reflection. It is *jouissance*, enjoyment, and egotism. It is mine. It does not belong to the Aristotelian categories. It is neither act nor potency. That which I do and that which I am are that in which I live and which I enjoy. This is *jouissance*, happiness (*bonheur*), more than mere being. It is not just the tone of my existence, but a passage into something, the value of my life for me. The supreme nourishment is the nourishment of life itself. Society requires more than reason. This term "reason" has no plural. Of what would an entirely reasonable being talk to another entirely reasonable being. Society would vanish in this case. In Kant the self comes back to itself in feeling the need of happines, *bonheur*.

Levinas has a good account of representing and thinking. There is something in Husserl's notion of constitution; the intentional relation of *sui generis*, is not causal, not synthetic nor analytic. It is clear and distinct. That is, insofar as it is true it is perfectly adequate to what is thought about, which loses itself in becoming a noema, perfect correlate of the thinking of it. Here the noesis is master over the noema. The externality of what is thought of becomes a meaning given by the noesis. This is constitution. In the tradition there is this complete mastery by thinking over its object which is absorbed by clear and distinct ideas. In this way, the object becomes a pure work of thought. This is the constant temptation of idealism in all Western thought.[w] Representation is full of illusions, though they may be useful. For example, it thinks only in the present, which it may confuse with eternity. It does not recognize its past, but uses it by objectifying it, and also the future. Becoming does not appear in this horizon. All becomes timelessly present. Tenses go. This is the Husserlian

---

v. "I should say something about this distinction; [it] seems to be right, and Heidegger does leave it out. I live in these activities. Perhaps it is here that in my existence I assimilate and take over these acts."[51]

w. "I can make use of this. This uncritical use of reason has its uses in giving us mastery and control over things, and achieving an initial correspondence in certain respects. Until we confront the truly other and our self-same reason is challenged by the radical other. Then we see the limits of absorption into the self-same system, and emerge into ethics."

epoche. The noesis and the noema become identical. The self-same assimilates all its object in a one-way determination of the other by the self. (Cf. Merleau-Ponty.) Reality is reduced to its thought content. To be intelligible is to be represented. There is here no anteriority of the given.[x] Truth means being determined formally by the object, but in such a way that thinking retains its spontaneity and is not really touched by the object.[52] But ultimately the real opposition of the same and the other disappears through the determination of the other by the same. Levinas admits that the body is a constant opposition to this constitution of thought. Here nourishment conditions thinking. Here otherness enters into the same. The world in which I live is not simply a set of noemas. It nourishes me and bathes me. The body recognizes a past in its future, and never gets outside of time.[y] On page 130 (of *Totality and Infinity*) he has a section on the element and tools.

Here he gives some good phenomenology of the earth, the sky, the wind, the air, and the sea. They present only a face to us. They give us adjectives, no substance. They seem indeterminate, but they precede the distinction of the finite from the infinite. They seem to have no origin in a being. We are familiar with them in enjoying them. Liquid manifests its qualities without support. They seem to determine no thing. The element seems to come to us from nowhere. We bathe in it. It engulfs us and surrounds us. We cannot fix it as an object. This enjoyment accompanies all our usage of things and instruments. Heidegger leaves it out. I enjoy the cigarette I am smoking without any sense of utility. There are no for-structures here. Man becomes disinterested. He can play with them. This is the truth in the moralities of hedonism. I am purely egoistic here (*jouissance*) with no reference to the other. I am without ears like a famished stomach. To live is to play without the biological and technological finality on which it is easy to focus. It shows the egoistic sovereignty of man over himself and the things of the world; that is, the inversion of food instincts in the gourmet, etc. Nourishment is not a tool except in a system of exploitation.

He says sensibility is being within the world, being contained. This is the finite without the infinite, totality. Levinas defends Descartes on the irrationality of the sensible, and also appears to accept Kant's distinction between thought and sense. He says that sensibility is *jouissance*.[z] Phenomenology has shown a continuity between sense and thought. Sense is not a defective kind of understanding with a strong tone of feeling. Sense is content with the given. It is finite without the infinite. Is it immediately

---

x. "My problem is how to see this as anything more than an illusion. But it does reveal within limits."

y. "But he [Levinas] splits up the whole experience here."[53]

z. "I think that he is wrong on this."[54]

at its term—*jouissance*? An insecurity pointing to otherness is present even in sensibility, sense is beyond instinct and this side of reason. Levinas objects to the notion of unconscious horizons. He defends matter vs. form in sense things, but not in all experience. (Cf. the visage.) He says art is a return to jouissance and the elemental. Man does not find himself in an absurd world where he is thrown as in Heidegger. The disquiet we feel in *jouissance* leads not to angst, etc., but to work. There is a basic agreement of self and world which is happiness, play, *bonheur*. The world of enjoyment has no strangeness, no secret. Levinas says that according to *jouissance* there is a hidden uncertainty about the future. But this is a hidden uncertainty about the future. But this is corrected by labor, economics, money, etc., so that the remedies pre-exist the evils. He is against *geworfenheit*.[aa] The internality and separation of *jouissance* is independent of desire for the infinite. There is no dialectical opposition here. I am independent, enjoying, sensing satisfied before the infinite comes into play. The tragedy of suicide shows the basic character of the love of life.[56] At first we are in agreement with and enjoying the world. But it is flawed by the need of care for the tomorrow. This leads to the household, labor exchange, and money.

The home is not an instrument (against Heidegger). The house is the beginning of independent human action—its origin. It does not belong to the world of objects; it is their source. The house is a basic condition for seeing the world of objects. It belongs to the separated being who is responsible for culture, work, civilization. It makes work and labor possible. Man achieves his separation in the dwelling. The home gives solitude and intimacy in an already human world. Here language takes the form of silence. Words do not have to be said. It is the intimacy of the feminine.[57] Buber really has described this. It is before the questions of critical language with the genuine other. The separate self now lives his own internal life in the home and gathers himself together, ready to go forth for possession and labor.[bb] Work is impossible for a being without a home. Work comes from the manipulating hand that grasps and takes. It is a movement towards the self, for possession not outwardly directed, but centripetal. It is through the hand that we first grasp the depths of matter. It moves towards the self not towards the thing and the infinite exteriority. The obscurity of matter presents itself to labor as resistance. That which is grasped by the hand gives solidarity and substance. Here the thing arises, not in the sensible world of jouissance, nor in the concept.

---

aa. "But I don't think he understands it [*geworfenheit*]. He calls it abandonment, dereliction, a very negative view. He misses it as pure human thrownness, facticity. He is really defending a divine creation *ex nihilo* with some providence."[55]

bb. "He says the world is born from this. Wrong."[58]

Work and the hand come between. We play with the elements, with adjectives lacking substance and solidity. This grasp comes out of *jouissance* and presupposes it. This is the organ of grasp and possession by the master self of enjoyment.

All manipulation of a system of tools presupposes an original grasp of things, which has its source in the home. The world is a possible possession? Contemplation comes after the home and possession. Then the world can become a spectacle, but not at first. In enjoyment the self bathes in the elements. It is both sovereign and suffers influence. But this ambiguity is part of the joy of living. The body is both master and slave. The healthy can become sick. But it does not suffer necessarily in thrownness as in Heidegger. This comes from an idealistic freedom. It is an independence in dependence. To enjoy, in the body on earth among things, and at the same time depend on them, is an ambiguity of the living body expressed by the notion of living in something, or living on other things than the self. There is constant risk of betrayal to which the fear of death bears constant postponement. Consciousness is the ambiguity of the body [English text p. 165, French text p. 139]. The body can work from the center of the home.

To be free is to construct a world where one can be free [English text p. 166, French text p. 140]. To labor comes from being menaced, from fear, the feeling par excellence. To have consciousness is to have time. Nothing is finished. There is always more time to come. But time presupposes a relation which is not offered in work, a relation to the radically other—the infinite. After a bodily act is finished, it may be understood as cause. But in being carried out it is "final cause." The hand is always adventure, however. There is always chance or mischance. Groping is not a technical defect, but the condition of all technology. The hand always gropes. The end does not attract us, does not draw us, but develops itself *s'attraper*.[59] The hand is the source of technology. To envisage the end and to reach out for it are parts of one and the same movement on the part of a being in the world who comes into it from an internality this side of it. This being is integrated in the things of the world, but dwells in its interstices. Representation comes after life is already going on, in which it is implanted. But representation then pretends afterwards to have constituted this life.

Heidegger analyzes the home only as part of a system of implements, but can man act in view of himself without a place of retirement, where he can be disengaged *chez soi*, at home? The groping hand traverses an empty distance from a place where I am living at home. Through labor I or we may come to possess, but the face of the other can challenge all possession, not from the outside, but ethically from on high. I cannot suppress this ethical challenge of the other, which places me in question. Being placed in question by the other is language [English text p. 171, French text p. 146]. Language is contact over a distance. We do not see or seize the other. Truth is not here in the modes of *jouissance* nor in possession. It is in the transcendence of an absolute externality which makes itself present and expresses itself. But this takes place in the world, in the dwelling which must be open and hospitable to the other—ready for him. We can forget the other and close our dwelling to any hospitality in egotism. This is always possible. The doors and windows may be tightly closed or open. The ring of Gyges signifies separation, and the possibility of deceit and trickery and crime. We must first possess the world before we can speak it, give it to another. Universality is a gift of what we have to the other. Transcendence is not an optics, a seeing, but an ethics, a giving, which happens in the world and presupposes an economy. My works conceal me as much as they reveal. They are not like language which opens and reveals. They are signs that must be deciphered (like all phenomena). In taking up what I have willed and done, I see in them many consequences that I have not willed. My works have a destiny independent of me, merged with the works of others and chance. It does not express adequately the internality from which they emanate. This is shown by the distrust of the individual for the tyranny of the state which is achieved by works, including my own from which I am absent as from my roles. I am not expressed by my life and by my works. I am absent from them. Freud shows this absence in what I do that is mixed with dream and hidden forces.

Our intellectual questions concern the quiddity, what is it? But this always means placing it in a system. It means what is it in this context? It presupposes someone who is asked the question (the whole linguistic situation). It is the correlate of metaphysical desire. It is anterior to all specific questions. Who is it? Often the answer is some quid—the President of the Council. But in back of this there is someone present without referring to any system of relations. The who expressed in action is not strictly present in this way, assisting in the interpretation. This who is absent as well as present in his acts. The same is true of works. In making myself available to the other in speech, I open myself to his question, and make myself responsible, under the obligation to respond. This ability to respond is my last reality. My existence as thing in itself begins with the presence in me of the idea of infinity, which leads me to seek for this last reality of myself which is able to respond.[cc] Here, in response to the other questioning me, I must gain command of the whole world in relation to me, and become responsible for it. The other in questioning me calls me

---

cc. "My point here. Here, in response to the other questioning me, I must gain command of the whole world in relation to me and become responsible for it. The other in questioning me calls me to a world mastery."[60]

to a world mastery. Death is not this master. It determines the flight from responsibilities. Courage is in spite of death. Only through the other does death call me to my last reality.[dd] I can be with him and experience his death. He departs from the world and I remain. He goes into death, "the source of all myths." Now he speaks only in the mode of silence. Is it like the passing of a part of myself, an alter ego? No, it is only insofar as we have been taken up into a total system. A total world has vanished— something with a relation to the infinite in it has passed. This is something separate and unique, that cannot ever be recaptured. This relation to the infinite cannot pass, for the infinite remains. And the infinite can still speak to me in the mode of silence. But the uniqueness cannot be recovered. This should be connected with what Levinas says about murder and the irrevocable command "thou shalt not murder." Something not recoverable has been lost, but something of it, the relation to infinity remains.

It is the idea of the infinite that breaks into our interior life and shows it to be insufficient, not by any lack or need of an unfulfilled totality, but by an infinite desire. This is a non-possession more precious than any possession, which feeds on its own hunger. It is beyond all satisfaction and unsatisfaction. Nothing can drown it, once it occurs, nothing can put it to sleep. This desire alone stops egotism and leads to ethics.

It makes us see the difference between phenomenon and being. This difference is concerned with a real order of other beings, anterior to the Socratic order. Real dialogue, against the sophists, is without rhetoric, whether it is in prose, flattery, or seduction. A phenomenon is a being which appears, but which is absent from its appearance. It is real, but infinitely far from its being. One may penetrate into the phenomena of the inner life. But he is absent. One understands him as one understands a primitive man who has left behind his hatchets and designs, but no words. These are essential for the revealing of being. (Cf. Heidegger, who writes language is the house of being. It is only through speaking that being is revealed.) Society is the presence of being, but the thing in itself is hidden. It is to the phenomenon as this is to the appearance. Expression makes manifest the presence of being. It reveals not a sign but the signifying itself. This is the speaking word, not the written word which has to be deciphered as an activity. From this word activity, which may happen in many ways, I am absent. Human existence remains phenomenal as long as it remains as an internal life. Between subjectivity badly understood, there is the assistance of the subjectivity which speaks.

---

dd. "Cf. the death of the other. Heidegger and Søren Kierkegaard leave this out. Here is a theme for me to develop."[61]

SECTION III. EXTERIORITY AND THE FACE*

Levinas holds that there is a pure quality of sensation neither purely an object nor the quality of an object. It precedes this distinction. Augustine and Heidegger are right in seeing how we refer to the other senses in terms of sight. Touch is basic also. In sight especially, sensation and concept seem to correspond. All things are englobed in a field of light. But Levinas wants to question this whole picture. Insofar as touch traverses the nothingness of space, it is like sight, in bringing forth objects on a ground of nothing. But sight requires the sun which is an object. Isn't light also objective? We can see light and its source at night. According to Heidegger this light is not a being, not something. But Levinas questions this, is it not something? This field is not the equivalent of nothing. But the vast empty spaces are terrifying. But when all definite 'qualifiable' things disappear, there is this emptiness. The chasing away of things brings out this impersonal there is. It leads to a kind of vertigo [English text p. 191, French text p. 165]. Vision in light is the possibility of forgetting this horror of the constant return of this apeiron. *Jouissance* expresses this contentment with definite things. Vision makes relations possible, discovered by the hand. It is not transcendent. It reveals no radical other. All is included, englobed, in the horizon. (But does this horizon not point beyond?) Levinas seems to say no. This is *jouissance*. Awareness returns to itself from the elements and the "there is," though it flees from itself in vision. But it has no care for what is beyond all beings and definiteness. Levinas says that science does not break with sensation. Even mathematics does not get away from the characters of sense. (It does not get us to the things in themselves apart from the subjective.) It does not reveal the radically other. The message of phenomenology says 'No.' But, I think that he is often doing a phenomenology of the other. Compare what he says about visage and language.[ee] It is only our relation with the other which opens us to transcendence and to an experience totally different from relative and egoistic sensible experience.

Visage and the Infinite

Vision dominates beings, has a power over them. The thing is given, is offered to me. I hold myself in the same and englobe them. The other is distinct not by a relative comparison as in the species hierarchy where in spite of the differences they are all under a common genus. There is no absolute difference here as when I am face to face with another person and

---

* This section begins on page 187 of the English edition of *Totality and Infinity*.
ee. "This is what I shall try to do. This is very interesting. I can make more out of this."[62]

world. Language related radical others of this kind, in which they absolve themselves from this relation. In seeing, the act appropriates the objects, though this act cannot be seen, and gives them a meaning. In discourse the other contests the sense that I give him. He is ethically inviolable. The solipsistic dialectic is interrupted (unless there is a lecture). I am placed in question. The presence of the other does not belong to me. I do not englobe him. This is experience par excellence. It is like radical empiricism where I actually can learn something new.[ff]

Kantian finitude involves sensibility: Heidegger's being to death. And the Kantian infinite simply enlarges the finite and presupposes it. This is not true of Descartes'. Hegel's infinite does not permit any relation to the finite. It englobes all relations. We feel that it cannot include the freedom of the individual in opposing the tyranny of the state, etc. But in discourse the idea of the infinite constantly produces itself in finite thought, running beyond all its capacities in content. My relation to this other is peaceful. No violence is exercised. The other with whom I speak does not restrict my liberty. He elicits it.[gg] This infinite does not trick me by cunning. There is no force. The face of the other invites me to a relation without common measure. This visage offers me the only matter for murder, for complete annihilation. (Thou shalt not kill is a first and basic command. This stands for utter negation of a powerless power.) I can kill only this radical other. He offers me no resistance except that of the infinite. It is ethically impossible to kill this other. War comes only from peace and presupposes it. The face of the other presents itself in its nudity, emptiness, constantly beyond all specific form that it takes. It is beyond the neutrality of the image. It appeals to me and thus assists its manifestation. The expression does not radiate without the help of the radiant being. Is this aesthetic beauty? It expresses itself and assists the manifestation of itself, speaks prose. The being which I am aware of may be only an appearance. In expressing itself in discourse the other imposes itself in its misery and nudity, appeals to my freedom, and helps it come forth. It freezes the smile in the harsh seriousness of benevolence. This is the beginning of language, an ethical act, an appeal which I cannot retire from. It is neither true nor false. To refuse nourishment to man is neither voluntary nor involuntary [English text p. 201, French text p. 175]. It obliges me to speak (though I may not know the answer . . .). This appeal and my response to it come before all unveiling of being. It is social and ethical. This is the beginning of intelligibility, which later can give itself up to a system which it merely repeats and elaborates. This presupposes an initial epiphany which later can give

---

ff. "All this is against the learning paradox of Plato et al., which presupposes that I know already. Here I can learn and be taught."[63]

gg. "I can make something out of this."[64]

itself up to a system which it merely repeats and elaborates. This presupposes an initial epiphany which is like a word of honor. The self opens up
and expresses itself by itself. This establishes the ethical relation of language. It is completely independent. (Cf. my point on freedom.) In art the
artist may be inspired and carried on by his work. (Cf. possession by the
gods.) But language is against all such rapture. It speaks in the form of
prose. The other is not a scandal which inaugurates a dialectic movement
to overcome it. In its culpability and arbitrariness, the self rises to its responsibility. It is peaceful and without violence. It is temporal and so constantly beyond itself.[hh]

Language conditions the functioning of thought. It gives thought a beginning in being, a first identification of meaning in the visage of the
other. It conditions thought not in its physical being, but rather as an attitude of the same to the other which is irreducible to a representation of
the other or to a consciousness of the other. Language is not an intention.
It does not develop in the interior of a consciousness. This does not mean
to disincarnate language, but it takes account of its difference from any
egological idealistic constitution.[ii] Present philosophy stresses incarnation
of language. But it often misses the peculiar structures that go with it.
Meaning is the infinite [English text pp. 206–7, French text p. 181]. It is this
infinite that obliges me.

The first volume of Husserl's *Logical Investigations* is still valid against
naturalist psychologism. In this light it is always possible to think of reason as an internal order of coherence which assimilates the irrational individual and all particularity, into this system or into the state. But Levinas says this is not so, reason lives in language. The first rationality
begins with the face to face. Society precedes the impersonal structures
and forms. (This is more existential than phenomenological.)[67] Universality comes first in the eyes of the one regarding me.

Language and Objectivity

To objectify is to thematize. It is to offer the world to the other through the
word. Levinas stresses the distance that comes with language.[jj] This distance of the self from itself comes from time. He holds himself at a distance from being and from death as an inexhaustible future coming from
the infinite, although this is not explained very well. This liberty of look-

---

hh. "This is the ethics of language. Levinas does not go into the sins of language except
very casually. I can refuse to speak, lie, dissimulate, refuse to answer. I can break my word,
evade questions and merely joke. Cf. thought and word and deed."[65]

ii. "Is society and obligation before intentionality?"[66]

jj. "I think this is true . . . I have often said this. Cf. Dufrenne. Language is distance from
the world and even from the self. Yes—this is so."

ing and thematizing comes from the other. Husserl has a *cogito* that is absolutely subjective and monadic. It is independent of the other. This is not true of Descartes. At the end of the *Third Meditation,* Descartes makes the certainty of the *cogito* depend on the divine existence as infinite. Levinas cites Descartes: The idea of the infinite contains more being and it comes first before the finite. How could I know my imperfection if I did not already have an idea of infinite perfection in me?[kk] At the end of the *Third Meditation* Descartes says we can admire and adore the infinite. He connects it with Faith.

The whole world presented in language is in the light of day, public and open. This is a common world, which I can command. And the other orders me also to command. The whole of social life depends on my confrontation with the other through no mediation of sign or image. A direct confrontation, equality, comes only when the other commands and reveals himself in his responsibility. It is active, and not a mere result of static similarities. It depends on the assuming of responsibilities, not on passive similarities. The interpersonal is asymmetrical.[ll] The word does not take me to a separate abstract realm but into a world where it is necessary to help and to give.

Will and Reason

The essence of discourse is ethical. Here we reject idealism which cannot admit this. Here will is reason and any separation of the two is illusory. For according to idealism, in the end all ethics becomes politics. (This I think is correct, regarding idealism.) The self and the other play roles in a system they have not originated. Will is what can be affected by the universal. All rests here on the hope of happiness. Each individual wills only the universal of an impersonal reason. Discourse is achieved with no questioners. Each person denies his particularity. Hegel and Spinoza speak for this view. All the suffering experience of humanity is relegated to the subjective and the imaginary. In reality the individual and the personal are not required for an absurd freedom of the arbitrary. They are required that the infinite may produce itself as infinite.[mm] It is in the individual that we find always imperfection and becoming. Life is not a

---

kk. ("For Husserl there is no such externality. The self gives itself this notion as an object, and thus makes itself infinite. With Descartes there is a way out of this subjectivism. The idea of the infinite is not an object. For Descartes this is rational, not a religious feeling. Here is a relation to something external—God is the Other—which does not depend on my internal life. Cf. James here.")

ll. "I question this."[68]

mm. "The social levels down (the individual). This is close to my point. Only the transitory individual is open to the infinite. He seems to be saying this."[69]

function of being. We see this in Bergson where the *durée* does not imitate an immobile eternity and in Heidegger where possibility no longer refers to a completion in an ergon. There is a more than being which we see in the notion of creation, in a God who is not eternally satisfied with himself. We find this in the God of Plato which is beyond being—not in Aristotle. In the separated individual—egotist and atheist, we find this possibility. It is related to an absolutely other, not to an englobing system. He becomes responsible. Here is the infinite related to the finite though absolving itself from it. The ethical presence is both other and imposes itself from it. The ethical presence is both other and imposes itself without any violence. The Socratic maieutic lacks this. It is closely related to the monad of Leibnitz which has no windows, is utterly self-enclosed.

The Ethical Relation and Time

Individuals can absolve from rational relations. In discourse the speaker does not give up his uniqueness. Language is reason, and it is response to the questioning other. He tolerates only a personal response.

Metaphysics arises between absolute terms (free persons) who absolve from their relations and do not yield to an inclusive system.[nn] But this is apt to happen as it has in the West; metaphysics comes down as an objective system, with the great prestige of a panoramic view and tends to absorb the plural individuals. If the many are to maintain themselves they must recognize the impossibility of a total reflection which will absorb the subjective and the objective into a single system beyond the subjective vs. the objective. Thought can never coincide with the existence of the thinker. (In a way I can recognize this. Thought cannot coincide exactly with being, cannot assimilate it.)

While maintaining themselves, the many individuals nevertheless remain in commerce or in war. At no moment are they causes of themselves. This would enclose each one into its interiority, windowless. But our analysis opens up another possibility. Neither war nor commerce is the original mode of this relation. Limitation unites as well as separates in a whole, so limitation is not violence. Each definition is part of a whole system [English text p. 222, French text p. 197].

But we have a pluralism of wills and concepts. They are not parts of a single totality. Here war and peace are possible. Individual wills here transcend the totality. Here he is trying to show utter independence in war and peace which means non-acceptance of fixed places in a world system. (A phenomenology of independence, coming from the will is

---

nn. "Compare arguments between different worlds and ways of life. This is metaphysics, I say."[70]

needed.) No calculation in terms of an inclusive whole can decide a war. There is a supreme risk. There must be confidence in a separated self. But while those at war are not parts, they seek each other, as they are in relation. Violence is possible only among independent beings who are at once seizable (can be attacked) and yet separate. This means that they are not *causa sui*. These terms are partially independent and yet partially in relation. This living contradiction makes violence possible.

In present philosophy there is much talk of a limited freedom, part free and part determined. But this idea has difficulties. How does the free part submit to the determined part, especially if it, the free part, is *causa sui*? Independence does not mean *causa sui*. We must grasp it in a different way. (We need a phenomenology of war and peace. Levinas has begun it. Has he finished it?) *Causa sui* is inconsistent with thrownness.[oo]

A being independent of the other and yet offered to him is a temporal being. It is time that gives meaning to the notion of a limited freedom. Facing the violence of death, which is sure, we take our own time which is a postponement. It is in this way that violence then becomes possible. In war we bring death to what, for the time being, exists completely (in its own world). If they were *causa sui* these beings would be immortal, and there would be no war or peace. As we are, we are exposed, but opposed to violence. It is not an accident which comes to a sovereign freedom. Mortality is an original and basic fact.

Freedom is an adjournment of necessity. (I question this. It can be better formulated. Human beings can be remade or unmade. This is responsibility, taking over, not necessity.) Ethics always can be otherwise. Obligation is not necessity. Man can remake himself creatively in time. Death is always there. Surprise and ambuscade are essential to war. The enemy must catch me where I am absent and exposed. The body is open in this way; it is both present and absent. As a living body I am not all there. I am both present and still to come, in the postponement of death. Violence happens only where discourse is possible, between separated beings before the infinite. Violence involves a visage. The other is unpredictable, that is, transcendent.

The visage resists the violence of murder [English text p. 225, French text p. 201]. Liberty manifests itself only outside of the totality. To think of freedom as in a totality (as a crack or a hole) is to integrate it as a bit of indetermination in this whole which englobes it. We can always reform this totality around the gaps and holes. We must now show how the self and the other can become equal and interchangeable in commerce. I can lose my liberty in this, or I can revive it.

---

oo. "Compare my notion of independence as taking over—not *causa sui*. Responsibility is not a cause of any sort. I am right in this."[71]

Commerce: The Historical Relation and the Face

The will operates in its works but is mute in them. They become anonymous as merchandise, and even the worker can disappear in his salary. A separated being can always enclose himself in his internal life (this is true in epicureanism . . .). But his body is always inserted among other things. This is a first alienation of self-being—which is necessary. This separated will is atheist in refusing itself to the other, and enclosing itself in a home. Fate limits heroism, and makes the hero always play a role in a drama beyond his control. Here is the source of the idea of fate. The sovereign will is subject to this fate through his body (thrown among others) and his fate. The source of this is the separation of every will from its works (my distinction between acts and works . . .). The author of a work cannot foresee its consequences which are beyond his control. This is not a mere ignorance which might be corrected by a greater calculation. It is due to the utter unpredictability of the other (his infinity), and the way he may interpret our works, which are subject to an utterly alien giving of sense. This is a necessary limit of my power. He who expresses aids his expression. But the work goes on in the absence of the author who cannot help it or sustain it in its original meaning. It goes on as a purely plastic form subject to other interpretations. It is a mere merchandise which can be bought and sold and used by others for their purposes. The will through its works is caught up in a destiny of history. There is no purely internal history, which is concerned with objective works. The reign of history is concerned with objective works. The reign of history is concerned with results, complete works of wills which are dead. What I actually do and produce never quite agrees with my desire for the infinite here. It was always something else I wished to do, beyond the objective result. Hence the unlimited field for psychoanalysis and sociology. Destiny does not precede history. It follows it. It is the history of the historiographs, the survivors who interpret and use the works of the dead. They are the conquerors who come after the creative inner life which is created.[pp] They bring about a kind of slavery, and forget the struggle against this slavery.

In relation to his works we must in a sense approach the worker. But he becomes anonymous. He is not face to face with us. In war we fight not against him but against the masses. The eternal truth of materialism is that the will can be attacked and even conquered through its works. The subject can be excluded from the world by intimidation and through the sword and torture. The will itself is open to such attack through its

---

pp. "Though there is the struggle of true history as one may call it which sometimes penetrates to the inner life of an author and to some degree recaptures it. Getting back to the living sources . . . I can say more about this struggle."[72]

body. It is constantly betraying itself, selling itself in this way. My body is not a thing. But neither is it solely my own. Merleau-Ponty goes too far here. It is not a pure *je peux*. The body is a coincidence of these points of view, on the one hand a thing; on the other my own. The body is constantly turning into a thing. It lives constantly between sickness and health. The will can sell itself and betray itself. The human will is not heroic. (But perhaps it knows that it should be. It feels this urge of desire for the beyond which is heroic.) In its move towards egotism the will is exposed to the others. It is mortal as we shall see. Is it not true that courage can refuse the will of another up to death? Only in part, because in suffering death I satisfy the murderous will of the other. By not serving him in life, I may serve him even more in my death. The other cannot be contained in my thoughts. He transcends me. I must recognize this even in yielding to his attack on my life. I have to recognize it as absolutely external to me. In escaping from the other by death I have to recognize him as other.

But the will can know its own betrayal and therefore remain at a distance from it. It can escape to itself and renew itself. The internality of the will sees itself under a jurisdiction that takes account of its total inner life. From this comes pardon, repentance and the undoing of history (here is possible a new order beyond history that escapes from its judgment). Levinas mentions prayer and the religious life here in the unmaking and remaking of history from an external source. Time is the mode of existence of a separated being in relation with an other.

The Will and Death

We think of death as Heidegger does, as an alternative of either nothingness or another life like this, with other surroundings. This is because we see only this world, where death is certainly a departure. Levinas approaches death from the point of view of the other in murder. The eyes say that murder is morally impossible. Of course it is strictly possible. But the eyes still remain and tell me this, as the eyes of Abel look at Cain from the ground. Does this mean that there is some middle between being and nothing? Perhaps this is not the ultimate opposition.[73] If I look at my own death I can see something else, neither being nor just nothing. I sense the coming of my death apart from my watching the deaths of others. This is a fear of a threat from another that constantly approaches me. It comes from no particular point in the future, no special threat. We cannot foresee the time when it is a threat approaching me that comes from no horizon. It offers me no grip, no approach. It gives me no chance to struggle. The other comes from the situation from which death comes. Here I am exposed to absolute violence, to murder in the night.

For primitive people death is never natural. It always requires a magi-cal explanation. It comes in an interpersonal order where it gains a signif-icance, even though absurd. The other appears even in the solitude of death. So I can appeal to this other, can ask for help and for medicine. It is utterly unknown like the empty spaces that inspire fear. Death comes from out there beyond. (It is not immanent. It breaks every system and every order. It cannot be englobed. In this it is like the infinite.) One does not know when it comes. Who is coming? Is it death or recommencement? I cannot know. I cannot grasp the instant of death. Over this instant I have no power. It is not an obstacle I can meet or surmount or anticipate. It can-not be integrated into my life. It approaches me as a mystery. It offers me no chance to take it over.[qq] This last instant will be performed without me. As Levinas observes, it is like Poe's story ["The Pit and the Pendulum"] where the walls come closer and closer together but always leave me some time. There are here two movements, one more time for me, and the other coming towards me ever closer. This is the main difference between time and space. (In space the last boundaries can be transcended.) In death I am menaced by not only nothing in my being but by another will in my will. (Cf. the death wish.) This enemy utterly apart from me re-mains in relation to me and still permits me to will in a non-egoistic man-ner, apart from myself. Thus it cannot take away all the sense from my life. This will grows from the desire that does not arise from need. It can be pure benevolence—for the other. Here I can will for institutions that as-sure a sensed world but an impersonal one.

The Will and Time

The human will is not heroic. But this does not mean that Levinas is ar-guing for weakness and laxity. The will in time unites a contradiction. On the one hand there is an inviolable immunity against all external attack, to the point of thinking itself to be uncreated and immortal, and on the other hand a permanent fallibility which is subject always to torture and seduction. The will moves always on this boundary line between triumph and degeneration. This fall of the will is worse than sin, because it affects its essential identity as will. Awareness is resistance to violence, adjourn-ment, distance from the present, not flight from it, but distance, as not yet already there. To be free is to have time to prepare for its own fall. Liberty is always in the future where we can achieve a distance from the present. I can maintain a distance from my own thrownness, and never be com-pletely thrown. I can take a position towards it, I can take it over at least

---

qq. "This is not mine. I am not responsible for it."[74]

in part. So I can be beyond tears and suffering. They are never the last word—not the end. Notice how freedom lies in the future. It is the future that enables me to gain distance and to be detached. To be conscious is to have time [English text p. 237, French text p. 214]. This temporal existence is always in some sense a preparation.

Suffering is where this distance becomes impossible where I cannot go back; I cannot escape. It touches me. In fear the future can be perhaps prepared for or avoided, but in suffering the enemy touches me here in the present. Here that which menaces the will is extremely close. I myself am a thing. I lose my freedom but I still remain free. There still is a future. A minimal distance at least is conserved. This ultimate passivity which moves desperately in act and in hope is patience, a disengagement at the heart of engagement which opens up a new possibility of non-egoism. Here I almost give up myself and will for the other. Here I am at least on the boundary of a mode of existence which is no longer centripetal. The final proof of freedom is not death but suffering. Hate knows this. For it does not will just death, nor just suffering. But it wants the hated being to be aware of its 'thingification.' Hence hatred is infinite and insatiable. But to will that the other should be both an object and retain his subjectivity is impossible, a contradiction. Violence does not stop discourse. It remains open to sense. I can bear it in patience. This places death in a new context, empty of the pathos which focuses only on my death. I am still in relation to another. Here the self ceases to be the center of gravity and is open to desire and to benevolence. (Now we return to politics.)

The Truth of Willing

The will has absolutely no power over death, which is violence and alienation against the will. But in patience I can live against someone and for someone. Here death does not touch the will. But is this true or only subjective?

Here we do not take the interior life to be a mere epiphenomenon, but an event in being, opening a new dimension, the production of the infinite (the infinite is not a thing, but a constant process—a production). Apology holds to the inner life. It demands justice.[75] Apology demands judgment, and this confirms its original movement in the production of infinity (as infinite responsibility). In apology I place myself under judgment which situates me under the infinite. The judgment of history kills the will and keeps it as silence. But the will seeks an ultimate judgment to confirm itself against death.

(Now Levinas first states Hegel's case and then attempts to refute it.) Hegel shows that the good will as such is not true freedom unless it organizes the means of its realization which requires social life and institutions.

Internality cannot replace the universal. Freedom must have institutions realized in history. Apolitical freedom is an illusion which is more than a mere error of reason (the will also is involved). To contrast liberty with violence and the absurd one needs an education! Freedom is inscribed on the tablets of the law. It requires gradual processes and developments. The worker gains freedom by fashioning implements, and storing up habits that can be transmitted. Individual intentions are not enough, in life which is exposed to torture and murder and death. Objective judgment comes from institutions that protect the individual by universal laws. These only give equality.

But here the will is dead, and exists only by its inherited works. The will must get beyond the arbitrariness of the purely inner life (*subjectiver Geist*).[76] It must also get beyond another tyranny of the universal and the impersonal. The singular man must rebel against this also. In the judgment of history the individual is present only in the third person. This word of the singular man is apology. It is ignored and useless to the judgment of history. It wills to be judged beyond its apology. It is not the nothingness of death that must be surmounted but the passivity of the will before torture and murder. Here the unicity and singularity of the individual person must be maintained. He must defend himself against universal laws and impersonal judgments. This judgment of history announces itself in the visible. This forms a coherent whole to which history is constantly tending. This leaves out the individual who is ever inserting his subjectivity. This must be asserted against the judgment of history and against philosophy if this accords with history (as in Hegel). The invisible must be expressed if history is not to have the last word. (History does not have the final word. Judgment on history, the judgment of God, comes only through the individual, as is true of Socrates.) The individual subject must speak this judgment. The judgment of history is objective and cruel. It silences the subject, and does not repair the offense of history. This occurs even when history rolls along reasonably. The judgment of history translated all apology into visible arguments, and silences the ultimate source. The singular cannot find any place in a totality. It calls for a judgment of God (through the individual) which takes account of the offense of history in silencing apology, even though it makes use of universal and objective principles. God sees the invisible, and sees without being seen (Cf. Gyges). But how is this accomplished in the concrete? The will is under the judgment of God when the fear of death turns into the fear of committing a murder—of the poor, the sick, the stranger, the widow and the orphan. This judgment is not based merely on universal principles and laws which silence the rebellion and the apology. It takes account of the singular and calls for an answer in terms of the infinite responsibility of the single person.

This is not an immense quantity, but a growing obligation, growing without limit to the infinite insofar as it is really taken over. Insofar as duties are fulfilled, they grow in this way. Also, the separate self ceases to be the center of gravity. It goes on more and more in emptying itself of this self-centeredness. The self can perhaps be defined as that center where this growing responsibility is possible. Justice does not englobe me in its universality. It summons me to go beyond the straight line of the just. Beyond this line the land of benevolence lies ahead, infinite and unexplored. This justice needs me and all my resources [English text p. 245, French text p. 223]. I alone can go beyond the universal law. Truth cannot be in tyranny nor in arbitrary will. In this growth nothing can replace me. Only I can do these things. As I become myself morality is achieved. The two processes are one and the same. The individual is not placed in a totality. He is confirmed but not by flattering his arbitrary tendencies nor consoling him from the fear of death, but by existing for the other—a new orientation of his inner life. This judgment is invisible, and lies under the judgment of history. This means a tension between the invisible sense and the seen events. This invisible judgment is more harsh than the judgment of history. It recognizes me in my endless responsibilities and leaves me intact. My subjectivity is hidden. It bears witness to the offense of universal history to the singular and particular. In this way the self need not fall into a being to death. The judgment of conscience cannot renounce all visibility.

I must make the other count more than myself. This clandestine judgment runs against the judgments of history. It must appear to something beyond history and its end. We must here remember the first origin of time in the "not yet." This is basic. Time is more than an image of eternity, or paternity and its fecundity.[rr]

---

rr. "This is somewhat like my moral views. It is not utilitarian. It means more and more responsibility, taking over, though my analysis is sharper. It stresses the other more than I do, and creative finding of meaning less than I do. It seems to resemble an existential ethics of the strenuous life. The individual is more open than the group. It does not envisage my conception of democracy. Also it rejects heroism. There is patience instead. But though man is not heroic, perhaps he seeks it and must try."[77]

SECTION IV: BEYOND THE FACE*

The relation to the other does not annul their separation. It does not presuppose a universal system which takes them up and into itself which
makes communication possible. Communication begins with this alterity
in the face to face. The two are unequal because there is no third englobing point of view. This is inequality. It does not come from two, A and B,
each of which is self-identical, and so different from the other. He is identical because of his otherness. Impersonal thought in the third person
comes out of this original speaking face to face. Reason, thus, comes from
singularity and presupposes it. I communicate my world to the other. I
give it, or apologize to him for my self and my acts. In apology, I appeal
to the judgment of the other, so he does not limit me. Freedom is not to be
causa sui. (It is to take over, to be responsible.) If freedom is finite or partially denied, it would be totally denied. (But does this mean that my responsibility is unlimited. Levinas says yes—in a sense, but this may be
dubious. My responsibility is limited from the start by the situation into
which I have been thrown, not due to me. He does not see this, though he
may be right on infinite responsibility). Historical existence consists in
taking a point of view beyond my consciousness, and destroying my responsibility in destiny. If the individual thought is only partial and inco-
herent, how can adding these incoherencies together lead to a coherent
impersonal discourse? Apology is a coherent discourse from me to the
others. I am in truth as I act out myself in history under a judgment that
is not hidden but that allows me to speak. Truth comes to being through
my subjectivity. Now we must get beyond the other and his visage. This
is the field of life and of fecundity.

Love can be thought of in terms of immanence, of a thing, a book, an
abstraction, as well as a friend, a brother. (Cf. Aristophanes' myth of the
two in one in the *Symposium*.) It is, however, really transcendent, the adventure par excellence in going to the other. It seems to be ambiguous—
both the need and desire. But as the latter it goes to what glimmers beyond the visage of the other, the wrath of the future, the ever not yet.
There is both concupiscence and transcendence. They are simultaneous in
love.

Phenomenology of Love

Love sees the other in his feebleness. To love is to fear for the other, for his
weakness, to bring help. Tenderness manifests itself towards a fragility

---

* This section begins on page 251 of the English edition of *Totality and Infinity*.

and vulnerability. There is also an utter ambiguity, an incompleteness of meaning. The combination of the two is feminine. The lover moves towards this in compassion, expressed in the caress. To caress means not to seize anything, to solicit that which escapes all form towards the future— not yet. It expresses love but suffers from an incapacity to speak. The carnal correlative to the caress is not the objective body the surgeon sees, not the body of myself, the *je peux*. It is neither the one nor the other. The caress sees neither the person nor the thing. It happens in the erotic night, of the hidden, the clandestine, the mysterious, where profanation is always near. The tender refers to a manner of being in the no man's land between being (here) and there. Its intention does not go towards the light, towards sense. It does not turn to possibles. It is close to passivity and to suffering, being all passion. It is a pity which completes itself, a suffering which turns into happiness, the voluptuous. It does not satisfy desire. It is desire itself. Shame makes us lower the eyes at the nudity, not to look at it. It is strange to all expression, and mysterious, like a strange object in relation to a clear word that does not really express it. The voluptuous is a pure experience that goes beyond any concept.

In existing for the other I exist differently from existing for myself. This is the essence of morality. And moral consciousness is transcendence, and therefore metaphysics. The epiphany of the visage is the origin of externality. Real externality is significance. It does not form a matter. There is nothing behind it. When it becomes formed it is death, the mortuary mask. To signify does not add to a being, it is to be present in person, as in the face. Any sign presupposes the expression which it signifies (and thus gives as a sign). I respect only the visages. Things call forth neither respect nor disrespect. Nudity is the opposite of meaning. It is clarity converted into ardor and night. It is an expression that ceases to express. It is a word that gives no sense but exhibition. Finally the visage becomes impersonal, it simply goes on in ambiguity and animality. The relation excludes universalization. It is not a social relation. It is the solitude of the two, the non-public par excellence, without language.

Levinas says the result, the child, is beyond any project.[ss] It is a transsubstantiation. Beyond all meaningful power, is the engendering of a child. This brings us to new categories and new logic.

Fecundity

In my child I am another. Hegel could write in his youth, the child is the parents. (Does this agree with the same in the other of Hegel? I think not.)

---

ss. "I question this."[78]

My child is a stranger. He does not merely belong to me. He is me [English text p. 267, French text p. 245]. No anticipation represents him or projects him. A project comes from a solitary head. It brings my ideas into the world if it is realized. But the child is not just my possibility, but the possibility of another. It comes from a future that is neither Aristotelian nor Heideggerian. The relation to this future, which is not just mine, is fecundity. It is like the infinite, a constant renewal. It continues history without finally producing old age.[79] To be infinitely means to make yourself being constantly at the origin. This is an alteration of substance in which an identity remains, a self-transcendence, transubstantiation. The being makes itself as divided into the self and the other. It is society and therefore time. We have come beyond the philosophy of Parmenides which says that all is one and unchanging. The other which desire desires is itself desire. Here is desire which is not a lack. It does not satisfy itself as a need, but transcends itself.[tt]

Subjectivity in Eros

This is not heroism, though there is a return to this which stops the anonymity of the mere "there is." But a being is produced not as definitive of a totality but as a constant renewal, an incessant recommencement. But the I returning to itself finds itself not free as the wind, but as aging and losing his powers. This means responsibility, which should surprise us since nothing is more far from freedom than this non-freedom of responsibility. The eros does not only go beyond other objects and things in its thoughts, it goes towards a future which is not yet and which I shall not possess but be. It does not return to its home, like Ulysses. It has another structure of absolute adventure. Levinas says it is not intentional for it does not rest on my powers.

Eros is ambiguous, both need and desire. It has its place as need among the other satisfactions of life. But as desire producing more insatiable desire it has another structure. It absolves itself, maintains itself in its other. It is benevolence giving rise to benevolence. In many thinkers of the West we find an identity back of the self, behind it—the daimon of Socrates, Mephistopheles of Faust, social of Durkheim, unconscious of Freud, the existential of Heidegger, which are not faculties of the self. They are not necessarily opposed to the self, but they are strange to it. In this view of eros, it is no force behind me of this kind. It is I myself who surpass my identity in infinitely recommencing (but not just in sex). Fecundity gets beyond the tragic egotism of the self, but does not disappear in the col-

---

tt. "This is rather obscure and mystical . . . I think Levinas is trying to get too much out of this."[80]

lective. Here is a unity which does not oppose the multiple, but engenders it. The classic notion of self-transcendence involves a contradiction. If I really advance beyond myself I lose my identity, my substance. In the tradition being always goes with unity. Plurality never appears in the existence of an existent. It is a plurality of different ones that exist and which, therefore, can be numbered. So quantity, a superficial category, becomes ontologically basic. All can be counted. Plurality never is existential. The philosophy of becoming (not being) is trying to make transcendence existential and fundamental. It makes being temporal. Opening on the future, and being to death are ways of expressing that do not conform to the classic logic of unity and counting. These people try to revive and change the notion of the possible. There can be plurality here. But this emphasis on the possible turns into a philosophy of power and domination. Man tries to be divine and thus solitary.

This is now a dominant trend (Heidegger). In late Heidegger there is an element of mystery and ignorance. But this powerlessness is described in terms of power. Is the subject only a bearer of ideas and powers? In love we have sought to find something else in this subject. The erotic relation has been neglected and thrown down simply to the biologists. It is ignored that the stream of life involves a specific dualism, and must be interrupted by sexual intervals. It develops only by the separation of individuals. Sexuality has never been studied in depth for its ontological implications (Cf. Freud). The sexual relation cannot be reduced to relations of genus and species, part to whole, action to passion. Here the subject enters into a relation with something radically other. This remains other in the relation and never becomes mine. Also there is no ecstatic union here. Voluptuousness is still dual. It is relation with another who is absent—who does not know. Nor is it power, for the initiative does not come from an active spurting force. It is neither knowledge nor power. These categories do not describe my relation with my child. Fecundity is neither power, nor domination. I do not have my child. I am him. He is a self that is not myself. The fecundity of the self is its transcendence. This structure goes beyond the details of biology. Rupture, denial of the father, then the son repeats the father. Here is a history without destiny. Genuine novelty is not wiped out by the weight of the past. The continuity with the past is broken. There is a constant revolution in the *ipseity* of the son. Renewal is not the same as continuity with the full weight of the past always there. The child takes up the uniqueness of the father but remains exterior to him. He is unique not by the number but by choice and election. He is my unique chosen son. Creation contradicts freedom only if it is confused with causality, but the child is not only unique, he is also one among his brothers. With them he is equal, and turned by this to the face of the other. All men are brothers by their very self-hood, not by any theological discovery. Here in the family the I is called for apology and benevolence.

The Infinity of Time

The indefinite anarchy of the there is, is a limit. But against this the being is origin and power. It has its own beginning, its own identity. It can gain a distance from being though still linked with it. This develops as time, as infinity, as anticipation of the possible.

This being is incomplete. It remains in suspense, at each instant is ready to commence. In memory we do not regret the lost possibilities in view of the unlimited future. Without multiplicity and discontinuity (fecundity) adventure would be reduced to the adventure of one destiny (there would be no possibility of beginning again). But under fecundity a being is always capable of a new beginning—another destiny. Now in spite of death a being can prolong itself in another who is yet the same, and thus triumph over old age and death. This is not a change in time which cannot transcend self-identity, nor metempsychosis where I may be another being. The discontinuity is essential. This possibility of recommencement is a pardon involved in the structure of time. Pardon always means a reversal of time. We can act as though we have not done what has been done (like a new beginning). The past is not forgotten; it remains, but in a purified form. There is a surplus of benevolence—in reconciliation, the *felix culpa*. After reconciliation we can say that the fault was better than if it had not been done. Time adds something radically new to the being. But the new spring has the fringe of past lived springs. There is in the son an always recommencing.[81] There is a discontinuity, a constant rupture, but a continuation over this rupture. Time is a drama in many acts. What is now will be pardoned and taken up again. It is not finitude that constitutes the essence of time as Heidegger thinks. It is its infinity. Death is not just the end of being, but an unknown which suspends power. Between the father and the son there is the nothingness of death, dead time. The principle of time is resurrection from this interrupting death. Time is discontinuous. Time is constituted by death and resurrection which presupposes the relation of the self to the other. The infinity of time makes judgment possible which is the condition of truth. But the infinity of time means placing all in question. The dream of a happy eternity in man is no accident. Truth means also a time achieved and infinite. The perpetual needs to be converted into the eternal, the messianic triumph is eternity, a new structure of time or an extreme vigilance of the messianic consciousness. We cannot deal with this question in our work now.[82]

CONCLUSION

In this book the infinite, the containing of something exceeding the container has been described as the logical plot of being. Individuation is not really achieved by classical logic using the notion of a last difference (property, etc.) because this is general. The individuals obtained in this way are really indiscernible. Hegel can show that these individuals really fall under a concept. If I show with my thumb "this," it presupposes a situation which can identify the movement of the thumb from the outside. Identity comes from the inside, not the outside, from an inner life related to the outer as the concave to the convex. Formal logic of observation cannot deal with such relation as that of the infinite without falling into absurdity. This relation is not seen. It is accomplished from the self to the other in the face to face. Being is externality. This does not mean an attack on the sands of the arbitrary subjective. For this will englobe the internal, turning it into a moment of the objective and thus eliminating itself because this needs a contrasting subjective that is legitimate. But we cannot agree either that the external is confronted with a subjectivity which actually opposes it, for then it is subject to an all embracing system which would include both, and turns the external into the same. We are referring to a subjectivity which is utterly separate and holds itself as I. Truth comes from this subjective.

The true essence of man is present in his visage, where he is not a violence to myself taken up into the system of history. He stops my violence by an appeal from above. He leads me to see subjectively or rather intersubjectively from a higher view which makes truth possible.[uu]

This curving of space is perhaps the presence of God. The face to face we have described makes possible the pluralism of society. The tradition has been wholly given over to the one. Multiple beings represent a fall from this, and through philosophy we may return into it. Now we need not think this. The desire for the infinite (not yet) calls for a separation and a constant new beginning. We do not deny or ignore the other because he cannot be absorbed in a system. We talk to him. Externality is not a negation but a marvel (we respect it). Transcendence ignores the totality. We now get beyond this panoramic being. We are lifted above the categories of being to those of the good. We recover the Platonic conception of a good beyond being. Creation means a common source but also a radical difference among them—created out of nothing means this. So the idea of creation can be restored to respectability. We are confronted with an anarchy of the many (where anything can happen), but a principle appears in this vertigo when a visage comes before us and claims justice.

---

uu. "This seems all right, but he speaks of a deforming or curving space subjectively which I do not like."[83]

Exteriority and Language

We have indicated a mode of action and an ontology which is not equivalent to the panoramic view which is that of common sense as well as of the philosophies of Plato and Heidegger. Here the uncovering of being is the essential virtue of a being. Even modern technology is a way of producing things which brings them into the light. Levinas questions this intellectualism. (Can I question it?) This means we must reject intentionality as the seen of seeing, as idea. This expresses the domination of the panoramic view. In spite of this we refuse the analysis of intentionality into noesis-noema as the primordial structure. (Does this mean substituting ethics and direct self-awareness in the act? If so, perhaps I can accept it.) We say being is revealed in touching, coming from the outside (Cf. empiricism). In holding this we modify the current conception of truth and intentionality as noesis-noema. Vision is characterized by an internal dominance. But discourse is totally different, from this kind of givenness accompanied by a dominating giving of sense. The questioner is always outside. The relation between separated beings is never totalized. He who thinks it or totalizes will simply add a new dualism, i.e., this point of view. Back of what he thinks, a questioner will arise. (Cf. the critique of all philosophy.) The face to face of discourse is not between a subject and an object. It is never adequate and finished. A questioner always arises.

We hold that this externality of being is not provisional, but is inescapably infinite. It will always be there. It will never be thematized. It is I who am speaking and I am ultimate in the presence that expresses itself. It cannot be absorbed into another that will assimilate me. Sight gives only images to the seer. The person is never self-expressed as in the word where he is presenting himself face to face. Language is the constant passage beyond the giving of sense to active signifying. Discourse is with God, from the outside, and not among equals, as Plato says in *The Phaedrus*. God keeps his distance. (And as I say, language is always distance.) Metaphysics is the essence of this language with God. The visage is never an image, because of its presence. All intuition depends on signifying which is irreducible to intuition.[vv] History is concerned with works where the person is not present. To work is never to express myself. The maker of a work is always anonymous. This is the source (necessary) of economic alienation. Politics also considers works.[ww] In the history of states man appears only as an ensemble of words. Justice consists in making expression once more possible (Cf. the Black revolt in

---

vv. "I question this. Signifying is measured by desire of the other, relation to the infinite."[84]
ww. "Levinas never speaks of Marx."[85]

which the person becomes unique and speaks his own word: justice is the right to his word) [English text p. 298, French text p. 274]. Blanchot has criticized the neutral impersonal being of Heidegger, and shown that it is similar to the Hegelian *Geist* which fools us by cunning. This is the philosophy of the neuter, which Levinas is against.

The pre-Socratics understood desire as need. This leaves philosophy and leads to the violence of the act. It completes itself only in art or politics. This neuter can present itself as a 'we' anterior to the self, or as the situation anterior to the persons caught in it. These absorb the self as in Hegel or what we call reason. Materialism lies not in the primacy of sense but in the primacy of this neuter, the impersonal. To place being apart from beings and directing them in some way is to fall into materialism. And the last philosophy of Heidegger falls into this sort of materialism. Being is revealed in the habitation of men between heaven and earth while waiting for the infinite (the gods) in the company of men. This is the land where man can originate from dead nature. The being of beings is a *logos* which is the word of no person. But we start from the visage as from a source where all sense appears, in its bare nudity, a head in misery which has no place to rest, which expresses a desire, not a need, an aspiration which does not proceed from a lack but a metaphysical desire from a person.

Subjectivity

Separation is achieved positively as inner life, self-sufficient and opening to critical knowledge. In metaphysics a finite being has an idea of the infinite. Intentionality for us means awareness of the other. Awareness of self is not a dialectical counterpart of my awareness of another. I do not think of or represent myself. Before all vision of self, I uphold myself. The subject implants itself as body, and holds itself in its internality, in its house. Thus it is not a negation, but a host. Language is openness, hospitality. It defines itself not through relations to a whole, but by itself. It starts of itself, and this is equivalent to separation. But this cannot happen without opening a dimension of internality.

The Sense of Subjectivity

When the self is before the other, a metaphysical relation, this is achieved through service and hospitality. When this relation places us before a third, it becomes we, and we seek for institutions and political order. These proceed by universal rules. If left to itself the state becomes a tyranny.[xx]

---

xx. "Yes this is right, but he says nothing of democracy."

How can we show subjectivity as the only source of benevolence? The state must model itself after the individual person. The internality opened up by separation is not clandestine and ineffable (phenomenology has shown us how to get at this internality, and to speak of it). It enables us to think of the actual as a vestibule to the future. Fecundity opens up a time that is infinite and discontinuous. It liberates the subject from its facticity[86] [English text pp. 300–301, French text p. 277]. By placing him beyond the possible, which is based on facticity and does not get beyond it, it gets rid of the last trace of fatality.

Beyond Being

Thematizing does not get rid of the external, the solid (Cf. remote depths). The external can be desired. Such a desiring being does more than care for Being. It exists in another way. We pass beyond death not in thought of the whole as Spinoza thought, but in a pluralist relation, in being for another, in justice. This passing beyond being is not measured by time. Duration itself becomes visible in our relation to the other where a being surpasses itself (this is opaque). Freedom is invoked.

Liberty comes with Separation. It can develop and deepen itself as benevolence (and responsibility). But without the other, if left to itself liberty becomes utterly arbitrary (which Hegel sees), a mere chaos in which each denies all the rest. No one regards the visage of the other. This turns into power and the seizure of one by another. This marches to unity, a reasonable system in which each will have its place. Philosophy has been part of this liberation from the many by suppression. Knowledge is power (I say), the suppression of the other by seizure, or the seizing vision that comes before. We have presented a different idea. If a human being desires the transcendent he does not want to seize what exists. He respects it. This is the truth of metaphysics.[yy] In the light of the infinite we can let all things be without controlling them or forcing them. They all can be free.

But this does not mean mysticism and irrationalism. It is not irrational to think of knowledge as not being power, and of freedom as requiring justification. Truth does not rest on liberty, as the present philosophy says, but liberty rests on truth. Freedom is not independent of all that is external to it. (I do not have to negate a thing to be free. I can be free with it.) Freedom should justify itself (as responsibility). In Sartre the other threatens and negates my liberty. But does the other not rather put my liberty

---

yy. "I can develop this."[87]

in question because it is arbitrary? In thinking of it critically, do I not see its arbitrary character and become ashamed? If alone by itself does it not turn into usurpation? It does not justify itself. To be in truth is not to comprehend, nor to seize on something, but to face the other without allergy to justice. 'Thou shalt not commit murder in the face of the other' submits my liberty to judgment. Clear ideas should be placed in question by morality. What is the justification of liberty? It is neither certain nor uncertain. It is not knowledge nor power. It is action, achievement. It means making infinite demands on this liberty (responsibility?). This means to be judged, in a social situation. Not by a system but in the face to face. Ethics designs the structure of externality. Ethics is not a branch of philosophy, but philosophy itself. (I can accept this.)[88]

Being as Benevolence

Generosity in my sense is desire engendering desire. To make being, is to be for another. All universality is derived from the social and thus ultimately from the face to face. The revelation of the third is inseparable from the face to face. Real benevolence concerns not a collective mass, but a being who shows himself in a visage.[89] It relies on no natural principles. It must respond to a visage. It is absolute adventure going towards the unexplored, without clarifying thought. The other is not the negation of the self as Hegel thought. It is founded on a positive non-allergic relation. To seize my inner life is also by the same gesture to turn outward [English text p. 305, French text p. 282], to respond, to express. The essence of language is friendship and hospitality. It is not to be alone inside myself and to seek for a beyond. The unity of this plural society is not a coherent system of elements, but peace. Here the self must not only maintain itself, but exist without egotism. I must be sure of the convergence of morality with reality. Judgment is from those outside of me, not from an impersonal reason. I must place myself in the infinite time of fecundity. This becomes concrete in the marvel of the family. This is not a step towards the state, even if the state makes a place for it. It has its own life apart from the state. It is the source of human time. It respects the individual, and allows him to be placed under judgment that lets him be and speak. It cannot be replaced as in Plato, nor made to exist from its disappearance as in Hegel.

The last word of Levinas is against the heroic of existential philosophy.[90] His view is the opposite of this which struggles for the state and its virile virtues. The hero seeks an eternal life of his own as if he could never be replaced by another self. But this infinite time is subject to boredom.

ENDNOTES

1. Jean Wahl helped to pioneer the existential approach to philosophy in France. It is to Marcelle and Jean Wahl that *Totality and Infinity* is dedicated. Levinas also expressed his gratitude to Wahl in *Ethics and Infinity: Conversations with Philippe Nemo*, translated by Richard A. Cohen, Duquesne University Press, Pittsburgh, 1985. Also worth noting is the substantial interview with Jean Wahl conducted in the work *Philosophical Interrogations: Interrogations of Martin Buber, John Wild, Jean Wahl, Brand Blanshard, Paul Weiss, Charles Hartshorne, Paul Tillich*, edited by Sydney and Beatrice Rome, Holt, Rinehart & Winston, New York, 1964. This book is also valuable in showing John Wild in dialogue with many of the leading philosophers of the post-war generation.

2. Wild, commenting on Levinas's reference to Hegel, is cryptically noting that Levinas is aware of the Hegelian dialectical presentation of the self as an identity, which is maintained through difference, a fundamental thesis of Hegel's *Phenomenology of Mind*. Here, Wild is implying his own well-known opposition to the idealistic claim that there can be no understanding gained from immediate experience. For Hegel, every immediate sense-experience is mediated by perception, then understanding, through a series of affirmations and negations. Wild holds that the content of experience gained through the senses is retained in perception, which in turn forms the basis of understanding. The locus of understanding for Wild is in fact in the act of sensing itself. Both Wild and Levinas distrust the Hegelian concept of self-knowledge, although for different reasons. Levinas categorically rejects the Hegelian concept of negation, which as an existential category means annihilation, i.e., in the case of the other, murder. Wild, rather, sees the problem here as an insufficient recognition on Hegel's part of the informative capacity of sense experience as a cognitive category. The shared objection of Wild and Levinas is to Hegel's idealism, which ends in the subordination of the existent to the idea, of existing to Being, of other to self, of experience to thematization, of reality to Totality.

3. Wild agrees with Levinas's critique of the formalism implied in the tautological presentation of the self, where A remains A throughout interior alterations. The concept of "world" is introduced by Wild as a possible expansion of the *chez soi* which, for Levinas, covers the realm of interiority. The self, then, for Wild remains as the center of a circle with the intentional structures of the world radiating to and from the periphery. For Levinas, the phenomenon of the *chez soi* remains more equivocal.

4. Wild wishes to retain the absolute difference between the "I" and the "You" introduced by Levinas, while at the same time raising the question of the place of the political dimension of Levinas's thought. In a democracy, a plurality of others must be addressed without forming a static system. This means taking account of ethical action in which the pronoun "we" can be employed. Here as in his introduction to the English version of *Totality and Infinity*, Wild seems intrigued but perplexed as to how Levinas can account for a plurality of political associations based upon a mutuality of respect. Hence, a reference in the original manuscript to a "most peculiar common concept." Again, Wild implies the necessity of appealing to a concept of "world."

5. The persistent reference to world or life-world on Wild's part represents an attempt on his part to preserve the central place of the *Lebenswelt* without surrendering the originality of Levinas's description of interiority.

6. Here, Wild merely restates Levinas's suggestive notion that "Religion" in the broad sense "is that relation with the other which does not constitute a totality" (*Totality and Infinity*, 40). Levinas amplifies the meaning of his characterization of religion in numerous places. These include but are not limited to *Nine Talmudic Readings* (trans. Annette Arnowicz, Indiana University Press, 1990), *Of God Who Comes to Mind* (trans. Bettina Bergo, Stanford University Press, 1998) and *Alterity and Transcendence* (trans. Michael B. Smith, Columbia University Press, 1999). (Cf. *Difficile Liberté*, Emmanuel Levinas, Albin Michel, 1963, and originally *Quatre Lectures Talmudiques*, E. Levinas, Minuit, 1968.) See also "God and Philosophy," trans. Richard Cohen, *Philosophy Today*, 1978; "The Hardness of Philosophy and the Consolations of Religion" (included in *Ethics and Infinity: Conversations with Philippe Nemo*, Emmanuel Levinas, trans. Richard Cohen, Duquesne University Press, 1985). Still, there is a great reserve which Levinas expresses in keeping his religious writings distinct in general from his purely philosophical reflections. This is noteworthy, especially given the non-Greek, that is, Hebraic, path which Levinas sets for philosophy. Cf. Derrida's comments in "Violence and Metaphysique," included in *Writing and Difference*, J. Derrida, University of Chicago Press, 1978.

7. Levinas is making the observation that Kierkegaard was mistaken in thinking that Hegel had left himself out of his system. Hegel, according to Levinas, represents the consummation of that kind of system building which embodies totality. Kierkegaard, presenting the case for subjectivity in opposition to Hegel, nonetheless, deepens and radicalizes the concept of self-reference, thereby centering future existential thought in the self. Levinas charts a new way of speaking, which while absorbing Kierkegaardian reflection, commences from the other rather than the self. It is this reversal that is alluded to in revision of the maxim concerning Hegel's presumed forgetfulness of self. Another way of putting the matter: It is the other, not the self, that Hegel omits from his system.

8. Here, Wild's commentary is actually somewhat longer than the section presented in *Totality and Infinity*. Wild wishes to preserve both the concepts of "dialectic" and "system," which he believes Levinas rejects completely. At the same time, Wild here introduces suggestions animated by Levinas's thinking which would introduce a creative or generative dialectic and preserve the possibility of an "open" as opposed to a closed "system." In a creative dialectic, for Wild, the end of the dialectical process over against Hegel, the end of the dialectical process, over against Hegel, is not and cannot be known in advance.

9. Here, Wild raises the question of the place and importance of perception. He notes ("Cf. perception") "Does it (i.e., theory) do this? I guess I shall have to say no." For Wild, perception informs theory of its contents through the disclosure of immediate contact with the phenomenon. Wild is attempting to blend a phenomenology of perception (as in Merleau-Ponty) with Levinas's description of the relation of theory to project.

10. Wild adds in the original manuscript: "I must think about this . . . " The reference is "wholeness" and again the question that Wild is asking of Levinas refers to what is lost in giving up on the notion of even an "open" system. If the notion

of "system" disappears or is rejected altogether, then it becomes more difficult to understand what Levinas means by "Totality." For something to be part of something else, that of which it is a part must be approachable and/or knowledgeable. Otherwise, the figure-ground relation in perception is threatened and neither the figure, nor the ground from out of which it emerges, can be discerned.

In the same way, an event of history cannot be rendered meaningful unless there is, anterior to this event, time unfolding in a way that can be recognized as historical. Here, Wild has already given an example of what he means in his response to a question asked of him in *Philosophical Interrogations* (Rome: Beatrice and Sidney; New York: Holt, Rinehart and Winston, 196). Wild stakes out a position, here, that the wisdom of philosophy is lived out while it is reflected upon. The history of philosophy is a dialogue that originates with concerns born out of the present in relation to the thinkers and ideas of the past, mediated through the data of texts. The very constant imposed upon such dialogue makes such an infllow conversation able to be spoken and heard in a finite way.

This in no way implies privileged access, the end of such history or the closure of such discourse as in Hegel. Hence, the notion of an "open" system. Wild does not develop the distinction between "open" and "closed" systems introduced here. However, the nature and importance of such a distinction is adumbrated. Nothing less than the integrity of a unified life-world that permits multiple versions is at stake.

In the language of Levinas, Wild is struggling to preserve the insights of "totality" within the broader horizon of "infinity." Clearly, this is not a subject unknown to or unreflected upon by Levinas. It may be that the "and" (or *et*) is, for Levinas, the ever-recurring transitive relation between *Totality and Infinity* (cf. Crispe, Ashley, "Emmanuel Levinas's *Metaphysics of Promise*," honors thesis, Department of Religion, University of Vermont, 1995).

Most succinctly, Wild wants to hold out for a system that is promissory in characters where the contingency of the future can be linked to enduring time of the past. In this way, totality is not reduced to infinity. Still, discrete, finite actions are able to be made discernible, articulate, thereby to solicit other philosophers who can elaborate the radically original project of Levinas.

11. Wild's reference to "God" here is not Levinas's notion of the Infinite but rather to a theological construct which would close questions before they could be asked, thus neutering the questioner and presenting a "closed" system. This would reduce speaking to God to speech about the construct. This is reminiscent of a remark Wild once made about "heaven." When asked his thoughts about the subject, Wild replied that "heaven" as a construct was just another closed system (remark to R. Sugarman in the summer of 1970). However, neither Wild in his earlier writing nor Levinas in his later works refrain from using the name "God" to characterize the infinite.

12. The turn in Wild's thinking from realism to existentialism derived, in good part, from the observation frequently cited by Wild that for Aristotle "there is no science of the individual." It was through the method of phenomenology that Wild came to believe that the interior life of the human subject could be explored in a discplined manner, disclosing the patterns of human subjectivity. In a sense, the fascination with Levinas's "An Essay on Exteriority," the subtitle to *Totality and*

Infinity, represents a last turn on Wild's part, where the surmounting of subjectivity in the irreducible reality of the other and "exteriority" is explored.

13. There is a way of reading Sartre's *Being and Nothingness* as an inversion of *Totality and Infinity*. Impled in *Being and Nothingness* and implicit in *No Exit*, "Hell is other people." The other limits my freedom. In *Totality and Infinity*, the other, in limiting my freedom, presents me with the possibility of responsibility. In Levinas's later writings the other has an almost messianic dimension. It is worth noting that Sartre learned of phenomenology from Levinas, who was his immediate contemporary.

14. Wild interjects here his long-held view that Berkeley is, when read carefully, searching for a radical kind of empiricism.

15. Wild notes in the original manuscript "Cf. James. For him (i.e., James), the individual is essential. Cf. fringes. Does ethics take the place of metaphysics? Perhaps. He stresses the importance of knowing the other individual and the need for perception and concepts. He sees remote depths in the individual facts, never exhausted, and their independence from us. He rejects the transcendental reduction." Wild's last published book, *The Radical Empiricism of William James*, was published in 1969. Since the Levinas manuscript very likely dates from 1969–1970, it can be safely assumed that Wild is measuring Levinas's thought against that of James, at least James as systematized by Wild. In James's steadfast rejection of idealism, Wild is noting certain similarities between Levinas and James. At the same time, Wild is indicating again the necesssity for elaborating a phenomenological description of perception in which the notion of "horizon" is given a favored position. Here, James's notion of fringes is invoked where the facts perceived always are accompanied by "fringes," which point away from the facts in isolation and, thereby, toward a context in which the sense of the perceived facts are oriented within a compass of meaning. Wild, in fact, is asking whether the notion of fringes might be less susceptible to idealisitic abstraction than the concept of horizon. The notion of fringes insists on the non-reducibility of facts (in Wild's sense of "world facts" as opposed to scientific facts). There is a reservation expressed on Wild's part concerning the apparent reduction of metaphysics to ethics by Levinas. Laconically, Wild notes "perhaps." As the commentary resumes, we can see Wild, the philosopher, at work arguing with himself in the presence of Levinas, buttressing Levinas's position where Wild believes it can be strengthened while at the same time asking questions, by which Wild reserves for himself, the right to stake out a position of his own.

16. Wild begins with an exposition of Levinas's criticism of Heidegger. Levinas's own critique is powerfully presented, although in a very condensed form. In fact, the whole of *Totality and Infinity* may be viewed as an attempt to chart an alternative to Heidegger's claim that ontology is first philosophy. In earlier works Wild pressed for the substitution of the phenomenon of "world" for Being, without losing the valuable insights gained from Heidegger's existential analytic, the systematizing of existential thought that forms the first part of *Being and Time*.

17. Levinas, in his subsequent work *Otherwise Than Being*, in fact, begins to expand the notion of responsibility to a place of primacy within his ethical metaphysics. For Wild, responsibility is a way of existing before its assumption in any concrete situation. Levinas speaks of freedom as "invested" or "installed," thereby marking its limits while permitting its just expression. There is, then, a virtual

convergence of views between Levinas and Wild here, a convergence that precedes influences, relation before dialogue. Wild acknowledges in the manuscript that "I must look into the relation between responsibility and justice." For Wild, Levinas has rescued the purity of the eidos of justice by redefining it as an action of justification.

18. Heidegger asserts that we have lost track of Being by attending to specific beings. This is what is meant by the difference between the "ontological" and the "ontic." For Wild, such "ontologism" divests beings of their irreducible existence, otherness, and transcendence of the knowing subject. This paves the way for an "intellectualism" in which understanding dominates existence, thereby superimposing a specious monism on a pluralistic reality.

19. This is a very straightforward statement on Wild's part, registering the unquestionable impact that Levinas is making on Wild's philosophic attention and orientation.

20. The distinction between the *je pense* and the *je peux* is not sufficiently clarified either in the text or in the commentary to make such a serious inference. Merleau-Ponty, for example, also argues for the perceptual primacy of the *je peux* as founding the *je pense* in *The Phenomenology of Perception*. Wild, following the lead of Levinas is arguing against an ontology of power and its tyrannical implications. In Merleau-Ponty, the *je pense* refers to a perceptual grasp, without any necessary ontological implications. As for example, the insufficiency of perceived potency of childhood, the "I cannot yet" as opposed to the parallel frailty of age, "the I can no longer."

21. Heidegger's ontology of power is nonetheless rejected utterly by both Levinas and Wild, each of whom sees a direct link to the violence of the tyrannical state. Wild goes one step further in suggesting a question that implicates Heidegger's relation to Hitler on a philosophical basis: "Isn't this for a final obedience to a personal self?" It is not accidental, for Levinas, that the ontology of power can culminate in the vile expression of the tyranny of the state. Moreover, the disregard for beings can manifest itself with impunity as a neutral relation to the finitude of the other, as an indifference to the murder of the other.

22. The learning paradox occurs in Plato's *Meno*, 80 ff. In essence, the paradox is this: "How can I properly be said to learn anything at all? If I do not know what I am searching for, then I will not recognize the object of my search when I come upon it; if, on the other hand, I can be said to know what I am searching for, then why should I begin to look for it?" Here, we see Wild unraveling the ancient paradox while sketching a creative hypothesis of his own. This hypothesis is a practical application of Levinas's primordial distinction between totality and infinity, and in a more immediate way the distinction between "need" and "desire." Need fills a lack within the sameness of totality; desire is propelled by that which is recognized in advance as being beyond the grasp of the knower. Teaching, then, moves beyond the eternally recurring questions and answers scripted in advance of their enactment in speaking philosophy. This is why both Levinas and Wild use the code word "maieutics" as an implicit criticism of Plato, alluding to the midwife metaphor in *The Theaetetus*. In maieutics what can be learned from the other is already present in the self to be eternally recollected. Levinas and Wild envision a richer different relation of time and the other.

23. Levinas has, according to Wild, established the basis for a radical phenomenology of lived existence, where the immediacy of the visage acts as a continual source of disclosure of sense. The visage provides a referent for all conceptualizing. What Wild cannot accept is Levinas's apparent disavowal of signifying power of the immediacy of sensory experience. However, the argument appears to be one of differing interpretations of the levels of sensory experience. Levinas argues that the face-to-face relation comes first. In fact, this is what mandates the immediate "as the imperative of language." Here, Wild emphasizes his doubtfulness of Levinas's assertion concerning the relation of language to the immediate by the following comment, which in the commentary is punctuated with three question marks: "But then Levinas says this is an imperative of language???" The question that remains to be answered by Levinas concerns the completely equivocal relation between contact and discourse. For Wild, the primacy of contact would be measured by the visage. At least, this is the direction in which Wild appears to move.

Speaking, as Levinas more clearly shows in *Otherwise Than Being*, can be divided between the "saying" and the "said." Wild is not so much taking issue with the radical position of Levinas that the saying has priority over the said, but with securing a philosophical foundation for the "said." Partly to this end, Wild stresses James's notion of knowledge by acquaintance in relation to "familiarity with my very existence" insisting on "coincidence" of the subject with itself. Also, from this same knowledge by acquaintance we have direct access to beings, and to the other. As Wild has indicated in his introduction to the English edition of *Totality and Infinity*, he expresses a reluctance to grant the other a primacy over the self. His reservation is grounded in the phenomenon of contact and the reliability of the immediate. From this it could be inferred, although Wild does not say this, that the relation with the other has a priority over both the self and the other, thus establishing a phenomenological ground for ethical equality, compatible with a theory of political democracy. In writings postdating *Totality and Infinity*, Levinas shows himself to be extremely sensitive to the kinds of questions Wild is raising here and gives his own responses in *Otherwise Than Being*, especially in the end of chapter 3 on "Proximity" and chapter 4, called "Substitution." In addition, Levinas takes up the question of political democracy in *Entre Nous: Thinking of the Other*, as well as in *Outside the Subject*, especially chapter 8, "On Inter-Subjectivity, Notes on Merleau-Ponty" and in chapter 10, "The Rights of Man and the Rights of the Other." In "Sensibility and Proximity," chapter 3 of *Otherwise than Being*, Levinas directs himself to exploring exactly the appearance of infinity within perception. In a very late work, *Alterity and Transcendence*, Levinas treats the subject historically within the history of modern philosophy as well as thematically.

24. Wild is searching for the infinite within perception, thereby seeking to ground the infinite as a phenomenological datum, rather than as a metaphysical construct. Moreover, he again joins with Levinas in the battle against Heideggerian ontologism; the world, unlike being, is adumbrated by an infinity of different versions. (Cf. J. Wild, *Existence and the World of Freedom*.)

25. As opposed to Sartre, Levinas speaks in the language of absence as opposed to nothingness. Cf. R. Sugarman, *Rancor Against Time*, Felix Meiner Verlag, 1980, p. 120 ff.

26. The language of "final causation" derives from Aristotle and is compatible with the movement of realism that preceded John Wild's turn toward phenomenology. The language in context appears to reflect Wild's desire to establish the reality of final causation, independent of classical realism, by appealing here to a phenomenological argument. The argument indicates the way in which the future conditions and establishes the present in the same way the effect that follows the cause chronologically conceals an intentional structure in which the cause aims at an effect. How this establishes "a new way of being," as Wild says, remains to be demonstrated.

27. John Wild remarks in the original manuscript: "I have not seen this." The description of freedom beginning in detachment and moving toward project, as elaborated here by Wild, suggests that Wild has found in Levinas's view of freedom one that is very close to Wild's own. The meaning of the aside would appear to indicate that Wild has not seen such a confirming view presented prior to *Totality and Infinity*. The elements of distance and illusion, particularly, help clarify Wild's own view of human freedom. Such a view of human freedom, Wild argues, is indistinguishable from responsibility when it becomes freedom for rather than freedom from. This is very close to Levinas's own view of responsibility and freedom as developed later in greater detail in *otherwise than being*.

28. ("At least its meaning . . . ") John Wild indicates that reclaiming the event as opposed to the meaning of the event must be distinguished. The philosophic challenge is to show how the existence of the past, in addition to its meaning, can be said to be reclaimed. Cf. *Rancor Against Time*, 74–92.

29. Levinas implies that the death of the other, rather than merely estranging me from own my being-toward-death, as in Heidegger, is a subject for genuine ethical reflection. The infinite dimension of the other is accompanied by the radical finitude of the other in which the ethical bond is established, permitting the recognition of the way in which he exceeds my thematic grasp of him. Hence, the ethical impossibility of murder is revealed by the vulnerability of his visage. There is here, then, an ethically infinite relation with the finite other and a finite relation with the theoretical infinity of the other. From Levinas's perspective the knowledge of the death of the other takes moral precedence over my own being-toward-death. This is the metaphysical origin of his concept of infinite responsibility where cognition originates in facing the other, which dominates Levinas's later thinking and writing.

30. "Can use some of Heidegger on death here." Given everything that Levinas has to say regarding death, Wild's position regarding Levinas's description of death, as opposed to that of Heidegger, is not developed. However, it is possible to speculate that Wild is concerned with a phenomenology of beginnings and endings that would situate birth and death within the horizon of the life-world.

31. In the original manuscript, Wild remarks here, "The I separates itself on its own." Wild may be suggesting that the "I" engages in the act of separating itself from historical time.

32. Wild notes in the original manuscript: "I say yes . . . " What Wild appears to be affirming is the phenomenon of lived history, different from that of the historiographer can be elaborated. Such a lived history would position human subjects facing the future without knowing its outcomes in advance.

33. Wild implies that Levinas is rejecting the idea of humankind. However, Levinas appears already to have qualified this notion. It is as a "totality" that the notion of humankind is rejected. Cf. p. 58 Engl. text; p. 30, French. The question Wild poses, nonetheless, remains an important one, i.e., how can a non-totalizing idea of a universal, in this case mankind, be accounted for?

34. Levinas resists the radical existential notion that truth is contact. He insists that it is "tangency," which permits distance. This, in turn, allows Levinas to distinguish truth from error, judgment from perception. Wild sees this as leading to formalism, an idealistic dimension to Levinas thought, which he rejects here and questions in what immediately follows. For Levinas the cognitive relation may be symbolized as follows: Distance-Relation-Contact (DrC); for Wild the cognitive may be symbolized as Contact- Relation- Distance (CrD).

35. "I question this." Then John Wild adds cryptically "Touch forms."

36. Cf. Plato's *Republic*, 359c.

37. Again, Wild refuses to abandon what William James called "knowledge by acquaintance." In addition to the epistemic question, Wild is very much concerned with the metaphysical consequences following from the apparent rejection by Levinas of the cognitive claims that derive from the coinciding of knower and known. For Wild, Levinas's tearing "everything to parts that are unrelated" leaves the problem of how the transcendent relation of the self and the other manifests itself in the more ontic dimension of the life-world. Moreover, Levinas's radical metaphysical pluralism must remain defensible against charges of anarchy. This objection illustrates an essential difference between Wild and Levinas, which reappears in many different guises throughout Wild's commentary. The difference concerns what appears to be the radically equivocal character of Levinas's metaphysics. There is, for example, no third term inclusive of both "totality" and "infinity." This also applies to other pairs of terms self vs. other, interiority vs. exteriority and individual vs. universal.

38. After this statement the original manuscript contains three question marks. It is unclear whether John Wild is signaling disagreement or incomprehension. It is more likely disagreement, given the primacy accorded by the concept of the "visage" by Levinas. As becomes clear, it is the visage of the other that, for Levinas, is the locus of certitude. There is nothing more compelling than the face of the other person in determining the clarity of discourse, the orgination of ethical responsibility and the genesis of thinking-speaking, which originates with the other who faces me, and thereby compels my attention, infinite responsibility, and serves as the guarantor of my thought.

39. John Wild notes here in the original manuscript: "Yes, this is so."

40. John Wild notes here in parentheses (also freedom I say . . .). Wild appears to be suggesting that, at a minimum, human freedom is a necessary if not sufficient condition for meaningful social and political equality.

41. Wild's question is a prescient one. Much of Levinas's next major work, *Otherwise than Being: Beyond Essence*, aims at clarifying the distinction between what Levinas there characterizes as "the saying" as opposed to "the said." The preliminary language of *Totality and Infinity* makes plain the primacy of approaching the other through language. Nonetheless, what is said (the point of the question Wild poses here to Levinas) remains to be clarified. Clearly, "the said," as Wild indicates,

must have an integrity of its own. In *Otherwise Than Being*, Levinas will try to demonstrate what Wild believes is only affirmed in *Totality and Infinity*, that is, how the said can be preserved in a philosophically comprehensible way within what Levinas refers to as the saying.

42. Stresses his agreement with Levinas's insistence that the alter ego of Husserl's *Cartesian Mediations* is not real alterity. This is also the case with Heidegger's analysis of *mitsein* in *Being and Time*.

43. Here, it is worth noting that Sartre's conception of the other as the one who limits my freedom, and thereby would through his look steal my existence, is radically inverted by Levinas. Cf. Sartre, *Being and Nothingness*. One could, in fact, view the whole of *Totality and Infinity* as a response to Sartre's presentation of the relation of self and other in *Being and Nothingness*.

44. Wild, in the manuscript, ends this sentence with two question marks. As Wild has already indicated in his English introduction to *Totality and Infinity*, the asymmetrical relation which establishes the other over the self is not easily accepted. Always in the background the consequences of devaluing formal equality appear to weigh heavily in Wild's reluctance to follow Levinas.

45. For Levinas, it is not man who is the measure of all things but rather the infinite that transcends man. What Wild, the author of two classic sympathetic works on Plato, is reflecting here is a fundamental question raised by Levinas to Plato concerning the primacy of the speaker over that which is said and a priority of the auditor over that which he hears. Cf. Robert Anderson's sympathetic portrait of Protagoras in "The Dramatic Unity of Plato's Theatetus," Yale University, Doctoral Dissertation, 1976.

46. Wild is pointing to a general philosophic problem in *Totality and Infinity*, that is, the necessity to show how shared, common public discourse can be accounted for. For example, in the case of an "agreement" that includes a mutiplicity of others, a commonly shared description of the facts must be possible. Levinas's extreme emphasis on difference must be able to show how agreement is possible without becoming totalized, that is, belonging to the realm of the same, which appears to characterize the very essence of agreement. In this sense Wild is pointing to the problematic place of objectivity in general for Levinas. More concretely, each person is potentially an other for every other person. Speaking philosophically signifies discourse with the other who addresses me. The transposition of such intimate communication into the third person is "natural," "objective," etc. The challenge is to demonstrate how speaking about the other does not compromise speaking to him.

47. "Yes this is important. Here is my dualism . . . " This statement appears in the original manuscript at this point. The reference is unclear. Clearly, there is a dualism that appears by dividing the world into the categories of "Totality" and "Infinity." If Wild is offering a criticism of Levinas, then this statement makes sense and needs to be further explored by critics who can bring the objection of dualism to *Totality and Infinity*. It is more doubtful that Wild is moving toward accepting a dualistic metaphysics at this stage in his reflections. For such a view would be at variance not only from his earlier insistence, during his Realistic period, on the analogy of Being, but also on the later attempts to secure a position free from dualism by asserting, in his Existential phase, that there is one world with many versions.

48. "This is better." Here Wild seems to be indicating that the "dualism" of *Totality and Infinity* is more sophisticated than it might first appear to be. For Levinas, existence is generative of discourse, and therefore, it may be argued that the horizon of infinity includes the category of "totality" without totalizing it.

49. Wild makes more explicit the Kantian thrust of Levinas's distinction between the moral relation, that is, the noumenon, that which can be intended toward the other, and the numinous, i.e., the "holy," which belongs to the language of theology and is interpreted as being sacred. Levinas explores the concept of atheism within the broader concept of theism, which remains perhaps an unspoken premise of his philosophy. The sense of this concept is perhaps most precisely captured in an expression from *Difficult Freedom*: "It is the glory of the Creator to have created a being capable of atheism." The isolated "I" recognizes its own limitation, thereby engendering the possibility of its self-transcendence. The infinite, which is irreducibly other, produces the recognition of the possibility of atheism and the prospect for self-transcendence. What remains most essentially religious for Levinas, as it does for Kant, is the moral relation. As Wild observes, for Levinas: "God is revealed in justice; in ethics, not in theology." However, this does not exhaust the realm of the religious for Levinas.

50. Wild can be seen here attempting to absorb some of Levinas's insights without making such a radical break from the existential phenomenological tradition in general. The primacy of world over language is emphasized. Heidegger's concept of conscience is revisioned in such a way as to indicate that it, too, may serve as a bridge to the infinite. Wild in the manuscript comments: "The infinite can help here." Clearly, this is a notion that could be further explored.

51. Wild here appears to be searching for a third term that will incorporate both instrumental action and enjoyment. Wild's reference is to existence. The thought, as acknowledged by Wild, remains to be completed.

52. Here, Wild is describing a position that he does not accept, i.e., the Husserlian notion of pure constitution of the object by the intending subject.

53. Wild notes that on page 130 of the English edition (103 of the French edition) Levinas "has a section on the element and tools." Wild's point is that while Levinas clearly modifies Husserl's concept of constitution by demonstrating the dependence of pure thinking on the body, on nourishment, the elements and time; what is required, in Wild's view, is a phenomenological description of thinking that evidences this very kind of embodiment.

54. Wild is insistent on securing a cognitive status for the realm of the sensible. Wild makes this point clear in what follows. This does not, however, preclude *jouissance* as an expression of sensibility. For example, the apple I see, I can also enjoy in seeing.

55. Wild is clearly correct in pointing out that Levinas rejects the Heideggerian notion of throwness. Labor, economics, embodiment, time and the other express an exteriority that resists a notion of pure idealistic constitution in the Husserlian sense. However, it is not as clear that Levinas "misses" this point in Heidegger. If Wild is correct concerning the implicit notion of creation *ex nihilo* in Levinas, then there is no room for throwness on an ontological level, as the two concepts appear contradictory.

56. Wild notes Levinas's strenuous position "against suicide." Levinas says, "Suicide is tragic, for death does not bring a resolution to all the problems to which birth gave rise, and is powerless to humiliate the values of the earth— whence Macbeth's final cry in confronting death defeated because the universe is not destroyed at the same time as his life" (*Totality and Infinity*, 146). Wild here appears to be anticipating Levinas's position that suicide does not bring an end to responsibility. Moreover, even the would-be suicide cannot undo, as MacBeth recognizes, or repeal, existence with his own intended death.

57. De Beauvoir, in *The Second Sex* (xvi, n. 3) criticizes Levinas's concept of the feminine. Taken in isolation, her criticism is understandable, although in need of elaboration. However, it must be kept in mind that, for Levinas, the home as well as the child does not belong to a subhistorical domain. It is, rather, a category that belongs to the infinite. In this respect, it is transhistorical in character. For Levinas, history itself, of necessity, belongs within the realm of totality. As such, Levinas's exalting of the feminine has a virtually religious significance. His argument is not only with Hegel but also with Plato. Otherness takes precedence over sameness, the ethical over the political and the sanctity of the home over the power and cunning of dialectical history. For a much more searching, balanced and current discussion of the literature on the place of the feminine in Levinas's thinking, see *Elevations* by Richard Cohen, chapter 9, "The Metaphysics of Gender."

58. John Wild is expressing his emphatic disagreement with Levinas's substitution of "home" for "world." For Wild, the phenomenon of world is primordial and irreducible; hence, it is inconceivable that the phenomenon of "home" could generate world. It is for this same reason that Wild rejects what he regards to be Levinas's privative description of thrownness, where world is, for Wild, the ultimate expression of such thrownness.

59. The sentence, "The end does not attract us, does not draw us, but develops itself, *s'attraper*," is followed in the original manuscript by a question mark. The problem posed by this assertion, for Wild, concerns the absence of intentionality in groping. If there is no sense of that which one is groping towards, then the concept is not able to be explained philosophically. Cf. John Wild, *Plato's Theory of Man*, Harvard University Press, 1945, chapter on Techne.

60. Cf. John Wild, *Existence and the World of Freedom*, where Wild speaks about world, "versions" of the world and human responsibility. In *Otherwise Than Being*, the views of Levinas and Wild appear to converge on the infinite reach of responsibility. The fundamental difference concerns Wild's insistence on the interposition of "world" and Levinas's emphasis on the infinite expressing itself through the other who approaches without the neutral, mediating concept of world. The givenness of world, in Wild's view, makes the phenomenon of responsibility more finite, more social and more open to being shared.

61. It is Levinas, rather than Wild, who will expand on the centrality of the death of the other, a central thesis of *Otherwise Than Being*, holding that it is to the other and his finitude for which I am infinitely responsible. The contrast with Heidegger's concept of achieving authenticity in my own being-toward-death could not be more dramatic. For Heidegger, the other, in his finitude, is merely an inauthentic distraction from my own authenticity. For Levinas, on the other hand, my responsibility toward the other in his finitude governs the possibility of just dis-

course and, therefore, speaking philosophy in a responsible way. Both friends and critics of Heidegger who try to explain his statements and behavior during the reign of the Third Reich would do well to reflect upon the political consequences that follow, however unintended, from Heidegger's egocentric description of being toward death in *Being and Time*.

62. Here, Wild clearly seems to be establishing the groundwork for a phenomenology of the other, which would incorporate the voluminous insights of Levinas, while at the same initiating a projected systematic book of his own. We can see the directions that such a work would pursue. Clearly, the repeated questions Wild puts to Levinas, most often deriving from what Wild conceived to be the stable results of phenomenology.

63. Here, John Wild is elaborating the radical phenomenology of Levinas in relation to the learning paradox in Plato's *Meno*: "How can learning be accounted for? In advance I must know that for which I am searching; if, I know what I am looking for, then there is no reason to begin to search for it. If I do not, then I will not be able to recognize that for which I am looking." For Levinas, the other, even including other things to be known, are radically different and, therefore, do not depend upon a prior comprehension of the same. Hence, the doctrine of *anamnesis* (recollection) is exposed as operating under a metaphysics of totality. Radical empiricism, which takes the contingency of experience, earnestly asks without knowing in advance and can do so because the subject, in the act of encountering the other, derives its signification from the exteriority that manifests itself in the visage of the other. (The reader may wish to compare Wild's statements here with his defense of the doctrine of anamnesis in Plato's *Theory of Man* and in his other writings on Plato.)

64. Clearly, Levinas has already made a great deal out of this. Levinas has shown that the other, in limiting my freedom, transforms it into concrete responsibility. This is a further indication that Wild is preparing to elaborate on Levinas's insight and very likely appropriating this insight, along with many others that he sees so clearly in *Totality and Infinity*, into a future but never finished work of his own.

65. John Wild adds here in the manuscript: "I can do a lot with this." Among the unpublished papers of John Wild, which he noted as "finished," is one called "Some Phenomenological Reflections on the Other," incorporating some of the points which Wild makes here. It is twenty typed pages clearly dating from 1968–1970, being readied for publication by him. See chapter 12 above.

66. The question, for Wild, is whether Levinas's position that society precedes intentionality is defensible. The clear implication is that Wild is unwilling to surrender the primacy that every other thinker in the phenomenological movement ascribes to the doctrine of intentionality. However, Wild is most sympathetic with Levinas's phenomenological description of the peculiar structures that express embodied language. He joins with Levinas in rejecting every variant of linguistic idealism, including the Husserlian notion that consciousness is constitutive of language. In the manuscript, Wild specifically notes that "idealism is transcendental a priori thinking . . . "

67. John Wild, in stating "This is more existential than 'phenomenological' . . ." remains unshaken in his position that the phenomenological approach should aim at clarifying the patterns of human existence.

68. In his introduction to *Totality and Infinity* Wild has already expressed his reservation concerning the absolute priority of the other over the self to the reader: "Furthermore, he may wonder about the strange asymmetry, the complete supremacy of the other, that the author finds in the self-other relation" (19). This question is important to Levinas's vision of society and the possibility of political democracy. Again, it refers to the necessity of being able to give a philosophically grounded explanation of ethical relations between a plurality of others.

69. Here Wild emphasizes the radical individualism that stamps his existential thinking. He indicates that he finds confirmation for his view in Levinas. The careful reader will note that now Wild, as well as Levinas, is forced to confront the problem of just, social relations with a plurality of others. This is the same question that he has just previously put to Levinas. In other words, how does the infinite inform the social realm of existence without becoming absorbed into totality or reducing the political to the ethical?

70. Wild is urging a view of metaphysics that is compatible with a phenomenological description of the life-world and its multiple versions. Metaphysics proceeds after careful phenomenological description, and its new role remains to be revisioned. Levinas, on the other hand, has metaphysics present at the beginning of his reflection, positioned as the relation between finite desire and the infinite other. The difference between these two views warrants further exploration and calls for further research into the question of the relationship between phenomenology, metaphysics and ethics. Again, Wild appears to be challenging Levinas to extend the metaphysical foundations of his ethics so as to found a place for a phenomenology of the life-world.

71. Wild is here speaking in his own name in the first person, as emphatically as anywhere else in the manuscript. His statement on his comment regarding "my notion of independence as taking over" is a clear reference to an idea Wild advanced from an insight of William James to clarify responsibility as a continuing, dynamic way in which the self chooses to lay claim to his own past actions. In other words, the choice that I make is, in this phrase Wild borrows from James, to take myself over from the past into the present for the sake of the future. However, Wild is suggesting that I am responsible not only for my discrete acts but also for my own appropriation of the life-world I inhabit with others. It is this life-world that also is subject to being claimed as my own by being "taken over." It is for this reason that Wild speaks of "my notion of independence" and asserts that responsibility is not a "cause of any sort." However, the only essential difference between Wild and Levinas concerns the irreducibility of the life-world for Wild. When Wild says "I am right in this . . . ," he is indicating the argument which he first makes in *Existence and the World of Freedom* and later takes up in *The Radical Empiricism of William James* that argues for a continuing, contextual response in relation to time. In this respect Wild indicates that Levinas's description is noncontextual and, in this way, unable to explain the continuing responsibility of the self for the other, which Levinas affirms.

72. Wild speaks of a "true history" in which the "inner life of an author" can be thematized without distortion. Such an approach must be phenomenological in character and proceed prospectively, viewing the world as the author did. Moreover, the implication is that this can extend to history as a whole. Such an "au-

thentic history" could enhance and deepen the intentions of the historical agents situated in the historical hour, which they did not themselves create. This would make it possible for Levinas to address the realm of the historical and the political without doing violence to the ethical.

73. Here Wild notes in the manuscript (Cf. "transcendence and immanence"). There are metaphysical oppositions within the text that remain to be clarified on Wild's view. These include, but are not limited to, transcendence and immanence, presence and absence, totality and infinity. We might wish to consider presence and absence as ontological categories to replace being and nothingness.

74. This is an ambiguous reference. It may be read as Wild implicitly disavowing Levinas's own unorthodox existential position, that is, "I am not responsible for my own death." However, it is more likely, given that he believes Levinas has advanced an original reflection on death, distinguishing the responsibility I have for the other as primary, that my responsibility for the death of the other takes precedence over my own. Wild is surely aware that this runs directly counter to the thought of Heidegger, Sartre, Merleau-Ponty and others and needs to be further explored. Levinas will continue to explore the philosophical centrality of the death of the other in his texts which postdate *Totality and Infinity*.

75. Here Wild notes in the original manuscript, "I guess this refers to Socrates . . ." He refers the reader to page 240 of the English edition, 217 of the French edition, where Levinas writes, "But does not apology of itself, precisely in escaping itself in death, call for a confirmation, in which it escapes death?" In the manuscript, Wild transposes this to read, "Is this not a sign that the self comes to itself in death?" The reference then, to Socrates, while oblique, makes sense. Socrates is presented by Plato in the *Apology* as not so much being vindicated by history but rather as demonstrating that there is a justice that transcends political history, which is the subject matter of historians and historiographers.

76. *Subjectiver Geist* is a term that Hegel uses to describe the inner dimension of the spirit of history. Wild indicates, against Levinas, that something analagous to this notion must be preserved in order to account for historicality. However Wild, in general, shares Levinas's antipathy to Hegel's totalizing concept of history where philosophy becomes identical with its own history. How Wild or Levinas would reconcile these two positions is problematic and is in need of further explanation.

77. This is an important general statement by Wild illustrating basic disagreements with Levinas while acknowledging his own desire to adapt Levinas's general perspective on the centrality of the other. Wild is particularly straightforward in stating, "It stresses the other more than I do, and creative finding of meaning less than I do." Also, Wild, unlike Levinas, is unwilling to give up on the concept of heroism, at least as an ideal purged of self-delusion. Here the key point is that for Levinas heroism and justice have no necessary relation at all. The last sentence of *Totality and Infinity* makes this clear: "The heroic existence, the isolated soul, can gain its salvation in seeking an eternal life for itself, as though its subjectivity, returning to itself in a continuous time, could not be turned against it . . . " The deeper division between Wild and Levinas here remains unspoken and in need of exploration. Wild, in holding out for the possibility of authentic heroism, appears

to maintain a position in which knowledge can govern power, in the Platonic sense. Levinas rejects this attempt to subject the existence of the other to thematization and, therefore, must clarify the relation that would obtain between knowledge, power, meaning and the other.

78. "I question this." Wild questions the very radical assertion by Levinas that the human child is beyond all other projects. Levinas's position represents the first fundamental challenge to the metaphor sketched out in Plato's *Symposium* where human progeny are subordinated to honor and to philosophy. For Levinas this is the subordinating of an idea to an existing human being. Wild, in his question, wishes to retain the centrality of the Socratic-Platonic task in which the project of philosophy is always first.

79. In the original manuscript this statement is punctuated by three question marks. Wild seems to be asking Levinas to demonstrate his assertion that the child "continues history without finally producing old age." Wild is asking Levinas for whom is this true, the child or the parent or both?

80. It is not clear whether Wild would be satisfied with a more grounded presentation by Levinas of his very radical notion that existence is produced through the child rather than discovered within the context of a broader thematic horizon. The agreement with Levinas is over the failure in philosophy to adequately distinguish between need and desire which failure originates with Parmenides and dominates philosophical thought in the West. The disagreement comes from Levinas's unstated Biblical perspective that creation is a philosophical category challenging the phenomenological concept of the human life-world as the ultimate expression of the human situation. Nonetheless, Wild's presentation of Levinas's concept of fecundity possesses a clarity and a richness that makes it an extraordinarily valuable contribution to Levinas scholarship. He does this by leaving a more Socratic-Platonic version of "progeny" (offspring, works or ideas) as a possible substitution for the child, which can be read in a more restrictive fashion in Levinas's somewhat ambiguous formulation.

81. Wild adds in the original manuscript, "Cf. My notion of remaking." This is a concept that John Wild repeatedly refers to in his commentary on Levinas. Wild's notion of "remaking" refers to the capacity of the self to reclaim its own past and thereby to transform its future through time. It is close to, but should not be confused with, the contemporary rhetoric of "reinventing the self." It is different in the sense that it insists upon the responsibility that I presently have for the continuing effects of all of my past actions and the way in which they open possibilities for my future. Wild here sees a similarity between Levinas and William James regarding these notions of self, freedom and responsibility. What he is suggesting is that his own idea of taking myself over can help to show the interconnectedness of these central themes in Levinas's thought.

82. Wild refers to Levinas's description of the messianic dimension of time. In the original manuscript, Wild punctuates his statements with question marks, which indicate either disagreement or, more likely, just plain difficulty in this portion of *Totality and Infinity*. However, Wild has already shown a remarkable appreciation of Levinas's radical reconceiving of temporality. Furthermore, Wild has already intimated that Levinas's use of the term "messianic" incorporates an ontological conception of time, self and other, which emphasizes the breaking out

of the frozenness of totalizing time (as in Hegel). This messinaic concept of time begins with the self recognizing the other and continues infinitely through progeny. Wild indicates that this is not a subject with which he wishes to deal in his commentary.

83. Here the key word governing Wild's reservation is "subjectively" in Levinas's characterizing of a curving space. Phenomenology has already secured a description of spatiality in the patterns that govern its appearance in the lifeworld. Any implication to the contrary would be, for Wild, to surrender one of the essential discoveries of the phenomenological approach to space.

84. John Wild places much greater emphasis on the knowledge gained from immediate existence than does Levinas. Signifying, for Wild, depends upon a preconceptual understanding, which is the locus for certainty in knowing. Levinas does not so much dispute this axiom of existential phenomenology, but rather affirms that it proceeds from an anterior relation to the infinite where signifying, measured by desire for the other, corrects the knowledge of immediate existence. It is this relation with the other, especially the face of the other, which for Levinas, is the source of knowing.

85. Wild notes correctly that Levinas does not refer to Marx directly. (See 146–47, *Totality and Infinity*, for references to Marxist views.) This is especially surprising given the careful and brilliant phenomenological description of labor and the body in section II, "Interiority and Economy" in *Totality and Infinity*. Clearly this is no mere oversight on the part of Levinas. Why, then, does he enter into an unspoken dialogue with Marx without referring explicitly to him? In *Difficile Liberté*, Levinas states explicitly that "only the hunger of the Third World limits philosophical reflection." Moreover, Levinas's insistence that justice founds truth has no more powerful advocate than Marx. Still, in resisting the primacy that Marx, following Hegel, attaches to history the way divides between the paths pursued by Levinas and Marx. Levinas remains responsible for his near reduction of the political to the ethical in a way that makes a description of class conflict understandable. It is clear that Wild is troubled by this inability of Levinas to situate the realm of the political and a number of his asides in the remainder of the manuscript are taken up with this question. On the other hand, Levinas's description of work, justice and the other radically challenge the Marxist concept of ethical analysis, while absorbing Marx's critique of alienated labor as expressed particularly in the 1844 manuscripts.

86. Wild perceptively comments that Levinas's description of the subject from its facticity follows from his view on fecundity. In the manuscript Wild comments "Yes, note that he has to say this . . . " Wild expresses a last cryptic reservation on this subject: "Can this be said?" Wild is not contesting the internal consistency of Levinas's position on fecundity. However, he appears to remain uncertain that this really overcomes or liberates the subject from his own relation to his finitude.

87. Here Wild indicates for the last time a fundamental agreement with Levinas's concept of metaphysics. In a certain sense he shows that he has been won over to Levinas's essential position regarding the possibility of a revisioned metaphysics. Still, the insistence on securing what for Wild are the stable results of phenomenology remains to be incorporated within such a metaphysics.

88. For students of John Wild, and the careful reader of this text, Wild's acceptance of Levinas's stance that ethics is the very root of philosophy represents more

than a startling climax to his dialogue with Emmanuel Levinas. It may be viewed as indicating the direction Wild envisioned for future philosophical reflection and a radical advance within the phenomenological turn in his philosophical career. On the other hand, it is likely that Wild himself would acknowledge that his philosophical reflections have come full circle. The adamant insistence that the thinker be held responsible for what he says marks the realistic as well as the existential phase of his career. Viewed this way, the movement from realism to phenomenology, now informed by Levinas's thinking, is the conclusion of a thinker who is radically self-referential and consistent, while remaining open to the perpetual task of beginning the project of philosophy, in the presence of the other, anew.

89. Wild questions Levinas's rejection of the notion that benevolence is always individual and cannot be given over to the social domain.

90. In the manuscript Wild asks whether Levinas is protesting against the heroic stance "of existential philosophy." As has already been noted, Wild holds out for the possibility of a heroic stance that is to be measured by its compatibility with justice.

Appendix I: Letters

LETTER FROM HARVARD COLLEAGUES TO JOHN WILD

HARVARD UNIVERSITY

DEPARTMENT OF PHILOSOPHY

EMERSON HALL
CAMBRIDGE 38, MASSACHUSETTS

April 14, 1960

Dear John:

Your friends and colleagues have only very recently been definitely enough aware of the temptations you have been wrestling with so that we could talk of the matter frankly with each other. But now we can unite to tell you of our deep concern and our hope that it is not yet too late to influence you in behalf of Harvard and us. Time is of the essence, we know, and those of us 'senior members' who are in the Greater Boston area today have consulted hurriedly to write you this letter.

The gist of what we would say, of course, is that we shall be very glad if you decide to stay and very sorry if you do not. We should miss you, John, more than the somewhat raucous style of some of us would lead you to guess. We value the unique and powerful contribution you make to the department's curriculum and to its councils, to our relations with other groups in the university, to the university as a whole, to philosophy at large, and to that great part of the wider public who are serious about the things you are so admirably serious about. We are grateful for your humanity, your scholarship, your widely searching thought, and your kind and whimsical humor. When it comes to a showdown, where could Harvard find your equal in the important and prophetic parts you have so effectively taken? (And who knows, conversely, how many roots you have in the alkaline Harvard soil which would be none the better for transplanting?) We value you, in fine, for your inimitable John-Wildness and your long friendship.

Whichever way you go, you may be sure, of course, of our affection and esteem, and our warm good wishes. But we hope sincerely that you can be persuaded to decide in favor of Harvard and of all those in the Harvard community who would suffer if you left us.

Ever truly yours,

Henry Aiken

Roderick Firth

Raphael Demos

Donald Williams

LETTER FROM EMMANUEL LEVINAS TO JOHN WILD

Emmanuel LEVINAS
6 bis, rue Michel-Ange
75 - PARIS XVI°
UNIVERSITÉ DE PARIS-X
———
LETTRES
ET SCIENCES HUMAINES
AVENUE DE LA RÉPUBLIQUE
92 - NANTERRE
———
TÉL. : 204.54.32
204.59.87 à 29.91
204.59.87 à 29.91

Référence à rappeler

N°......................

NANTERRE, LE 19 novembre 19 70.

Monsieur le Professeur John WILD
1516 N.W. 14 th Ave
Gainesville
FLORIDA, U.S.A. - 32601

Cher Professeur John WILD,

J'ai reçu votre lettre qui me permet, avant tout, de m'acquitter d'une dette de reconnaissance qui me pesait lourdement. J'ai lu, en son temps, la remarquable préface que vous avez bien voulu écrire pour la traduction anglaise de "Totalité et Infini". Je ne savais pas comment vous remercier, au sens propre du terme et j'ai laissé passer ainsi le délai où ces remerciements étaient naturels. J'ai donc l'occasion, avant tout, de vous exprimer ma gratitude et pour l'intelligence qui anime votre texte et pour le coeur qui y est toujours présent.

Croyez, très cher Collègue, à mes sentiments les meilleurs.

E. LEVINAS

LETTER FROM EMMANUEL LEVINAS TO JOHN WILD, ENGLISH TRANSLATION

Emmanuel Levinas
6 bis, rue Michel-Ange
75 – PARIS XVI°
UNIVERSITE DE PARIS – X

LETTRES
ET SCIENCES HUMAINES
AVENUE DE LA REPUBLIQUE
92 – NANTERRE
Tel: 204.34.32
   204.29.87 a 29.91
   204.39.87 a 39.91
Reference a rappeler
N°.........................

NANTERRE, LE 19 novembre 1970.

Monsieur le Professeur John WILD
1516 N.W 14th Ave
Gainesville
FLORIDA, U.S.A. – 32601

Dear Professor John WILD,

I received your letter, which allowed me, before anything else, to fulfill an obligation of gratitude that was weighing heavily on me. I read, in due time, the remarkable preface that you agreed to write for the English translation of "Totality and Infinity." I did not know how to thank you in the proper meaning of the term, hence I let the extension of time pass when these thanks were natural. Therefore, I have the opportunity, before anything else, to express my gratitude to you, both for the intelligence that animates your text and for the spirit, which is ever present. . . .

With best regards, very dear colleague.
E. LEVINAS.

LETTER FROM EMMANUEL LEVINAS
TO RICHARD SUGARMAN

Emmanuel Levinas   Paris le 20 août 72
112, rue Michel Ange
     Paris 16e
Tel: 46 51 62 91

Cher Professeur Richard Sugarman,
    Vous m'avez adressé, il y aura bientôt deux ans,
toute une documentation relative à l'oeuvre de
votre maître et ami John Wild.. Parmi ces papiers
figurait le manuscrit d'un compte-rendu élo-
quent consacré à mes modestes travaux dont
la publication en livre exigeait d'après vous,
quelques pages de ma propre plume.
    Malgré l'importance que j'attachais à votre
demande — ou à cause de cette importance — je
n'ai pas pu, dans l'embarras matériel de mes
occupations immédiates quotidiennes, aborder
le travail demandé et témoigner à la mémoire
de John Wild la sympathie que son texte
méritait. D'ajournement en ajournement, le
temps passant. Vous serait-il possible de faire
paraître le texte excellent de John Wild sur "Totalité et Infini"- sans compter sur mes pages?
    Recevez, je vous prie, tous mes remerciements
pour l'attention que vous m'avez témoignée par
votre envoi d'il y a deux ans et croyez à mon
admiration   et à mes sentiments les meilleurs.

LETTER FROM EMMANUEL LEVINAS TO RICHARD SUGARMAN, ENGLISH TRANSLATION

Letter translated by Lisa Obrentz

Emmanuel Levinas   Paris, August 20,1992
112, rue Michel Ange
Paris 16e
Tel: 46516291

Dear Professor Richard Sugarman,

Almost two years ago, you addressed to me a full documentation that was relative to the work of your professor and friend John Wild. Amongst these papers there was the manuscript of an eloquent review devoted to my modest works which, according to you, the publication into a book required a few pages from my own pen.

Despite the importance that I gave to your demand – or because of this importance – I was not able to, in the true embarrassment of my daily immediate occupations, approach the expected work and express in the memory of John Wild the congeniality that his text deserved. From postponement to postponement, time passed. Would it be possible for you to publish John Wild's excellent text on "Totality and Infinity" without relying on my pages?

Please accept all of my thanks for the attention that you have brought to me from your letter two years ago, and believe in my admiration and my best wishes.

Emmanuel Levinas

Appendix II: Bibliography of John Wild's Posthumous Papers

The following is a bibliography of the posthumous papers of John Wild located at the Beinecke Rare Book Library at Yale University, New Haven, Connecticut. These papers were compiled by Richard Sugarman and Roger Duncan. These papers are open to the public beginning January 1, 2006. The bibliography of the unpublished papers is divided into two parts, A and B.

A. This portion includes those papers that were given to Professor Richard Sugarman, University of Vermont. These papers were given to Professor Sugarman either by John Wild in the two years preceding his death in October of 1972 or by Catherine Wild in the winter of 1973. The cataloguing, indexing and description of the contents is by Richard Sugarman.

1.

1.00. Notebooks (1936). Notes and Commentary on Aristotle's *Metaphysics*. 337 pp., handwritten (quite legible). Hardbound.

Extensive commentary, interpretation and occasional translation by John Wild. This volume clearly represents, along with the companion volume on the *De Anima*, the first in-depth explorations of Aristotle that were to form the basis of Wild's neo-Aristotelian writings published in mid-/ late 1940s and early 1950s. These two volumes are self-contained commentaries. On the whole they follow the texts very closely. At the same time John Wild offers original and brilliant interpretations. The fact that he had studied with Heidegger firsthand in 1930–1931 and chose to return instead to Aristotle is noteworthy.

1.01. Notebooks (1938). Aristotle's *De Anima*, notes and commentary. 250 pp. Hardbound. See remarks on *Metaphysics* (1.00).

1.02. Notebooks (1934). Aristotle's *Ethics, et al.*
    Contents: Notes and commentary on:
a. *Nichomachean Ethics*—45 pp., handwritten.
b. N. Hartmann—53 pp., handwritten.
c. *Moral Theory*, G. C. Field—9 pp., handwritten.
d. Jaspers—38 pp.
e. *Les Deux Sources de la Morale et de la Religion*, H. Bergson—4 pp., handwritten.
Same notebook (1936, summer):
a. Jager: Greek Political Ideas. 73 pp., handwritten.
b. Thucydides. 17 pp., handwritten.
c. "Ideas to be Developed." 17 entries spanning 40 pp., handwritten.
    These entries are aphoristically stated. Many of the themes, riddles and paradoxes stated here are developed in John Wild's later writings.

1.03. Notebooks. Notes and commentary on Aristotle (date uncertain, probably early 1930s*). Condition: poor.
    Contents:
a. *Nichomachean Ethics*.
b. *Logic*.
    Ethics: 7 pp.; *Categories*: 7 pp.; *De Interpretatione*: 7 pp.; *Prior Analytics*: 16 pp.; *Posterior Analytics*: 18 pp.
    * These are most likely the earliest of the notebooks. Wild relies exclusively on English translations, not true of the later notes and commentaries on Aristotle. John Wild's serious interest in the Greeks commenced in 1931 as a result, in good part, of his visit to Germany on a Guggenheim Fellowship. His attendance at the lectures of Heidegger and Jaspers played an important role in this development, convincing Wild of the necessity to return to the beginnings of philosophy, particularly Aristotle. According to Catherine Wild, John Wild taught himself Greek ca. 1932.

1.04. Notebooks (undated, probably early 1930s). Ca. 50 pp., handwritten. Notes and commentary on Aristotle's *Politics*. Hardbound. Condition: good.
    Notes are chronological following chapters of the *Politics*. Much sketchier than notes on *Ethics, Logic, De Anima*, etc.

1.05. Notebook (undated, probably late 1930s). 150 pp., handwritten. Hardbound. Condition: good.

It is difficult to assay the purpose and place of this volume without thorough study. This is especially difficult given John Wild's later antipathy to the Hegelian concept of philosophy in general. On the most palpable level it represents an attempt to study Hegel's philosophy against the background out of which it emerges philosophically and historically. If Wild's reconstruction of the missing chapters of this projected study exist, I have not been able to locate them.

Projected table of contents: *Completed or reasonably developed

1–16	Hegel and Present*
17–37	Kant in General
38–68	Romantic Atmosphere
69–89	Fichte
90–110	Schelling
111–30	Schleiermacher
131–45	Jugendschriften (Dilthey)
146–56	Phenomenologie*
156–67	Encyl. and Later Period

Logik

168–95	? . . . 3 Positions*
196–216	Kant and Old Logic*
217–37	Hegelian Logic vs. Old (Logic)—Hartmann
238–68	Sein*
269–300	Wesen*
301–31	Begriff*
332–42	Philosophy of Nature
343–58	Philosophy of Spirit

2. Included among John Wild's last papers is a sheet entitled "Papers for Florida." Although it bears no date, it is almost certainly from the spring or summer of 1969, the period immediately preceding John Wild's move to the University of Florida.

This is the clearest statement of materials John Wild appeared to be readying for publication. I have been able to locate nine of the ten essays (averaging approximately 30 pp. each). All of the essays with one exception post-date 1960 and most were begun at Yale (i.e., 1963 or later).

2.00. The essays are demarcated into two categories: "finished" or "almost finished." In the case of four essays it is unclear as to whether John Wild considered them "finished" or "almost finished."

"I have already finished"
a. Belief

b. The Other (Phenomenological Reflections)
c. Rights of the Other (Drew University)

"Almost finished"
a. "Secondary Qualities and the L. W. (Life-world)—9 pp. of conclusion needed Life-world."
b. "The Time-lag—Sharpen and Re-organize."
c. "O.K. The Existential A Priori. Focus it on Life-world and Freedom."

"Finished or almost finished"
a. "Democracy." A final draft, ca. 25 typed pp. Originally delivered in 1966 or 1967 in New Haven, Connecticut, to a small group of Yale faculty and graduate students who met at Wild's house to deliver and discuss subjects in phenomenology. Almost certainly unpublished.
b. "The World and Its Versions—needs horizon, contrast with Being." 6 pp.
c. "The Phenomenological Method or Phenom. Philosophy." "Needs to be corrected. Bring out observation by phil."
d. Existential Realism. "Attack on Ess. and E. My Views. Existential Realism." 31 pp. A transitional essay dating from 1959. John Wild was probably intending to update. Rethinking of essence-existence controversy. Relation of a realistic metaphysics and epistemology to phenomenology.

2.01. "Phenomenology of Belief" (fall 1967) (subtitle: "William James and the Phenomenology of Belief"). 25 typed pp. Completed first draft either read or intended for conference. (Includes several handwritten pp. outlining essay.)
   Contents: Part of the essay is incorporated verbatim into John Wild's book *The Radical Empiricism of William James*. While it draws its impetus from James, John Wild's essay is more systematic and philosophically sophisticated than James's own treatment. The essay is much more elaborate by some 20 typed pp. than material included in John Wild's book on James.

2.02. "Rights of the Other" (subtitle: "Rights of the Other as Other"). 17 typed pp. of an apparently final draft. It may have originally been given as a talk at Drew University before John Wild left Harvard. This is Catherine Wild's guess. This could probably be documented by internal evidences and contacting Drew, etc.
   Contents: Several pp. of penciled notes and reflections on the essay, and 7 additional typed pp. are probably a later supplement to an earlier talk.

2.03. "Lebenswelt and Berkeley"* (summer 1969) or "Primary and Secondary Qualities."* Includes 20 typed pp. (apparently first draft); 12

typed pp. (apparently final draft)*; 6 penciled pp. of notes outlining essay. May have been given or intended as public talk at the University of Florida.

John Wild's comment: "Needs correction and completion"

*Final draft bears title: "Primary vs. Secondary Qualities: Science vs. the Lebenswelt—An Historical Analogy."

Comment: I have not yet had an opportunity to study this document.

2.04. "The Perceptual Time-lag and Lived Time" (undated, probably late 1960s). 26 typed pp. with carbon copy. Clean copy. John Wild's comment: "Sharpen and reorganize."

Contents: "An examination of 'certain temporal paradoxes in the light of what is now known phenomenologically about lived time'" (John Wild).

2.05. "The Existential A Priori" or "An Empirical Approach to the A Priori."

***There are at least four different finished versions of this essay, each about 30 typed pp. in length. Wild became so convinced of the importance of this subject that he taught a seminar in spring 1968 at Yale on the general subject of the a priori. Wild's assertion is that unless the a priori can be disclosed as already at work in the *Lebenswelt*, philosophy cannot lay claim to a domain of enquiry over which it exercises autonomy.

Wild initiates his discussion with an historical reconstruction of the problem. He proceeds to develop an argument. Though clearly influenced by *Being and Time* and familiar with M. Dufrenne's treatment of the same subject, he takes a different tack from either. The argument presents an original systematic examination of the problem from a phenomenological viewpoint. It is, in addition, a substantial contribution to the problem of the a-priori in the history of philosophy.

(An abridged version was published under the title "Is There an Existential A Priori?" in *The Eisenberg Memorial Lectures*, Michigan State University, 1969.)

3.
3.00. Levinas: "notes" (undated).

Contents: 79 typed pp. A commentary and interpretation of *Totality and Infinity*, for which John Wild wrote the preface to the English translation by A. Lingis, 1969.

Best guess is that the bulk of the writing was done between 1968 and 1970. Wild taught courses on *Totality and Infinity* at Yale in 1969 and at the University of Florida in 1970.

Wild's exploration of *Totality and Infinity* is the first sustained, systematic commentary on *Totality and Infinity* in English. This commentary has already been published as a manuscript in *Phenomenological Inquiry: A Review of Philosophical Ideas and Trends* (24: October 2000. Published by *The World Institute for Advanced Phenomenological Research and Learning*, Belmont, MA, ed. Anna-Teresa Tymieniecka). Wild's exposition follows the text of *Totality and Infinity* closely. Wild sees *Totality and Infinity* as the most profound critique of Heidegger's *Being and Time* to date. He presents *Totality and Infinity* as a positive, philosophically revolutionary work in its own right.

Still, John Wild appears to see Levinas's vision as partial—one which he thought could be incorporated into a broader philosophic horizon, with apparent gaps to be filled in.

There are notes, probably among John Wild's last, which indicate that he was planning to write a last book drawing heavily on Levinas—but more systematic than *Totality and Infinity*. Emphasis was to be given to social political philosophy left undeveloped in *Totality and Infinity* and to philosophic problems that Levinas does not specifically address, for example the relationship of the order of "totality" to that of "infinity."

**This original manuscript is self-contained, although the typed manuscript begins on p. 3, preceded by 7 pp. of notes. This manuscript will be useful to students of John Wild, Emmanuel Levinas and contemporary Continental philosophy.

There is a letter written in French from E. Levinas to John Wild expressing his thanks and admiration for his introduction to the English version of *Totality and Infinity*.

4.

4.00. "The Frontiers of Phenomenology and Existential Philosophy" (fall 1962). 24 typed pp.—One paragraph added in longhand, penciled corrections. Given, initially at least, as a public lecture. Folder in which essay is found specifies "Yale—Important Papers."

Contents: Essay represents John Wild at his clearest, discoursing on phenomenological themes. Some of these themes are carried over and developed in *Existence and the World of Freedom* (1963); especially John Wild's argument that distinguishes "world facts" from "scientific facts."

** The essay contains what John Wild believed to be an original phenomenological approach to the appearance-reality problem. This portion of the essay is illustrated by what Wild believed to be the beginning of the resolution to the "bent-stick" argument, drawing on Husserl's theory of profiles.

In addition, the essay contains a striking description and valuable summation of recent work on the phenomenology of the lived body. Also, Wild elucidates the mind-body problem within competing philosophic frameworks. This essay is perhaps John Wild's clearest, best-written introduction to phenomenology.

4.01. "A Phenomenological Approach to Relativism." 24 typed pp. A talk (46 minutes) given in Ohio (unclear where). Probably early or middle 1960s. 4 pp. of penciled summary and outline.
   Contents:
a. An examination of the invariant patterns in the claims advanced by historical, cultural and ethical relativism.
b. A phenomenological development of the concept of world and versions of the world as a framework within which to adjudicate the claims of relativism and absolutism.
   Comment: It is a lucid and original essay. It is a clear contribution to the controversy over relativism. This is a rare essay on a vital subject. From a polemical standpoint alone, it turns the tables on its critics. Its main thrust is very positive, non-polemical.

4.02. "Contemporary Phenomenology and the Problem of Existence." 28 typed pp. (2 pp. of corrections, mainly omissions). "Yale—Feb. 24" (year not given—probably delivered as a talk in 1963 or 1964).
   Contents:
a. Classical, that is, Aristotlian-Thomist, essence-existence distinction developed.
b. Phenomenological reformulation of this distinction developed with general consideration of the question: "How (do) I know my own existence?"
c. Comparison of ordinary language accounts with those of existential phenomenology, especial consideration of sense-reference, fact-meaning distinctions.
d. "How (do) I distinguish real from fictive existence?"
   i. Historical meaning of the problem in Hume and Kant.
   ii. Original arguments presented by John Wild on criteria for distinguishing "real" from fictive or imagined existence.

4.03. "Existentialism as a Philosophy." 25 pp. final draft, typed. Talk may have been delivered at the Fullerton Club on April 19, 1959. It is based on an address given before the Conference on Methods in Philosophy and the Sciences.
   Comment: Have not studied.

4.04. "Christian Existentialism" (undated, probably 1960). 22 and 1/2 typed pp. Clearly first intended as a talk to a public audience (notation "50 mins.").
Comment: Have not studied.

4.05. "Christian Existentialism and Social Problems." 31 typed pp. Originally given as public talk at Trinity College (November 19, 1960).
Comment: Cf. 4.05.

4.06. "Notes on Heidegger," notes on *Being and Time* (undated—may have been in conjunction with graduate seminar on *Being and Time* given at Yale in fall 1966, or within the preceding seven years). About 50 handwritten pp. of systematic exegesis. Clearly not intended for publication.

4.07. "My Development of Certain Themes in Ricoeur's Lectures on Finitude at the Sorbonne" (spring 1957?). 12 pp., typed (1 and 1/2 spaced), 2 pp., handwritten.
Contents include:
a. "Finite—in Language"
b. "Finitude of Perception"
c. "Finitude of Desire"
d. "Finitude and Power"

4.08. "Kierkegaard and Existential Philosophy." 20 typed pp.—rough copy.
Also included in folder: John Wild's selections from Kierkegaard. Ca. 10 pp. typed, single-spaced. And notes for a course, apparently at Harvard (middle or late 1950s).
Comment: May intentionally form companion piece to a published article on "Kierkegaard and Classical Philosophy," *Philosophical Review*, September 1940. Have not studied.

5.
5.00. Interviews (1957). 40 pp. (11 typed, 29 handwritten).
The interviews contain a series of fascinating diary-like entries and reminiscences. They were conducted by John Wild while on a Guggenheim Fellowship in England, France, Holland and Germany.
Contents include:
a. Visit to Oxford, November 12–14, 1957. Discussions with Charles Taylor.
b. Wild's reactions to a lecture by J. L. Austin on "Reality and the Real."
c. Description of an hour-long conversation between Austin, Gilbert Ryle and Wild. John Wild pressed Austin and Ryle on certain phenomeno-

logical concepts, the life-world in particular, and philosophers, especially Heidegger.

d. Conversation with L. De Raeymaeker—Louvain, May 18, 1957. Reactions of an important Thomist to the developing "New Philosophy," that is, phenomenology.

e. Fascinating comparison of Barth and Jaspers at work in classroom, how each has aged, etc.

f. Conversation with Van Peursen (The Hague, May 25, 1957).

g. Long series of conversations with Peter Brunner who studied with Brightman at Boston University.

h. Long, vividly described conversation with Georges Gusdorf on philosophy, religion, Merleau-Ponty, Heidegger, etc.

i. Roger Mehl, conversations. Mehl influenced John Wild significantly in developing interest in "the inauguration of a truly Christian philosophy."

j. Lecture notes on talk by Karl Barth.

k. Visit to Göttingen—conversations with Hermann Wein.

l. Conversation with Eugen Fink. Detailed account of Fink discoursing on Heidegger with respect to three issues: "Can the Thomistic distinction of essence and existence be found in *Being and Time*?"; Heidegger on *Sein*; and "Is Heidegger anthropocentric?"

5.01. a. "Things I Am Clear About in Philosophy." 10 typed pp.

Statement of philosophic confession on the *Lebenswelt*, philosophy,

Aristotle, motion, human freedom, truth and history, substance, philosophy, anthropology (John Wild sets out what he believes is an original idea), being and meaning of consciousness.

A most important, revealing statement at a transitional point in John Wild's philosophic life, it consolidates his move from neo-Aristotelianism to phenomenology. Likely completed after his trip to Europe in 1958.

b. "Things I Am Clear About in Religion and Theology." 2 and 1/2 typed pp.

A statement of personal, philosophic confession framed as eleven dogmas, arguments, reflections. Very revealing of John Wild's beliefs at the pinnacle of his Anglicanism, which without question subsided in the middle and late 1960s.

5.02. Further Criticisms of the Tradition after Mehl. 4 typed pp.

Contents: "Reading Mehl, April and May 1957, has been a most stimulating experience. It has opened up the possibility of writing a Christian philosophy, always denied in the tradition which has really assimilated theology into philosophy . . . I must try to work out Mehl's suggestions further—a philosophy which shall be utterly free and autonomous, in no sense subordinated to revelation, but open to it."

5.03. "Plans" (1957–1958).
a. "Plan for Philosophic Anthropology"
b. "Phenomenology of Theory"
c. Essay on evil
d. Essay on error and illusion
These plans are detailed, along with some others, in 4 typed pp. Some of these plans were realized in later essays, such as number 4. Cf. 4.03.

5.04. Religious talks (undated, probably mid- or late 1950s).
Mainly devotional invocations, prayers and brief sermons. Ca. 30 pp. of notes, all but one handwritten.

5.05. Speeches (academic) (dates very uncertain— range could be as much as 25 years). 35 pp. of penciled notes.
Contents include:
a. "Mind, Guilt, and Responsibility of the Scholar" Phi Beta Kappa talk
b. "Natural Law"—Yale
c. "World Philosophy"—Honolulu
d. Haverford speech
Others unclear, need to be studied. Almost illegible.

5.06. Northwestern speeches. Several handwritten pp., almost illegible. Includes talk at Hillel, Northwestern on "Religion and Philosophy." A separate version of this essay was given at St. Louis University.

5.07. "Boston University Talk" (December 7, 1960). 5 pp. of handwritten notes on "Reason and Existence."

5.08. "Garret Talk" on existentialism and phenomenology (January 14, 1963). Several pp. of handwritten notes. Largely illegible.

5.09. "Talk on James," North Park College (May 14, 1963). 10 pp., typed and handwritten. Could be pieced together.

5.10. Folder ("Projects—Summer 1963").
Contents include:
a. Essay on "Guilt." 12 typed pp. Approach is phenomenological. There are notes indicating directions for longer treatment of the subject.
b. 12 pp. of thesis topics. It is unclear whether John Wild was designing projects for students, such as dissertation ideas, or rather intending to work on these subjects himself.
c. Notes for intended articles on "inner-outer" and "philosophy as therapy."
d. Notes on Husserl's "Krisis."

5.11. "Psychiatry" (spring 1959). Notes taken by John Wild on seminar in which he participated with a number of psychiatrists at Massachusetts General Hospital.

Contents include: About 5 pp. of penciled notes by John Wild and 2 single-spaced typed pp. of notes on Wild's talk: "Basic Themes of Existential Philosophy," submitted by Dr. John Parks.

5.12. "Talk at Vanderbilt" on "The Individual and the Group" (February 8, 1963). 1 p. penciled notes and correspondence.

5.13. "Moral Choice and Personal Identity" (incomplete) (date uncertain—late 1950s?).

Apparently 24 pp. of a first draft, typed and handwritten. The first 14 pp. are missing.

5.14. Eulogy of John Wild (October 28, 1972). 3 pp. (1 and 1/2 sp.).

Given by Professor Henry Jordan of Connecticut College at a memorial service held October 28, 1972, at Yale Divinity School.

6.

6.00. Lecture and Seminar Preparations.

Wild seems to have developed a different set of notes (usually between 40 and 100 handwritten pp.) afresh for each of the many and varied courses in philosophy he taught. Some, as in the case of seminars on Plato taught at Harvard in the early 1940s, show the natural evolution of first drafts of books, occasionally even a modified chapter as in the case of Wild's interpretation of Plato's Allegory of the Cave—later produced in slightly modified form in Plato's *Theory of Man.*

Very often the notes contain Wild's syllabi for the course given. The quality and richness vary considerably. Still, they are invaluable primary source documents of a philosopher's self-education. In some cases, as in a course (seminar) on James given by John Wild at the University of Florida in the spring of 1970, Wild completely rewrites and rethinks his way through James. Only three years previously he had published *The Radical Empiricism of William James*, a comprehensive treatment of James's philosophy. (See addendum for a list of contents of lecture notes and seminar preparations.)

7.

7.00. There are three folders containing material, which in one form or another are undoubtedly included in Wild's "realistic" writings, especially "Introduction to Realistic Philosophy" and "The Return to Reason."

7.01. "Science of Philosophy—Metaphysics." 80 pp. typed, single-spaced. Subtitle: "Introduction to Metaphysics." A self-contained treatise developing a complete, systematic, realistic metaphysics. It represents John Wild at his philosophically most rigorous. It is, of course, not representative of his later phenomenological critique of realism.

7.02. "Human Cognition." 45 pp. typed, double-spaced. First draft of chapter 5, "The Nature of Human Cognition," of *Introduction to Realistic Philosophy*.

7.03. "Realism and Its Subjective Alternatives." 40 pp. typed, double-spaced. First draft of chapter 7 of *Introduction to Realistic Philosophy*.

7.04. Translation of *Sein und Zeit* by John Wild along with R. Trayhern, B. Dreyfus and C. de Devga.
   "An informal English paraphrase of sections 1–53 with certain omissions as noted." This translation (ca. 1959), though never published, has been widely circulated. John Wild used this translation in a course given at Yale in the fall of 1963. By the time he taught a graduate seminar at Yale in the fall of 1966 on Heidegger, Wild himself returned to the McQuarrie-Robinson translation.

Lecture Notes: Addendum

6.01. Readings in Plato (Harvard, 1940–1941), Phil. 12. Ca. 40 handwritten pp. with syllabus. Includes "Platonic Aletheia: An Interpretation of the Cave," 20 typed pp.

6.02. Seminar in Phenomenology and Linguistic Analysis (Harvard, fall 1958). Ca. 40 handwritten pp. Includes syllabus and student papers.

6.03. Ethics and the Philosophy of Religion (Harvard, fall 1960), Phil. 191, Theology 103. Ca. 80 handwritten pp.

6.04. Philosophic Rebels (Northwestern, spring quarter, 1962), course on Plato, Pascal and Kierkegaard. Ca. 40 handwritten pp., syllabus.

6.05. Ethics (Yale, fall 1964). Includes 40–50 handwritten pp., several charts and a one-page typed book review.

6.06. Existentialism and William James (Yale, spring 1964). Ca. 40 typed pp. Includes summaries of books by James and citations of letters from James to others.

6.07. James seminar (University of Florida, Spring, 1970). Ca. 40 handwritten pp.

B. The second portion of these papers were donated by Catherine Wild to Beinecke in the fall of 1974. These papers are found in six folios numbered by Professor Richard Sugarman and Roger Duncan on February 6, 1977. The placement of the folders was probably determined by either Professor David Carr or Professor Edward Casey, formerly at the Department of Philosophy at Yale. The numbers on the side indicate the folders found in each folio. The description of the contents are by Richard Sugarman and Roger Duncan. The number of pages included in each folder are estimates.

Box 1, no. 11. Seminar notes for a course on "the other" given by John Wild at Yale in spring 1969. Ca. 75 pp., handwritten.

Box 1, no. 12. Seminar notes for a course given by John Wild on "Marxism and Existentialism," numbered Philosophy 24 B. Almost certainly given as an undergraduate course by John Wild at Yale in fall 1966. Ca. 75 pp., handwritten. Several typed pp. on "the "other," probably the beginnings of an essay.

Box 1, no. 13. Lecture notes for course on "Epistemology and Metaphysics," numbered Philosophy 150, given at Yale in 1963. Includes syllabi and grades. Ca. 75 pp., handwritten. Note: Most of Wild's course notes run to 75 pp. Length hereafter will not be specified unless noteworthy.

Box 1, no. 14. Seminar notes for a course given on the "Philosophy of Power," numbered Philosophy 609. Almost certainly given at the University of Florida in 1969–1970. Major thrust of the course appears to concentrate on Levinas's critique of traditional ontology. Includes a syllabus on politics and Marxism that may belong to another course.

Box 1, no. 15. Lecture notes for a course given by John Wild on "Philosophy of Religion," at Yale in fall 1967. Includes grades and syllabi.

Box 1, no. 16. Lecture notes for a course on "the other," numbered Phil. 609, fall 1970. Probably given in sequence with 14, above. Concentrates on the problem of other minds with special emphasis on Levinas.

Box 2, no. 17. Lecture notes for a course given on existential philosophy at Harvard, numbered Philosophy 13B. Special emphasis on James and Heidegger. Includes syllabi and grades. Also some lecture notes for a course given at Harvard in 1960–1961 with similar content.

Box 2, no. 18. Notes (rough) for an essay on education and democracy. Correspondence with Prentice-Hall concerning the publication of *Existence and the World of Freedom*.

Box 2, no. 19. Miscellaneous manuscript notes. Very provocative but condensed 20 pp. including: plan for a book on value premised on the notion that the Good is beyond Being; criticism of Levinas; remarks on philosophy in the present age; notes on the concept of "the inner life."

Box 2, no. 20. Annotated typescript (carbon) of parts of the *Challenge of Existentialism*. Incomplete draft with corrections includes pages numbered 6 through 10, 12–19, 23–26, 26a, 27–196. Published by Indiana University Press, 1955.

Box 2, no. 21. "The Structure of Immediate Experience," subtitled "Naturalism and Immediate Experience." 51 pp. typescript with manuscript corrections, called chapter 1. Likely post-1949.

Box 2, no. 22. "My Book—Levels of Awareness" Typescript with corrections (part 2, chapters 3, 4). Deserves most serious scrutiny. Dating uncertain, probably mid- or late 1950s.

Box 2, no. 23a.* "New Views on Logic and the Theory of Signs." Annotated typescript. 51 pp. from the *Introduction to Realistic Philosophy*. Published by Harper and Row, 1948.

*Marked 23a simply because of an error in which two folders are noted as 23.

Box 3, no. 23b. "What I Hold." Subjectivism and the World of Meaning. Numerous drafts of APA speech. Variously titled "The Life-world and Its Meaning for Contemporary Thought."

Box 3, no. 24. An article submitted to John Wild by one F. Zurdeeg. "An Analytical Philosophy of Religion," with a letter to John Wild by the author.

Box 3, no. 25. Lecture notes for course in Existential Philosophy, Philosophy 30a, at Yale in 1965–1966. Quite extensive. Includes syllabus.

Box 3, no. 26. Essay: "Some Phenomenological Reflections on the Other" (1968). 26 pp. Very promising. Proceeded by a shorter five-page essay on "the other." Folder includes correspondence with Prof. Hanna re: Florida move.

Box 3, no. 27. "The Other Person and Otherness." 25 fragmentary pp. on "the other." Notes for a phenomenology symposium held at Yale, probably 1969.

Box 3, no. 28. William James and Existential Authenticity. Clean carbon of a completed essay, date uncertain, probably prior to the publication of *The Radical Empiricism of William James*, Doubleday and Co., 1969. Special emphasis on *The Varieties of Religious Experience*.

Box 3, no. 29. "Turn from Realism to Phenomenology Is Complete" (1957). 12 typed pp. (legal size), typed in red, on possible topics for articles reflecting changed views.
   Topics include:
a. History of the Life-world
b. Christianity and the Life-world
c. Christianity and Philosophy
d. World or Ordinary Language
e. Life-world and Its Meaning for Philosophy
f. "War of the Worlds"—"outline of my 90 pages." Subsequently included in a condensed version in *Existence and the World of Freedom*.
g. Christian Philosophy and Its Moral Implications

h. Philosophy and Freedom
i. "Anthropology"
j. Ethics.
   Folder also includes notes from a visit to London with observations, 1957.

Box 3, no. 30. Bibliography of John Wild's works and works about him to 1959. Bibliography is very extensive and should be helpful in framing a complete bibliography. Includes a photograph of John Wild.

Box 3, no. 31. "Talks on Philosophy and Existential Philosophy." 15 pp. Notes for speeches at Boston University, Haverford and various churches.

Box 3, no. 32. "The Other Person: Some Phenomenological Reflections." 2 copies, pp. 1–2, 7–20. Check with box 2, folder 27.

Box 3, no. 33. "My Philosophical Ideas" (November 1957). 14 pp. Notes for an essay (emphasis on life-world).

Box 3, no. 34. "Some Reflections on the Life-world." Why the life-world is not a system. Pp. 1–10, incomplete. Promising. Syllabus, 1956–1957. A one-page entry "On Death"—must be much later because it shows that John Wild has already read Levinas.

Box 3, no. 35. "The Lived Body," (late 1960s, early 1970s). 25 pp. Carbon of typescript. Attempts to position the concept of the lived body within the history of philosophy. An original essay, one of Wild's last. Wild was readying it for publication.

Box 3, no. 36. Two typed pp. on James.

Box 4, no. 37. Lecture notes for a course on the Philosophy of Christianity given by John Wild, at Harvard in spring 1956. Ca. 70 pp.

Box 4, no. 38. "The Human Lebenswelt." Typescript (carbon) with corrections and annotations. Incomplete, pp. 2, 5–11, 14–19, 23–29. Draft for Machette lecture, 1959. Also several pp. for the draft of an article on "Hobbes, the Individual and Society."

Box 4, no. 39. Notes for a talk on "Existential Philosophy and Its Implication for Politics," April 9, 1961, at the home of one Harold Guetzkow, probably in Evanston, Illinois, in connection with work while at Northwestern University.

Box 4, no. 40. "The Uses of Philosophy," summary of Mahlon Powell lecture by John Wild in March 1961. 3 pp. Summary of talks by Blanshard and Max Black with marginal notes by John Wild.

Box 4, no. 41. "Existentialism and Realism" (date uncertain). 6 pp., handwritten. Notes for two talks at Lamoine and Weston.

Box 4, no. 42. "Problems of Epistemology and Metaphysics." Manuscript notes in conjunction with a course given by John Wild in spring 1964, Phil. 150. Annotated copy of course outline. Ca. 40 pp.

Box 4, no. 43. "Christianity and Existentialism." Two clean drafts, 18 and 20 pp. respectively, of a talk given at Wheaton College in Illinois, December 14, 1961. Postdates *Human Freedom and the Social Order: An Essay in Christian Philosophy*, Duke University Press, 1959.

Box 4, no. 44. Bibliography of the writings of John Wild through 1966 from a master's thesis written in France. Very extensive.

Box 5, no. 45. Outline for an article "inner vs. outer"—analysis of inner-outer as special metaphor for two modes of understanding. 2 pp.

Box 5, no. 46. "Is There an Existential A Priori?" (1967). Carbon, one of several versions.

Box 5, no. 47. a. "The Rights of the Other as Other" (1967–1968). 26 typed pp. Based on the distinction between need and desire; grounds the notion of right not on utility but on fullness.
b. "The Right of the Other as Other." 17 typed carbon pp. 3. "The Ethics of Language" (1968). 1 p. pencil notes, various entries on James and existentialism; several untitled pp.

Box 5, no. 48. "Projects"—pencil notes, notes for an article "fact vs. meaning" (1960–1964).

Box 5, no. 49. "The Other Person—Some Phenomenological Reflections." 20 typed pp. (carbon and copy). The recognition of the radical otherness of the other through dialogue as pointing directions for steering between the dilemma of chaos and the tyrannical categories of finished systems.

Box 5, no. 50. "The World and Its Versions." Typescript. The world understood not as a construction or a fact but the ground of any possible construction or fact.

Box 5, no. 51. "The Problem of God" (date uncertain). 4 pp. Notes in pencil and ink.

Box 5, no. 52. "Critique of Dialectic." Deals with power. Late lecture notes: Ricoeur notes—2 pp., existential epistemology—1 p.

Box 5, no. 53. Miscellaneous notes for classes on Dewey and Bergson; correspondence for a lecture at Shimea(?) College (1961).

Box 5, no. 54. "The Death of God and the Life of Man" (date uncertain). 25 typed pp; 18 typed pp. of another draft. Does the 'death of God' mean the end of the life of man?

Box 5, no. 55. Book Reviews:
a. Barrett—*Irrational Man*. 4 typed pp.
b. Ortega—*Man and Crisis*. 5 pp.
c. *New Knowledge in Human Values*. Several versions, 2 pp. each.

Box 5, no. 56. "Critique of Heidegger." 10 pp., handwritten.

Box 5, no. 57. "Collective Existence" (late 1960s). 40 pp. manuscript notes on subject; Yale syllabus.

Box 5, no. 58. "Existential Themes in the Thought of William James" (late 1950s). 48 pp. corrected typescript. Early piece, Harvard.

Box 6, no. 59. Seminar "On the A Priori," about 100 pp. notes for a course given at Yale in spring 1967.

Box 6, no. 60. Seminar on "Freedom and Responsibility," around 100 pp. notes for a course given at Yale in fall 1966.

Box 6, no. 61. Existential Structures (probably late 1960s). Pp. noted 8–27.

Box 6, no. 62. Lecture notes on *Philosophy of Existentialism*, Philosophy 509, probably given at Northwestern in 1962–1963. Ca. 75 pp.

Index A: Names

Adenauer, Konrad, 104
Aiken, Henry, xviii, 252
Allport, Gordon, 106, 121
Anderson, John, xxix
Anderson, Robert, 242n45
Aquinas, Thomas, 31, 90–92, 105
Arendt, Hannah, 124
Aristotle, xviii, xix, xxi, xxv, xxxii, 4, 95, 109, 184, 216; on change and causation, 103, 114, 135; on consciousness, 116; on dualism, 12, 14; on knowledge, 31; *Nichomachean Ethics* and, xxxiii; other and, 170, 188; reason and, 193; on truth, xxxiv, 111
Augustine, 20, 97, 135, 137, 212
Austin, J. L., 81, 84, 85, 87–89, 121
Ayer, A. J., 87, 100, 121

Barth, Karl, 81, 82, 93, 97, 99, 100–101, 104–5, 111, 122
Bekenithms, 104
Bergson, Henri, 216
Berkely, George, xxv, 133, 191, 237n14
Bernstein, Richard J., xxix, xxx
Biemel, Walter, 102, 103, 104, 107–8, 122
Blanchard, Brand, xxii, xxix
Blanchot, Maurice, 231
Bleuler, 105

Bollnow, Otto, 103
Boman, Thorleif, 95
Brentano, Franz, 36
Brightman, E. S., 97
Brumbaugh, Robert, xxix
Brunner, E., 93, 96–98, 104, 106
Buber, Martin, 124, 145, 201
Bugbee, Henry, 89
Bultmann, Rudolph, 97, 98, 100, 104–6, 122, 133
Buytendijk, F. J. J., 106, 122

Cairns, Dorion, xxiii, xxiv
Carnap, Rudolf, 22
Carr, David, xxix
Casey, Eduard, xxix
Cowgill, Cynthia Wild, xxvii

de Beauvoir, Simone, 244n57
de Chardin, Pierre Teilhard, 100, 122
Demos, Raphael, xxviii, 252
de Raeymaeker, Louis, 90–92, 102, 122
Derrida, Jacques, 235
Desan, Wilfred, xxxi, 100
Descartes, René, xxii, 12, 20, 30, 103–4, 189, 192–93, 195, 207, 213, 215
de Walhens, Alphonse, 94, 100, 107, 122
Dostoevsky, Fyodor: *Brothers Karamazov*, 155

275

Index B: Categories

a priori, x, xxi, 11, 12, 18, 19, 27, 29–44, 49, 82, 85, 88, 111, 116, 118

absence, xxvi, xxxii, 51, 57, 60, 119, 166, 176, 210, 211, 217, 227, 240n25, 247n73

absolute, 25, 26, 48, 50, 63, 64, 66, 67, 78, 83, 88, 96, 138–39, 143, 154, 187, 233

absurd, 155, 195, 215, 222

action/active, xxxiii, 14, 17, 18, 19, 20, 21, 22, 25, 26, 27, 30, 41, 42, 49, 50, 51, 53, 73, 86, 88, 91, 92, 94, 95, 109, 148, 152–53, 162, 167–68, 175–77, 181, 230, 234

alienation, xxxii, 190, 218, 221, 230

alterity, 185, 188, 242n42

ambiguity, xxii, 27, 39, 46, 55, 57, 84, 85, 109, 134, 142, 173, 225

analytic philosophy, 121

anthropocentrism, xxxiv, 169, 184

anthropology, xxxiii, xxxiv, 23, 63, 64, 65, 73, 76, 78, 90, 95, 102–4, 106–8, 115, 127

anxiety, xxiii, 78, 114

appearance, 21, 22, 27, 211

argument, 8, 132, 135–36, 140, 165, 167, 177, 179–80

artificial intelligence, xxxi

Association for Realistic Philosophy, xx, xviii

atheism, 194–99, 204, 216

attention, 21, 33, 38–39, 59, 78, 131

Auschwitz, 135

awareness, 18, 19, 20, 21, 24, 26, 32, 35, 36, 41, 42, 46, 47, 49, 50, 53, 64, 68, 71, 75, 88, 117–18

becoming, 6, 31, 60, 198, 206, 215, 227

behavior, 14, 18, 22, 37, 146

Being, xviii, xxii, xxix, xxxi, xxxii, xxxv, 3, 4, 5, 6, 7, 14, 21, 23, 26, 29, 34, 35, 60, 69, 71, 87, 88, 90, 91, 92, 94, 95, 96, 98, 102–3, 107–10, 114–17, 119, 123, 151, 154, 175–76, 185, 190–93, 197, 198, 201, 202, 209, 211, 215, 216, 217, 218, 221, 226, 228, 229, 230–34, 238, 243n47; in-the-world, 188; toward-death, 213, 219, 223, 240, 245n61

Beinecke, xiii, xv, xxvii, xxxiii, xxxiv. *See also* Yale

belief, x, xi, xx, 35, 42, 64, 79, 87. *See also* faith

body, xxxiii, 4, 11–15, 17, 18–19, 20, 22, 24, 25, 26, 27, 29, 30, 36–37, 38, 39, 40, 41, 47, 48, 49, 50, 51, 78, 90, 91, 94, 95, 122, 125–26, 187, 209, 217, 219

bracketing [*epoche*], 115, 207

279

psychology, 12, 17, 23, 38, 59, 91, 103–4, 106–7, 122

quality, 212
quantity, 52, 223, 227

rationalism, 11, 33–34, 65, 74, 77, 88, 103, 115, 131, 176
rationality, 6, 193, 214
realism, xxi, xxii, 3 88, 94, 115–16
realistic movement, the, xx, 113
reality, 7, 12, 25, 27, 42, 87, 94, 109, 138, 143, 193, 207, 211, 215, 233
reason, 6, 33–34, 40, 64, 72, 77, 166, 175–76, 190–91, 193, 202, 205–6, 208, 214–16
reductionism, 63, 83
reflection, 3, 12, 93, 113, 151, 154, 160–61, 169–75, 184, 216
relativism, 25, 28, 63–78, 99, 115, 140, 169
religion, 95–96, 98–101, 105–6, 139, 148, 169, 188, 199, 204
rerum natura, 6
responsibility, xxxi, 210; death of God and, 134, 135; eros and, 226; ethics and, 191–92; freedom and, 232–33; guilt and, 146–55; infinite, 214–15, 241n38, 244n60; judgment and, 221–23; Levinasian, 185, 195, 240n27, 248n81; other and, 167–68, 173; relativism and, 64, 78; religion as, 199
rights, human, 159–64

science, 4, 19, 22–23, 25–27, 31–32, 50, 54, 57–58, 66–67, 71, 73, 75, 77, 86–87, 92, 94, 102–3, 105–8, 114, 116, 133–34, 153, 175–76, 191, 195, 197; human, 50; of the individual-as-such, 4, 176, 191; natural, 50, 175; objective, 22, 25, 66; perspectives of, 77; philosophy of, 27; point of view of, 54, 58; systems of, 153; world of, 134
self, 13–14, 37, 39, 95, 103, 108, 114, 120, 152, 154–55, 160, 162–65, 168,

170, 174–75, 184, 187–88, 190–92, 198, 201, 205, 207–9, 214, 216, 218, 224, 226–27, 229–30; active, 13; other and, 188, 226, 231; presence of the self to the self, 187; self-consciousness, 162, 164, 187; self-identity, 170, 187; self-responsibility, 154; self-same, 165, 168; self-transcendence, 155, 226–27; system of the, 165; towards the, 208
sensation, 17, 33, 198, 212
sensory perception, 185
signification, 78, 98, 205, 220
skepticism, 12, 35, 72, 142–43, 155
society, 63–64, 145, 147, 168, 174, 178–79, 185, 201, 205–6, 211, 214, 226, 229; closed, 168; free, 147, 178; human, 179; open, 185; pluralism of, 229
Society for Phenomenology and Existential Philosophy (SPEP), xviii, xxviii, 233
solipsism, 68, 70, 170
soul, 12, 14, 17, 90–91, 142, 197
space, 6–7, 12, 16, 19, 26, 30, 33–34, 37–39, 40–41, 48, 52, 56, 58–59, 77–78, 86, 114–15, 118, 135, 212, 220, 229; geometric, 6, 118; human, 78, 114; intervals of, 58–59; lived, 11, 16, 29, 36, 37, 41, 118; movement of, 30; oriented, 19, 37–38, 77; perceptual, 26; position in, 86
spatiality, 99
speaking, 13, 41, 56, 70, 82, 132, 134, 174, 177, 179, 201, 202, 224, 230. *See also* Levinas, *Speaking Philosophy* (Index A)
Stalinism, xxv, xxvi
subject, 27, 39, 50, 88, 108, 137, 152, 162, 167, 174, 199, 202, 218, 222, 227, 230–31; individual, 162, 167, 174; isolated, 50; mind of the, 152; spiritual, 27
subjectivism, xxiii, 215
subjectivity, 37, 86, 191, 211, 221–24, 226–29, 231–32

About John Wild

John Wild (1902–1972) achieved a degree of international eminence rare among American philosophers. He was the most prominent figure associated with phenomenology and existential philosophy on the American scene. He was twice the recipient of the prestigious Guggenheim Fellowship and served, during the course of his career, as president of several of the major philosophical associations in the United States. John Wild impressed upon his readers and his students the importance of making philosophy "less academic" by bringing it closer to the concrete patterns of everyday experience. He was a fearless, courageous, rigorous and independent thinker who guided the American phenomenological movement for a generation.

He taught at Harvard for thirty-four years and moved to Northwestern University in 1960, where he served as chair of the Department of Philosophy. He spent seven years teaching at Yale and concluded his academic career at the University of Florida. He cofounded the Society for Phenomenology and Existential Philosophy (SPEP). He served as general editor of the Northwestern University series in phenomenology and existential philosophy.

In addition to his many books and published articles he left some 5,000 pages of posthumous papers. The posthumous papers chosen for the present book include articles that Wild was readying for publication toward the close of his career and an intriguing journal that he kept while on his second Guggenheim Fellowship (1957–1958) in England and the continent. The journal records his reflections on his conversations with some of the most important figures in British and continental philosophy. Among Wild's posthumous papers included in this volume is an instructive and inspiring commentary on Emmanuel Levinas's *Totality and Infinity*.

About the Editors

Richard I. Sugarman and **Roger B. Duncan** were introduced to phenomenology and to each other by John Wild while students of philosophy at Yale University. Together, they compiled a bibliography of Wild's posthumous writings. They collated, edited and annotated his posthumous writings in preparation for this book. It is their hope that Wild's previously unpublished papers will help to stimulate a resurgence of interest in phenomenology and existential philosophy.

Richard I. Sugarman currently teaches religion and philosophy at the University of Vermont. He is the author of *Rancor Against Time: The Phenomenology of Ressentiment* (Felix Meiner Verlag) and writes extensively on the philosophy of Emmanuel Levinas. Roger B. Duncan taught for many years at the University of Connecticut and presently teaches philosophy and religion at various colleges and seminaries. He is the author of articles on ancient, medieval and contemporary philosophy.